Mastering Microsoft Dynamics 365 Business Central

Discover extension development best practices, build advanced ERP integrations, and use DevOps tools

Stefano Demiliani
Duilio Tacconi

BIRMINGHAM - MUMBAI

Mastering Microsoft Dynamics 365 Business Central

Copyright © 2019 Packt Publishing

Commissioning Editor: Richa Tripathi
Acquisition Editor: Alok Dhuri
Content Development Editor: Tiksha Sarang
Senior Editor: Storm Mann
Technical Editor: Ketan Kamble
Copy Editor: Safis Editing
Language Support Editor: Safis Editing
Project Coordinator: Francy Puthiry
Proofreader: Safis Editing
Indexer: Rekha Nair
Production Designer: Deepika Naik

First published: December 2019

Production reference: 2210420

Published by Packt Publishing Ltd.
Livery Place
35 Livery Street
Birmingham
B3 2PB, UK.

ISBN 978-1-78995-125-7

www.packt.com

Subscribe to our online digital library for full access to over 7,000 books and videos, as well as industry leading tools to help you plan your personal development and advance your career. For more information, please visit our website.

Why subscribe?

- Spend less time learning and more time coding with practical eBooks and Videos from over 4,000 industry professionals

- Improve your learning with Skill Plans built especially for you

- Get a free eBook or video every month

- Fully searchable for easy access to vital information

- Copy and paste, print, and bookmark content

Did you know that Packt offers eBook versions of every book published, with PDF and ePub files available? You can upgrade to the eBook version at www.packt.com and as a print book customer, you are entitled to a discount on the eBook copy. Get in touch with us at customercare@packtpub.com for more details.

At www.packt.com, you can also read a collection of free technical articles, sign up for a range of free newsletters, and receive exclusive discounts and offers on Packt books and eBooks.

Contributors

About the authors

Stefano Demiliani is a Microsoft MVP (Most Valuable Professional) in Business Applications, a Microsoft Certified Solution Developer and Azure architect, and a long-time expert on different Microsoft technologies. He has a master's degree in computer engineering from Politecnico di Torino, he works as a CTO for EID/Navlab (one of the main Microsoft partners in Italy), and he has recently moved many customers from around the globe to the cloud.

He has worked with Packt Publishing on many IT books, and he's the author of some of the most successful books in the Microsoft Dynamics world. You can reach him on Twitter (@demiliani) or on LinkedIn.

> *We hope that this book will help you to master Microsoft Dynamics ERP and embrace the cloud world. Thanks to all the wonderful staff who have worked with me on this book (especially Duilio for consenting to be on board), and thanks also to my family (I'll return to you all the hours spent working on this project). I would like to dedicate this book to my little daughter, Sara: I love you. Maybe one day you will be proud of me for this.*

Duilio Tacconi is a Microsoft Dynamics NAV/Microsoft Dynamics 365 Business Central Escalation Engineer at Microsoft EMEA **Customer Support and Services** (**CSS**). He joined Microsoft in 2008 after working in a customer IT department with a focus primarily on system administration and development. Despite graduating with the highest score in agricultural science in 1996, he has been on the ERP circuit since 1998 as a developer and a system implementer for several companies with Microsoft and non-Microsoft technologies. Currently, he is an SME at EMEA, one of Microsoft EMEA CSS references for Managed Service for Partners, and a three-time Iron Man finisher. Duilio lives in Cernusco Sul Naviglio (Italy) with his beloved wife, Laura, and his son, Leonardo.

> *Born with the heart and soul of Microsoft Dynamics NAV, Microsoft Dynamics 365 Business Central has all the features, tools, and power needed to dominate the SMB market over the next few decades. Thanks to all the Packt guys for all the professional help, and a warm thank you to Stefano for dragging me into this project. I dedicate this book to Laura: my love, my life, and my special half.*

About the contributors

Tobias Fenster started as a developer 20 years ago. Holding different positions including Head of Technical Consulting and Head of Development before becoming CTO, Tobias is now the CTO for COSMO CONSULT. He writes about Dynamics NAV/Business Central in connection with Docker and Windows containers on his blog, as well as tooling such as Azure DevOps and the new development environment. He holds a Microsoft MVP award for Business Solutions and one for Azure. You can find him on Twitter: @tobiasfenster.

Luc van Vugt stepped into the NAV world in 1999, training hundreds of developers. After Microsoft acquired Navision, he joined the Dynamics localization team, GDL, as a tester, UA specialist, and project lead. For 6 years, he was closely involved with all successive releases. Since leaving Microsoft, he has become an active community member through his blog. He is also the co-founder of Dutch Dynamics Community and a speaker at conferences. For this, he has been awarded a Microsoft MVP since 2011. In 2014, he co-founded *NAV Skills*, supporting NAV professionals around the globe with, among other things, webinars.

Kamil Sáček (*Kine*) graduated from the Brno University of Technology in 2001. Following this, he began working as a Navision developer with NAVERTICA a.s. (formerly, FUTURE Engineering a.s.), now as the department manager of software development.

Since 2005, he has been consecutively awarded MVP status in Microsoft Dynamics NAV (now Dynamics 365 Business Central). You can find his many posts on the mibuso.com forum; and tweets under the handle @MVPKine.

In the last few years, he has been focusing on supporting his team of developers by creating tools for them such as the PowerShell module NVRAppDevOps, and a preconfigured template for new Business Central projects.

Douglas Romão is a Microsoft MVP in Office Apps and Services and a technology solution expert. He has been working in software development and consulting since 2007, across different project types and sizes, integrating Microsoft technologies that focus on collaboration and productivity all over the world. As a speaker and community manager, he is responsible for the PowerApps, Flow, and SharePoint technical communities in Brazil. He is passionate about discovering new ways to solve problems using technology as the main driver.

Dmitry Katson is an all-round Microsoft Dynamics NAV specialist with more than 15 years of experience. He started as a Navision developer in 2004 with the biggest gold-producing company in Russia, and then moved to the customer side as a leading support specialist. In 2010, he co-founded NavDesign. The main business of the company was ISV solutions design and maintenance. In 2016, *NavDesign* was bought by Consyst Business Group – one of the largest IT integrator companies in Russia. In 2018, he founded AirApps. The main focus of the company is to extend Microsoft Dynamics 365 Business Central with modern AI-ready apps and help partners to move their IP to the cloud. On May 18, he was awarded an MVP.

Eric Wauters is one of the founding partners of iFacto Business Solutions and Cloud Ready Software. With his 18 years of technical expertise, he is an everyday inspiration to development teams. As a development manager, he continually acts upon the technical readiness of iFacto and CRS. Apart from that, Eric is also very active in the NAV community, where he tries to solve technical issues and shares his knowledge with other Dynamics enthusiasts. Surely, many among you will have read some of Eric's posts, which he invariably signs with Waldo. Lots of people have been using and even contributing to the tools he shares for free on GitHub. His proven track record has earned him a Microsoft MVP since 2007.

Packt is searching for authors like you

Table of Contents

Section 2: Developing Extensions for Dynamics 365 Business Central

Preface

This book is for Dynamics 365 Business Central developers who need to create applications and customizations on top of Microsoft Dynamics **enterprise resource planning** (**ERP**).

The book starts by explaining the Microsoft Dynamics 365 Business Central platform (the focus is on the **Software-as-a-Service** (**SaaS**) platform) and the modern development environment (Visual Studio Code, the AL language, and other tools, such as Docker). Then the book covers all the developer-oriented topics that you need to know about in order to extend and customize the ERP, with a focus on how to write better code following best practices, how to debug and deploy extensions, and how to write automatic testing.

The book also covers advanced topics related to integration, cloud services, and serverless processing (with Azure Functions, web services, and APIs) using Dynamics 365 Business Central with Office 365 apps such as Power BI, Flow, and PowerApps; integration with machine learning functionalities; and how to apply DevOps techniques to your development process.

The book ends with an *architectural* topic by analyzing the best ways of moving existing solutions to the new development model based on extensions.

Who this book is for

This book is aimed at Microsoft Dynamics NAV/Dynamics 365 Business Central developers and solution architects with advanced knowledge of business processes and C/AL programming. Knowledge of web service programming (APIs) and C# would be a plus.

What this book covers

Chapter 1, *Microsoft Dynamics 365 Business Central Overview*, provides a technical introduction to the Dynamics 365 Business Central architecture (cloud and on-premises) and to the new development platform.

Chapter 2, *Mastering a Modern Development Environment*, provides an overview of the modern development environment for Dynamics 365 Business Central as well as tips and tricks on how to efficiently work with Visual Studio Code when developing extensions.

Chapter 3, *Online and Container-Based Sandboxes*, covers all the details about how to create a sandbox environment with Dynamics 365 Business Central for development, how to use an online sandbox for testing, and how to use Docker to improve your development process.

Chapter 4, *Extension Development Fundamentals*, provides an overview of the new extension model, the differences with the past, the new object types, and how to create objects with AL.

Chapter 5, *Developing a Customized Solution for Dynamics 365 Business Central*, guides you in developing a complete solution with Dynamics 365 Business Central using Visual Studio Code and the AL language, starting from a real-world business case. In this chapter, you will see how to create a complete solution and how to customize the solution for a customer without modifications to the base code.

Chapter 6, *Advanced AL Development*, covers the advanced programming topics that you need to know about when developing extensions, such as file management, using .NET objects, calling web services with AL, handling XML and JSON, handling media files, handling notifications, asynchronous programming, and more.

Chapter 7, *Report Development with AL*, introduces you to how to handle reports in the new extension model (the creation of new reports and the customization of existing reports).

Chapter 8, *Installing and Upgrading Extensions*, shows you how to handle install and upgrade logic for your Dynamics 365 Business Central extensions.

Chapter 9, *Debugging*, shows you how to debug an extension and how to inspect code and variables.

Chapter 10, *Automated Test Development with AL*, covers the details of how to write and execute automated tests for Dynamics 365 Business Central extensions.

Chapter 11, *Source Code Management and DevOps with Business Central*, covers how to efficiently handle source code management techniques when developing solutions for Dynamics 365 Business Central, and it will give an overview on how to handle **continuous integration/continuous delivery (CI/CD)** and DevOPs techniques for your extension's projects.

Chapter 12, *Dynamics 365 Business Central APIs*, introduces the Dynamics 365 Business Central API framework. It shows you how to use existing APIs, how to create new APIs to extend the platform, and also advanced API topics such as bound actions and webhooks.

Chapter 13, *Serverless Business Processes with Business Central and Azure*, describes how to use Azure Functions with Dynamics 365 Business Central to execute .NET code in the cloud and to implement serverless processing solutions.

Chapter 14, *Monitoring, Scaling, and CI/CD with Azure Functions*, shows you how to monitor Azure functions, how to handle scalability for improving performance, and how to implement a CI/CD process using Azure DevOps.

Chapter 15, *Business Central and Integration with the Power Platform*, shows the usage of Dynamics 365 Business Central in combination with the Dynamics 365 Power Platform. We'll see an overview of the Power Platform applications and some real-world applications by using the Power Platform with Dynamics 365 Business Central.

Chapter 16, *Integrating Machine Learning into Dynamics 365 Business Central*, gives an overview of how to integrate machine learning functionalities into Dynamics 365 Business Central extensions.

Chapter 17, *Moving Existing ISV Solutions to the New Extension Model*, covers taking an existing ISV solution (written with old C/AL code) and moving it to the new extension model. It covers in detail the architectural aspects and gives tips on how to start this process in the right way.

Chapter 18, *Useful and Proficient Tools for AL Developers*, presents a set of third-party tools that are useful to your development experience.

To get the most out of this book

You should be comfortable with programming using C/AL for Dynamics NAV or Dynamics 365 Business Central, as well as with using tools such as PowerShell and the Azure portal. Knowledge of cloud concepts will help you a lot in understanding some of the topics.

The book will guide you through how to create complete solutions and how to solve tasks. Following the provided samples by using at least a trial environment is a must if you want to get the most from this book.

Download the example code files

You can download the example code files for this book from your account at www.packt.com. If you purchased this book elsewhere, you can visit www.packtpub.com/support and register to have the files emailed directly to you.

You can download the code files by following these steps:

1. Log in or register at www.packt.com.
2. Select the **Support** tab.
3. Click on **Code Downloads**.
4. Enter the name of the book in the **Search** box and follow the onscreen instructions.

Once the file is downloaded, please make sure that you unzip or extract the folder using the latest version of:

- WinRAR/7-Zip for Windows
- Zipeg/iZip/UnRarX for Mac
- 7-Zip/PeaZip for Linux

The code bundle for the book is also hosted on GitHub at https://github.com/PacktPublishing/Mastering-Microsoft-Dynamics-365-Business-Central. In case there's an update to the code, it will be updated on the existing GitHub repository.

We also have other code bundles from our rich catalog of books and videos available at https://github.com/PacktPublishing/. Check them out!

Download the color images

We also provide a PDF file that has color images of the screenshots/diagrams used in this book. You can download it here: `https://static.packt-cdn.com/downloads/9781789951257_ColorImages.pdf`.

Conventions used

There are a number of text conventions used throughout this book.

`CodeInText`: Indicates code words in text, database table names, folder names, filenames, file extensions, pathnames, dummy URLs, user input, and Twitter handles. Here is an example: "Here is the output of a `docker run` command where the image was not locally available."

A block of code is set as follows:

```
mcr.microsoft.com/businesscentral/onprem:1910-cu1-au-ltsc2019
```

Any command-line input or output is written as follows:

```
docker network create -d transparent transpNet
```

Bold: Indicates a new term, an important word, or words that you see onscreen. For example, words in menus or dialog boxes appear in the text like this. Here is an example: "Simply browse through `https://dynamics.microsoft.com/en-us/business-central/overview/` and click on **Find a partner** under the desired licensing module."

 Warnings or important notes appear like this.

 Tips and tricks appear like this.

Get in touch

Feedback from our readers is always welcome.

General feedback: If you have questions about any aspect of this book, mention the book title in the subject of your message and email us at `customercare@packtpub.com`.

Errata: Although we have taken every care to ensure the accuracy of our content, mistakes do happen. If you have found a mistake in this book, we would be grateful if you would report this to us. Please visit `www.packt.com/submit-errata`, selecting your book, clicking on the Errata Submission Form link, and entering the details.

Piracy: If you come across any illegal copies of our works in any form on the Internet, we would be grateful if you would provide us with the location address or website name. Please contact us at `copyright@packt.com` with a link to the material.

If you are interested in becoming an author: If there is a topic that you have expertise in and you are interested in either writing or contributing to a book, please visit `authors.packtpub.com`.

Reviews

Please leave a review. Once you have read and used this book, why not leave a review on the site that you purchased it from? Potential readers can then see and use your unbiased opinion to make purchase decisions, we at Packt can understand what you think about our products, and our authors can see your feedback on their book. Thank you!

For more information about Packt, please visit `packt.com`.

Section 1: Dynamics 365 Business Central - Platform Overview and the Basics of Modern Development

In this section, we will introduce you to the Dynamics 365 Business Central architecture (cloud and on-premise) and to the new development platform.

This section comprises the following chapters:

- Chapter 1, *Microsoft Dynamics 365 Business Central Overview*
- Chapter 2, *Mastering a Modern Development Environment*
- Chapter 3, *Online and Container-Based Sandboxes*

1
Microsoft Dynamics 365 Business Central Overview

Microsoft Dynamics 365 Business Central is one of the best-in-class pieces of cloud-based **Enterprise Resource Planning** (**ERP**) application software that's targeted at the **small and medium business** (**SMB**) market. The application is based on the **Software-as-a-Service** (**SaaS**) model, and it is sold through **Cloud Solution Provider** (**CSP**) partners.

Potential customers can spin up a trial tenant at any time and/or contact a CSP partner to purchase and assign a per-user license.

In this chapter, we will cover the following topics:

- **Customer perspective**: What Dynamics 365 Business Central is, what functional areas it covers, and licensing
- **Partner perspective**: An overview of Business Central Admin Center and its use
- **Microsoft perspective**: A deep dive under the technological skin of Microsoft Dynamics 365 Business Central
- **A future perspective**: What to potentially expect in the upcoming years and how to contribute to making it happen

By the end of this chapter, you'll have a clear and in-depth overview of the Microsoft Dynamics 365 Business Central platform.

Understanding the customer perspective

Targeted at SMBs, the core design of Dynamics 365 Business Central relies on Microsoft Azure and the Office 365 platforms. The application's core code and business processes come from the evolution of 30+ years of feature enhancements of Microsoft Dynamics NAV (mostly known as *Navision*): one of the most solid pieces of on-premise ERP software in the SMB domain.

Potential customers – or those who simply want to give the application a spin—can subscribe for fast setup with a trial version through `https://trials.dynamics.com/Dynamics365/Signup/BusinessCentral` by providing an email address that's bound to an Office 365 subscription and a phone number. After 30 days, when the trial period ends, the product needs to be purchased.

Official licensing is assigned exclusively through Microsoft Partners that are credited and certified by the CSP program. Simply browse through `https://dynamics.microsoft.com/en-us/business-central/overview/` and click on **Find a partner** under the desired licensing module, as shown in the following screenshot:

Microsoft Dynamics 365 Business Central delivers out of the box functionalities in modules with a fixed price per month, per user. There are three types of per user/month choices with different capabilities and application modules: Essentials, Premium, and Team Members. Essentials and Premium are full users, while Team Members are just additional users with limited capabilities.

These are the properties (collection of capabilities) of the *Essentials* module (from $70 per month):

- Financial management
- Customer relationship management
- Project management
- Supply chain management
- Human resource management
- Warehouse management

These are the properties of the Premium module (from $100 per month):

- Financial management
- Customer relationship management
- Project management
- Supply chain management
- Human resource management
- Warehouse management
- Service management
- Manufacturing

Currently, it is not possible to have a mixed user experience of both Essential and Premium within the same tenant. It is possible to move from the Essential to the Premium module, but you can't downgrade from Premium to Essential. If you have already at least one user licensed as Essential or Premium, it is possible to have an external user added as a named license *Team Member* within the same module (Essential or Premium).

This is what you get as a Team Member (from $8 per month):

- Essential or Premium (depending on the module of the user that has added the Team Member).
- The ability to consume data or reports, complete light tasks such as time or expense entries and HR record updates, and use PowerApps for Dynamics 365.
- Technically, they might have read access to all the tables but only have insert/update access to a maximum of three tables.

All the details related to the licensing types and what they include are described in the official Microsoft Dynamics 365 Business Central Licensing Guide (the latest review at the time of writing was October 2019), which can be found at `https://mbs.microsoft.com/Files/public/365/Dynamics365BusinessCentralLicensingGuide.pdf`.

Once the customer gets started with their trial or production tenants, they will be offered a productive, intuitive, and user-friendly web client interface, as shown in the following screenshot:

The best browser experience is offered by Microsoft Edge or Google Chrome.

Customers can also benefit from the universal app deployment type in almost every modern device, such as tablets, phablets, and phones. This is achieved by downloading an app (known as Dynamics 365 Business Central Universal App) from the Windows Store, Google Play, or the Apple Store. To install the mobile app, go to `https://docs.microsoft.com/en-us/dynamics365/business-central/install-mobile-app`.

Upon opening this website, we get three options for installing the mobile app. You can install it from Microsoft, download it from the Apple Store, or get it from the Google Play Store. The following is a snippet of the screen you'll see when you select to install the app from Microsoft:

Microsoft Dynamics 365 Business Central

Microsoft Corporation • Business > Accounting & finance

♡ Wish list

Microsoft Dynamics 365 Business Central is a business management solution that helps companies connect their financials, sales, service, and operations to streamline business processes, improve customer interactions and make better decisions.

More

 PEGI 3

At the time of writing, Microsoft Dynamics 365 Business Central has been officially localized and released by Microsoft in 18 countries (sorted by release date):

April 2018	July 2018	October 2018
United States	Australia	Mexico
Canada	New Zealand	Norway
United Kingdom		Iceland
Denmark		
Netherlands		
Germany		
Spain		
Italy		
France		
Austria		
Switzerland		
Belgium		
Sweden		
Finland		

Starting from the October 2018 update, CSP partners can now create their own localized versions for countries where Dynamics 365 Business Central has not been released or is not on the radar as a Microsoft localization.

These localizations start with the worldwide standard application base (called W1) and are distributed as extensions through the Microsoft Dynamics 365 Marketplace, called AppSource. Like any extension (or app) that's deployed through AppSource, all the application and technical support is provided by the partner who sells the app through AppSource.

You can read more about this at `https://docs.microsoft.com/en-us/dynamics365/business-central/dev-itpro/developer/readiness/readiness-develop-localization#service-availability-in-additional-countries`.

The following is a list of current extra CSP localized countries (at the time of writing) with the app and the publisher's name:

Country	Application Name	Publisher
Estonia	Estonian language for Estonia VAT Reporting localization for Estonia Business Register localization for Estonia Banking Formats localization for Estonia Intrastat Reporting localization for Estonia	Estonian Dynamics Partners
Hong Kong SAR	Chinese (Traditional) Language Pack for Hong Kong Traditional Chinese Pack for Hong Kong Traditional Chinese Language for Hong Kong	Tectura Hong Kong Limited Pacific Business Consulting, Inc. K-Solve IT Solutions Limited
Indonesia	Tax Calculation Localization for Indonesia	Wahana Ciptasinatria
Japan	Japanese Language for Japan J-Pack – Japanese Localization	Pacific Business Consulting, Inc.
Malaysia	ADS Reporting (Starter) Localization for Malaysia ADS Local Tax (Starter) Localization for Malaysia	ADS Global SSO Sdn Bhd
Poland	Polish Language for Poland Polish Functionality – Starter Pack	IT.integro sp. z o.o.
Portugal	SOFTSTORE Localization Language for Portugal SOFTSTORE Localization Pack for Portugal	Softstore SA
Serbia	Serbian Language for Serbia Localization for Serbia	Adacta d.o.o.

Country	Application Name	Publisher
Singapore	Localization for Singapore AFON GST Localization for Singapore Dalstech GST Localization for Singapore	IBIZ Consulting Pte Ltd AFON Systems Pte Ltd Dalstech Pte Ltd
South Africa	South African Invoice	Braintree by Vox
South Korea	Korean Language for South Korea Korean Localization for VAT	DEEX Korea Co Ltd MAVEN Korea Co., Ltd.
Taiwan	Traditional Chinese Language Pack for Taiwan **Government Uniform Invoice** (GUI) for Taiwan Payroll System for Taiwan	Knowledge & Strategy Information Co., Ltd.
Thailand	Tax Localization for Thailand (VAT and WHT) VAT and Withholding Tax Localization for Thailand VAT and WHT Localization for Thailand	Triple P Application Co., Ltd. AVISIONTH Ubiz Solution Co., Ltd.
United Arab Emirates	VAT Localization for the United Arab Emirates	Alfazance Consulting

 You can read more about this at `https://docs.microsoft.com/en-us/dynamics365/business-central/dev-itpro/compliance/apptest-countries-and-translations` and `https://appsource.microsoft.com/en-us/marketplace/apps?product=dynamics-365%3Bdynamics-365-business-centralpage=1`.

Now that we know about what Dynamics 365 Business Central is and what it provides to a customer, let's have a deep dive into the partner's perspective.

Understanding the partner's perspective

CSP enables partners to access a portfolio of Microsoft cloud services to be sold. Within this program, there are tools for managing and supporting these cloud services. One of these online services is Dynamics 365 Business Central.

You can find out more about the Partner Center at `https://docs.microsoft.com/en-us/partner-center/csp-overview`.

In the SaaS proposition, it is only through the CSP partners or their resellers that a potential customer could purchase licenses for Dynamics 365 Business Central and convert the trial license into a pay-per-use license or start by directly paying the monthly fee for the users.

In every CSP, a partner or reseller is technically represented by a unique tenant record in the **Azure Active Directory** (**AAD**). AAD is a multi-tenant authentication service that offers identity and access capabilities for applications running in Microsoft Azure and Microsoft on-premises environments.

Within this specific AAD tenant record, a partner can define a different type or class of users (often called supporting agents) that are mainly categorized into two different groups (so-called agent groups): *Admin* and *Helpdesk* groups.

Like partners, customers also have their own AAD tenant unique record. When subscribing to an Essential or Premium plan within a Dynamics 365 Business Central tenant, every customer gives consent for a special trusted relationship between the CSP partner and the customer AAD tenants.

The relationship's direction goes from customer tenant to partner tenant, and it can be revoked and/or managed by the customer if needed.

In the customer environment, AAD tenants, user, role, and subscription entities are defined and managed. Roles are assigned to users by the customers and these roles reflect their capabilities in the products that they subscribe to. Subscribing to an online product such as Dynamics 365 Business Central in the customer AAD tenant requires the further important step of the CSP partner assigning the specific online product license to the users.

These tasks are performed through the **Business Central Admin** portal. This portal can be accessed directly by the customer or the CSP partner. The CSP partner may also have access to the **Admin Center** via the **Partner Center** portal with the following options:

1. With the Partner Center portal, there are several ways to browse to the Dynamics 365 Business Central Admin Center portal. One of these is from the **Service Management** tab. The **Service Management** tab contains links to various admin portals related to a specific customer AAD tenant, such as Exchange or Office 365. It also displays the service health status for products that the portals or administrator consoles refer to, such as Exchange Online, Identity Service, and Dynamics 365 Business Central.

2. By clicking on the Dynamics 365 Business Central link, the partner will be redirected straight to the Dynamics 365 Business Central Admin Center portal. Back in the Partner Center portal, the CSP partner is also able to check the customer's order history and see which subscriptions they belong to. It is also possible to select the Dynamics 365 Business Central billing frequency – such as monthly or once per year – and subscribes to different online services on behalf of that customer.

3. The subscriptions are divided per offering type (level). As an example, within Dynamics 365 Business Central, it is possible to choose the Essential or the Premium plan.

4. In the **Users and licenses** section, the CSP partner can add users manually or upload many of them from a file. For every user, a different service license can be assigned.

5. Once a license has been assigned, the user can start working with Dynamics 365 Business Central and will have the app listed on their home page at `home.dynamics.com`. Clicking on the Dynamics 365 Business Central icon redirects the user to their first login, and they can start working immediately in the production tenant. You may notice that the URL definition benefits from an easy to identify fixed client endpoint and customer tenant, and its Dynamics 365 Business Central Admin portal should look like this:

   - Customer tenant: `https://businesscentral.dynamics.com/<GUID>`
   - Customer tenant admin portal: `https://businesscentral.dynamics.com/<GUID>/admin`

GUID identifies the same customer environment that you came from in the Partner Center portal.

 Since the Fall 2019 update, if you have multiple production environments, when you click on the Dynamics 365 Business Central icon on the home page (`home.dynamics.com`), you will be prompted to select which environment name to choose. The environment endpoint should look like `https://businesscentral.dynamics.com/<EnvironmentName>`.

So, who can access the Dynamics 365 Business Central Admin Center portal? The answer is as follows:

- CSP Partner Admin and Helpdesk agents who have an active entitled relationship with the customer tenant
- The customer's AAD Global Administrator

 Dynamics 365 Business Central licensed users won't be able to access the administration portal. There is no relationship between the product license and Dynamics 365 Business Central Admin Center portal access.

The customer's AAD tenant Global Administrator can sign in, and partner AAD tenant Administrators and Helpdesk users can access as a Delegated Admin. Delegated Admins can perform elevated tasks as Partner, but they do not have the same rights that the customer's Global Administrator has. In short, Delegated Admins are not Global Administrators of the tenant.

An example of Dynamics 365 Business Central Admin Center portal

As a quick example, a Delegated Admin cannot create a new company in the customer tenant but should ask the customer administrator (with SUPER rights) to create a new company or be promoted by the customer in order to add the appropriate Dynamics 365 Business Central permission rights. Once the new company has been created, the Delegated Admin can sign in and perform the administrative tasks they are entitled to.

Partner Delegated Admins can sign in to a specific customer tenant that they have a relationship with by just typing the Dynamics 365 Business Central fixed endpoint, `https://businesscentral.dynamics.com`, followed by the customer tenant's AAD name (for example, `https://businesscentral.dynamics.com/customerAADtenantname.onmicrosoft.com`). This is necessary because the partner may be dealing with several customer administrative tasks and may need to connect, disconnect, and reconnect as quickly as they can during their daily activities.

The Dynamics 365 Business Central Admin Center portal currently contains four sections (**Environments**, **Notification recipients**, **Telemetry**, and **Reported Outages**), as depicted in the sidebar in the following screenshot:

We'll look at each of these in the upcoming sections.

Environments

Environments list all the Dynamics 365 Business Central production and sandbox tenants for a specific customer. For each of these, it shows the status, provisioning country, version, and upgrade window.

At the time of writing, the possible actions are as follows:

- **New**: Create a new production or tenant sandbox. Currently, it is possible to create up to three production tenants for the same or different countries and up to three sandbox tenants for the same or different countries. It is possible to create sandboxes as copies of production databases.

Depending on the amount of data in the production tenant, the operation of creating a sandbox from the production tenant could be a lengthy process.

- **Delete**: You could select a sandbox or production tenant for deletion.

At the time of writing, the possible actions for a specific tenant are as follows:

- **Set update window**: Configure an update window in local time for a specific tenant. The update window lets you select a start time and an end time. It is down to Microsoft to send a notification right after the update happened. The notification typically contains details of whether the update has been performed successfully or if it failed, and for what reason it failed. If the update failed, an actionable report of the failure will be added in the notification in order for the partner and/or customer to act upon it.
- **Schedule Update**: When a new update is available, a notification is sent by Microsoft to the admin center recipients and through this action, it is possible to schedule the update.
- **Delete**: Delete the current production or sandbox tenant.
- **Report Production Outage**: This is a new addition since the Fall 2019 update. If users are not able to connect to a production environment, just by pushing the production outage button, it is possible to file a record (ticket) into the request for immediate help to the Dynamics 365 Business Central operations center. This ticket will be highly prioritized so that the issue can be resolved in a timely manner.
- **Manage Support Contact**: This is used to add the support contact for one specific environment. Users will see this information on the **Business Central Help & Support** page. It is possible to choose different support contacts for each tenant or just one that fits all.

Since Microsoft is constantly adding new actions, it has been announced that the ability to download an Azure SQL backup (BACPAC) of a production tenant will come after the official release in October 2019. This could be restored on-premises for further offline troubleshooting, data analysis, and **Business Intelligence** (BI)-driven tasks.

-

To find out more, visit `https://docs.microsoft.com/en-us/ dynamics365-release-plan/2019wave2/dynamics365-business- central/planned-features`.

Notification recipients

Notification recipients list all the Dynamics 365 Business Central notification recipients for a specific customer. The list shows the recipients' names and email addresses. These users will be notified when a special life cycle tenant task is completed, such as when a minor update is applied or when an upgrade to a new application version is available.

This is useful if you want developers and testers to be notified when something has happened, or will happen soon, to a specified tenant in order to give them enough time to review their custom development against the new standard application code.

Telemetry

This shows a filter pane with date, time, and event types for a specific customer.

It is possible to set filters to a specific environment (production or sandbox) and go back in time by specifying the number of minutes to look back. The list reports the following:

- **Timestamp**: A value that represents when exactly the operation was logged.
- **Level**: An integer value that shows errors, warnings, and information.
- **Opcode Name**: The type of application operation (for example, start or stop).
- **Object Type and ID**: This represents the type and ID of the object that generated the log.
- **Object Extension Name and ID**: If no value is displayed, it means that the telemetry log comes directly from legacy application code (C/AL).
- **Function Name**: This represents the name of the object function that generated the log.
- **Failure Message**: If no value is displayed, this typically means that this is an information message about a start or stop operation that happened to a specific object function.

For the specified time range, it is also possible to search in columns for a specific operation or an error message. This is frequently used in sandbox or staging environments to find out whether there are inconsistencies or runtime errors between the standard base app and custom extensions that have been developed.

Reported production outages

This is a new addition with the Fall 2019 update. It reports a list of the production outage tickets and their status. It is possible to filter for the last 30, 14, or 7 days.

 More information on this is available at `https://docs.microsoft.com/en-us/dynamics365/business-central/dev-itpro/administration/tenant-admin-center`.

Aside from client logins and performing activities through the portal's **user interface** (**UI**), the Partner Center and Dynamics 365 Business Central Admin Portals expose a set of powerful APIs that could be used to create a custom façade to handle customer creation, license assignment, and other tasks in a modern and fully automated way.

Even with basic knowledge of PowerShell or Visual C# and without any high-level development skills, it is possible to take the first step toward creating your own tailored dashboard and an automated way to create new customer users, assign or revoke licenses, and so on.

For example, we could use the following endpoint: `https://api.businesscentral.dynamics.com/v1.2/admin/applications/BusinessCentral/environments/Sandbox`.

How it works behind the scenes

The fixed web service endpoint global service is called and redirects the information to the global tenant manager global service, which will do its broadcast and find out which regional control plane, data plane, and tenant the request belongs to.

After retrieving the required information, the fixed web service endpoint will pass requests back and forth directly to the regional control plane that was selected. In other words, the global services only performed the first routing information task (a simple proxy task).

The fixed web service endpoint, when routed to communicate with the specific regional control plane, will start interacting with the tenant admin backend service.

You can find out more about this at `https://docs.microsoft.com/en-us/partner-center/develop/` and `https://docs.microsoft.com/en-us/dynamics365/business-central/dev-itpro/administration/administration-center-api`.

At the time of writing, some partners have already implemented the Dynamics 365 Partner Center SDK in their own projects and have consumed these APIs within Dynamics 365 Business Central on-premise environments (using .NET interoperability) in order to have a fully integrated customer tenant management dashboard. This can also be done for demonstration purposes.

Now that we have unleashed some of the best features that are provided to Microsoft's partners, let's have an overview of what Dynamics 365 Business Central is under the hood.

Under the skin of Dynamics 365 Business Central

Microsoft invested a lot in the last year and continues to invest in a modernized and streamlined Dynamics 365 Business Central architecture in order to have an ERP cloud service solution that is easy to deploy and upgrade.

At the time of writing, statistics are very encouraging and even exceed expectations.

Basically, a new Dynamics 365 Business Central tenant is created every 180 seconds. 400,000 metrics are emitted per minute, with approximately 8 TB of logs generated per day. These logs are then pre-processed, aggregated, and approximately 4 TB data is uploaded to Cosmos DB for big data analysis via the Azure Data Lake service.

These are just some of the numbers that Dynamics 365 Business Central is producing, and just a few of the Microsoft cloud services that are used to provide the best online ERP experience in the world.

At this pace, in the near future, it might be foreseeable that **Artificial Intelligence (AI)** could be used to self-trigger microservice tuning at all platform and application levels.

Going a bit deeper, considering that Azure technologies are involved, at the time of writing, there are 20 resources that are orchestrated together in every single microservice collection. This goes to show what a complex environment is provided to users and developers in the simplest way possible.

The Dynamics 365 Business Central development team's main goal is to move the extensibility burden to the partners and the customers. Partners and customers have to completely forget about where and how the data is stored, as well as the technologies that are required to gather, transform, and upgrade it. Instead, they should simply concentrate on extending the application. No platform skills are required; simply hit refresh and repeat "developers, developers, developers..."

Here is a tabular overview of the Azure resources that are used to build each platform service, their purposes, and links to more information about each resource:

Azure resource	General-purpose	Link
Azure Service Fabric	Distributed systems platform that makes it easy to deploy and manage scalable microservices and containers.	`https://docs.microsoft.com/en-us/azure/service-fabric/service-fabric-overview`
Azure Key Vault	To encrypt and decrypt data within the application and several other security-related features.	`https://docs.microsoft.com/en-us/azure/key-vault/key-vault-whatis`
Application Gateway	Web traffic load balancer that makes an intelligent load distribution of the application calls.	`https://docs.microsoft.com/en-us/azure/application-gateway/overview`
SQL Elastic Database Pools	Resource optimizer for Azure SQL databases that's used for customer and application tenants.	`https://docs.microsoft.com/en-us/azure/sql-database/sql-database-elastic-pool`
Application Insights	Set of tools for gathering log information and sending it as telemetry data.	`https://docs.microsoft.com/en-us/azure/application-insights/app-insights-overview`
Azure **Machine Learning** (**ML**) service	SaaS-based lab for developing and applying machine learning models and their outcomes.	`https://docs.microsoft.com/en-us/azure/machine-learning/service/overview-what-is-azure-ml`
Azure Search	APIs for advanced search to be implemented inside applications and microservices.	`https://docs.microsoft.com/en-us/azure/search/search-what-is-azure-search`

Azure Storage	Provides the storage layer abstraction to preserve data according to security and privacy. These reflect regional legal models.	`https://docs.microsoft.` `com/en-us/azure/storage/`
Azure **Active Directory** (**AD**)	Microsoft's cloud-based identity and access management service. Guaranteed secure and solid sign-in and resource access.	`https://docs.microsoft.` `com/en-us/azure/active-` `directory/fundamentals/` `active-directory-whatis`
Azure Function	Provides APIs for specific routines/functions in isolated environments. Suggested replacement for Dynamics 365 Business Central and .NET interoperability.	`https://docs.microsoft.` `com/en-us/azure/azure-` `functions/functions-` `overview`
Traffic Manager	DNS-based traffic load balancer, the main purpose of which is to distribute traffic load optimally to services across global Azure regions, all while providing high availability and responsiveness.	`https://docs.microsoft.` `com/en-us/azure/traffic-` `manager/traffic-manager-` `overview`
Azure Load Balancer	Used to guarantee high availability for microservices. Load Balancer supports inbound and outbound scenarios and provides low latency and high throughput. It scales up to millions of flows for all TCP and UDP applications.	`https://docs.microsoft.` `com/en-us/azure/load-` `balancer/load-balancer-` `overview`
Azure SQL Database	A relational database for managing data in and out of cloud storage.	`https://docs.microsoft.` `com/en-us/azure/sql-` `database/sql-database-` `technical-overview`
Azure Container Registry	Stores base images for all types of container deployments. Typically used to store sandbox images to be downloaded for development purposes.	`https://docs.microsoft.` `com/en-us/azure/` `container-registry/`
Azure Data Lake Storage Gen1	Used to analyze the huge amount of telemetry data that's created.	`https://docs.microsoft.` `com/en-us/azure/data-` `lake-store/data-lake-` `store-overview`

Azure Service Bus	A message broker solution that's used to decouple applications and services from each other. Data is transferred between different applications and services.	`https://docs.microsoft.com/en-us/azure/service-bus-messaging/service-bus-messaging-overview`
Health Monitoring	Azure Service Fabric introduces a scalable set of analytics tools to monitor system and/or service health. Alerts can be created with specific rules and sent to on-call operation engineers.	`https://docs.microsoft.com/en-us/azure/service-fabric/service-fabric-diagnostics-overview`
Azure Virtual Network	Enables many types of Azure resources, such as Azure virtual machines, to securely communicate with each other and the internet.	`https://docs.microsoft.com/en-us/azure/virtual-network/virtual-networks-overview`
Azure Data Factory	A cloud-based data integration service that allows the creation of data-driven workflows for automating data movement and data transformation.	`https://docs.microsoft.com/en-us/azure/data-factory/introduction`
Cosmos DB	Used to aggregate telemetry data and further analysis.	`https://docs.microsoft.com/en-us/azure/cosmos-db/introduction`

Global services are just a few services that don't store any data and only perform processing activities. They are just proxies that don't hold any data and are used to redirect requests to the appropriate control and data planes.

Global services are mainly used to redirect requests to the appropriate control planes; in fact, they are simply routing the information when users are logging in. The fixed client endpoint is responsible for routing to the appropriate control and data plane based on credentials. No other extra information is needed.

There are several global services in different world regions with multiple instances, but they are all accessed from within the same endpoint. A traffic manager in front of them redirects the call to the closest instance where the calls come from. This makes the Dynamics 365 Business Central service very efficient and performant. Statistically, 30,000 calls per hour are routed through Dynamics 365 Business Central global services. Next, let's understand where and how these work.

Regional control planes

These are collections of microservices that have their own purposes and perform specific tasks (provisioning, scale, monitoring, and authentication, for example) to manage application access, distribution, and runtime. They are all built-in and managed by Azure Service Fabric. Each region has a subset of these services, and they are called regional services because they follow the same privacy and legal guidelines of the country or region of the world they belong to.

There are two benefits of this:

- Privacy and security laws in that specific region are respected when it comes to data handling.
- Closeness to data storage means that latency is reduced and network performance is increased.

A control plane is a collection of services that manage a specific data plane. For this reason, they are located and distributed in the same region as the data planes.

The following are the services that currently make up a control plan:

- **Database Monitor**: Used to monitor a tenant's and application databases' health and upload telemetry and statistics into the internal analysis tool.
- **Elastic Pool Optimizer**: Extracts statistics from elastic pools and uploads them into internal tools.
- **Extension Management Service**: This is the core service of the control plane and is where the sync daemon routes and finalizes service calls. Roughly speaking, it is an information container. It has a registry of all the data plane clusters and inventories (which tenants are in which cluster, and so on). Its duty is to create, upgrade, and manage tenants on demand. Typically, this service acts upon sync daemon requests or from other services in the regional control plane.
- **Extension Validation Service**: Compiles the per-tenant extensions against upcoming application services. This will determine whether the changes in the base application that are coming will break the private IP that was created for that tenant. These errors could be surfaced to the partner through the CSP partner portal.
- **Health Monitor**: Keeps track of the state of the tenant and, if it detects an unhealthy ping, it sends an internal alert.

- **Management Portal**: Internal dashboard portal based on the Dynamics 365 Business Central web client platform. It manages customer tenants and provides a UI to perform actions over these tenants.
- **Management Service**: The heart of service orchestration. It contains a catalog of what kind of activity could/should be performed by the tenant. Some of these include create, copy, upgrade, and delete.
- **Provisioning Service**: Historically, it was made of a collection of PowerShell scripts for Azure VM provisioning. Nowadays, it is mainly used to perform extension validations.
- **Sync Daemon**: This is one of the oldest services for Dynamics 365 Business Central. Global services typically talk to this service in the regional control planes and it determines whether to create a new tenant or route to the appropriate data plane. It has an operations database that is used to enqueue requests of creating new tenants, just in case it cannot be served immediately.
- **Tenant Admin Backend Service**: Performs activities related to the admin center. For example, it is responsible for validating web service requests, such as the integrity of the content and the business logic of the content.
- **Tenant Buffering Service**: This is typically handled by the management service. It is constantly checking how many tenants have been created and replaces the number of buffer tenants with new ones to cope with peak periods and maintain the right balance between brand new tenant creation and the assignment of existing tenants.
- **Tenant Maintenance Service**: Used for tenant maintenance. For example, when a customer decides to move from a trial to a paid subscription, this service kicks in. The maintenance service will then move the tenant from the Standard tier to a more performant Premium tier. If a trial expires or a license is removed in the AAD, or the customer stops paying, the maintenance service will put the tenant in a suspended state. There is a 90-day period to redeem the tenant, but this may vary, depending on the data retention policy in each country. After this grace period, the tenant is dismounted from the service tier and, after a while, it's deleted.
- **Tenant Upgrader**: Schedules and triggers update jobs in a time upgrade window specified by the CSP partner. Currently, the date when the tenant will be upgraded is decided by Microsoft and cannot be changed.

The development team is constantly adding new services or splitting existing ones to make room for new features or to optimize the maintenance and scalability of Dynamics 365 Business Central. In the next section, we will see what regional data planes work with these.

Regional data planes

Regional data planes are collections of services that enable safe customer data storage. It is important to save data in the same country in Azure data centers that are close to the customers, as well as in the same privacy and compliance region of the customer. Data safety is very important. As an example, two data planes have been created in the Western Europe region, both of which are supported by four data centers. They are standard and publicly available, and everyone – including the development team – can make use of them and unleash the potential of the Azure services, their APIs, and their extensibility.

In SaaS solutions, it is very important to work on isolated microservices in order to quickly deploy updates and changes in segments. The same applies to data planes, where scheduled updates can be applied with the required atomicity through what are called internally safe deployment practices.

Data plane resources are all reserved for handling customer data. These are constantly measured using an amazing number of telemetry parameters. All the management of data planes, such as creating and upgrading tenants, is performed by other regional entities called control planes.

Here is a list of the current regional data planes (as of October 2019) and the localized version they are hosting:

WEST EUROPE	NORTH EUROPE	UNITED STATES	CANADA	ASIA/MIDDLE EAST	AFRICA	OCEANIA
Austria	Denmark	Mexico	Canada	Hong Kong (CSP)	South Africa (CSP)	Australia
Belgium	Estonia (CSP)	United States		Japan (CSP)		New Zealand
France	Finland			Malaysia (CSP)		
Germany	Iceland			Thailand (CSP)		
Italy	Norway			South Korea (CSP)		
Netherlands	Sweden			Taiwan (CSP)		
Serbia (CSP)				United Arab Emirates (CSP)		
Spain				Indonesia (CSP)		
Switzerland				Singapore (CSP)		

United Kingdom						
Poland (CSP)						
Portugal (CSP)						

A data plane cluster contains all the redundant VMs and Azure SQL databases for the application and customer tenants. Currently, high availability is guaranteed by load balancing five Azure VMs per data plan.

Since these statistics demonstrate the generation of a tenant roughly every three minutes, how is it possible to cope with and scale to such a high volume when multiple requests come simultaneously within the same data plane? This is handled in a pretty intelligent way. When a regional control plane is instructed to create a new tenant, the management service reserves a buffer tenant in the data plane cluster. What is a buffer tenant? Basically, it is a tenant that's already been created, with a demo data company inside the database that acts as sort of pre-packaged template. Buffer tenants are not bounded to any application service (dismounted).

When a buffer tenant is reserved, it is not able to be taken by any other management service call and it is transformed into a production tenant by simply changing some configuration parameters and adding the production company name for a specific customer. Once this is done, the tenant is mounted against a production service and, when it's operational, connections are good to go.

In short: reserve, configure, mount, operational, and it's good to go. No lengthy database creations or restore processes.

Currently, data plane cluster environments in production and sandbox environments are different. This is because of the different environment's natures and their needs. They are mainly different in terms of performance because of the different Azure SQL database tier. Trial and sandbox tenants currently belong to the Azure S-tier. When switched to production, these are moved to the more performant, and recommended by Azure SQL Team, P-tier.

A single data plane cluster is an aggregate of Microsoft cloud technologies that's logically divided into the Compute and Data tier. Let's explore the anatomy of a data plane:

Service Name	General Purpose
Public IP Addresses	These are different depending on user calls (browser/web service) or are instantiated internally by the control plane.
Application Gateway	This is a smart, intelligent, and sophisticated Layer 7 load balancer that's capable of analyzing cookies and inspecting payloads. It's used for user calls and only supports HTTP calls.
Azure Load Balancer	This is used internally by regional control plane calls.
VM Scale Set	It is made up of five Azure VMs by default. More Azure VMs can be provisioned inside the VM scale set so that it has infinite scaling and can cope with high service load or isolation. The entire Azure VM set is defined inside the same availability set. This means that if there is a hardware failure, it won't affect all the VMs at the same time, guaranteeing high service availability. Every VM inside a VM scale set contains a Dynamics 365 Business Central Web Server and Dynamics 365 Business Central. This helps optimize traffic between web servers and Dynamics 365 Business Central. Every Azure VM also contains a monitoring service to collect telemetry data and licensing services to avoid storing certificate private keys that are used to access AAD tenants.
Virtual Network	This is used to let Azure VMs communicate with each other within the VM scale set.
Storage Account	This contains telemetry data from the VMs and service health data.
Azure Service Fabric Controller	This is used to manage and orchestrate service deployments in every cluster. For example, when needed, it could be instructed to provision a new VM in the scale set.
Application Database	This contains standard application code and is bound to the Dynamics 365 Business Central service in each VM. Even if this could look like part of the data tier, the application database doesn't actually store any customer data. This is why it has been listed with the other compute section items.

Network Security Group	This is mainly used to provide an extra security layer to each cluster. Typically, the development team doesn't allow any remote connection through Terminal Services, even from themselves. Dynamics 365 Business Central's telemetry service provides information on the VM or the service status and provides actionable insights through specific endpoints. In other words, the safety of data handling is totally guaranteed.

After understanding this exhaustive list, let's move on and look at the Data-tier level.

Data-tier

The simplest data tier is the so-called per-single or individual database. This is pretty easy to explain and understand: create an Azure SQL database, for example, within an Sx tier, and, if a customer needs more performance, you just have to scale it up to Sx+n, depending on how many resources you need (how fast you want your process to finish).

The drawback with individual databases is that, by the time you have created the database in Azure SQL, all the resources are allocated, not shared nor released, and the customer – or you – has to pay for them, whether you are using them or not.

When you have thousands (or hundreds of thousands) of databases to handle, like in every multi-tenant class A product, the resource placement design should be smart enough to know when to assign or release resources at need. Otherwise, this will turn into a cost-killer product for everyone: customers, partners, and Microsoft itself.

Dynamics 365 Business Central database resource allocation is intelligent. It relies on the Azure SQL Elastic Pools technology. Basically, with Azure SQL Elastic Pools, it is possible to define a total amount of resources to be shared within the pool and a range (min and max) value for every database tenant. The cloud resource governor will distribute the resources wisely within the pool. This is very efficient, performant, and cost-effective.

It's worth mentioning that there are **Standard** (**Sx**) and **Premium** (**Px**) Elastic Pool data tiers. When needed, tenants from Sx are moved to a more performant Px pool.

All the production databases are currently running in the Px elastic pool data tier.

The data tier is accessed through a WCF-based **Navision Service Tier** (**NST**) that's installed inside another microservice called VM Scale Set. The following is the current anatomy of a single VM scale set:

Web Server	Dynamics 365 Business Central Web Server components
NST	Dynamics 365 Business Central Server service. For security reasons, it is isolated in host mode in a Hyper-V container (such as a small VM). This prevents malicious code accessing a user's secrets.
Monitoring Agent service	Used to collect telemetry data coming from the current status of Azure VMs. This service also collects telemetry data from platform and application logs for both web server and server service components.
Licensing service	This is a service that was introduced in the Fall 2018 update for security reasons. This service is responsible for checking the existence of a valid license within AAD, and its APIs are called by the NST component.
Tenant Directory	This is a collection of tenant names and their connection strings. It is typically accessed by another service, such as the Licensing service, to avoid spoiling attacks or direct calls from NST through the application database tenant list.
Hybrid Proxy	This enables hybrid replication so that we can move on-premise data to the cloud. You can find out more about this at `https://docs.microsoft.com/en-us/dynamics365/business-central/dev-itpro/administration/about-intelligent-edge` and `https://docs.microsoft.com/en-us/dynamics365/business-central/about-intelligent-cloud`.
Extension Service	This allows per-tenant extensions to be installed asynchronously.
Delta Service	This enables delta queries to the Dynamics 365 Business Central OData service endpoint.
Browser Client	This hosts the static part of the webserver components (`.js` files and so on).

Gateway service	This is a performance-driven service artifact that's used for intelligent request routing. This service redirects calls to a so-called "warm" service if another session for the same tenant has already been created. It warms up the memory cache with application and data objects.
Task Trigger service	This service is used to optimize scheduled task execution and improve performance when they are executed (faster start) and in the context they are executed in (that is, routed to a warm NST, if one exists).

Now that we have unleashed the service and looked at what's under the hood of Dynamics 365 Business Central, let's have a quick overview of what will be in its future.

Understanding the future perspective

Azure and Office 365 are now considered solid and mature and have a considerable **Returns On Investment (ROI)** for customers.

They are among the best sources of revenue for Microsoft and where the most investment and capital is redirected. All Microsoft services are requested to align with Microsoft's strategy of increasing the consumption of these two flagship services.

Dynamics 365 Business Central perfectly fits into Microsoft's strategy: it brings new potential SMB ERP customers into this offering to accelerate the best-in-class Microsoft cloud service consumption.

In other words, potential Dynamics NAV and Dynamics GP customers are strongly encouraged to subscribe to Dynamics 365 Business Central's Essential or Premium tier instead of receiving a typical offering for an on-premise deployment.

A huge product transformation to drive online adoption has been announced at the latest Microsoft and non-Microsoft events. These actions are mainly aligned with existing Dynamics NAV and Dynamics 365 Business Central on-premise customers. The following is the current roadmap for the product that was recently presented at **Directions EMEA** (https://www.directionsemea.com/):

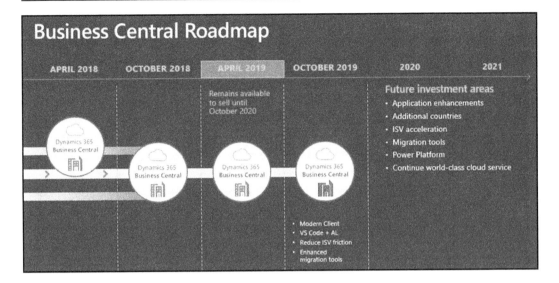

With the Fall 2019 release, Microsoft achieved the challenging goal of reducing the gap between on-premise and online deployment. Both products deployment capabilities are now almost the same:

- **Use Modern clients only**: No more Windows client deployment for on-premise releases.
- **Extension development only**: No more legacy code changes through CSIDE or mixed-mode for on-premise releases. Standard code changes can only be done on-premises, even if these should be avoided as much as possible. More information can be found at `http://www.waldo.be/2019/08/06/al-baseapp-customization-because-you-can-doesnt-mean-you-should/`.

The current plan from the development team, according to their announcement, is to move the existing legacy C/AL code into AL and provide standard code as Microsoft localized extensions or, more feasibly, as a series of dependent apps.

In this way, both on-premise and online client access will be roughly the same in terms of both user and development experience. The difference between on-premise and online, then, will be really small, and moving from on-premise to online in a single step will be far easier.

Since this journey is a continuous work in progress, Dynamics 365 Business Central's development team is wide open and listens to all customer and partner requests with a proactive and reactive service. This has been done to cover all the different perspectives and points of view. In the upcoming sections, we'll look at exactly how Microsoft listens to and acts upon customer and partner requests.

Proactive scenarios (Microsoft listens)

Let's look at a few proactive scenarios for Microsoft Dynamics features and versions:

- **Suggestions for new features and enhancing existing features and capabilities:** This directly creates an internal record to Dynamics 365 Business Central's engineering backlog. You can also vote for existing suggestions, and this elevates prioritization and rankings for that specific feature. It is directly handled by the development team (`https://aka.ms/bcideas`).
- **Bugs or errors found in application or platform PREVIEW or BETA versions:** Only for **Independent Software Vendor (ISV)/Value Added Resellers (VAR)**. Note that no advisory or consultancy requests are accepted (`https://docs.microsoft.com/en-us/collaborate/`).
- **Bugs or errors found in PREVIEW or BETA versions of AL in Visual Studio Code:** It should be noted that no advisory or consultancy requests are accepted (`https://github.com/microsoft/al`).

New event requests

Function Expose requests will be added to the release in preview and not to the current online version. A reactive request should be raised to backport the changes to the current online stack (`https://github.com/microsoft/ALAppExtensions/`).

Reactive scenarios (Microsoft acts)

These are the Microsoft rules for reactive scenarios:

- **Bugs or errors found in applications or platforms for versions in General Availability (GA) and in mainstream support:** Only for ISVs/VARs that have an **Advanced Support for Partners (ASfP)** contract with Microsoft.
- **Backport new events or functions exposed in versions currently in GA and in mainstream support:** Online customers must contact their seller or CSP partner to receive support and/or ask them to file a reactive support request.

 More information can be found here: `https://community.dynamics.com/business/b/financials/archive/2018/12/04/find-the-right-resources-and-provide-feedback`.

All in all, considering the existing customers that still are on-premise with Dynamics NAV and Dynamics GP, the best suggestions we can provide to customer and partner organizations are as follows:

- Use and request events.
- Move all the existing private IPs outside the standard code with event-driven development as much as possible. If this requires new events in the standard application, request them through the appropriate channel.
- Move legacy code into extensions.
- Whatever can be isolated into event-driven development can also be packaged as an extension. Move as many private IPs as possible into an extension. This task has a widely accepted technical term called *SaaSification*.
- Refactor all the code to make it work in the web client and focus all the skills on web-based development.
- Make the web client your main client and switch your mind to web-oriented development.
- Train all your salespeople, installers, developers, functional application experts, and everyone else who's using or demoing the web client. Live and breathe using the Dynamics 365 Business Central web client.
- Collaborate and use social media.

- Stay up to date on LinkedIn, Twitter, and Yammer. Take note of your own business process showstopper and share it with the Dynamics 365 Business Central community and development team by actively participating in official and unofficial forums and dedicated product events.
- Last but not least, mainly for partners and freelancers, get used to and specialize in modern technologies.

We suggest that developers acquire skills related to the following topics:

- Visual Studio Code and AL
- JavaScript and web-based development
- AI and machine learning techniques
- Azure services for developers (such as Azure Functions and Cognitive Service)
- Git and Azure DevOps

Developers and architects should become familiar with the following:

- Docker containers
- Azure compute services (such as Azure VMs and Azure Storage)
- Office 365 services and Dynamics 365
- **Common Data Model (CDM)/Common Data Service (CDS)**

It is highly recommended for partners to subscribe to the Dynamics 365 Business Central *Ready to Go* program and benefit from its endless and constantly updated learning catalog. You can read more about it at `https://docs.microsoft.com/en-us/dynamics365/business-central/dev-itpro/developer/readiness/readiness-ready-to-go?tabs=learning`.

Summary

This introductory chapter provided an overview of what is now available in – and what will be in the future of – Dynamics 365 Business Central.

First, we focused on Dynamics 365 Business Central by considering the partner and customer perspective. This will be beneficial for you when it comes to understanding what the product is capable of offering in terms of localizations, features, and the SMB market segment you would like to target.

Next, we covered the Partner Center and Dynamics 365 Business Central Admin Center portals and how to use them. Then, we covered Microsoft Dynamics 365 Business Central's main technological characteristics and had an overview of the architectural elements. We finished this chapter with a short overview of what might happen in the future, how to contribute toward making this happen, and how to be part of the evolution of the Microsoft SaaS solution.

In the next chapter, we will thoroughly examine the Visual Studio Code, the AL language extension, and the modern development environment.

2
Mastering a Modern Development Environment

In the previous chapter, we introduced Dynamics 365 Business Central and revealed that its skeleton is Microsoft cloud microservices.

In this chapter, we will take a close look at the development environment. We will discuss the main shortcuts, tips, and tricks related to Visual Studio Code, the official development platform, and the AL language, the development language extension. The union between Visual Studio Code and AL defines the so-called modern development environment.

AL is the official extension provided by Microsoft, free of charge, through the online marketplace. Officially released in 2017 to extend what was then called Dynamics 365 for Financials, it is now a solid fully fledged development language that extends Dynamics 365 Business Central. It comes equipped with a lot of features that greatly enhance developers' productivity and coding quality.

The main goal of this chapter is to help Dynamics 365 Business Central developers understand what the development platform offers, unleash all their potential, and become proficient in their daily coding activities.

In this chapter, you will learn the following:

- What the Visual Studio Code user interface is composed of, and the purpose of each section
- How to be proficient in using the most powerful Visual Studio Code editing features
- What the AL language extension is, and what it consists of

Mastering Visual Studio Code

Visual Studio Code is one of the most widely used development environments worldwide. It is engineered to make it easy and quick to design cloud- and web-based applications, using a plethora of extensible languages. The application is focused on maximizing code editing and also unleashing the developer's potential by providing useful shortcuts to provide quick access to all that is needed in a specific development context.

When you start Visual Studio Code, freshly installed, it will show you the typical **Welcome** page:

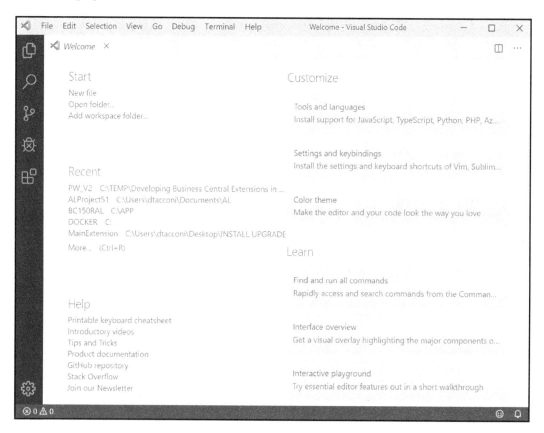

The **Welcome** page contains the following:

- **Start**: Shortcuts for creating and opening files and folders
- **Recent**: A list of recently opened files and folders
- **Help**: A list of documentation sheets, product docs, videos, and useful resources
- **Customize**: How to customize Visual Studio Code through extensions, keyboard shortcuts, background color themes, and so on
- **Learn**: Additional shortcuts to learning resources that are related to the most widely used commands, and how to master the user interface

The Welcome page is loaded whenever you run the Visual Studio Code as a new window (*Ctrl* + *Shift* + *N*). It is possible to change this behavior by unchecking **show welcome page on startup** or clicking **File | Preferences | Settings** and searching for Welcome page.

The Visual Studio Code environment is divided into five main areas:

- Code editor
- Status bar
- View bar
- Sidebar
- Panels area

Let's look at each of them in the following sections.

Code editor

The code editor is where you write your code and where you spend most of your time. It is activated when creating a new file, or when opening an existing file or folder.

You are allowed to edit just one single file, or you can even load and work with multiple files at the same time, side by side:

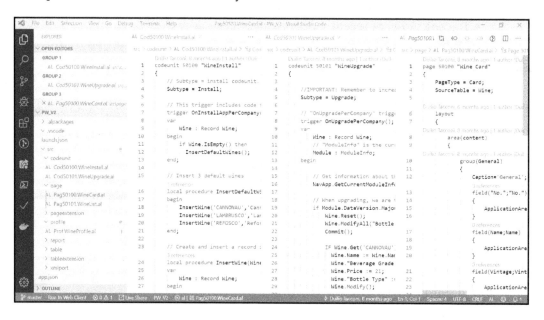

There are different ways to have multiple file views; three are mentioned here:

- Select a filename in the **EXPLORER** bar, then right-click and select **Open to the Side** (*Ctrl + Enter*).
- *Ctrl* + click on a filename in the **EXPLORER** bar.
- *Ctrl* + \ to split the editor into two parts.

It will accommodate several files, dividing the space equally between them. You can move through the different file editors by simply pressing *Ctrl + 1*, *Ctrl + 2*, *Ctrl + 3*, ..., *Ctrl + N*.

Editor windows can be resized, reordered, and zoomed in/out according to your needs. To zoom in/out press *Ctrl + +* / *Ctrl + -*, or **View | Zoom in / Zoom out**.

Zooming applies to all Visual Studio Code areas, not only to the code editor.

Visual Studio Code also provides an easy way of navigating between files with shortcuts. The quickest way is to press *Ctrl + Tab*. This will open the list of files that have been opened since Visual Studio Code started.

Status bar

The status bar typically contains information about the currently selected file or folder. It also provides some actionable shortcuts:

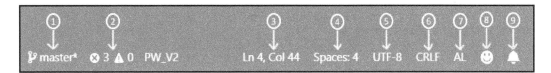

From left to right, the status bar contains the following information:

1. If Git is enabled, it will report version control information, such as the current branch.
2. Number of errors and/or warnings detected in the current code.
3. Cursor position (line position and column position).
4. Indentation size and type (spaces or tabs).
5. Encoding of the currently selected file.
6. Line terminator: **Carriage return (CR)** and/or **line feed (LF)**.
7. Language used to process the code in the selected file. If you click on the language, a menu will appear, and you should be able to change the processing programming language.
8. Feedback button, which you can use to share your feedback about Visual Studio Code on Twitter.
9. Notification icon. This shows the number of new notifications, which are typically related to product updates.

 The status bar has a conventional colorization, and it changes depending on what's processing. It is purple when opening a file, blue when opening a folder, orange when debugging, and so on.

View bar

This is on the left side of the workspace, and contains shortcuts to the sidebar. If a shortcut is clicked, the sidebar that belongs to the tool that has been chosen becomes visible. Clicking again, or pressing *Ctrl + B*, makes it disappear.

Sidebar

The sidebar is the place where you will interact the most with the code editor. It is context-sensitive, and you will find five standard activities, each enabled by the corresponding icon in the view bar.

EXPLORER (Ctrl + Shift + E)

EXPLORER provides a structured and organized view of the folder and files that you are currently working with. The **OPEN EDITORS** sub-view contains the list of active files in the code editor. Below this section, there might be another sub-view with the name of the folder that is open:

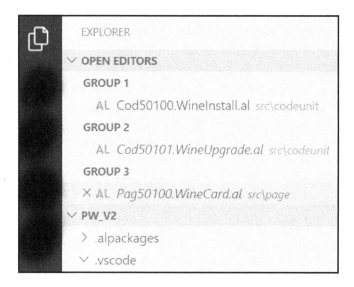

If you hover over the **OPEN EDITORS** sub-view, three action buttons will be shown: **Toggle Vertical/Horizontal Editor Layout** (*Shift + Alt + O*), **Save All** (*Ctrl + K + S*), and **Close All Files** (*Ctrl + K* or *Ctrl + W*). They are all self-explanatory:

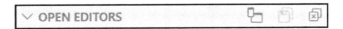

Hovering over the folder name (in this example PW_V2) will make four action buttons visible:

From left to right, these are **New File**, **New Folder**, **Refresh**, and **Collapse All**. They are self-explanatory.

Right-clicking on a folder or filename will open a context menu that shows common commands such as **Reveal in Explorer** (*Shift + Alt + R*), which opens the folder that contains the selected file. You can also copy the file path via **Copy Path** (*Shift + Alt + C*).

Down in the **EXPLORER** bar, there is another section called **OUTLINE**. It gives a very useful tree-view of members and types for a specific file. Consider the following screenshot:

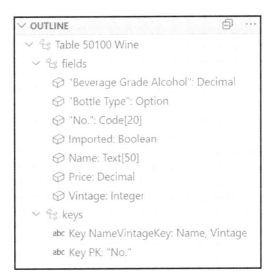

This is indeed a powerful option when you are developing complex objects and you want to jump into a specific area in one click.

SEARCH (Ctrl + Shift + F)

This is a powerful tool for searching for and replacing text in files. It is possible to opt for a simple search with one or more keywords, and you can use wildcards such as * and ?. Alternatively, you can opt for creating a complex search based on regular expressions (regex). There are also advanced options to include and/or exclude files or file types.

This is really helpful for developers when searching the *where used* field or variables in all files within an extension folder. Consider the following screenshot:

Search outputs are listed in a tree-view that lists all files containing the search keyword, and shows a small piece of code related to the line that they belong to in the file. The keyword match is highlighted in the tree-view, as well as within the code editor. These can be all collapsed by clicking the **Collapse All** button.

It is possible to reset the search results by clicking the **Clear Search Results** button.

SOURCE CONTROL (Ctrl + Shift + G)

Visual Studio Code provides native integration with one of the most widely known source control management systems: Git. The basics and integration of Git will be discussed in `Chapter 11`, *Source Control Management and DevOps with Business Central*.

DEBUG (Ctrl + Shift + D)

Visual Studio Code is not just a code editor for editing flat files. It also ships with an out-of-the-box integrated debugger framework that can be extended to debug different platforms and languages.

Visual Studio Code does not provide any debugging capability for Dynamics 365 Business Central. This comes embedded in the AL language extension for Visual Studio Code, which extends the existing .NET core debugger. In `Chapter 9`, *Debugging*, we will discuss this argument in detail.

EXTENSIONS (Ctrl + Shift + X)

Extensions are used to browse the online marketplace for extensions for Visual Studio Code, which include a growing plethora of additional languages, debuggers, tools, helpers, and much more. AL is an extension for Visual Studio Code that was developed by Microsoft. In the Visual Studio Code marketplace, you can also download several helpful extensions that extend (extensions for an extension) the AL Language extension and help Dynamics 365 Business Central developers be more efficient and productive and write code professionally.

Consider the following screenshot, which shows typical Visual Studio Code extensions installed for Dynamics 365 Business Central:

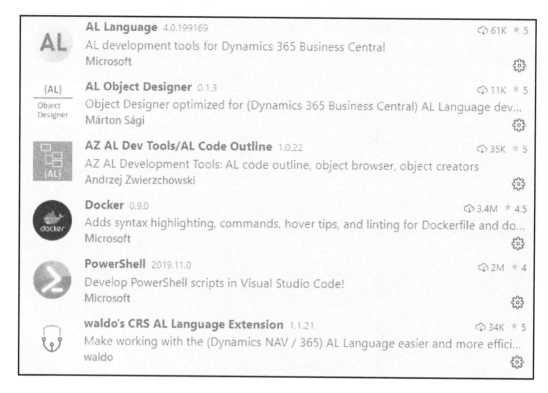

In the **EXTENSIONS** bar, it is possible to search the online marketplace or install an extension manually. You can also see the list of installed, outdated, recommended, and disabled extensions and sort them according to different criteria.

Some extension packages are meant to download and install a set of extensions. With Dynamics 365 Business Central, you might think of downloading and installing AL Extension Pack from `https://marketplace.visualstudio.com/items?itemName=waldo.al-extension-pack` or SD Extension Pack for Dynamics 365 Business Central from `https://marketplace.visualstudio.com/items?itemName=StefanoDemiliani.sd-extpack-d365bc`.

It is also possible to perform actions on a single extension by right-clicking on it. An extension could be enabled, disabled, disabled per workspace (a workspace could be a project or a folder), and so on. One of the newest – and coolest – features that has been added is the ability to install another version of the extension.

This is very useful for Dynamics 365 Business Central developers, in case there are regression behaviors or bugs in high-AL Language extension versions. Consider the following screenshot, which shows the current online AL Language extension versions:

EXTENSIONS	Select Version to Install
Search Extensions in Marketplace	4.0.182565 13 days ago (Current)
	3.0.168874 1 month ago
∨ ENABLED	3.0.152816 2 months ago
AL Language 4.0.182565	3.0.145991 3 months ago
AL AL development tools for Dynamics 36	3.0.126610 5 months ago
Microsoft	

This is also useful when developments target a specific platform version.

Manage

The **Manage** button is shown with a gear icon at the very bottom of the view bar:

If you click on it, a pop-up menu with a list of commands appears. These commands are used to customize Visual Studio Code, or to search for updates.

Command Palette

The Command Palette is one of the most important tools in Visual Studio Code. Its purpose is to give quick access to standard and extended commands. There are different ways to run the Command Palette:

- **Manage | Command Palette**
- **View | Command Palette**
- Keyboard shortcut: *Ctrl + Shift + P* (mostly used by all developers)

The Command Palette is not only good for showing menu commands, but it can also perform other actions, such as installing extensions. You can browse through it to review the huge list of available commands. Commands are indexed and searchable. Just type a few letters to get a filtered list. It's worth mentioning the long list of keyboard shortcut(s) that are available for most of these commands.

One very important thing to know about the Command Palette is the use of the > sign. When you press *Ctrl + Shift + P*, the Command Palette pops up with the > sign and shows the list of commands available. Consider the following screenshot:

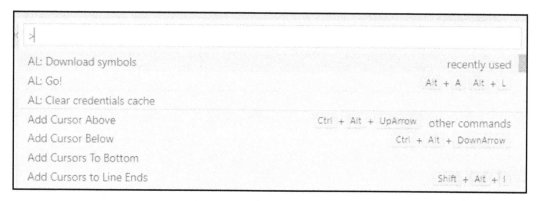

If you remove the > symbol, Visual Studio Code uses the Command Palette to show a list of the recently opened files. The following screenshot shows this:

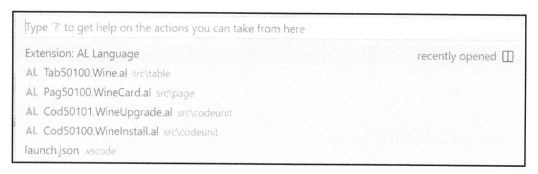

The power of this feature is that, without using the mouse, you can open the Command Palette, run a command, remove the **>** character, and select a file to edit. That's fantastic for development productivity.

Panels area

Visual Studio Code not only shows detailed analysis and information related to your code, but also has access and display information coming from other sources such as Git, installed extensions, and debuggers. These outputs are logged into the panels area, which, by default, is at the bottom, but could be easily moved to one side of the workspace using the **Move Panel Right** button, enabled by right-clicking on the panel's title bar. It is possible to restore the original layout with the **Move Panel to Bottom** button, or even **Hide Panel** (*Ctrl + J*).

The Panels area is not visible by default. It is typically enabled and shown when the information needed is requested, such as when the debugger is enabled.

In the Panels area, there are four different windows: **PROBLEMS, OUTPUT, DEBUG CONSOLE**, and **TERMINAL**. Let's examine them in the following sections.

PROBLEMS

With languages that have advanced editing features, such as AL, Visual Studio Code is able to identify code problems while typing. Problems lines have a specific colorization. There are three types of notifications: errors, warnings, and info. All of these can be shown in the **PROBLEMS** window. The following screenshot shows an example of the **PROBLEMS** window showing three errors:

```
              6 references
    18        field(3;"Vintage"; Integer)
    19        {
    20            Caption = 'Vintage';
    21            DataClassification = ToBeClassified;
    22            ThisIsNotAPropertyButAnError
    23        }

PROBLEMS  3     OUTPUT   DEBUG CONSOLE   TERMINAL

∨ AL  Tab50100.Wine.al  src\table  3
    ⊗ The property 'ThisIsNotAPropertyButAnError' cannot be used in this context AL(AL0124) [22, 13]
    ⊗ Syntax error, '=' expected AL(AL0104) [23, 9]
    ⊗ Syntax error, ';' expected AL(AL0104) [23, 9]
```

Typically, blocking errors are shown in red, while warnings are marked in green.

OUTPUT

The **OUTPUT** panel is the place where Visual Studio Code typically displays messages during or after command execution.

Because built-in tool actions and multiple extension commands can run concurrently, it is possible to make use of a drop-down box in the **OUTPUT** panel to change the view, and see the output for each standard or extension-based command.

The following screenshot shows the **OUTPUT** window in the Panels area:

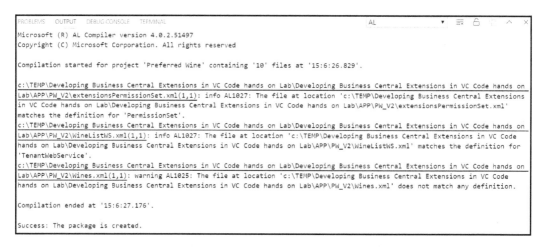

Typically, when working with Dynamics 365 Business Central extensions, the AL language is selected.

DEBUG CONSOLE

This is a special window used by native and extension-based debuggers, such as the AL language debugger, to display information about code execution. This window and its output will be analyzed in detail in Chapter 9, *Debugging*.

TERMINAL

Visual Studio Code allows us to execute commands in the same way as the Command Prompt, directly from within the development environment. The Terminal session is based on PowerShell by default.

Now that we have all elements that are in related to Visual Studio Code place, we can move onto the next section and analyze the powerful editing features that it offers.

Visual Studio Code – the editing features

Visual Studio Code provides many of the features that you would expect from the best-in-class code editor. If you are familiar with Visual Studio, you might have noticed that some features have been inherited from this IDE, or engineered in a similar way.

Developed by developers for developers, Visual Studio Code has keyboard shortcuts for almost every editing command, giving you the option to edit code faster, and completely forget about the mouse.

Let's study these features in the following sections.

Comment lines

Visual Studio Code provides out-of-the-box commands for text selection and professional editing in the **Edit** menu. The **Edit** menu also includes **Toggle Line Comment** (*Ctrl + U*), which adds a line comment for the selected line. This means that if you select 10 lines of code, Visual Studio Code will add 10 comment lines. The beauty of this command is that it works in reverse as well. If you select the 10 commented lines and press **Toggle Line Comment**, the comments will be magically removed.

For developers working with CSIDE, the old legacy language for on-premises Dynamics 365 Business Central, this command is the equivalent of **Comment Selection** (*Shift + Ctrl + K*) and **Uncomment Selection** (*Shift + Ctrl + O*).

Delimiter matching

Visual Studio Code is capable of detecting pairs of delimiters, such as brackets and parentheses. This feature is really helpful if you want to delimit code blocks, and it kicks in when the mouse is placed near one of the delimiter pairs:

```
Caption='General';
0 references
field("No.";"No.")
{
    ApplicationArea = All;
}
```

The preceding code is an example of delimiter matching.

Text selection

The **Selection** menu also has commands that relate to text selection, but most of them are used to move or duplicate lines of code above and below the selected line.

If you position the cursor near an AL function, variable, or constant, you can use **Add Next Occurrence** (*Ctrl + D*), **Add Previous Occurrence**, or **Select All Occurrences** (*Shift + Ctrl + D*) to select occurrences of the selected item, and occurrences will be highlighted in a different color.

In the code editor, you can also press *Ctrl + D* for a word or identifier selection on the right of the cursor. You can then easily expand (*Shift + Alt + →*) or shrink (*Shift + Alt + ←*) text blocks within delimiters.

Code block folding

If you hover over line numbers in the code editor, a – will appear close to the initial part of a code block. Click on it to fold it, and a + will appear. Click on this, and the code block unfolds:

```
 6        // This trigger includes code for company-related operations.
 7        trigger OnInstallAppPerCompany();
 8  +     var ···
10  +     begin          ···
13        end;
14
15        // Insert 3 default wines
          1 reference
16        local procedure InsertDefaultWines();
17  +   ' begin ···
21        end;
```

The preceding screenshot shows the code block folding depicted with +.

Multiple cursors (or multi-cursor)

Each cursor operates independently. *Alt* + click will generate a secondary cursor at the desired position.

The most common development situation in which you want to go for multiple cursors is when you need to add or replace the same text in different positions, but within the same source file. The following screenshot shows three cursors in action when editing the DataClassification property:

```
 6        fields
 7        {
              6 references
 8            field(1;"No."; Code[20])
 9            {
10                Caption = 'No.';
11                DataClassific
12            }
              12 references
13            field(2;"Name"; Text[50])
14            {
15                Caption = 'Name';
16                DataClassific
17            }
              6 references
18            field(3;"Vintage"; Integer)
19            {
20                Caption = 'Vintage';
21                DataClassific
22            }
23
```

This is a great feature for AL language developers, especially when they have to write down the same sentence many times in the same place (for example, `Caption` or `DataClassification` in a table object and for each table field).

Mini-map

Sometimes, when working with very long files such as report source files (RDLs) or codeunits, it is pretty difficult to know where the pointer should be positioned – or is positioned – within a source file. Visual Studio Code has a full-fledged mini-map feature: a small preview of the source code file. The following is an example of an RDL:

The mini-map feature can be disabled/enabled through **View | Toggle Minimap**, or by running the **Command Palette** (*Ctrl + Shift + P*) and selecting **View: Toggle Minimap**.

Breadcrumbs

The **Show Breadcrumbs** command is available in the **View** menu. With AL files, there is an icon in the top-left corner of the code editor. This can be expanded to double-check the definitions of properties, functions, fields, keys, and so on:

If you click on an element in the expanded list, the cursor will jump to its primary definition, making code navigation quite fast.

IntelliSense

In visual editors, IntelliSense is a word completion tool that appears as a pop-up list while you type. Visual Studio Code IntelliSense can provide smart suggestions, showing the definition and purpose – like online help – related to a specific element. The following screenshot shows IntelliSense in action:

```
     6 references
38      field(6;"Price"; Decimal)
39      {
40          Caption = 'Price';
41          DataClassification = ToBeClassified;
42          MinValue = 0;
43          DecimalPlaces = 2;
44
45      }    Access                        Access property              ×
46           AccessByPermission
     10 re   AutoFormatExpression          Sets the fields accessibility level, which controls
47      fiel  AutoFormatType               whether it can be used from other code in your
48      {     AutoIncrement                module or other modules.
49            BlankNumbers
50            BlankZero                    Get help
51            CalcFormula
52      }     CaptionClass
53   }        CaptionML
54            CharAllowed
55   keys     ClosingDates
56   {
```

IntelliSense is context-sensitive, and if you need to enable it directly without typing anything, just press *Ctrl* + spacebar. Depending on the context where the cursor is placed, IntelliSense will show all the items that can be used in that context. For example, inside a `Table Field` declaration, it will list all the specific field properties, such as `Caption` and `CaptionML`, while in an empty codeunit definition, it will show all the properties that are exposed by a codeunit object.

Word completion

Through the IntelliSense feature, the code editor in Visual Studio Code implements word completion for all native (such as JSON) and extension-based supported languages (such as AL). Just press *Enter* or *Tab* to insert the suggested word:

```
 7        // "OnUpgradePerCompany" trigger is used to perform the actual upgrade.
 8        trigger OnUpgradePerCompany();
 9        var
10            Wine : Record Wine;
11            // "ModuleInfo" is the current executing module (installed app).
12            Module : ModuleInfo;
13        begin
14
15            // Get information about the current module.
16            NavApp.GetCurrentModuleInfo(Module);
17            M
18        / [⊚] Module                                    (local) Module: ModuleInfo
19        i  ⊗ MaxStrLen
20           ⊗ Message
21           ⊗ CurrentExecutionMode                       e Type"::"750 ml",false);
22           ⊗ GetCurrentModuleExecutionContext
23           ⊗ GetModuleExecutionContext
24           ⊗ StrMenu
25           ⊡ ExecutionMode
26           ⊡ TransactionModel
27           □ tcodeunit (CRS: Method - No UI)
28           □ tcodeunit (CRS: Method)                    e"::Magnum;
29               Wine.Modify();
```

The preceding screenshot shows an AL variable suggested by the word completion engine.

The Go To Definition

This is a super-cool, must-know feature. You can hover over a variable, constant, function, or whatever code element you want with the mouse, and if you press *Ctrl*, the word or identifier (known also as a symbol) will magically switch into a hyperlink.

If you click on the word while pressing *Ctrl*, you will be automatically redirected to the code that defines that word. *Ctrl* + hovering over a code element also enables the **Go To Definition** feature.

Other possible ways to enable this feature are as follows:

- Select a code element and press *F12*.
- Right-click on a code element and then select **Go To Definition** from the context menu.

Find All References

Find All References makes it very easy to parse how many times and where an object, a function, or any code element has been used across source code. You can simply right-click on any variable, function, or element name and then select **Find All References**, or use the keyboard shortcut *Shift + Alt + F12*.

When it's enabled, the code editor will create a result list in the activity bar showing how many times it has been referenced, and in which object files and position(s). A shortcut icon is created in the sidebar called **References**. The following screenshot shows how to find all references in AL files for a specific variable:

If you expand an occurrence in the reference list on the left and click on a record, the code editor will open the file where it is referenced and position the cursor in editing mode, selecting the element searched in that file.

The reference list can be cleared and refreshed, and you can collapse all the elements in it. If you clear the list, you can always run the previous search again, since the history is maintained for you.

Peek Definition

Imagine that you have a large number of code files, and you need to edit the definition of a variable or field that you are currently using. With many other editors – or development environments – you most likely have to save all the files in text format, then search through all these code files and be sure to replace that variable name. This task not only can be annoying, but can also distract you from the original code you were writing.

Visual Studio Code brilliantly solves this problem by providing the Peek feature, which can be enabled in different ways:

- Right-click a variable, field, or function name and select **Peek Definition**.
- Use the *Alt + F12* keyboard shortcut.

An interactive pop-up window should appear, showing source code that defines the selected element. The following screenshot shows the **Peek Definition** for a table source in a report:

```
src > report > AL Rep50100.WineList.al >  Report 50100 "Wine List" >  dataset > {} Wine: Record 50100 Wine
  4          UsageCategory = Lists;
  5          ApplicationArea = All;
  6
  7          DefaultLayout = RDLC;
  8          RDLCLayout = 'WineList.rdl';
  9
 10          dataset
 11          {
                 0 references
 12              dataitem(Wine; Wine)
Tab50100.Wine.al  C:\TEMP\Developing Business Central Extensions in VC Code hands on Lab\Developing Business Central Extensions in VC Code hands on          ×
       8 references                                                                        table 50100 "Wine"
  1    table 50100 "Wine"
  2    {
  3          LookupPageId="Wine List";
  4          DataClassification = ToBeClassified;
  5
  6          fields
  7          {
                 6 references
  8              field(1;"No."; Code[20])
  9              {
 10                  Caption = 'No.';
 11                  DataClassification = ToBeClassified;
 12              }
                 12 references
 13              field(2;"Name"; Text[50])
 13              {
```

You can then see what has been written, and also directly edit it.

Renaming symbols

For a developer, it is very common to rename a variable, constant, field, or function name. These coding elements are technically called symbols. Visual Studio Code provides a very powerful feature to rename symbols.

If you press *F2* on the coding element that you wish to rename, or right-click and then select **Rename Symbol**, a small interactive popup appears in edit mode. There, you can write the new element name without using a distracting dialog window, allowing you to concentrate on your coding. All references to that code element will be renamed accordingly. The following screenshot shows renaming the XMLport symbol reference:

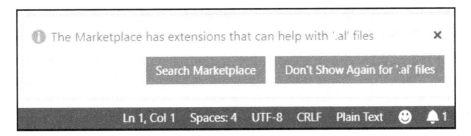

All of the features shown so far are the most useful features provided by Visual Studio Code that support proficient code editing for AL developers.

At this stage, it is important to take a closer look at the AL Language extension and see how to configure it.

Understanding the AL Language extension

AL is now a cross-platform language that is deployed through an extension for Visual Studio Code. This extension not only supports deployment on Windows OSes, but is also supported for the macOS version of Visual Studio Code.

The free AL Language extension (`https://marketplace.visualstudio.com/items?itemName=ms-dynamics-smb.al`) is available for download from the Visual Studio Code marketplace. This provides an optimized experience for Dynamics 365 Business Central extension development, and includes all the support and tools that you need to build apps (from now on, a synonym for extension), including the debugger.

The easiest way to get the extension installed without further information is by opening any Dynamics 365 Business Central code file (`.al`) and following the instructions shown by Visual Studio Code when it detects that an extension is available for that file type:

Similarly, you might want to install other extensions that add other languages (such as PowerShell), tools (such as Docker), or enhanced editing features to the AL Language extension. A list of the most useful marketplace extensions used by Dynamics 365 Business Central in combination with AL Language will be provided in Chapter 18, *Useful and Proficient Tools for AL Developers*.

Let's understand what these extensions are in AL Language in the sections ahead.

AL Language

Created by the Dynamics 365 Business Central development team, AL Language is the official Visual Studio Code extension for developing apps for small, single-tenant personalization's and complex add-on vertical solutions that are deployed through the online Dynamics 365 Business Central AppSource marketplace.

It can be deployed in two different ways:

- Directly, as a downloadable package from the Visual Studio Code marketplace.
- Manually, as an installable package (.vsix):
    - The installable package is dispatched when creating a Docker-contained sandbox from the official Dynamics 365 Business Central image.
    - Downloaded from Dynamics 365 Business Central on-premises DVD.

To start directly with AL Language, simply download it from the marketplace by following these simple steps:

1. Run Visual Studio Code.
2. Click on the **Extensions** view bar.
3. In the search field, type Dynamics 365 Business Central.
4. Select **AL Language**.
5. Click on **Install** and when the installation finishes, reload Visual Studio Code as requested. It shows the following AL Language extension:

The AL Language build number, also known as the development build, is shown close to the title. In the preceding screenshot, the AL Language development build (or runtime) is `4.0.182565`.

The development build is very important, because new language features and enhancements are typically not backported to older builds, so they could be outdated and not compatible with the more recent Dynamics 365 Business Central platform updates.

 AL developers should always select the latest AL Language development build in order to benefit from the latest enhancements and stability features.

The AL Language development model relates to creating, editing, and organizing flat text files with the typical `.al` extension. In short: AL Language development is simply folder and file based.

It's worth mentioning that the Visual Studio Code terminology calls a root folder a workspace. The AL Language root folder represents the source code container for an extension. Therefore, the AL Language root folder is also called the Visual Studio Code development workspace.

When creating whatever kind of extension, the workspace consists of the following items:

- `launch.json` file
- `app.json` file
- Symbol files
- `.al` object files (such as table, page, report, and codeunit)
- Complementary files (such as `WebService.xml` files, the extension logo in `.bmp` format, and the `permissions.xml` file)

We will analyze AL Language objects and complementary files in more depth all throughout this book and in later chapters. We will focus now on the backbone of the app development: `launch.json`, `app.json`, and symbol files.

launch.json

This file is stored in the extension workspace in a subfolder called `.vscode` and mainly determines the specific parameter settings for downloading and uploading AL Language commands.

The following table shows the download and upload AL commands:

Download commands	Upload commands
`AL: Download symbols`	`AL: Publish` (*F5*)
`AL: Download source code` (*F7*)	`AL: Publish and open in the designer` (*F6*)
	`AL: Publish without debugging` (*Ctrl + F5*)
	`AL: Rapid Application Publish` (*Alt + F5*)
	`AL: Rapid Application Publish without debugging` (*Ctrl + Alt + F5*)

It is also used just to establish a connection, as in the case of AL: debug without the publishing (*Ctrl + Shift + F5*) command, or to launch a specific debugging feature such as AL: open Event Recorder. The Event Recorder feature will be covered in Chapter 9, *Debugging*.

The `launch.json` file is a JSON array that might have different JSON values, each representing a set of attributes targeting different deployment: on-premises or SaaS. Attributes could be mandatory or optional, depending on the target deployment.

The following table shows the `launch.json` attributes:

Attribute	Mandatory	Deployment type	Description
Name	Yes	All	Name shown in the debugger window to identify the set of launch parameters.Default values: Publish to your own server (on-premises), Publish to Microsoft cloud (SaaS).
Type	Yes	All	Constant value: `al`.
Request	Yes	All	Constant value: `launch`.
startupObjectType	No	All	Object type to run after publishing: Table or Page.
startupObjectId	No	All	Used together with `StartupObjectType`.Defines the object ID to run.
tenant	No	All	AAD tenant (SaaS) or tenant name (on-premises with multitenancy) to connect to extract symbols and/or publish the app package.
sandbox	No	Online	Specifies the sandbox name in case of multiple online sandboxes created for the same AAD tenant.
breakOnError	No	All	Specifies whether the debugger should stop when an error occurs.Default value: `true`.
breakOnErrorWrite	No	All	Specifies whether the debugger should stop on record changes (insert, modify, and delete).Default value: `false`.

Attribute	Mandatory	Deployment type	Description
schemaUpdateMode	No	All	Determines the data synchronization mode.Synchronize: This is the default value. If there is already data deployed for this extension, it will be preserved and not removed. The extension metadata will be synchronized with the existing one, if any.Recreate: Wipe out previous metadata (tables and table extensions, typically) and use the new metadata from scratch.ForceSync: Force the schema synchronization. This should be used with extreme caution since it might lead to data loss scenarios.
DependencyPublishingOption	No	All	This parameter was introduced with the Dynamics 365 Business Central Fall 2019 update. It applies in complex environments where multiple dependent apps are loaded from the same root folder. Possible values are as follows:Default: Enable rebuilding and publishing of all dependent apps.Ignore: Does not apply dependency publishing. This option should be used quite carefully since it risks breaking existing interdependent solutions.Strict: Publishing will fail if there are any installed extensions that have a dependency on the startup folder.

Attribute	Mandatory	Deployment type	Description
Server	Yes	On-premises	Server name. Default value: http://localhost.
serverInstance	Yes	On-premises	Dynamics 365 Business Central Server service name.
authentication	Yes	On-premises	Authentication type: Windows or User Password.At the time of writing, AAD is not supported for on-premises deployment and it is the default, and only, value for online deployments.
Port	No	On-premises	Dynamics 365 Business Central port number.Default value: 7049.
applicationFamily	No	AppSource	Used to develop an embedded extension for AppSource. This is a tag for Microsoft to determine the targeted upgrade operation if specific AppSource extensions have been deployed in the tenant.
launchBrowser	No	All	Specifies whether or not to launch a browser when publishing extensions.
enableLongRunningSqlStatements	No	All	Enable the capability of displaying long-running T-SQL statements while debugging. This feature is planned to work for on-premises and online sandbox environments.
enableSqlInformationDebugger	No	All	Enable the capability of retrieving T-SQL query info. This feature is planned to work for on-premises and online sandbox environments.

If you have set up more than one value in the JSON array, when you perform upload or download AL Language commands, you will be prompted to choose one of the parameter set names defined in the JSON array.

The following screenshot is an example of a `launch.json` file:

```
launch.json    ×

.vscode > launch.json > ...
 1   {
 2       "version": "0.2.0",
 3       "configurations": [
 4           {
 5               "type": "al",
 6               "request": "launch",
 7               "name": "FCORP Online",
 8               "startupObjectId": 22,
 9               "startupObjectType": "Page",
10               "breakOnError": true,
11               "launchBrowser": true,
12               "tenant": "sandboxIT"
13           },
14           {
15               "type": "al",
16               "request": "launch",
17               "name": "FCORP On-premise",
18               "server": "http://localhost",
19               "serverInstance": "BC150",
20               "startupObjectId": 22,
21               "startupObjectType": "Page",
22               "breakOnError": true,
23               "launchBrowser": true,
24               "enableLongRunningSqlStatements": true,
25               "enableSqlInformationDebugger": true,
26               "port": 15049
27           }
28       ]
29   }
```

This shows the file with two parameter set values.

app.json

Typically stored in the extension workspace root folder, this represents the app manifest written in JSON. Inside the JSON file, there are parameters referencing base and system applications, and platform and runtime definitions.

These terms need to be well understood when developing for Dynamics 365 Business Central.

System and base application

With the Fall 2019 update, Microsoft converted all legacy C/AL code into AL objects. Currently, the big application monolith has been split into two apps:

- **System application**: with approximately 200 objects.
- **Base application**: depending on the localized version, it spans from 6,000 to 8,000 objects.

To be extended, these need to be referenced as dependencies in the `app.json` file, and their symbols pulled on-premises or from an online sandbox through the `AL:Download symbols` AL Language command.

When pulled in the `.alpackages` folder, they are typically referenced through a version number in the major, minor, build, and revision notations, and this is reflected in the name of the symbols that are downloaded (for example, `Microsoft_System Application_15.0.36560.0` and `Microsoft_Base Application_15.0.36626.36918`).

The major version digit typically corresponds to the Dynamics 365 Business Central major update release.

The October 2019 (or Fall 2019) release update is major version 15. The Spring 2020 (or April 2020) update release will be major version 16, and so on.

The minor version typically corresponds to minor updates. The November 2019 update 1 is minor version 15.1, December 2019 update 2 should be minor version 15.2, and so on.

The build number is a progressive number that is incremented by Microsoft as soon as there are changes committed to the branch that is related to feature enhancements or bug fixing.

When developing an extension, you must be aware of what system and application object level is needed as a minimum requirement, as defined in the dependency parameter of the app.json file.

Platform

Platform represents the results of the final compilation of the Dynamics 365 Business Central platform components (client, server, web server, and so on).

It is shown with the same notation as the application. Application and platform builds typically have a different build number, since platform code changes and application code changes are following different compilation paths and are merged together in the end.

When targeting a platform development, you must be aware of the minimum requirement that files and APIs should have to make use of the features, properties, and functions that they expose in order to avoid unpredictable behaviors from the application.

Runtime

Runtime represents the results of the final compilation of the Dynamics 365 Business Central AL Language extension file.

The notation is simpler and consists of a major, minor, and build version. For example, the Spring 2018 update (or the April 2018 update) is named major version 1, while the Fall 2018 update (or the October 2018 update) is version 2, and so on. The current major version that targets the Dynamics 365 Business Central Fall 2019 update is version 4.

When developing extensions, within the app.json file, you can define what runtime version the application is targeting. This enables or disables different sets of features that cannot be part of the target platform deployment, and the AL Language extension's runtime will detect that.

The following table shows the `app.json` attributes:

Attribute	Mandatory	Description
Id	Yes	**Global Unique Identifier (GUID)** of the extension.
Name	Yes	Extension name.
Publisher	Yes	Publisher name.
Version	Yes	Version of the extension package (for example, 1.0.0.0).
Brief	No (Yes for AppSource)	Short description of the extension.
Description	No (Yes for AppSource)	Long and verbose description of the extension.
privacyStatement	No (Yes for AppSource)	URL to the privacy statement.
EULA	No (Yes for AppSource)	URL to the license terms and conditions for the app.
Help	No (Yes for AppSource)	URL to app helpdesk support.
url	No (Yes for AppSource)	URL to the extension package's home page.
Logo	No (Yes for AppSource)	Relative or full path to the app logo from the root directory of the extension
Dependencies	Yes	List of dependencies from other extensions. Since the Fall 2019 update, it is mandatory to reference at least system application and base application extensions.
Screenshots	No	Relative or absolute path to app screenshots.
Platform	Yes	Minimum platform version supported (for example, 15.0.0.0).
idRanges	Yes	Range of application object IDs or an array of object ID ranges.

showMyCode	No	Enables viewing extension source code while debugging and/or downloading source code from the extension management page. Default value: `false`.
Target	No	Default value: `Cloud`. Extension with the same font as Cloud. It's one of the possible values for Target option (`Cloud` for the new version, `Extension` for the previous version).. These are the only two values allowed by Dynamics 365 Business Central SaaS. Set this value to `OnPrem` or `Internal` if you need to target the extension to on-premises.
helpBaseUrl	No	URL for the extension's online help.
contextSensitiveHelpUrl	No (Yes for AppSource)	URL for the context-sensitive help for an AppSource extension.
supportedLocales	No	Comma-separated list of the local languages supported by the app.
features	No	Optional features in preview that could be enabled by the compiler. An example is `TranslationFile`. Adding this parameter flag in the features enables the generation of a directory called **Translations** in the extension folder and a `.xlf` translation file containing all the labels used in all extension objects.
Runtime	No	Minimum runtime version targeted by the extension.

The following screenshot is an example of an `app.json` file:

```
app.json        ×

app.json > ...
    1    {
    2        "id": "56ddd910-3aa8-4c3e-936c-be20edeaf6a9",
    3        "name": "Preferred Wine",
    4        "publisher": "Tacconi Inc.",
    5        "brief": "version 2.0",
    6        "description": "version 2.0",
    7        "version": "2.0.0.0",
    8        "privacyStatement": "",
    9        "EULA": "",
   10        "help": "",
   11        "url": "",
   12        "logo": "",
   13        "dependencies": [
   14            {
   15                "appId": "63ca2fa4-4f03-4f2b-a480-172fef340d3f",
   16                "publisher": "Microsoft",
   17                "name": "System Application",
   18                "version": "1.0.0.0"
   19            },
   20            {
   21                "appId": "437dbf0e-84ff-417a-965d-ed2bb9650972",
   22                "publisher": "Microsoft",
   23                "name": "Base Application",
   24                "version": "15.0.0.0"
   25            }
   26        ],
   27        "screenshots": [],
   28        "platform": "15.0.0.0",
   29  >     "idRanges": [ ···
   34        ],
   35        "showMyCode": true,
   36        "runtime": "4.0",
   37    }
```

With all of this information, we should now be able to master app configuration files and tweak them according to the runtime version. In the next section, we will introduce symbols and explain their vital importance in extension development.

Understanding symbols

Like in all other languages, symbols represent references to a collection of standard objects, properties, and functions. They are a special extension file themselves with the typical `.app` naming convention and are used to maintain object reference consistency while compiling, and they also populate valid IntelliSense entries.

Symbols are typically stored inside the database in a BLOB field in JSON for each object record. It is worth mentioning that in multitenancy, the `Object Metadata` table is part of the application database, so in customer tenant databases there are no system symbols or metadata stored, only data.

With Dynamics 365 Business Central, symbols are already preloaded inside the application database, and these can be grouped into two classes:

- Standard symbols
- Extension symbols

Prior to the Fall 2019 update, standard application symbols were all generated by Microsoft through a special compilation of standard legacy objects using the CSIDE development environment. The same happened for the on-premises version: symbols were generated asynchronously, or could have been imported as a normal extension through PowerShell scripts.

Standard application symbols were stored in the Symbol Reference BLOB field in the `Object Metadata` table.

 Find out more on this topic by reading the following official reference:
`https://docs.microsoft.com/it-it/dynamics365/business-central/dev-itpro/developer/devenv-running-cside-and-al-side-by-side`

The following table shows us the standard symbols. Understanding what they are and their importance is vital for the successful compilation and deployment of any kind of extension prior to the Fall 2019 update:

- **Application**: Contains symbols for all the application objects described in the CSIDE object designer, except system tables in the 2000000004 to 2000000199 ID range and standard Test Toolkit objects. With an on-premises version or Docker-contained sandbox, if you're making changes to a standard legacy object, you must opt for (re)generating symbols through the CSIDE development environment, as described in the following blog post: Generate Symbols in a Modern Development environment with Microsoft Dynamics NAV 2018 (`https://blogs.msdn.microsoft.com/nav/2018/01/16/generate-symbols-in-a-modern-development-environment-with-microsoft-dynamics-nav-2018/`). With the upgraded on-premises version, symbols coming from earlier versions must be extracted from a standard on-premises database (or from the product DVD), imported in the upgrade database, and regenerated, as described in the following blog post: `https://blogs.msdn.microsoft.com/nav/2018/02/02/import-symbols-in-new-or-upgrade-databases-with-microsoft-dynamics-nav-2018/`.

- **System**:
    - Contains symbols for system tables in the 2000000004 to 2000000199 ID range, and also virtual table definitions.
    - System and virtual table structures cannot be modified through extensions.
    - System and virtual table symbols cannot be regenerated.
    - For this reason, if you are developing extensions, they should never be considered for any changes within the CSIDE development environment.

- **Test**: Contains symbols for application Test Toolkit objects. Standard application Test Toolkit object symbols cannot be regenerated. Developers should create their own test objects. For this reason, in a modern development environment for SaaS deployment, they should never be considered for any changes within the CSIDE development environment.

Whenever you extend an application, you always need to have the appropriate symbols in place. You can achieve this in two ways:

- Connect to a sandbox environment, run the Command Palette (*Ctrl + Shift + P*), and type and select `AL: Download Symbols`.
- Download the required symbols from another place (such as the product DVD, for on-premises deployment) and store them in the defined symbol storage directory.

For on-premises deployment, you will find the `System.app` and `Test.app` symbols on the Dynamics 365 Business Central Spring 2019 product DVD in the following directory: `\ModernDev\program files\Microsoft Dynamics NAV\140\AL Development Environment`. In the Dynamics 365 Business Central Fall 2019 DVD you will only find `System.app` in the following directory: `\ModernDev\program files\Microsoft Dynamics NAV\150\AL Development Environment`. Since the Fall 2019 update, application and test symbols are no longer downloaded automatically by the AL Language runtime, and they no longer need to be stored inside the database, since all of the objects that belong to the application, including Test Toolkit ones, have been converted into AL objects. These AL objects are now part of standard extension packages. Extension packages contain symbols natively.

If you have a multiuser environment with developers that are working on the same staging tenant, you might think of downloading symbols through the Command Palette once and then setting a common path for storing the symbols for all users. In this way, it is possible to avoid downloading the same set of symbols every time, thereby increasing the development productivity.

The default symbol-storing path can be changed using one of the following shortcuts:

- From the **Menu** bar, go to **File** (*Alt + F*) | **Preferences** (*P*) | **Settings** (*S*) and then select AL Language settings.
- Use the settings shortcuts (*Ctrl*) and then select AL Language settings.

The parameter to change is *Al: Package Cache Path*, the default value of which is set to the relative path, `./.alpackages`.

Alternatively, you could run the Command Palette (*Ctrl + Shift + P*), type and select **Preferences: Configure language specific settings…**, then choose **AL**. The settings.json file will open, and you can then add or change the values of the al.packageCachePath parameter. The following screenshot shows the AL settings symbol path when it has been changed to a storage location:

```
{} settings.json  ✕

C: ▷ Users ▷ dtacconi ▷ AppData ▷ Roaming ▷ Code ▷ User ▷ {} settings.json ▷ abc al.packageCachePath
  1    {
  2        "files.autoSave": "afterDelay",
  3        "terminal.integrated.rendererType": "dom",
  4        "workbench.colorTheme": "Default Light+",
  5        "window.zoomLevel": 0,
  6        "editor.minimap.enabled": false,
  7        "breadcrumbs.enabled": true,
  8        "workbench.activityBar.visible": true,
  9        "[al]": {
 10        },
 11        "al.packageCachePath": "\\\\storagesrv\\SHARED\\ALSymbols"
 12    }
```

Later in this chapter, we will also discuss other AL Language configuration settings.

Together with system application extension, base application extension, and standard symbols, your extension might also depend on other custom or third-party extensions. These extensions, then, should emit symbols that you should be able to download from the application database when invoking **AL: Download Symbols** from the Command Palette.

Extension symbols are stored in the Symbols BLOB field in the NAV App table.

To specify that your extension has a dependency on another extension(s), you must populate the relevant JSON array parameter in the app.json file. This is what the app.json file parameter looks like for an extension that depends on two other apps:

```
"dependencies": [
    {
        "appId":  "63ca2fa4-4f03-4f2b-a480-172fef340d3f",
        "publisher":  "Microsoft",
        "name":  "System Application",
        "version":  "15.0.0.0"
    },
```

```
{
    "appId":  "437dbf0e-84ff-417a-965d-ed2bb9650972",
    "publisher":  "Microsoft",
    "name":  "Base Application",
    "version":  "15.0.0.0"
},
{
    "appId": "99ddd910-3aa8-4c3e-936c-be20edeaf777",
        "name": "Preferred Wine Basic"
        "publisher": "Tacconi Inc."
            "version": "1.0.0.0"
},
{
    "appId": "77ddd910-3aa8-4c3e-936c-be20edeaf888",
    "name": "Preferred Wine Tools",
    "publisher": "Tacconi Inc.",
    "version": "2.1.0.0"
}
],
```

If you have installed the CRS AL language Extension toolbox from Cloud Ready Software (`https://marketplace.visualstudio.com/items?itemName=waldo.crs-al-language-extension`), you could type `tdependency` to enable the code snippet to easily edit each JSON array element for this parameter. This will make your coding faster and prevent syntax errors. We will discuss the standard and custom code snippet features in the last section of this chapter.

The version parameter of the dependent extension(s) represents the lower bound for the compiler to accept the symbols. In other words, symbol versions of the dependent extension lower than the one reported are not considered valid for download or compile operations.

Inside symbols

Symbols are the result of a compression (`.zip`) operation of several files that are used by the AL Language extension. To demonstrate what is under the hood, just use the most common decompression tool (for example, 7-zip) to extract their content after renaming the `.app` package with the `.navx` extension.

The following tables show the standard symbol components (files and directories) for the base application extension:

File name	Description
[Content_Types.xml]	Specify the content of the package: XML and JSON files.
MediaIdListing.xml	Specify the extension logo filename and its ID.
navigation.xml	It contains an entry for the **Departments** menu.
NavxManifest.xml	It will report the manifest for the standard symbol or extension. The most relevant parameters for the base application symbols are as follows: – version: Identify the application version of the JSON file (such as 15.0.36626.36675) – platform: Target the recommended major platform version that's compatible with these symbols (such as 15.0.0.0) – runtime: Recommended runtime version to be used for these symbols (such as 4.0) System symbols typically only specify the version and the runtime.
SymbolReference.json	Contains all references in JSON notation to AL objects. These JSON files are heavily used by the AL Language extension to maintain reference integrity while compiling/building the app package and to enable all IntelliSense-related features. Basically, it is structured as an array containing a list of valid AL object parameters, as shown in the following snippet: "Tables": [], "Codeunits": [], "Pages": [], "PageExtensions": [], For each of these object elements, there are specified fields, properties, functions, and so on.

Symbol JSON files cannot be hacked/changed to manually generate or modify a symbol file.

Next, let's also have a look at what the various directories do:

Directory name	Content description
addin	Controls add-ins definitions.
layout	RDL and DOCX report layouts.
logo	Extension logo.
ProfileSymbolReferences	Symbols for profiles and related page customizations.
src	AL files. Their content is used typically to show the code while debugging.
Translations	Translation files in the XLIFF format.

Symbols are the beating heart of the extension validation mechanism and, as shown in the previous tables, they also carry out the code (if the showmycode parameter has been set to true in the extension app.json file).

Based on AL symbols, in the Visual Studio Code marketplace you could find very useful extensions that are targeting AL development environments.

The most commonly used ones are as follows:

- AL Object Designer by Marton Sagi
- AZ AL Dev Tools/AL Code Outline by Andrzej Zwierzchowski

Both are very easy to use and are useful for inspecting symbols and their content.

After learning about symbols, we have completed an overview of the main items that are needed to build an app. Let's have a look now at AL Language extension configuration, and how to set them up in order to have a more productive development environment.

Understanding AL Language extension configuration

General and per workspace settings can be easily shown through the shortcut key, *Ctrl+*. An intuitive menu will be shown, and by selecting **Extension | AL language extension configuration**, a set of configuration parameters is listed. The following screenshot shows the AL Language extension configuration parameters:

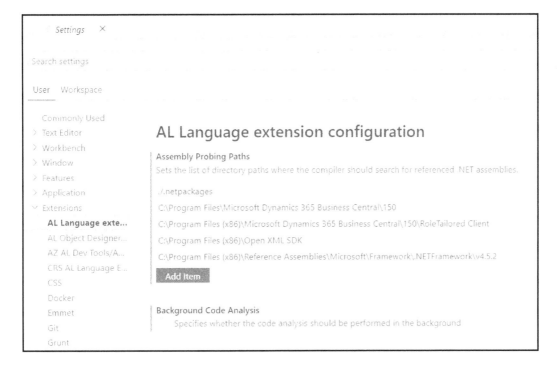

Basically, these configuration values are saved into a file called `settings.json`.

The following is a list of the description and values of the most common ones:

- For the following Path parameters:
    - `"al.packageCachePath":  "./.alpackages"`: It is possible to change the default value to a local folder or to a shared folder for multi-developer environments. It represents the path to store and look for symbols.
    - `"al.assemblyProbingPaths":  ["./.netpackages"]`: This parameter is fundamental to compiling extensions when there are references to external assemblies. Its data type is a JSON array, so the developer has to specify a comma-separated list of paths where the assemblies are stored.

    - `"al.ruleSetPath":  null`: This is used if developers would like to provide a custom override of standard code analyzer rules. It will be discussed in more depth in Chapter 9, *Debugging*.

- For the following Code Analyzer parameters:
    - `"al.enableCodeAnalysis":  false`: This helps to enable code analysis and is discussed in more depth in Chapter 9, *Debugging*. In large projects, with several thousands of objects, it would be better if it was turned off, in order to prevent performance issues while coding or compiling.
    - `"al.codeAnalyzers":  []`: This has the type of code analyzers. It will be discussed in more depth in Chapter 9, *Debugging*.
    - `"al.enableCodeActions":  false`: Enables code actions such as automatically converting multiple `if` statements to a `CASE` statement or spell check. It is disabled by default.
    - `"al.backgroundCodeAnalysis":  true`: This is enabled by default. In large projects, this could be a real performance killer, and it is recommended that it is turned off in such scenarios.

- For the following Compilation parameters:
    - `"al.compilationOptions"`: `{"generateReportLayout": true, "parallel": true}`: Used to specify if a report layout should be generated or not when compiling, if it does not exist, and to have a serialized or parallel build of the package.
    - `"al.incrementalBuild"`: `false`: In complex extension development environments, where multiple extension folders are loaded from a root folder, this parameter specifies if the reference resolution will happen from the referenced project, instead of happening from the symbols that are stored in the package cache path. Switching this parameter to true will result in an increase in performance in such scenarios.

- For the following Service Log parameters:
    - `"al.editorServicesLogLevel"`: `null`: This is very useful for debugging situations where compilation reports unhandled errors or crashes. Logging could include errors up to a very verbose description of what is happening behind the scenes. It will be discussed more in deep in `Chapter 9`, *Debugging*.
    - `"al.editorServicesPath"`: `"bin/"`: If the service log is enabled, it determines the log path.

- For the following Browser parameters:
    - `"al.browser"`: `"Edge"`: Choose your preferred browser to launch your Dynamics 365 Business Central application from Visual Studio Code. Options are **SystemDefault**, **Edge**, Chrome, or Firefox. This is useful if you have multiple browsers installed.
    - `"al.incognito"`: `false`: Choose to start the browser in a normal session that stores existing credentials or use private/incognito browsing.

After exploring the core settings that are needed to develop an extension, let's analyze one of the best code-editing features that is provided with AL Language: code snippets.

Mastering AL Language code snippets

AL Language standard code snippets in Visual Studio Code are available after installing the AL Language extension. These are triggered as you type within the code editor, and you can recognize them by a squared prefix symbol.

Typically, they start with the letter t and are followed by a meaningful name that describes what the snippet is about, for example, `ttable` or `tpage`. A tooltip shows a preview of the code snippet.

The following screenshot shows the standard snippet for an if-then-else conditional sentence:

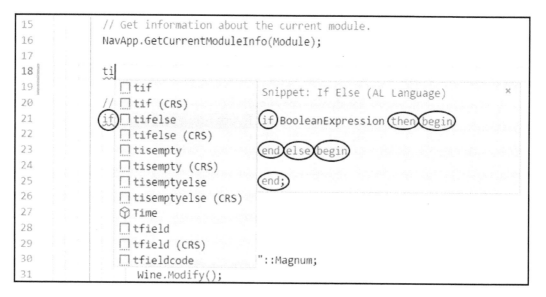

Notice that if the snippet contains variable names or code identifiers, they could be highlighted, suggesting that you should give them a different name and that they act as a sort of placeholder. When you rename a highlighted identifier, all occurrences will be also renamed, making snippet usage very flexible. This will not only reduce coding time, preventing writing or copying and pasting repeating sentences, but it also uses the appropriate complex structure syntax that a developer might not keep in mind.

It is possible to download code snippets that have been produced by other developers in the form of extensions directly from the Visual Studio marketplace. Typically, many of the extensions that extend support for AL Language also include a series of code snippets of their own.

A typical example is the free CRS AL Language extension.

Together with several very useful developer tools, this extension also implements a set of AL code snippets that integrate with and enrich the existing standard ones. Currently, it implements 68 extra AL code snippets, and the list is growing with every extension update.

The following screenshot shows all the available extra snippets that appear if you type CRS in an `.al` file:

```
0 references

crs
        □ tfield (CRS)                    Snippet: Table FlowField (Count) (CRS   ×
        □ tfieldcode (CRS)               AL Language Extension)
        □ tfieldgroup (CRS)
        □ tfieldgroups (CRS)             field(id; "MyField"; Integer)
        □ tfieldoption (CRS)             {
        □ tfieldtext (CRS)                   Caption = 'MyField';
        □ tflowfield (CRS)                   Editable = false;
        □ tflowfieldcount (CRS)              FieldClass = FlowField;
        □ tflowfieldexist (CRS)              CalcFormula = Count (LookUpTable
        □ tflowfieldlookup (CRS)         where (FieldToBeFiltered = const
        □ tflowfieldsum (CRS)            (Filter)));
        □ tfor (CRS)
```

Another way to search for code snippets while coding is to run the Command Palette (*Ctrl* + *Shift* + *P*) and then type snippet or insert snippet to bring up a drop-down list of the AL snippets that are available.

The following screenshot shows the drop-down list of AL snippets from the Command Palette:

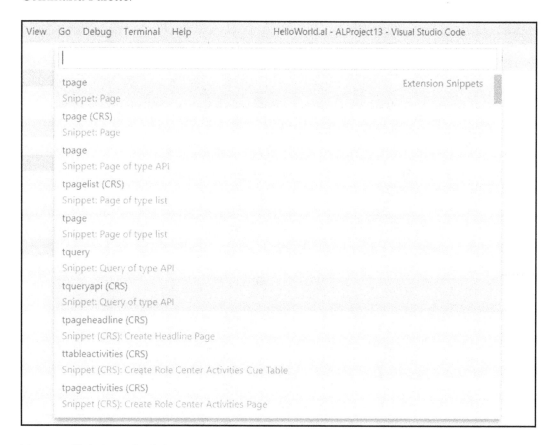

If you still did not find the code snippets that are useful to you in the marketplace, with Visual Studio Code it is also possible to manually add new code snippets from scratch. To accomplish this, you have to click on the **Menu** bar and go to **File** (*Alt + F*) | **Preferences** (*P*) | **User Snippets** (*S + S*).

The shortcut sequence, *Alt + F, P, S, S, Enter* will bring you straight there without needing to use the mouse.

You can then select whether to create a global snippet for all languages, a local snippet for the current workspace, or one that's specific for a target language. In this example, we will create a new snippet to be used with AL Language files by choosing **al (AL)** from the language list.

The following screenshot shows the available options when creating a specific code snippet:

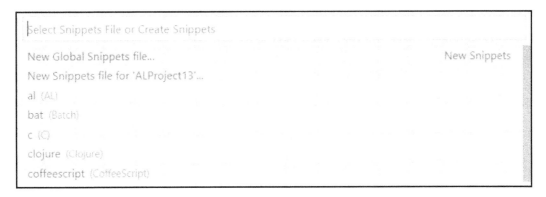

If you have enabled the breadcrumb feature, you might have noticed that a specific configuration file is open in editing mode for custom AL Language snippets. Typically, the file is called `al.json`, and it is stored in the following location:

```
C:\Users\<username>\AppData\Roaming\Code\User\snippets
```

Each snippet is defined by a unique name and is composed of three elements:

- **Prefix**: Used to search and trigger the snippet in the editor
- **Body**: The section that is pasted inside the editor
- **Description**: A verbose description of what the snipper is for

Inside the body, you could use a specific syntax to enable placeholders:

- `$1`, `$2`, `$3`, ..., `$n` are used to move the cursor position within the snippet by pressing the *Tab* key.
- `$0` is used as the final cursor position.
- `${1:labelX}`, `${2:labelY}`, and `${3:labelZ}` are used for placeholders. Placeholders with the same IDs are connected to each other, enabling the multiple cursors feature.

Now, we'll go through a simple example.

Imagine that you would like to add a standard code header block on top of the object, like it was in the old designer (the CSIDE development environment), and you need a smart way to implement this repeatedly and quickly on every object.

The easiest solution is to create an ad hoc custom snippet to be invoked on every new object file creation, as follows:

1. Add the following code to the `al.json` file and save it:

```
{
  "Create standard comment block": {
  "prefix": "tcomment (Custom)",
  "body": [
  "//",
  "// ${1:YY.MM.DD} Initialization",
  "// ${1:YY.MM.DD} ${2:Modification Description}",
  "//"
  ],
  "description": "Standard header comment block"
  }
}
```

You can enable the amazing autosave feature by simply going to the **Menu** bar and selecting **File** (*Alt + F*) | **Auto Save** (*U*). A check mark will appear beside the Auto Save menu item. Another way to accomplish this task is to run the Command Palette (*Ctrl + Shift + P*) and type `File: Toggle Auto Save` (or type part of it and select the entry from the drop-down action list).

2. Create a new file inside your extension and save it with the `.al` extension (for example, `MyCodeunit.al`). The cursor should be automatically positioned in the first line and column of the file.

3. Start typing `tcomment` and IntelliSense will detect the existence of your custom snippet. Select it.

4. The cursor will be placed in the first placeholder element. Just type the current date in the `YY.MM.DD` format and press **Tab**. You might notice that since two placeholders share the same ID, they are edited together, enabling the multiple cursor feature.

5. Now, it is time to write down something useful that is related to the object description, and what it is for.

The following screenshot shows the custom comment block snippet in action with multiple cursors:

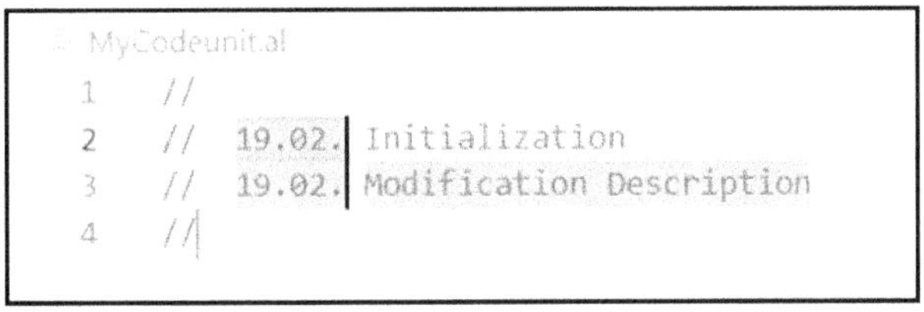

```
MyCodeunit.al
1    //
2    //  19.02.| Initialization
3    //  19.02.| Modification Description
4    //
```

These code snippets make it easy to understand Visual Studio Code. Try them out and master them!

Summary

Visual Studio Code is a code-centric tool that supports, out of the box, a wide variety of languages, providing coding features such as syntax colorization, delimiter matching, code block folding, multiple cursors, code snippets, IntelliSense, and so much more.

By installing the AL Language extension, this modern development environment is fully set up as an app playground for beginner and skilled developers. We have unleashed some tips and tricks in this chapter that enable you to be proficient in the developer's daily work of creating modern apps for Dynamics 365 Business Central.

We then moved on to learn about the powerful coding features that this modern development environment offers. After all of this, it is time to see the AL Language in action throughout this book. But before moving to structured and advanced extension development, it is important to understand how to implement and maintain a sandbox/staging environment. This is what we will do in the next chapter.

3
Online and Container-Based Sandboxes

Dynamics 365 Business Central allows us to set up sandboxes for development and testing purposes. There are two general options for these sandboxes: online sandboxes (SaaS-based) and Docker-based sandboxes (self-deployed).

Online sandboxes can be created very easily because they run as a service, which is the same as Dynamics 365 Business Central production environments. The only requirement is an existing production tenant.

Docker-based sandboxes are based on Docker containers and can run either on Azure or on-premise.

In this chapter, we will cover the following topics:

- Creating online sandboxes
- The basics of Docker images and containers and how to work with them
- Setting up local Docker environments
- Mastering the `navcontainerhelper` PowerShell utility
- Choosing the right Docker image for your development purposes
- Creating your own Docker image

Creating online sandboxes

When subscribing to a trial tenant or directly purchasing Dynamics 365 Business Central, you also have the ability to create online sandbox environments.

You can create online sandboxes in two ways: from a production environment client and/or from Dynamics 365 Business Central Admin Center.

When creating them from a production environment, search (*Alt + Q*) for `sandbox` and choose **Sandbox Environment (Preview)**:

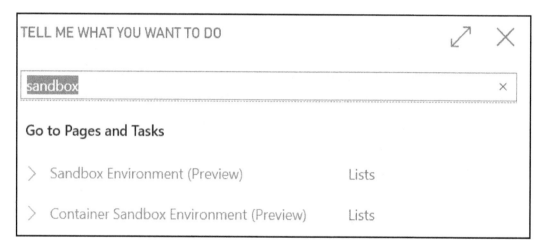

You will then be prompted to create a new sandbox environment or open or reset an existing sandbox. If there are no sandboxes and you choose open or reset, a new sandbox will be created. Online sandboxes that are created using a production environment client have the following properties:

- They are named **sandbox** by default and are also visible in the Dynamics 365 Business Central Admin Center.
- They do not contain any customer data and just have data coming from a standard demo/evaluation Cronus company.

It is very important to carefully read the Microsoft disclaimer when subscribing to an online sandbox tenant, and it's worth mentioning that this feature is still marked as being in preview:

SANDBOX ENVIRONMENT (PREVIEW)

A new sandbox environment (preview) only contains the CRONUS demonstration company. Actions that you perform in the sandbox environment (preview) do not affect data or settings in your production environment.

This Sandbox environment feature is provided as a free preview solely for testing, development and evaluation. You will not use the Sandbox in a live operating environment. Microsoft may, in its sole discretion, change the Sandbox environment or subject it to a fee for a final, commercial version, if any, or may elect not to release one.

You can also create up to three sandbox environments from Dynamics 365 Business Central Admin Center. With the appropriate credentials, log into the Admin Center through a supported browser at `https:\\businesscentral.dynamics.com\GUID\Admin,` where `GUID` is the tenant ID of your environment.

The following shows what it looks like in the Admin Center:

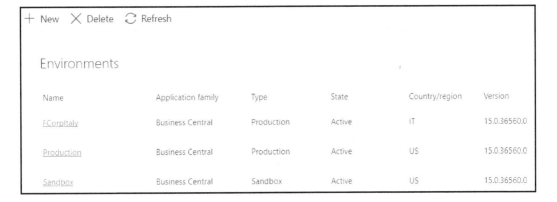

+ New   × Delete   ↻ Refresh

Environments

Name	Application family	Type	State	Country/region	Version
FCorpItaly	Business Central	Production	Active	IT	15.0.36560.0
Production	Business Central	Production	Active	US	15.0.36560.0
Sandbox	Business Central	Sandbox	Active	US	15.0.36560.0

Click the **New** button and then give the new online sandbox a valid name. Check the option for copying production data:

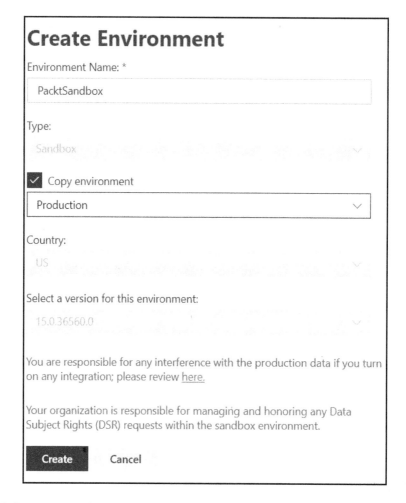

After a while, your sandbox, with a copy of the production data, will be up and running and ready for testing and development tasks.

Online sandboxes–pros and cons

According to the Microsoft disclaimer, online sandboxes are still a preview feature, and we recommend using them for demo purposes or spot development activities only. Online sandboxes have the following properties:

- They are supported by a different priority than production environments.
- Tenants are created in Azure SQL Database S-level pools, which are less performant than production P-level pools.
- They are still marked as Preview, so they are frequently subject to change.
- During upgrades, currently all per-tenant extensions are uninstalled and you/your CSP partner are required to install them once again.

You can find out more about the background of this by reading the following articles:

- `https://demiliani.com/2019/01/24/dynamics-365-business-central-te nant-upgrade-extensions-disappeared-in-sandbox-environment/`
- `https://demiliani.com/2019/03/14/dynamics-365-business-central-on line-sandbox-makes-you-crazy-maybe-remember-these-points/`

For professional development, container-based sandboxes are far more appropriate and we encourage you to use Docker-contained sandboxes in your company when developing either AppSource or per-tenant extensions.

From the online production environment, you can also search (*Alt* + *Q*) for sandbox and click on **Sandbox Environment (Container)**to easily set up an offline local or Azure-hosted Docker-contained sandbox.

You can find out more about this at`https://demiliani.com/2018/03/29/d365bc-container-sandbox-environment/`.

Let's move on to the next section and learn how to work with Docker-based environments.

Introducing Docker

If you opt to use self-deployed sandboxes, they will be based on Docker. Docker is the leading cross-platform software container environment. Since this is a book about Dynamics 365 Business Central, this section will only be a quick introduction to Docker, but if you want to learn more, there are excellent learning resources in the official documentation by Docker (`https://docs.docker.com/`) and Microsoft (`https://docs.microsoft.com/en-us/virtualization/windowscontainers/about/index`), both of which are very good starting points.

Dynamics 365 Business Central runs *only* on Windows, so when you're looking for Docker documentation, make sure that it is intended for Windows. While most of Docker is platform-independent, there are some platform-specific sections as well.

In order to follow the content of the following sections, you need to know about the following Docker basics:

- A Docker image is like a pre-built template with the minimum amount of OS binaries, libraries, and application binaries needed. The image can be identified by a name, such as Business Central / Sandbox. The exact image version can be specified with a tag. For example, `1910-cu1-de` would give you the **October 19 release (1910)**, **CU 1 (cu1)**, **German version (de)**.
- A Docker container is an instance of an image with an immutable base (the files that are in the image) and its changes on top. A container is not a **virtual machine (VM)**. It doesn't have a GUI or anything you can connect to by using the **Remote Desktop Protocol (RDP)**.
- A Docker host is a (physical or virtual) machine where containers are running.
- A Docker registry is a place where you and others can upload (push) and download (pull) images. Specifically, images can be downloaded from repositories that are part of the registry.

All Dynamics 365 Business Central Docker images are available through the Microsoft Container Registry, which you can find at `http://mcr.microsoft.com` in the business central repository. It will be called **sandbox** or **on-prem**, so a typical address to pull a Dynamics 365 Business Central on-premise image from is `mcr.microsoft.com/businesscentral/onprem:1810-cu5-de`.

For previews of new and upcoming releases, there is also a special repository called `bcinsider.azurecr.io`, but you need credentials to access it. Microsoft provides those credentials through the Ready to Go! program on collaborate (`https://docs.microsoft.com/en-us/collaborate/`).

The scripts that are used to create and run the Dynamics 365 Business Central images are open source and available at `https://github.com/Microsoft/nav-docker`.

It is also worth noting that while these images are called business central, they also contain a SQL Server for the database, an IIS for the `Web Client`, and file sharing by default.

Some base mechanisms when using Docker

In the following sections, we will use a couple of mechanisms that cover most real-life scenarios. Let's go through each of them.

Environment variables

An environment variable is a way to parameterize a Docker container when it starts. Dynamics 365 Business Central images understand a lot of environments, for example, those used to set the authentication type or the username and password, or the SQL server and database you want to connect your Business Central Service Tier to. Environment variables are set using the `-e` parameter. If you need to set multiple environment variables, you can just use multiple `-e` parameters:

```
-e auth=Windows -e databaseserver=sql -e databasename=cronus
```

There is no list of all environment variables you can use to configure Dynamics 365 Business Central containers in line with your requirements, but the script for setting up those variables in the image is a good starting point, and the names of the variables give you a pretty good idea of what they do. You can find this script at `https://github.com/Microsoft/nav-docker/blob/master/generic/Run/SetupVariables.ps1`.

Volumes

With volumes, you have a way to map folders on your Docker host to your container, for example, to give it access to binaries or other files it needs to run your solution.

If you are not using volumes and you remove a container, all the changes you make to the filesystem inside the container will be lost because they will have been removed, along with the container.

Volumes are set using the -v parameter, followed by the path of your host, a colon, and the path inside your container. If you want to map the c:\data\containers folder on your host to c:\temp inside of the container, you would write the following command:

```
-v c:\data\containers:c:\temp
```

Networks and ports

Docker lets you use different ways to connect your containers to the network. If you configure nothing else, it uses a so-called NAT network. This means that your containers get an IP address known only on the Docker host, which also makes them reachable on the host. As an alternative, you can create a so-called transparent network, which means that the container will share the network connection of the host and will try to get its own IP address using either DHCP for dynamic IP assignment or a static IP address you configure. If you have a transparent network called transpNet, you would instruct Docker to use it with the following command:

```
--network transpNet
```

Dynamics 365 Business Central images use all the standard ports, so you have 7045-7049 for the Business Central Service Tier services, 443 for HTTPS, 80 for HTTP for the Web Client, and 1443 for SQL. They also share some files through port 8080, which is mapped to an IIS backend share.

If you don't want to use transparent networks but still want to make the ports available outside the Docker host, you can use a mechanism called port mapping with the`-p` parameter. With that, you can instruct Docker to make a port of the container that's available on the same or a different port of your host. If you want to make an HTTPS-based `Web Client` listening on port `443` available on port `4443` of your host, you would typically use the following command:

```
-p 4443:443
```

Since Dynamics 365 Business Central works a lot better if it knows which ports it is listening on, the best approach is to include `-e WebClientPort=4443`, which causes the `Web Client` to listen on that port instead of the standard port, `443`. Consequently, your port mapping parameter would be `-p 4443:4443`.

Scenarios where Docker is especially useful for Dynamics 365 Business Central sandboxes

There are a couple of scenarios where the use of Docker containers makes a lot of sense and can help solve common problems. Please note that, at the time of writing, there is no production support for Dynamics 365 Business Central running in a Docker container, so you can only use it for development and testing purposes. The scenarios that will be covered in this book are as follows:

- **Locally available scenarios**: You want to run the sandboxes on your local sandbox or on your own virtual machine.
- **Centrally available environments**: The sandboxes are provided on a central environment and are administered by some kind of operations team.
- **Containers hosted on Azure VMs**: If you don't want or can't have a VM in your own datacenter, you can use Azure **Infrastructure-as-a-Service** (**IaaS**) to host your sandboxes.
- **Serverless environments on Azure Container Instances**: You can also use the **Platform-as-a-Service** (**PaaS**) offering of Azure Container Instances if you just want to run your containers without worrying about Docker itself.

It is worth mentioning that there are other options, such as the **Azure Kubernetes Service** (**AKS**) or products from other cloud providers, but since Dynamics 365 Business Central tends to run with more Microsoft-oriented customers and Kubernetes only recently initiated support for Windows containers, they will not be covered here.

Docker is also very useful for automated builds in a **Continuous Integration/Continuous Delivery** (**CI/CD**) pipeline. This topic will be covered in depth in `Chapter 11`, *Source Control Management and DevOps with Business Central*.

Locally available environments using pure Docker commands

Having your Dynamics 365 Business Central sandboxes local makes sense if you want to give the person working with them full control or if you need to use them offline. It will, however, require the person using it to understand at least the basics of Docker, which is not very complicated but may or may not suit your requirements.

Your first container

The first step in running Dynamics 365 Business Central sandboxes is installing Docker. This is quite easy and documented at `https://docs.docker.com/install/windows/docker-ee/`. Once you have done that, it's time to run your first container. Microsoft has provided a very helpful PowerShell module called `navcontainerhelper`, which eases the process of creating containers. However, to give you some basic understanding of the underlying mechanisms and how Dynamics 365 Business Central images work, it makes sense to look at a couple of easy examples with just Docker.

The most basic way to run a Dynamics 365 Business Central sandbox is by using the following command:

```
docker run -e accept_eula=y mcr.microsoft.com/businesscentral/sandbox
```

This only works in what is called process isolation, which allows the container to use host resources such as memory as necessary. Depending on your configuration and whether you are running on an old version of Windows 10 or Docker, you may get an error stating that the container doesn't have enough memory. In that case, add `-m 3G` as a parameter, which will allow the container to reserve 3 GB of memory.

> More on process isolation can be found at `https://docs.microsoft.com/en-us/virtualization/windowscontainers/manage-containers/hyperv-container`.

Note that this will, by default, pull the image based on Windows Server 2016. If you want to run the much smaller and therefore quicker image based on Windows Server 2019, you need to add what is called a tag; in this case, this will be `ltsc2019`. More details can be found in the *Choosing the right image* section:

```
docker run -e accept_eula=y
mcr.microsoft.com/businesscentral/sandbox:ltsc2019
```

This instructs Docker to run a container using the specified image, that is, `mcr.microsoft.com/businesscentral/sandbox`. Running a container means that Docker checks whether that image has already been downloaded (pulled) and if not, it pulls it. If it is already available, or after Docker has downloaded the image for you, it creates a container for that image and starts it. You will see the output from the main process inside the console window where you ran that command.

With the `-e` parameter, you let Docker know that you want to set the `accept_eula=y` environment parameter inside the container, which means that you accept the **End User License Agreement** (**EULA**). This is necessary whenever you run a Dynamics 365 Business Central sandbox.

The following is the output of a `docker run` command where the image was not locally available:

```
docker run -e accept_eula=y -m 3G
mcr.microsoft.com/businesscentral/sandbox

Unable to find image
'mcr.microsoft.com/businesscentral/sandbox:latest' locally

latest: Pulling from businesscentral/sandbox

3889bb8d808b: Already exists

...

6d7321cdab15: Already exists
5c2abed3c0c2: Already exists
0bc14e36adef: Pull complete
4fd56667f5dc: Pull complete
...
4dd9d6309b80: Pull complete
Digest:
sha256:ca99037c70e1eedf21e8472a5d46efeb148dd46a7b16bdf2ddad864e2e4cb97
c
Status: Downloaded newer image for
mcr.microsoft.com/businesscentral/sandbox:latest
Initializing...
Starting Container
Hostname is 12cec5da3d89
PublicDnsName is 12cec5da3d89
Using NavUserPassword Authentication
Starting Local SQL Server
Starting Internet Information Server
Creating Self Signed Certificate
Self Signed Certificate Thumbprint
857B5A19C68D44BE3368CB96E2AFF6F540C0D957
Modifying Service Tier Config File with Instance Specific Settings
Starting Service Tier
Registering event sources
Creating DotNetCore Web Server Instance
Enabling Financials User Experience
Creating http download site
Setting SA Password and enabling SA
Creating admin as SQL User and add to sysadmin
Creating SUPER user
Container IP Address: 172.20.200.44
Container Hostname   : 12cec5da3d89
Container Dns Name   : 12cec5da3d89
```

```
Web Client           : https://12cec5da3d89/BC/
Admin Username       : admin
Admin Password       : Fuwu1800
Dev. Server          : https://12cec5da3d89
Dev. ServerInstance  : BC
Files:
http://12cec5da3d89:8080/al-4.0.192371.vsix
http://12cec5da3d89:8080/certificate.cer
Initialization took 164 seconds
Ready for connections!
```

As you can see, the log output lets you know where you can reach the `Web Client` and the Development Server service (for connections with Visual Studio Code with the AL Language extension) for your container (use the IP address for now; more on that later) and which username and password to use.

Pulling new image versions

Note that, by default, Docker doesn't check whether there is a new version of the image and tags you to try to download. If you want to make sure you have the current version, you can run the following command, which will always check if there is a newer image:

```
docker pull mcr.microsoft.com/businesscentral/sandbox
```

If there is a new version available, it will download it and produce some output that looks similar to what you saw previously. If no new version is available, you will see the following:

```
docker pull mcr.microsoft.com/businesscentral/sandbox
Using default tag: latest
latest: Pulling from businesscentral/sandbox
Digest:
sha256:ca99037c70e1eedf21e8472a5d46efeb148dd46a7b16bdf2ddad864e2e4cb97
c
Status: Image is up to date for
mcr.microsoft.com/businesscentral/sandbox:latest
```

We can also use more environment parameters, a volume, and port mapping to show you a more advanced example while using the mechanisms we introduced earlier:

```
docker run -e accept_eula=y -e usessl=n -v "c:\dev\addins:c:\program
files\Microsoft\Dynamics Business Central\150\Service Tier\Add-
ins\mine" -p 80:80 -name mycontainer
mcr.microsoft.com/businesscentral/sandbox
```

This achieves the following:

- It accepts the EULA and tells the image not to use SSL for the `Web Client` with the two -e parameters.
- It maps a local folder, `c:\dev\addins`, to the `mine` subfolder of the `Add-Ins` folder of the Business Central Service Tier with the -v parameter.
- It makes port 80 available as port 80 on your laptop with the -p parameter. You could also use-p 8080:80, which causes port 8080 on your laptop to go to port 80 on the container.
- It names the container `mycontainer` so that you can easily refer to it with the --name parameter.

Now that we have learned about running a local Docker environment, let's have a look at how to connect to an existing SQL Server instance.

Connecting to an existing SQL Server

You can instruct the container to connect to an existing SQL Server and database instead of using the SQL Server inside the container, which will also mean that the SQL Server inside the container will not be started. This is needed if you want to connect multiple instances to the same database, but also makes a lot of sense if you want to run a lot of containers on the same host. Otherwise, you will have one SQL Server running per container, which will need a lot of resources.

In this section, I am assuming there is a SQL Server (in a container or not) called `sqlserver` running in your local environment where the Business Central container can reach it. I have a SQL user called `sqluser`with a password of `1SuperSecretPwd!`, who has the necessary rights to access a Business Central database called `FinancialsW1` on that server. For this scenario, the `docker run` command would look like this:

```
docker run -e accept_eula=y -e databaseServer=sqlserver -e
databaseUsername=sqluser -e "databasePassword=1SuperSecretPwd!" -e
databasename=FinancialsW1 mcr.microsoft.com/businesscentral/sandbox
```

We get the following output:

```
Initializing...
Starting Container
Hostname is c9658bdbe7f0
PublicDnsName is c9658bdbe7f0
Using NavUserPassword Authentication
Starting Internet Information Server
Import Encryption Key
Creating Self Signed Certificate
Self Signed Certificate Thumbprint
87B2FC05A437AFE41966A3E99EFC75A2C2CAD537
Modifying Service Tier Config File with Instance Specific Settings
Starting Service Tier
Creating DotNetCore Web Server Instance
Enabling Financials User Experience
Creating http download site
Creating Windows user admin
Container IP Address: 172.26.151.47
Container Hostname   : c9658bdbe7f0
Container Dns Name   : c9658bdbe7f0
Web Client           : https://c9658bdbe7f0/BC/
Dev. Server          : https://c9658bdbe7f0
Dev. ServerInstance  : BC
Files:
http://c9658bdbe7f0:8080/al-4.0.192371.vsix
http://c9658bdbe7f0:8080/certificate.cer
```

The following is the final output:

```
Initialization took 116 seconds
Ready for connections!
```

Note that, in this case, the container will not create any users in the database because it assumes that, if you are using an existing database, you will also have existing users in that database. Also, note that the container will import its own encryption key into the database, which is used to encrypt passwords. So, if you want to connect multiple containers to the same database in that way, you need to make sure the encryption key is shared.

Handling your running containers with Docker cmdlets

If you need to get a PowerShell session into a running container, you have two options:

- First, you can use `Enter-PSSession`, as if you were connecting to another computer, except you need to give it the full ID of the container instead of the machine name. The easiest way to get there is to use a subcommand querying Docker for that container. Entering a PS session for the `mycontainer` container would look like this:

  ```
  Enter-PSSession -containerid (docker --no-trunc -qf
  "name=mycontainer")
  ```

  The preceding statement *only* works when you're running as an administrator.

- The second option is to execute the `powershell` command on your container and instruct Docker to open an interactive Terminal for it. This would look as follows for the `mycontainer` container:

  ```
  docker exec -ti mycontainer powershell
  ```

With both commands, you end up with a PowerShell session inside your container. If you want to run Business Central cmdlets, the easiest way is to call `c:\run\prompt.ps1`, which imports all the development and admin cmdlets.

To see all the currently running containers, you can write and execute `docker ps`, which gives you the following output:

```
docker ps
CONTAINER ID        IMAGE
COMMAND                     CREATED            STATUS
PORTS                                          NAMES
12cec5da3d89        mcr.microsoft.com/businesscentral/sandbox
"powershell -Comma..."    22 minutes ago       Up 21 minutes (healthy)
80/tcp, 443/tcp, 1433/tcp, 7045-7049/tcp, 8080/tcp
determined_shockley
9518e7e456de        mcr.microsoft.com/dynamicsnav:2017-cu22-de
"powershell -Comma..."    42 minutes ago       Up 41 minutes (healthy)
80/tcp, 443/tcp, 1433/tcp, 7045-7049/tcp, 8080/tcp    testcont
95959a311e54        mcr.microsoft.com/dynamicsnav:2017-cu22-de
"powershell -Comma..."    About an hour ago    Up About an hour
```

```
(healthy)     80/tcp, 443/tcp, 1433/tcp, 7045-7049/tcp, 8080/tcp
RKOS-18111
13057bf415cc          mcr.microsoft.com/dynamicsnav:2017-cu22-de
"powershell -Comma..."    22 hours ago        Up 22 hours (healthy)
80/tcp, 443/tcp, 1433/tcp, 7045-7049/tcp, 8080/tcp   VOEKOM
0e7970ce5318          mcr.microsoft.com/dynamicsnav:2017-cu22-de
"powershell -Comma..."    29 hours ago        Up 29 hours (healthy)
80/tcp, 443/tcp, 1433/tcp, 7045-7049/tcp, 8080/tcp   Buchau
6c1c44f170bb          mcr.microsoft.com/dynamicsnav:2017-cu22-at
"powershell -Comma..."    46 hours ago        Up 46 hours (healthy)
80/tcp, 443/tcp, 1433/tcp, 7045-7049/tcp, 8080/tcp   syAToekom
```

To see all currently existing containers, you can use `docker ps -a`, which also includes exited and/or stopped containers (the output also shows a container with a status of `Exited`):

```
docker ps -a
CONTAINER ID          IMAGE
COMMAND                 CREATED           STATUS
PORTS                                         NAMES
12cec5da3d89          mcr.microsoft.com/businesscentral/sandbox
"powershell -Comma..."    24 minutes ago      Exited (1073807364) 9
seconds ago
determined_shockley
9518e7e456de          mcr.microsoft.com/dynamicsnav:2017-cu22-de
"powershell -Comma..."    43 minutes ago      Up 43 minutes (healthy)
80/tcp, 443/tcp, 1433/tcp, 7045-7049/tcp, 8080/tcp   testcont
95959a311e54          mcr.microsoft.com/dynamicsnav:2017-cu22-de
"powershell -Comma..."    About an hour ago   Up About an hour
(healthy)             80/tcp, 443/tcp, 1433/tcp, 7045-7049/tcp, 8080/tcp
RKOS-18111
```

Stopping and starting containers is as easy as using `docker stop` and `docker start`, respectively. If you want to remove a container, you need to either stop (`docker stop`) and then remove it (`docker rm`) or use the `-f` parameter for `docker rm` to force the removal of the container, even if it's still running.

 Be aware that removing a container means that all the files inside that container are gone and can't be restored.

If the command is successful, it only returns the name or ID of the container as you specified it:

```
docker rm -f 12
```

Note that you can address containers either with their name or with their ID. You don't need to specify the full ID; you just need enough characters from the beginning of the ID so that Docker can uniquely identify the container. Also, note that `docker ps` gives you a truncated ID for each container, and you can use `docker ps -no-trunc` to get the full ID.

Creating locally available environments using navcontainerhelper

To make it easier to adopt and use Dynamics 365 Business Central Docker images, Microsoft has created a PowerShell Module called `navcontainerhelper`. It uses the same images and commands that you can use with pure Docker commands and, in a lot of places, you can see how the cmdlets translate to Docker commands. It also contains a very valuable collection of additional PowerShell scripts to help with common development, build, test, and release tasks in Dynamics 365 Business Central.

Installing navcontainerhelper and keeping it updated

To use the `navcontainerhelper` module, you need to install it from the PowerShell gallery, as follows:

```
install-module navcontainerhelper -force
```

If there is a new version of `navcontainerhelper`(which, at the time of writing, happens at least every couple of weeks) with new helpful features and bug fixes, just run the following command:

```
update-module navcontainerhelper -force
```

Your first container

To follow the same examples as in the previous section, you will learn how to run your first container using `navcontainerhelper`. However, `navcontainerhelper` expects you to give it a name and make a conscious decision about authentication. If you don't provide any other parameters, it assumes that you want to use Windows authentication and asks for your password so that it can create a user with the same username and password inside the container. This also enables **single-sign-on** (**SSO**). Consider the following command:

```
New-NavContainer -accept_eula -imageName
mcr.microsoft.com/businesscentral/sandbox mycontainer

NavContainerHelper is version 0.6.4.16
NavContainerHelper is running as administrator
Host is Microsoft Windows Server 2019 Datacenter - ltsc2019
Docker Client Version is 19.03.2
Docker Server Version is 19.03.2
Pulling image mcr.microsoft.com/businesscentral/sandbox:latest-
ltsc2019
latest-ltsc2019: Pulling from businesscentral/sandbox
3889bb8d808b: Already exists
e0718b11f512: Pulling fs layer
...
76a160cd3c52: Pull complete
Digest:
sha256:3eb2e9d87102c135c1b0c004523abbbe7bff53fc98fe5527a4e85e9ff198d1f
d
Status: Downloaded newer image for
mcr.microsoft.com/businesscentral/sandbox:latest-ltsc2019
Using image mcr.microsoft.com/businesscentral/sandbox:latest-ltsc2019
Creating Container mycontainer
Version: 15.0.36626.37711-w1
Style: sandbox
Platform: 15.0.37582.0
Generic Tag: 0.0.9.95
Container OS Version: 10.0.17763.737 (ltsc2019)
Host OS Version: 10.0.17763.678 (ltsc2019)
Using locale en-US
Using process isolation
Disabling the standard eventlog dump to container log every 2 seconds
(use -dumpEventLog to enable)
Files in C:\ProgramData\NavContainerHelper\Extensions\mycontainer\my:
- AdditionalOutput.ps1
- MainLoop.ps1
Creating container mycontainer from image
mcr.microsoft.com/businesscentral/sandbox:latest-ltsc2019
```

```
db420a5aec3da0b94b2a466432c160f3a28bd7da5ed83d5ea683ee5e7bd330ff
Waiting for container mycontainer to be ready
Initializing...
Starting Container
Hostname is mycontainer
PublicDnsName is mycontainer
Using Windows Authentication
Starting Local SQL Server
Starting Internet Information Server
Modifying Service Tier Config File with Instance Specific Settings
Starting Service Tier
Registering event sources
Creating DotNetCore Web Server Instance
Enabling Financials User Experience
Creating http download site
Creating Windows user tobias.fenster
Setting SA Password and enabling SA
Creating SUPER user
Container IP Address: 172.23.237.104
Container Hostname   : mycontainer
Container Dns Name   : mycontainer
Web Client           : http://mycontainer/BC/
Dev. Server          : http://mycontainer
Dev. ServerInstance : BC

Files:
http://mycontainer:8080/al-4.0.192371.vsix

Initialization took 311 seconds
Ready for connections!
Reading CustomSettings.config from mycontainer
Creating Desktop Shortcuts for mycontainer
Container mycontainer successfully created
```

As you can see from the last couple of lines, navcontainerhelper even creates convenient desktop shortcuts. They allow you to access the Web Client or open a PowerShell or Command Prompt inside your container with a simple double-click. The shortcuts actually use the same docker exec command that you saw in the previous sections.

`New-NavContainer` has a long list of parameters, which may either be just mappings for environment parameters or very helpful little functions. To give you an example, if you specify –updateHosts, then `navcontainerhelper` will add the name and IP address of the container to the hosts file on your laptop. This means that you don't need to use the IP address – you can use the container name as the address! There are, of course, ways to do this without `navcontainerhelper`, but none are as easy as specifying one single parameter in your startup command.

Pulling new image versions

Pulling new images works exactly the same for `navcontainerhelper` as it does for plain Docker; there's no special command there. However, you can specify –alwaysPull as a parameter for your `New-NavContainer` command, which will –as the name clearly implies –always try to pull a new image version before running your container.

But `navcontainerhelper` actually adds more convenient optimizations automatically. If you do not specify `ltsc2016`or `ltsc2019`as part of your tag, it will determine the best container platform and use that. It also automatically determines whether process isolation is possible and sets the memory limit, if necessary, to 4 GB.

Using more environment parameters, a volume, and port mapping

As we mentioned previously, `New-NavContainer` provides a lot of parameters that just set environment parameters. We did the following in our previous example using plain `docker run`:

```
docker run -e accept_eula=y -e usessl=n -v "c:\dev\addins:c:\program
files\microsoft\Dynamics NAV\150\Service Tier\Add-ins\mine" -p 80:80
-name mycontainer mcr.microsoft.com/businesscentral/sandbox
```

To achieve the same in `navcontainerhelper`, we would use the following:

```
New-NavContainer -accept_eula -PublishPorts 80 -additionalParameters
@('--volume c:\dev\addins:c:\program files\microsoft\Dynamics
NAV\150\Service Tier\Add-ins\mine') -containerName mycontainer -
imageName mcr.microsoft.com/businesscentral/sandbox
```

Let's compare the features:

- Accepting the EULA is done with `-accept_eula`, and not using SSL is the default for `navcontainerhelper`.
- The mapping of the local folder to the `Add-ins` folder in the container is done with the `-additionalParameters` parameter. This is the mechanism in `navcontainerhelper` that specifies any `docker run` parameter you may need that is not already covered.
- Port mapping is done with the `-PublishPorts` parameter.
- Naming the container is done with the `-containerName` parameter.

Again, `navcontainerhelper` adds more automatically: `c:\programdata\navcontainerhelper` is always shared with the container as the same folder inside the container. Also, every container has its own folder at `c:\programdata\navcontainerhelper\extensions\<containername>`, and everything local to this container is placed there.

Connecting to an existing SQL Server

`navcontainerhelper` makes this task just a bit more convenient than using Docker directly. You need to specify the same parameters, but you can give it a credential object instead of putting the username and password in as clear text. As a reminder, the following is what the `docker run` command looks like:

```
docker run -e accept_eula=y -e databaseServer=sqlserver -e
databaseUsername=sqluser -e "databasePassword=1SuperSecretPwd!" -e
databasename=FinancialsW1 mcr.microsoft.com/businesscentral/sandbox
```

The following is the same command but using `navcontainerhelper`. It will open a credential entry dialog where you can enter your SQL username and password. But instead of sharing the password as clear text in the environment variables, `navcontainerhelper` ensures that passwords are handled securely, as follows:

```
New-NavContainer -accept_eula -databaseServer sqlserver -
databaseCredential (Get-Credential) -databaseName FinancialsW1 -
imageName mcr.microsoft.com/businesscentral/sandbox:latest -
containerName mycontainer -auth NavUserPassword
cmdlet Get-Credential at command pipeline position 1
Supply values for the following parameters:
Credential

NavContainerHelper is version 0.6.4.16
NavContainerHelper is running as administrator
```

```
Host is Microsoft Windows Server 2019 Datacenter - ltsc2019
Docker Client Version is 19.03.2
Docker Server Version is 19.03.2
Pulling image mcr.microsoft.com/businesscentral/sandbox:latest-
ltsc2019
latest-ltsc2019: Pulling from businesscentral/sandbox
3889bb8d808b: Already exists
e0718b11f512: Pulling fs layer
...
76a160cd3c52: Pull complete
Digest:
sha256:3eb2e9d87102c135c1b0c004523abbbe7bff53fc98fe5527a4e85e9ff198d1f
d
Status: Downloaded newer image for
mcr.microsoft.com/businesscentral/sandbox:latest-ltsc2019
Using image mcr.microsoft.com/businesscentral/sandbox:latest-ltsc2019
Creating Container mycontainer
Version: 15.0.36626.37711-w1
Style: sandbox
Platform: 15.0.37582.0
Generic Tag: 0.0.9.95
Container OS Version: 10.0.17763.737 (ltsc2019)
Host OS Version: 10.0.17763.678 (ltsc2019)
Using locale en-US
Using process isolation
Disabling the standard eventlog dump to container log every 2 seconds
(use -dumpEventLog to enable)
Files in C:\ProgramData\NavContainerHelper\Extensions\mycontainer\my:
- AdditionalOutput.ps1
- MainLoop.ps1
Creating container mycontainer from image
mcr.microsoft.com/businesscentral/sandbox:latest-ltsc2019
db420a5aec3da0b94b2a466432c160f3a28bd7da5ed83d5ea683ee5e7bd330ff
Waiting for container mycontainer to be ready
Initializing...
Starting Container
Hostname is mycontainer
PublicDnsName is mycontainer
Using NavUserPassword Authentication
Starting Internet Information Server
Import Encryption Key
Creating Self Signed Certificate
Self Signed Certificate Thumbprint
583BDDBAB357DB4B4AB722284629195E27328B7E
Modifying Service Tier Config File with Instance Specific Settings
Starting Service Tier
Creating DotNetCore Web Server Instance
Enabling Financials User Experience
```

```
Creating http download site
Creating Windows user admin
Setting SA Password and enabling SA
Creating SUPER user
Container IP Address: 172.23.237.104
Container Hostname : mycontainer
Container Dns Name : mycontainer
Web Client : http://mycontainer/BC/
Dev. Server : http://mycontainer
Dev. ServerInstance : BC

Files:
http://mycontainer:8080/al-4.0.192371.vsix

Initialization took 99 seconds
Ready for connections!
Reading CustomSettings.config from mycontainer
Creating Desktop Shortcuts for mycontainer
Container mycontainer successfully created
```

Note that the default authentication mechanism when using `docker run` is `NavUserPassword`, while the default for `navcontainerhelper` is Windows, so in order to achieve the same result, we need to specify that as well.

Handling your running containers with NavContainerHelper

There is no special command in `navcontainerhelper` that lets you see your running containers, so you just use the same `docker ps` commands that were introduced in the previous section. There are commands for starting and stopping containers (`Start-NavContainer` and `Stop-NavContainer`, respectively), but they are very thin wrappers around `docker start` and `docker stop` with no additional benefits.

Removing containers, however, is done with `Remove-NavContainer`, which does a bit more: it cleans up the shortcuts and container-specific folders, and it removes entries in your hosts file if you specify `-updatehosts`.

There is also a command to get a session into your container called `Enter-NavContainer`. This gives you a PowerShell session inside your container with the added benefit of calling `c:\run\prompt.ps1`, which gives you all development and admin cmdlets immediately and a nicely formatted prompt so that you always know where you are. Consider the following command:

```
Enter-NavContainer mycontainer[MYCONTAINER]: PS C:\Run> Get-
NAVServerInstance
ServerInstance : MicrosoftDynamicsNavServer$BC
DisplayName    : Dynamics 365 Business Central Server [BC]
State          : Running
ServiceAccount : NT AUTHORITY\SYSTEM
Version        : 15.0.37582.0
Default : True
```

Centrally available on-premise environments

So far, we have only covered locally running containers but, depending on your scenario, you may want to set up one or multiple central VMs that are administered not by the developers and consultants but by an operations team. In this case, the same options that we explained previously exist, but you need to consider a couple of additional topics. You also need to decide whether you want a full self-service environment where a developer or consultant can self-provision a new sandbox or whether you want the operations team to handle creating and deleting the sandboxes.

If your operations team handles these operations, the only topic you need to think about is networking. You have the following two options to make your container ports available outside the Docker host:

- Port mapping lets you map container ports to host ports. However, this will become tedious over time as you need to find free ports for every container and tell your users which ports to use.
- Transparent networking lets the container get its own IP address (static or DHCP) and keep the standard ports. This method works with a lot less maintenance. We will look at this in more detail now.

So, creating a transparent network is quite easy. In the simplest scenario, you just write the following to create a transparent network called `transpNet`:

```
docker network create -d transparent transpNet
```

You can also set the subnet or IP range, but that is beyond the scope of this book. Check the online documentation for Docker or run `docker network create --help` to learn more about that. Telling a container to use a transparent network is also easy because there is a parameter called `--network`. Use it as follows when running pure Docker:

```
docker run -e accept_eula=y --network transpNet
mcr.microsoft.com/businesscentral/sandbox
```

`navcontainerhelper` doesn't have a specific network parameter on `New-NavContainer` at the time of writing, but you can use `-additionalParameters` parameter instead:

```
New-NavContainer -accept_eula -additionalParameters @('--network
transpNet') -containerName mycontainer -imageName
mcr.microsoft.com/businesscentral/sandbox
```

With that, your container will get its own IP address and you will probably be able to reach it by name from outside your Docker host as well. Please note that this very much depends on the setup of the network that your host is running in. It is similar to adding a new VM to the network and, depending on the security mechanisms that have been put in place by network administrators, this may not actually work without further setup.

If you want to have an environment where developers or consultants can create their own environments, you will have to solve two issues:

- **How would you like container handling to be done (create, start, stop, and delete actions)?** You could allow your users to access the host through RDP or PowerShell, but then it becomes difficult to handle permissions. You can also use tools such as Portainer (`https://portainer.io`), which is a GUI for handling containers. Here, users can manage their containers and you can, for example, create templates with predefined values for the container parameters. However, note that you won't be able to use `navcontainerhelper` in this scenario because that would mean running PowerShell scripts on your host. Another option is to create some kind of frontend application yourself, but that of course will take some time.

- **How will users access the filesystem in your containers?** It depends on your Dynamics 365 Business Central usage. Often, it is necessary to access the filesystem. If you are already running a full-cloud solution, this is not possible anyway, but if you still have on-premise customers, this may be an issue. The easiest solution is to always map a volume into your container, such as `c:\shared`, and allow users to access the folder on the host.

Containers hosted on Azure VMs

If you want to run your sandboxes in Azure VMs, the challenges you face are almost the same as they are with centrally available sandboxes on an on-premise VM. However, you can take some shortcuts: Microsoft provides standard VM images with preinstalled Docker, such as Windows Server 2019 Datacenter with Containers, so you don't have to worry about that.

If you want to use `navcontainerhelper`, you need to install it, and then you are ready to go. An even quicker way is to use one of the quick start templates provided by Microsoft, such as `http://aka.ms/getbc`. This will create an Azure VM, install Docker and `navcontainerhelper`, pull the latest Dynamics 365 Business Central image (defaulting to the on-premise image), and start it for you. And on top of that, you get a nice log showing you how all the magic that is happening is progressing. Afterward, you can use that VM to create additional sandboxes as you need them.

However, there is one issue in Azure VMs that makes handling them a bit more complicated: you can't use transparent networking. This makes sense for a number of reasons and likely won't change in the near future, so you have to consider other solutions. One would be port mapping, as we mentioned previously, but that also takes quite a lot of maintenance. The easiest way is to use a reverse proxy such as nginx or Traefik, but that is also beyond the scope of this book.

You can find a quick introduction on how to get started at`https://www.axians-infoma.de/techblog/running-multiple-nav-bc-containers-on-an-azure-vm/`.

Choosing the right image

Now that you know how to create and run your sandboxes, the only question is which version you want to use; making this decision may be quite complex. The basics for making a viable decision on that topic will be summarized in this section.

Officially, publicly released versions are always available on the registry (`mcr.microsoft.com`) with the following repositories and image names:

- `mcr.microsoft.com/businesscentral/sandbox`: The sandbox image of the SaaS version of Dynamics 365 Business Central
- `mcr.microsoft.com/businesscentral/onprem`: The on-premise version of Dynamics 365 Business Central
- `mcr.microsoft.com/dynamicsnav`: The old Dynamics NAV product, starting from Dynamics NAV 2016

Previews of unreleased versions are available on the `bcinsider.azurecr.io` registry with the following repositories and images names:

- `bcinsider.azurecr.io/bcsandbox`: A preview of the next minor release of the SaaS version of Dynamics 365 Business Central
- `bcinsider.azurecr.io/bconprem`: A preview of the next minor release of the on-premise version of Dynamics 365 Business Central
- `bcinsider.azurecr.io/bcsandbox-master`: A preview of the next major release of the SaaS version of Dynamics 365 Business Central
- `bcinsider.azurecr.io/bconprem-master`: A preview of the next major release of the on-premise version of Dynamics 365 Business Central

Note that, once again, you need login credentials for `bcinsider.azurecr.io`, which you can get from Microsoft's collaborate platform after you have registered for the Ready to Go! program.

When you have decided which image to use, you also need to decide on which tag to use, representing one of the specific releases by Microsoft. All images allow you to specify the language (`gb`, `de`, `dk`, and so on) and the base OS (`ltsc2016` for Windows Server 2016 and `ltsc2019` for Windows Server 2019). The released on-premise versions also allow you to use the same naming conventions that you can use with traditional installs by referencing them by their cumulative update name.

Consider the following examples, just to get some insight into the syntax:

- Dynamics 365 Business Central Fall 2018 (1810), CU 11, German version, based on Windows Server 2016:

```
mcr.microsoft.com/businesscentral/onprem:1810-cu11-de-ltsc2016
```

- Dynamics 365 Business Central Spring 2019 (1904), CU 5, Danish version, based on Windows Server 2019:

  ```
  mcr.microsoft.com/businesscentral/onprem:1904-cu5-dk-ltsc2019
  ```

- Dynamics 365 Business Central Fall 2019 (1910), CU 1, Australian version, based on Windows Server 2019:

  ```
  mcr.microsoft.com/businesscentral/onprem:1910-cu1-au-ltsc2019
  ```

- Dynamics NAV 2017, CU 28, British version, based on Windows Server 2019:

  ```
  mcr.microsoft.com/businesscentral/dynamicsnav:2017-cu28-gb-
  ltsc2019
  ```

The SaaS versions that have been released allow you to specify the update version instead of the cumulative update:

- Dynamics 365 Business Central SaaS Update 25, Spanish version, based on Windows Server 2016:

  ```
  mcr.microsoft.com/businesscentral/sandbox:update25-es-ltsc2016
  ```

The preview version allows you to only specify the language and the Windows Server version:

- The latest preview of the next minor release of the SaaS version of Dynamics 365 Business Central, German version, based on Windows Server 2019: `bcinsider.azurecr.io/bcsandbox:de-ltsc2019`
- The latest preview of the next major release of the on-premise version of Dynamics 365 Business Central, Danish version, based on Windows Server 2016: `bcinsider.azurecr.io/bconprem-master:dk-ltsc2016`

There are defaults if you don't specify everything, so `mcr.microsoft.com/businesscentral/onprem` will give you the latest cumulative update of the latest Dynamics 365 Business Central on-premise release, W1 version, based on Windows Server 2016. In order to avoid surprises, it almost always makes sense to specify as much as possible with tags.

Modifying scripts inside standard images

As you have seen, Dynamics 365 Business Central container images have a lot of configuration options, giving you the possibility to change a lot of their behavior. However, if you ever run into a situation where you need to run a different container configuration setup, images have one more ace up their sleeve: you can override any script in the container.

The mechanism for this works by placing a script with the exact same name as the one you want to override into the `c:\run\my` folder in your container. The easiest way to do that is through a volume. Assuming that you have a folder such as `c:\bc-override` with an`AdditionalSetup.ps1` file, you can do the following:

```
docker run -e accept_eula=y -v c:\bc-override:c:\run\my
mcr.microsoft.com/businesscentral/onprem
```

When the container gets to the place where `AdditionalSetup.ps1` is called, it checks whether a file with that name exists in `c:\run\my` and if so, calls it. If not, it calls the standard script with that name, which is stored in `c:\run`. This script may look as follows:

```
Write-Host "----- Hello from the override script --------------------"
```

If it does, you will get the following output when starting the container:

```
Initializing...
Starting Container
Hostname is 4e58d9587fb0
PublicDnsName is 4e58d9587fb0
Using NavUserPassword Authentication
Starting Local SQL Server
Starting Internet Information Server
Creating Self Signed Certificate
Self Signed Certificate Thumbprint
1462D57EE355D19018232160C396159313A20893
Modifying Service Tier Config File with Instance Specific Settings
Starting Service Tier
Creating DotNetCore Web Server Instance
Enabling Financials User Experience
Creating http download site
Creating Windows user admin
Setting SA Password and enabling SA
Creating admin as SQL User and add to sysadmin
Creating SUPER user
----- Hello from the override script --------------------
Container IP Address: 172.26.148.48
```

```
Container Hostname   : 4e58d9587fb0
Container Dns Name   : 4e58d9587fb0
Web Client           : https://4e58d9587fb0/BC/
Admin Username       : admin
Admin Password       : Rohy1060
Dev. Server          : https://4e58d9587fb0
Dev. ServerInstance  : BC
Files:
http://4e58d9587fb0:8080/al-4.0.192371.vsix
http://4e58d9587fb0:8080/certificate.cer
Initialization took 117 seconds
Ready for connections!
```

Using the `navcontainerhelper` utility, you would call it like this:

```
New-NavContainer -accept_eula -imageName
mcr.microsoft.com/businesscentral/sandbox -myScripts @("c:\bc-
override\AdditionalSetup.ps1") mycontainer
```

Alternatively, since `navcontainerhelper` has a more convenient way of doing things, you can just add your PowerShell script code inline:

```
New-NavContainer -accept_eula -imageName
mcr.microsoft.com/businesscentral/sandbox -myscripts @( @{
"AdditionalSetup.ps1" = "Write-Host '----- Hello from the override
script --------------------'" } ) mycontainer
```

With this very powerful feature, you can change every script in the container to suit your needs. To get an idea of what you can adjust, please check out `https://github.com/Microsoft/nav-docker/tree/master/generic/Run`.

Creating your own images

With the mechanism we just saw, we can change everything inside our containers. But what if you want to make sure that your colleagues, partners, or customers get exactly those same modifications without the need to get the my-scripts override right? Or what if you need some DLLs or other files inside your container and want to deliver them as part of your own image? The answer to that is building your own image, which, fortunately, is very easy as well.

Docker has a layering concept that makes an image a stack of layers. All you need to do is put your own layer on top of the standard image. You can do that by using a Dockerfile, which needs a reference to the standard image you want to extend and then the actions you want to take. Let's say you want to place some DLLs stored in c:\bc\dlls into the image Add-ins folder and put your own AdditionalSetup.ps1 script from the c:\bc\override folder into the c:\run image folder. Your Dockerfile would look as follows, stored in the c:\bc folder:

```
FROM mcr.microsoft.com/businesscentral/sandbox
COPY ["./dlls/*", "c:/Program Files/Microsoft Dynamics
NAV/150/Service/Add-ins/"]
COPY ./override/AdditionalSetup.ps1 c:/run/
```

To build this image, you need to run the docker build command in c:\bc and give your image a name using the -t parameter:

```
docker build -t myimage
```

The result will look something like the following:

```
Sending build context to Docker daemon 7.168kB
Step 1/3 : FROM mcr.microsoft.com/businesscentral/sandbox
 ---> 20f72db6c9a9
Step 2/3 : COPY ./dlls/* c:/Program Files/Microsoft Dynamics
NAV/150/Service/Add-ins/
 ---> f202642914a9
Step 3/3 : COPY ./override/AdditionalSetup.ps1 c:/run/
 ---> 1164c1273517
Removing intermediate container e9070e72cbaa
Successfully built 1164c1273517
Successfully tagged myimage:latest
```

With that in place, you can use your image like any other image:

```
docker run -e accept_eula=y myimage
```

The way to share this image with others is via a **Docker repository**. For an image that's been built on top of the official Microsoft image, this will be done with a private repository. How to set that up is beyond the scope of this book, but https://docs.docker.com/registry/ is a good starting point if you want to learn more.

Summary

In this chapter, we learned about the basics of online and Docker-based sandboxes and how to use them optimally. We stressed the need to master the fundamentals of Docker and how to create a basic container from a Dynamics 365 Business Central image from an online repository.

With the skills you've acquired from this chapter, you should be able to create your own containers, choose the right image, and be familiar with the `navcontainerhelper` tool when it comes to handling your custom sandbox environment.

You should also be able to master Dockerfile formats and perform in-depth modifications of standard images by overriding scripts and creating your own Dynamics 365 Business Central sandbox baseline.

In the next chapter, we will start our development journey by learning about AL language fundamentals.

2
Section 2: Developing Extensions for Dynamics 365 Business Central

In this section, we will give you a complete overview of developing a customized solution for Dynamics 365 Business Central with the new extension model.

This section comprises the following chapters:

- Chapter 4, *Extension Development Fundamentals*
- Chapter 5, *Developing a Customized Solution for Dynamics 365 Business Central*
- Chapter 6, *Advanced AL Development*
- Chapter 7, *Report Development with AL*

4
Extension Development Fundamentals

In the previous chapter, we had an overview of the new Modern Development Environment and we learned how to start a new Dynamics 365 Business Central extension project by using the AL Language extension and the Modern Development Environment.

In this chapter, we'll examine the details of the objects of the new extension's development model and how to create new objects with AL, extend standard objects, and handle an AL extension project. More specifically, we'll cover the following topics:

- The basics of extension development
- An overview of the main AL objects
- How to create basic objects in an extension project
- Best practices for handling your AL project
- Guidelines for AL objects

By the end of this chapter, you will have learned about the different AL object types, as well as how to create and use them, and (more generally speaking) you will be ready to start a Dynamics 365 Business Central extension project with the AL Language extension and the Modern Development Environment (Visual Studio Code).

Technical requirements

To follow this chapter and in order to experiment with basic object creation in the AL Language, you will need the following:

- A Microsoft Dynamics 365 Business Central sandbox environment (locally installed on a Docker container or an online one)
- Visual Studio Code
- The AL Language extension, which can be installed from the Visual Studio Code marketplace

Basic concepts regarding extensions

As you already know, with Microsoft Dynamics 365 Business Central SaaS, you don't have access to the database or to the standard base code (this is different in the on-premise version, where you can still have access to the base code, and modifying that core is your responsibility). In the SaaS world, you cannot alter the database schema and cannot alter the standard business logic.

In the previous versions of the Microsoft Dynamics ERP, we have always talked about *code modification*. In the SaaS world, we have to start thinking about a new concept: *code extension*. To customize Dynamics 365 Business Central, you have to create **extensions**.

An extension (according to Microsoft's guidelines) is defined as *an installable feature built in a way that it does not directly alter source resources and that is distributed as a preconfigured package.*

An extension interacts with the standard base code by using *events*. The following diagram shows how events interact between the different layers in a Dynamics 365 Business Central extension:

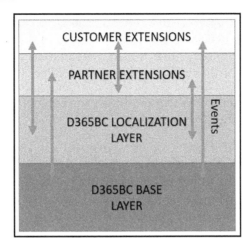

An event is essentially a function that is triggered by code when something happens in the business process. This function is normally defined as the *event publisher* function. It comprises only a signature and does not execute any code. The object that contains the event publisher function is defined as the *publisher*.

In Dynamics 365 Business Central, events are classified according to the following types:

- **Database events**: These are events that are automatically raised by the system during database operations on a table object (such as insert, modify, delete, and rename).
- **Page events**: These are events that are automatically raised by the system during operations in a page object.
- **Business events**: These are custom events that are raised by C/AL code. A business event defines a formal contract with an implicit promise not to change in future application releases.
- **Integration events**: These are custom events that are raised by C/AL code. They are similar to business events but they can change their signature in future releases of the application.
- **Global events**: These are system events that are raised by the application.

When an event is published and raised by code, it is available in the application for subscriptions. A *subscriber* is a code function that listens for and handles a published event. It subscribes to a specific event publisher function and handles the event by adding custom business logic to it. When the application raises an event, the subscriber function is automatically called and its code is executed.

Remember that you can have multiple subscribers to a single event publisher function. In this case, the order of the subscriber's execution cannot be determined (it's random), so be careful regarding the event chain when you architect your code.

Events guarantee that you can interact or modify the behavior of standard business processes without changing the base code.

 Dynamics 365 Business Central exposes a lot of events in its standard code and new events are added monthly. You can request new events by going to the following link: `https://github.com/Microsoft/ALAppExtensions/issues`. To get a complete overview of published events in Dynamics 365 Business Central, I suggest that you take a look at the following GitHub repository: `https://github.com/waldo1001/blog.CALAnalysis/tree/master/Published%20Events`.

In this section, we learned how events are the fundamental building blocks of every AL extension. In the next section, we'll have an overview of the available AL objects and learn how to create them with the AL Language extension.

Understanding the basics of the AL Language

An extension of Dynamics 365 Business Central is written using the **AL Language**. With AL, you can create new objects, extend standard objects, and create custom business logic for your application.

You create an extension for Dynamics 365 Business Central by using Visual Studio Code as your development environment and by using the AL Language extension (as we described in `Chapter 2`, *Mastering a Modern Development Environment*). When installed, you have full support for developing AL projects.

All Dynamics 365 Business Central functionalities are coded as objects (new objects or extensions of standard objects), and these objects are defined in `.al` files. A single `.al` file can define multiple objects (although we don't recommend that).

Extensions are then compiled as `.app` package files, and this file is the final extension that you will publish in your final environment.

At the time of writing, the following objects are available with the **AL Language** extension for Visual Studio Code:

- Table object
- Table extension object
- Page object
- Page extension object
- Codeunit object
- Report object
- Enum object
- XMLport object
- Query object
- Control add-in (JavaScript)
- Profile and page customizations

We'll look at the main objects in detail in the following sections. Some of these objects (such as reports, page customizations, and add-ins) will be covered in later chapters.

The AL Language extension contains a lot of snippets for defining objects and for handling the language's tasks. The main standard snippets are as follows:

- **Objects**:
    - `tpagecust`: New customization of a standard page
    - `tpageext`: New extension of a standard page
    - `ttableext`: New extension of a standard table
    - `tquery`: New query
    - `treport`: New report
    - `txmlport`: New xmlport
    - `tpage`: Here, we can choose whether we want to get a new List or a new Card
    - `tcodeunit`: New codeunit

- **Code**:
    - `tcaseelse`: Case statement with else
    - `tcaseof`: Case statement without else
    - `tfor`: For statement
    - `tforeach`: Foreach statement
    - `tif`: If statement with begin and end

- `tifelse`: If statement with begin and end else
- `tisempty`: Isempty statement with begin end
- `tisemptyelse`: Isempty statement with begin end else
- `trepeat`: Repeat loop with begin and end clause
- `twhile`: While statement
- `twith`: With statement

- **Profile**:

  - `tprofile`: Allows us to create a new profile with page customizations

- **Events**:

  - `teventbus`: Allows us to create a business event
  - `teventint`: Allows us to create an integration event
  - `teventsub`: Allows us to create a subscriber event

- **Fields and Keys**:

  - `tfield`: New field without a type (we need to put one in manually).
  - `tfieldbiginteger`: Big Integer type.
  - `tfieldboolean`: Boolean field.
  - `tfieldblob`: Blob field.
  - `tfieldcode`: Code field. You will need just to put the length of the field.
  - `tfielddate`: Date field.
  - `tfielddateformula`: Dateformula field.
  - `tfielddatetime`: Datetime field.
  - `tfielddecimal`: Decimal field.
  - `tfieldduration`: Duration field.
  - `tfieldguid`: GUID field.
  - `tfieldoption`: Option field. In this case, the `OptionMember` property is automatically added.
  - `tfieldrecorid`: RecordID field.
  - `tfieldtext`: Text field. You will need just to put the length of the field.
  - `tfieldtime`: Time field.
  - `tkey`: Adds a new key to a table.

- **Fields and Action on Pages**:
  - `tfieldpage`: Adds a field to a page
  - `taction`: Adds an action to a page
- **Triggers**:
  - `ttrigger`: Creates a trigger definition
  - `tprocedure`: Creates a procedure definition

After installing the AL Language extension in Visual Studio Code, you can start a new AL project by going to **View | Command Palette** and selecting **AL:Go!**.

Visual Studio Code asks you for a folder that it can create the project in and then asks you to select the target platform (Dynamics 365 Business Central version). Select **4.0 Business Central 2019 release wave 2**:

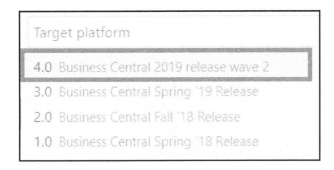

Now, Visual Studio Code will configure the project for you. It creates the `launch.json` file so that you can connect to your development environment and the `app.json` file with the extension's manifest file (as described in `Chapter 2`, *Mastering a Modern Development Environment*).

Now, you can start defining the objects that comprise your solution.

Table definition

With the AL extension, you don't have a graphical tool for designing tables (like we did previously in CSIDE); instead, you need to create a table using code.

A table definition can be created by using the `ttable` snippet:

```
table id MyTable
{
    DataClassification = ToBeClassified;

    fields
    {
        field(1;MyField; Integer)
        {
            DataClassification = ToBeClassified;
        }
    }

    keys
    {
        key(PK; MyField)
        {
            Clustered = true;
        }
    }
    var
        myInt: Integer;
    trigger OnInsert()
    begin
    end;

    trigger OnModify()
    begin
    end;
    trigger OnDelete()
    begin
    end;
    trigger OnRename()
    begin
    end;
}
```

To define a table, you need to specify an *ID* (which must be unique in your application) and a *name* (which must also be unique). Then, you can set the table's properties (use *Ctrl* + spacebar to discover all the available properties):

```
table 50100 MyTable
{
    DataClassification = CustomerContent;

        Caption                          Caption property ⓘ
        CaptionML
        DataCaptionFields
        DataPerCompany
        Description
        DrillDownPageId
        ExternalName
        ExternalSchema
        LinkedInTransaction
        LinkedObject
        LookupPageId
        ObsoleteReason
            Caption = 'Description';
            DataClassification = CustomerContent;
    }
```

A table object has the following main properties:

- `Caption`: The string that identifies the table in the user interface.
- `DataCaptionFields`: Sets the fields that appear to the left of the caption on pages that display the content of this table.
- `DataPerCompany`: Sets a value that indicates whether the table data applies to all the companies in the database or only the current company (when default = `true`, data is only available for the current company).
- `DrillDownPageID`: Sets the ID of the page to use as a drill-down.
- `LookupPageID`: Sets the ID of the page to use as a lookup.
- `LinkedObject`: Available for on-premise only; it specifies a link to a SQL Server object.
- `Permissions`: Sets whether an object has additional permissions that are required to perform some operations on one or more tables.
- `TableType`: Specifies the table type (Normal, CRM, ExternalSQL, Exchange, or MicrosoftGraph).
- `ExternalName`: This property appears when you specify CRM or ExternalSQL in the `TableType` property and specifies the name of the original table in the external database.

- `ExternalSchema`: This property appears when you specify CRM or ExternalSQL in the `TableType` property and specifies the name of the database schema in the external database.
- `ReplicateData`: Specifies whether the table must be replicated to the cloud service (the default value is true).
- `Extensible`: Sets whether the object can be extended or not.

A table object contains a set of fields. A table's field can be created by using the `tfield` snippet:

```
field(id; MyField; Blob)
{
    DataClassification = ToBeClassified;
    FieldPropertyName = FieldPropertyValue;
}
```

A field is defined by an *ID* (which must be unique within the declaring table and all its extensions), a *name* (which must also be unique within the declaring table and all its extensions), and a *type* (the data type of the field).

It's recommended to always set the `Caption` property (for tables and fields) and to set the `DataClassification` property (used for defining the data sensitivity for GDPR regulations) to a value other than `ToBeClassified`. A field can have its own specific properties that you can set as needed (optional properties, as shown in the following screenshot):

```
0 references      AccessByPermission     AccessByPermission property
table 50100       AutoFormatExpression
{                 AutoFormatType
    DataClas      AutoIncrement
                  BlankNumbers
                  BlankZero
    fields        CalcFormula
    {             Caption
        1 refe    CaptionClass
        fiel      CaptionML
        {         CharAllowed
                  ClosingDates

        }
}
```

A table also contains a set of *keys*. You can define keys using the `tkey` snippet:

```
key(MyKey; MyField)
{
}
```

A table's key is defined by a *name* and the *fields* that comprise the key (a comma-separated list of table fields). A key can have the `Clustered` property set to `true` if it's the primary key of the table. A clustered index is a special type of index that reorders the way the records in the table are physically stored, and so a table can have only one clustered index.

A table can also have triggers (`OnInsert`, `OnModify`, `OnDelete`, and `OnRename`), and inside a table, you can define your own methods.

Page object definition

A page object is the user interface for your users in Dynamics 365 Business Central. You can define a page object in AL using the `tpage` snippet:

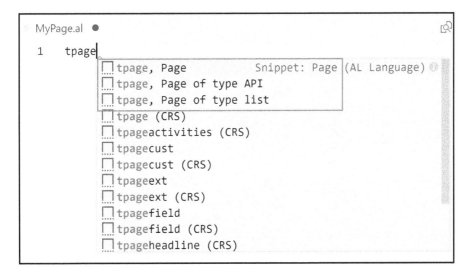

The first three options allow you to create the following page types:

- `Card` page
- `API` page
- `List` page

A `Card` page (the first option) is defined as follows:

```
page Id MyPage
{
    PageType = Card;
    ApplicationArea = All;
    UsageCategory = Administration;
    SourceTable = TableName;
    layout
    {
        area(Content)
        {
            group(GroupName)
            {
                field(Name; NameSource)
                {
                    ApplicationArea = All;
                }
            }
        }
    }
    actions
    {
        area(Processing)
        {
            action(ActionName)
            {
                ApplicationArea = All;
                trigger OnAction()
                begin
                end;
            }
        }
    }
    var
        myInt: Integer;
}
```

A `Card` page is identified by its *ID* and its *name* (both of which must be unique inside the application). A page also has its own properties. The main things to define are as follows:

- `PageType`: Identifies the type of the page.
- `SourceTable`: Sets the underlying table for this page.
- `SourceTableView`: Sets the key, sort order, and filter you want to use to determine the view of the source table presented to the user.

- `ApplicationArea`: Sets the visibility of the page inside the Business Central application. The standard values are All, Basic, Suite, and Advanced.
- `UsageCategory`: Sets the Departments column for the searched page in the web client.
- `Extensible`: Sets whether the object can be extended or not.

A page has a `layout` (which defines the page appearance in the UI) and an `actions` section (which defines the available menu items for adding code actions inside a page). Inside the layout, you have a content area, which contains a set of groups, and every group can contain one or more page fields. You can add a field inside a page group by using the `tpagefield` snippet:

```
field(MyField; FieldSource)
{
    ApplicationArea = All
    FieldPropertyName = FieldPropertyValue;
}
```

A field on a page is defined by a *name* (the field keyword inside the page) and a *field source* (the source expression of the page field, which corresponds to the physical fields defined in the underlying table).

A field can have its own properties and it must have an `ApplicationArea` set.

A `List` page (the third option) is defined as follows:

```
page Id PageName
{
    PageType = List;
    ApplicationArea = All;
    SourceTable = TableName;
    layout
    {
        area(Content)
        {
            repeater(Group)
            {
                field(Name; NameSource)
                {
                    ApplicationArea = All;
                }
            }
        }
    }
```

```
                area(Factboxes)
                {
                }
        }
        actions
        {
                area(Processing)
                {
                        action(ActionName)
                        {
                                ApplicationArea = All;
                                trigger OnAction();
                                begin
                                end;
                        }
                }
        }
}
```

A List page has the PageType property set to List and the layout section has a Content area and a FactBox area. The Content area has a repeater group, which contains all the fields you want to display on that list. After that, you have the actions section.

If your page contains a repeater control (for example, a List page), you can define actions that apply to the entire page or to the repeater control itself (a single record). For this, the action has a property called **Scope**, which can be defined as a *page* (the action is at the page level) or a repeater (the action is at the record level).

Table extension definition

As we mentioned previously, with Dynamics 365 Business Central, you cannot modify an existing table; instead, you need to create a table extension.

A table extension can be defined by using the ttableext snippet:

```
tableextension Id MyExtension extends MyTargetTable
{
        fields
        {
                // Add changes to table fields here
        }
        var
                myInt: Integer;
}
```

A `tableextension` object is defined by an *ID* and a *name* (which must be unique) and by the table that must be extended (or altered). Then, inside the fields group, you can add new fields or change existing field properties.

The following code is an example of an extension to the standard `Customer` table that adds some new fields and changes an existing field property:

```
tableextension 50100 CustomerExtSD extends Customer
{
    fields
    {
        field(50100; PacktEnabledSD; Boolean)
        {
            DataClassification = CustomerContent;
            Caption = 'Packt Subscription Enabled';
        }
        field(50101; PacktCodeSD; Code[20])
        {
            DataClassification = CustomerContent;
            Caption = 'Packt Subscription Code';
        }

        modify("Net Change")
        {
            BlankZero = true;
        }
    }
}
```

In a `tableextension` object, you can also add new keys to the extended table by adding a *keys* group, like you can in a table definition. For example, in our previous `tableextension` object, we've added two new fields, and we want also to create a secondary key on those fields in the `Customer` table. We can create a `key` group with the key name and the key fields:

```
tableextension 50100 CustomerExtSD extends Customer
{
    fields
    {
        field(50100; PacktEnabledSD; Boolean)
        {
            DataClassification = CustomerContent;
            Caption = 'Packt Subscription Enabled';
        }
        field(50101; PacktCodeSD; Code[20])
        {
            DataClassification = CustomerContent;
```

```
                    Caption = 'Packt Subscription Code';
            }
            modify("Net Change")
            {
                BlankZero = true;
            }
        }

    keys
    {
        key(PacktKey; PacktCodeSD,PacktEnabledSD)
        {
        }
    }
}
```

 You cannot create a key based on a new field or a standard field, and you cannot alter an existing key in an extended table.

Here, we have defined a secondary key called `PacktKey` in the `Customer` table, which consists of two custom fields (`PacktCodeSD` and `PacktEnabledSD`). Defining secondary keys is extremely useful for increasing the performance of some calculations, sorting records, and reports.

Page extension definition

Exactly like tables, with Dynamics 365 Business Central, you cannot directly modify an existing page; instead, you need to create a page extension (using the `pageextension` object in AL).

A `pageextension` object can be defined by using the `tpageext` snippet:

```
pageextension Id MyExtension extends MyTargetPage
{
    layout
    {
        // Add changes to page layout here
    }
    actions
    {
        // Add changes to page actions here
    }
    var
```

```
            myInt: Integer;
    }
```

A `pageextension` object is defined by an *ID* and a *name* (which must be unique) and by the page that must be extended. A `pageextension` object contains a `layout` block (where you can add changes to the standard page layout, such as adding new fields or new sections or changing standard fields) and an `actions` block (where you can add your new actions).

The following is an example of a `pageextension` object in which we have added a new field to the `Customer Card` page (the field is added at the end of the `General` tab) and we have modified the `Style` property of an existing field (the `Name` field):

```
pageextension 50100 CustomerCardExtSD extends "Customer Card"
{
    layout
    {
        addlast(General)
        {
            field(PacktEnabledSD; PacktEnabledSD)
            {
                ApplicationArea = All;
            }
        }

        modify(Name)
        {
            Style = Strong;
        }
    }
}
```

As you can see, we have added a field to the page and modified the `Style` property of the `Name` field so that it is in bold. Remember that not all the available field properties can be modified via a `pageextension` object.

Codeunit definition

A codeunit is a container of AL code, and this code can be triggered by directly executing the codeunit (with the `OnRun` trigger) or by calling the functions defined in the codeunit itself.

We can define a codeunit in AL by using the `tcodeunit` snippet:

```
codeunit Id MyCodeunit
{
    trigger OnRun()
    begin
    end;
    var
        myInt: Integer;
}
```

A codeunit is defined by an *ID* and a *name* (which must be unique inside your application). By default, the codeunit skeleton only contains the OnRun trigger definition, and inside this trigger, you can write the code that you want to execute when calling the Codeunit.RUN method.

A codeunit has its own properties that you can set:

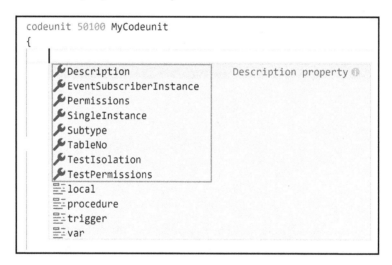

In a codeunit, you can define procedures (functions) that can be local to the codeunit or global (that is, publicly exposed to objects that instantiate the codeunit).

A procedure can be defined by using the `tprocedure` snippet:

```
local procedure MyProcedure()
    var
        myInt: Integer;
    begin
    end;
```

By default, this snippet creates a local procedure without parameters and without a return value. You can change the scope from local (the default value, meaning that it is visible only inside the object that declares the procedure) to global (so that it is also visible outside the object) by removing the `local` keyword.

As an example, this is a global procedure with parameters and a return value:

```
procedure CheckIfPacktCustomerIsEnabled(CustomerNo: Code[20]): Boolean
    var
     //Local variables here
    begin
      //Method code here
    end;
```

A codeunit can have more than one procedure (local or global) defined.

Event definitions

As we mentioned previously, events are fundamental building blocks when it comes to developing extensions for Dynamics 365 Business Central. When working with events, we have two main entities: the event *publisher* and the event *subscriber*.

An **event publisher** (an event that's raised by the application) can be defined in AL by using the **teventbus** (for a business event) or **teventint** (for an integration event) snippets:

A **business event** has the following schema:

```
[BusinessEvent(IncludeSender)]
    local procedure MyProcedure()
    begin

    end;
```

Here, `IncludeSender` is a Boolean value that specifies whether the global methods defined in the object that contain the event publisher method will be visible to the event subscriber methods that will subscribe to this event (this is `true` if the global methods must be visible and `false` (the default value) if not).

When the `IncludeSender` argument is set to `true`, the signature of the event subscriber methods that will subscribe to this published event will automatically include a `VAR` parameter (a reference value) for the published event object.

An **integration event** has the following schema:

```
[IntegrationEvent(IncludeSender,GlobalVarAccess)]
    local procedure MyProcedure()
    begin

    end;
```

Here, the `IncludeSender` Boolean parameter has the same meaning as we described previously.

`GlobalVarAccess` is a Boolean parameter that specifies whether the global variables defined in the object, which contains the event publisher method, are accessible to the event subscriber methods that subscribe to this published event (this is `true` if they must be exposed and `false` – which is the default value – if not).

When the `GlobalVarAccess` argument is set to `true`, all the event subscriber methods that subscribe to this event will be able to access the global variables in the object where the event publisher method is declared. You have to manually add the variable parameters to the event subscriber methods, and you need to use a name and a type that match the variable declaration in the event publisher object.

After an event has been published by an event publisher (your previously defined method), you need to raise that event in your code where needed (event subscribers will not react to the event until it's raised in your application code).

As an example, the following is a codeunit with a public method that raises a business event and an integration event:

```
codeunit 50100 MyCodeunit
{
    procedure CheckIfPacktCustomerIsEnabled(CustomerNo: Code[20]):
Boolean
    begin
        //Raising a business event
        MyBusinessEvent('XXX');
```

```
    //Other code here...

    //Raising an integration event
    MyIntegrationEvent('YYY');
end;

[BusinessEvent(true)]
local procedure MyBusinessEvent(ID: Code[20])
begin
end;

[IntegrationEvent(true,true)]
local procedure MyIntegrationEvent(ID: Code[20])
begin
end;

//Global variables
var
    myInt: Integer;
    Customer: record Customer;
}
```

An **event subscriber** (a function that handles a raised event in the application) can be declared using the `teventsub` snippet:

```
[EventSubscriber(ObjectType::ObjectType, ObjectID, 'OnSomeEvent',
'ElementName', SkipOnMissingLicense, SkipOnMissingPermission)]
local procedure MyProcedure()
begin
end;
```

From the preceding code, we can see the following:

- `ObjectType` is an enumeration that identifies the object type that publishes the event to subscribe to (the object that contains the event publisher method) or that raises the trigger event to subscribe to.
- `ObjectId` is an integer value that specifies the ID of the object that publishes the event to subscribe to (when declaring it, don't use the ID; use the `ObjectType::Name` syntax).
- `OnSomeEvent` is a text parameter that specifies the name of the method that publishes the event in the object identified by the `ObjectId` parameter.
- `ElementName` is a text parameter that's used for database trigger events. It specifies the table field that the trigger event pertains to.

- `SkipOnMissingLicense` is a Boolean parameter that specifies what happens to the event subscriber method when the Dynamics 365 Business Central license of the user account that runs the current session does not include the permissions on the object that contains the subscriber method (`true` if the method call must be ignored and `false` if an error must be thrown and the code's execution must be stopped).
- `SkipOnMissingPermission` is a Boolean parameter that specifies what happens to the subscriber method when the user account that runs the current session does not have permission on the object that contains the event subscriber method (`true` if the method call must be ignored and `false` (the default value) if an error must be thrown and the code execution must be stopped).

As an example, this is a codeunit with two event subscribers for the business and integration events we defined in the previous example:

```
codeunit 50101 MySubscriberCodeunit
{
    [EventSubscriber(ObjectType::Codeunit, Codeunit::MyCodeunit,
'MyBusinessEvent', '', false, false)]
    local procedure MyBusinessEventSubscriber(ID: Code[20])
    begin
    end;

    [EventSubscriber(ObjectType::Codeunit, Codeunit::MyCodeunit,
'MyIntegrationEvent', '', false, false)]
    local procedure MyIntegrationEventSubscriber(ID: Code[20])
    begin
    end;
}
```

When defining the event subscriber, if you press *Ctrl* + spacebar on the event parameters, you will see a list of the objects that the event can interact with (exposed by the publisher). In our example, the business event subscriber can see the event parameter and the sender object (because we've declared the event publisher with `IncludeSender` set to `true`), as follows:

```
[EventSubscriber(ObjectType::Codeunit, Codeunit::MyCodeunit,
0 references
local procedure MyBusinessEventSubscriber()
begin        [●] ID: Code[20]                    Event Parameter ⓘ
             [●] sender: Codeunit MyCodeunit
end;         ⩵ var
```

The integration event subscriber can see the event parameter, the sender object (because we've declared the event publisher with `IncludeSender` set to `true`), and the global variables of the sender object (because we've declared the event publisher with `GlobalVarAccess = true`):

```
[EventSubscriber(ObjectType::Codeunit, Codeunit::MyCodeunit, 'MyIntegrationEvent', '', false, false)]
0 references
local procedure MyIntegrationEventSubscriber()
begin                           [●]Customer: Record Customer        Global Variable
                                [●]ID: Code[20]
end;                            [●]myInt: Integer
                                [●]sender: Codeunit MyCodeunit
                                ≡ var
```

When using events, always remember the following:

- When the code that calls the event publisher method is run, all the event subscriber methods that subscribe to the event are run.
- If there are multiple subscribers, the subscriber methods are run one at a time in a random order (there's no way to specify the order in which the subscriber methods are called).
- If there are no subscribers to the published event, then the line of code that calls the event publisher method is ignored and not executed.

XMLport definition

XMLports are objects that are used for importing and exporting XML or text-based data between an external source and Dynamics 365 Business Central.

An XMLport can be defined in AL by using the `txmlport` snippet:

```
xmlport Id MyXmlport
{
    schema
    {
        textelement(NodeName1)
        {
            tableelement(NodeName2; SourceTableName)
            {
                fieldattribute(NodeName3; NodeName2.SourceFieldName)
                {
                }
            }
        }
```

```
            }
        }
        requestpage
        {
            layout
            {
                area(content)
                {
                    group(GroupName)
                    {
                        field(Name; SourceExpression)
                        {
                        }
                    }
                }
            }
            actions
            {
                area(processing)
                {
                    action(ActionName)
                    {
                    }
                }
            }
        }
        var
            myInt: Integer;
    }
```

As an example, this is a simple XMLport definition for importing some customer data (the No. and Name fields):

```
xmlport 50100 MyXmlportImportCustomer
{
    Direction = Import;
    schema
    {
        textelement(NodeName1)
        {
            tableelement(Customer; Customer)
            {
                fieldattribute(No; Customer."No.")
                {
                }
                fieldattribute(Name; Customer.Name)
                {
                }
```

```
                }
            }
        }
    }
```

The xmlport object has the Direction property set to Import (only used for importing data to Dynamics 365 Business Central) and reads the No and Name fields from an XML object called Customer.

Defining query objects

A query object allows you to define an object that can be used to retrieve data from a single table or from multiple tables by applying filters and joins between tables. The returned result is a single dataset.

You can create a query in AL by using the tquery snippet:

```
query Id MyQuery
{
    QueryType = Normal;
    elements
    {
        dataitem(DataItemName; SourceTableName)
        {
            column(ColumnName; SourceFieldName)
            {
            }
            filter(FilterName; SourceFieldName)
            {
            }
        }
    }
    var
        myInt: Integer;
    trigger OnBeforeOpen()
    begin
    end;
}
```

As you can see, a query object has an elements section, and inside that section, you define a dataitem and its column elements that must be retrieved (the table fields to be included in the resulting dataset).

You can also create links between dataitems to retrieve data from more than one table.

As an example, the following is a `query` object that's been defined in AL so that it retrieves a list of customers, along with their sales and profit data:

```
query 50100 "Customer Overview"
{
    Caption = 'Customer Overview';
    elements
    {
        dataitem(Customer; Customer)
        {
            column(Name; Name)
            {
            }
            column(No; "No.")
            {
            }
            column(Sales_LCY; "Sales (LCY)")
            {
            }
            column(Profit_LCY; "Profit (LCY)")
            {
            }
            column(Country_Region_Code; "Country/Region Code")
            {
            }
            column(City; City)
            {
            }
            column(Salesperson_Code; "Salesperson Code")
            {
            }

            dataitem(Salesperson_Purchaser; "Salesperson/Purchaser")
            {
                DataItemLink = Code = Customer."Salesperson Code";
                column(SalesPersonName; Name)
                {
                }
                dataitem(Country_Region; "Country/Region")
                {
                    DataItemLink = Code = Customer."Country/Region
Code";
                    column(CountryRegionName; Name)
                    {
                    }
                }
            }
        }
    }
```

```
        }
    }
```

The query loops through the `Customer` table and then (for every customer) retrieves data from the other tables specified in the `DataItemLink` property.

Query objects are extremely useful and powerful for retrieving records in your code. The first basic problem that you can solve with query objects is to avoid using nested loops when retrieving data from linked tables (joins). If you have `Table1` linked through a foreign key to `Table2`, instead of looping through `Table1` and, for every record of this table, going to `Table2` to retrieve the related data, you can use a query object and apply the pattern described in the following diagram:

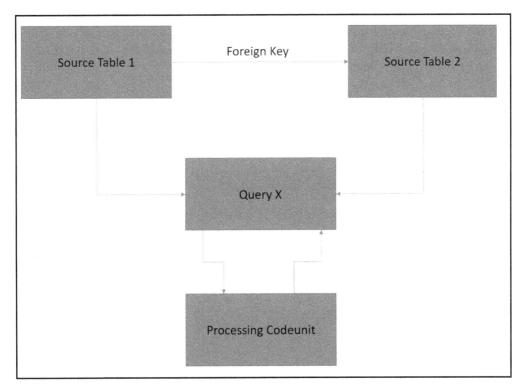

Here, you can define a query that returns the full filtered join of the two tables and then you can loop through the record set that's returned by the query object (this requires only one loop).

If (as an example) we want to use our previously defined Customer Overview query in our code, this is what we have to do in AL:

```
procedure UseCustomerOverviewQuery()
    var
        CustomerOverview: Query "Customer Overview";
    begin
        if not CustomerOverview.Open() then
            exit;
        while CustomerOverview.Read() do
        begin
            //Here we have all joined records to loop
        end;
    end;
```

Here, we execute the query object by calling the Open method, and then we loop through the returned dataset by using the Read method. Inside the loop, you have the complete record being returned by the query (the master table and the joined tables) and you can work on this data as needed.

Extending the options – enums

A field of the **option** type is used in Dynamics 365 Business Central to define a field that provides a fixed and predefined list of values.

When you define an option field, you define the admitted values for that field in the following way:

```
field(5; LicenseType; Option)
{
    OptionMembers = " ","Full","Limited";
    OptionCaption = ' ,Full,Limited';
    Caption = 'License Type';
    DataClassification = CustomerContent;
}
```

In the preceding code, we can see that the OptionMembers property contains the predefined value for the field. Here, the License Type field contains three values (blank, Full, Limited), and blank (the first value) is the default one.

But what if you want to extend these options, for example, by adding a new license type called *Teams*? This isn't possible! Option fields cannot be extended.

To create an extendable option field, AL introduced the enum object. An *enum* is a type that consists of a set of named constants, and it can be extended from other extensions if you set the Extensible property to true, as shown here:

```
enum 50100 LicenseType
{
  Extensible = true;
  value(0; None) { }
  value(1; Full) { }
  value(2; Limited) { }
}
```

You can define a field so that it has the enum type in the following way:

```
field(50100; LicenseType; enum LicenseType)
{
    Caption = 'License Type';
    DataClassification = CustomerContent;
}
```

This allows you to define a field that has the same behavior as an option: when a user clicks on that field, Dynamics 365 Business Central presents a list of possible values to choose from.

To extend the enum field from another extension and add a new possible value called Team, you need to create an enumextension object, as follows:

```
enumextension 50110 LicenseTypeEnumExt extends LicenseType
{
  value(50110; Team)
  {
    Caption = 'Team License';
  }
}
```

After that, your License Type field will have one more option value to choose from.

You can also use an enum object directly from AL code (as a variable):

```
var
    LicenseType: enum LicenseType;
begin
    case LicenseType of
        LicenseType::Full:
                //Write your code here...
```

You can also extend the `TableRelation` property of an `enum` value. For example, imagine you have the following table:

```
table 50120 LicenseDetail
{
  fields
  {
    field(1; Id; Integer) { }
    field(2; LicenseType; enum LicenseType) { }
    field(3; LicenseDetail; Code[20])
    {
      TableRelation =
      if (LicenseType = const (Full)) FullLicenseTable
      else if (LicenseType = const (Limited)) LimitedLicenseTable;
    }
  }
}
```

In this table, we have a field called `LicenseType` (which is an `enum`) and a field called `LicenseDetail`, which has a `tablerelation` property (to the `FullLicenseTable` and `LimitedLIcenseTable` tables) based on the value of the `enum` field.

Another app could extend both the `enum` field and the table relation so that it can handle the new extended enum. Here's an example:

```
enumextension 50110 LicenseTypeEnumExt extends LicenseType
{
  value(50110; Team)
  {
    Caption = 'Team License';
  }
}

tableextension 50110 LicenseDetailExt extends LicenseDetail
{
  fields
  {
    modify(LicenseDetail)
    {
      TableRelation = if (LicenseType = const (Team))
TeamLicenseTable;
    }
  }
}
```

Here, the new app creates the `LicenseType` enum extension (as we described previously) and creates a new `tableextension` object, where it modifies the `TableRelation` property of the `LicenseDetail` field by adding a new relationship to a `TeamLicenseTable` if the enum has the value of `Team`.

 The combined `TableRelation` is always evaluated from the top down, so the first unconditional relationship will prevail. This means that you cannot change an existing `TableRelation` from table A to table B if the original field has a relationship with table A.

By using `enums`, you can extend all your option's values. We recommend using this new approach in your extensions if you want extensibility.

In this section, you've had a complete overview of the available objects in the AL Language extension. In the next section, we'll learn about some of the best practices when it comes to creating and handling an AL project.

Creating a profile object

A `profile` object allows you to define the user experience (main page) of a particular user profile. You can create a `profile` object with the AL Language extension by using the `tprofile` snippet.

A profile object is defined as in the following example:

```
profile "SALES MANAGER"
{
  Caption = 'Sales Manager';
  ProfileDescription = 'Functionality for sales managers';
  RoleCenter = 9005;
  Enabled = false;
}
```

Here, we have defined a profile called **Sales Manager**, which uses the `RoleCenter` page with `ID = 9005` (standard Sales Manager role center object in Dynamics 365 Business Central).

To deploy a `profile` object from your extension, I recommend creating a `Profile` folder in your AL project and, inside that folder, placing all the `.al` files that define your profiles.

Understanding AL project structure best practices

As we mentioned previously, an AL project is file-based. You have all your `.al` files inside a project folder. The main problem that you encounter when you start working with a complex project is how to structure the project. How do we organize the objects and the `.al` files?

There's no written rule for this topic. What we wholeheartedly suggest is to avoid having all the objects (`.al` files) at the project root level, as shown in the following screenshot:

Here, none of the objects are organized, and if you have a large number of objects, your object list will grow a lot, causing difficulties with handling and retrieving files.

The most sought-after way of structuring your project could be to organize your files by object type, as shown in the following screenshot:

Here, all the extension's code is inside the SRC folder. Then, all the objects are organized per type, according to the objects that we have defined (there's a subfolder for every object type that we have in our solution). It's easier to find an object with this organization (just go to the object type folder), but this project structure has a drawback: it's not easy to recognize the objects that we need in order to implement a particular business functionality in our extension project.

Our suggestion is to try to organize your project tree first by functionality and then by object type, as shown in the following screenshot:

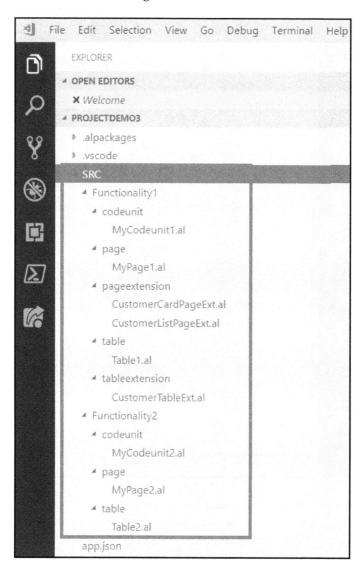

Here, in the SRC folder, there are two subfolders: `Functionality1` and `Functionality2`. In these folders, objects are organized by type. This is our recommended way of working, and this structure helps us find objects by functionality.

In the next section, we'll learn how to name objects in AL and how to use object ranges.

Naming guidelines and AL object ranges

When creating extensions for Dynamics 365 Business Central, you need to assign a numerical ID to your objects. The rules for assigning object IDs are as follows:

Range	Purpose
0 – 49,999	Business Central base application. It cannot be used by partners.
5,0000 – 99,999	Per-tenant extensions (resellers who want to customize the delivered solution to the individual needs of a customer).
80,000 – 99,999	Extended objects that you have to modify the permissions of in your development license.
100,000 – 999,999	Reserved for localizing Dynamics 365 Business Central for a specific country or region. It cannot be used by partners.
1,000,000 – 69,999,999	**Registered Solution Program** (**RSP**) range.
70,000,000 – 74,999,999	Business Central SaaS apps (AppSource).

Regarding file naming, each `.al` filename must start with the corresponding object type prefix and object ID and must be written only with characters [A-Za-z0-9]. The file naming notation (which is mandatory for `AppSource`) should be as follows:

- Full objects: `<ObjectNameExcludingPrefix>.<FullTypeName>.al`
- Extension objects:
  `<ObjectNameExcludingPrefix>.<FullTypeName>Ext.al`

For each object type, you can use the following abbreviation (prefixes):

Object Type	Abbreviation (prefix)
Page	Page
Page Extension	PageExt
Page Customization	PageCust
Codeunit	Codeunit
Table	Table
Table Extension	TableExt
XML Port	Xmlport
Report	Report
Query	Query
Enum	Enum
Enum Extension	EnumExt

As an example, here are some AL objects and their corresponding filenames:

- Table 50100 *Book* should be called `Book.Table.al`
- Page 50100 *Book Card* should be called `BookCard.Page.al`
- Codeunit 50110 *Book Management* should be called `BookManagement.Codeunit.al`
- Pageextension 50101 `MyCustomerCardExt`, which extends `Customer Card`, should be called `CustomerCard.PageExt.al`

You should also use a prefix/suffix to target your objects (reserved for you by Microsoft, as we'll explain later). This allows you to have objects that are named in a unique way between extensions, which avoids naming conflicts.

The rules for using the prefix/suffix are as follows:

- The prefix/suffix must be at least three characters long.
- The object/field name must start or end with the prefix/suffix.
- When you modify a core Dynamics 365 object using a table extension or a page extension, the prefix/suffix must be defined at the control/field/action/group level.
- Use a caption to handle the label that you want in the UI.

For example, if you have reserved the `PACKT` prefix and you want to create a field called `CustomerCategory`, the valid field names that you can use are as follows:

- `PACKTCustomerCategory`
- `CustomerCategoryPACKT`
- `CustomerCategory_PACKT`
- `CustomerCategory PACKT`

If you want to create the *Customer Category* table, the valid names for the table object are as follows:

- table 70000000 `PACKT Customer Category`
- table 70000000 `Customer Category PACKT`
- table 70000000 `Customer Category_PACKT`

Using the reserved name as a prefix or a suffix is absolutely your choice. We prefer to use it as a suffix because it's more natural to find the field with Visual Studio IntelliSense (if the field that appears to you in the UI is Customer Category, typing these words will present the real field name, along with its suffix).

These guidelines are mandatory for AppSource, but are not mandatory for your per-tenant extensions. Our suggestion is to always follow these guidelines.

To register a prefix/suffix for your objects, you need to send an email to `d365val@microsoft.com` specifying the name you want to reserve for your app. Remember that the prefix/suffix should be app-based and not company-based.

Working on AL coding guidelines

When creating your AL project (and your `.al` files), remember to always follow these main guidelines.

Inside a `.al` code file, the structure for all your objects must follow this sequence:

- Properties
- Object-specific constructs:
  - Table fields
  - Page layout
  - Actions

- Global variables:
    - Labels (old text constants)
    - Global variables
- Methods

Remember to always reference the AL objects by their object name and not by their ID. So, for example, this is how you reference a `Record` variable or a `Page` variable:

```
Vendor: Record Vendor;
Page.RunModal(Page::"Customer Card", ...);
```

In an event subscriber object, this is how you should reference the publisher object:

```
[EventSubscriber(ObjectType::Codeunit, Codeunit::MyCodeunit,
'MyIntegrationEvent', '', false, false)]
local procedure MyIntegrationEventSubscriber()
begin
end;
```

So, let's sum this up:

- **Format your AL code**: Take care of indentation and spacing (it keeps the code more readable). You can use *Alt* + *Shift* + *F* to auto-format your code.
- **Keep your .al files clean**: When using snippets, they automatically create an object skeleton with methods, properties, variables, triggers, or sections that you might not be using. Please remove all the code that isn't being used. A typical example is triggers definitions on tables (which you can remove if you're not handling them) or global variables inside objects (if you don't remove them, your app will be full of myInt: integer variables).
- **Method declarations**: Be as local as possible. Only use global methods if you need to expose them to other objects.
- **Use events to trigger business logic, but do not code in these triggers**: Putting a lot of code inside triggered events is just like putting a lot of code into field validation triggers. Identify your methods instead and call them from the triggered events.

For complex code, you can start using the *Generic Method* pattern:

- Declare each method on its class (table).
- Each method is a codeunit on its own (encapsulation).
- Invoke a method only from its class (table/codeunit).
- Each method's codeunit only has one global function.

- Local functions include the following categories (in this order):
  1. Main (one function; a method header in the form of a readable flowchart)
  2. Main business process (multiple functions)
  3. UI wrapper (two functions)
  4. Business extension (one or more functions to provide extensibility)
  5. Event wrapper (two functions)

This is an example of some AL code that's been organized according to this pattern:

```
codeunit 50113 CreatePalletMeth{
    procedure CreatePallet (PurchLine: Record "Purchase Line"; HideDialog: Boolean);
    begin
        if not ConfirmCreatePallet(PurchLine, HideDialog) then exit;

        OnBeforeCreatePallet(PurchLine, Handled);
        DoCreatePallet(PurchLine, Handled);
        OnAfterCreatePallet(PurchLine);

        AckCreatePallet(PurchLine, HideDialog)
    end;

    local procedure DoCreatePallet(PurchLine: Record "Purchase Line"; var Handled: Boolean);

    local procedure ErrorIfNotItemLine(PurchLine: Record "Purchase Line");
    local procedure ErrorIfEmptyNumber(PurchLine: Record "Purchase Line");
    local procedure DoInsertPallet(PurchLine: Record "Purchase Line");

    local procedure ConfirmCreatePallet(PurchLine: Record "Purchase Line"; HideDialog: Boolean) : Boolean;
    local procedure AckCreatePallet(PurchLine: Record "Purchase Line"; HideDialog: Boolean);

    [BusinessEvent(false)]
    local procedure OnBeforeCreatePallet(PurchLine: Record "Purchase Line"; var Handled: Boolean);SS
    [BusinessEvent(false)]
    local procedure OnAfterCreatePallet(PurchLine: Record "Purchase Line");

    [IntegrationEvent(false,false)]
    local procedure OnBeforeInsertPalletRecord(PurchLine: record "Purchase Line";var Pallet: record Pallet)
}
```

	Label
	Main
	Main Business Process
	UI Wrapper
	Event Wrapper
	Business Extension

 You can find more information regarding other coding rules to follow at https://docs.microsoft.com/en-us/dynamics365/business-central/dev-itpro/compliance/apptest-bestpracticesforalcode.

Respecting coding rules and guidelines is extremely important for increasing code readability, and many of these rules are mandatory for AppSource.

Summary

In this chapter, we looked at the fundamentals of extension development with the AL Language, along with an overview of the main objects for creating applications (tables, pages, codeunits, and so on) and how to create them in Visual Studio Code. Then, we had an overview of the best practices for handling an AL project (project organization, object IDs, naming conventions) and guidelines for writing better code by focusing on the extensibility aspect of our extensions.

We learned how to create objects, how to create an AL project, how to handle its structure, and how to stick to naming conventions with objects.

In the next chapter, we'll implement a real-word extension for Dynamics 365 Business Central by applying all these rules and best practices.

5
Developing a Customized Solution for Dynamics 365 Business Central

In the previous chapter, we saw the fundamentals of extension development for Dynamics 365 Business Central and we analyzed all of the building blocks for creating extensions, such as events and basic objects definitions, and how to extend standard objects.

In this chapter, we'll put all of these concepts together and create a real-world extension for Dynamics 365 Business Central. These extensions will be created by using **AppSource** guidelines and best code practices.

This chapter will cover the following topics:

- Translating a business case into a real-world extension
- Understanding dependent extension

Translating a business case into a real-world extension

In this section, let's imagine having a Dynamics 365 Business Central customer with various business requirements. We want to create an extension to satisfy this customer's needs.

Our customer is a big commercial company that has adopted Dynamics 365 Business Central as the company's ERP and has various business requirements that require customization of the standard features to be satisfied.

The business requirements are as follows:

- Sales: These requirements include the following:
    - The company wants to classify customers based on custom categories that they can define as needed and that can change in the future. Each `Customer Category` must have its own details that can be used for some business processes.
    - The sales office must be able to create a default `Customer Category` and assign this default value to a customer automatically.
    - The sales office needs the possibility to create gift campaigns for customer categories. A gift campaign is related to a limited period of time and a limited set of items.
    - A gift campaign can be set to inactive for a certain period of time.
    - When a gift campaign is active, the sales order manager must be able to automatically assign free gifts on a customer's sales order (they need a button on a sales order document that analyzes the order content, checks whether a campaign is active, and creates the free gift lines accordingly).
    - When a sales operator inserts a sales order line, they should be alerted if the customer is ordering an item quantity near to an active campaign promotion.
    - When a sales order is posted, the generated item ledger entry must store the `Customer Category` value (at the time of this order) for reporting purposes.
- Vendor quality: These requirements include the following:
    - The company has a quality process in place (CSQ, international institute for the certification of business quality) and they need to classify vendors according to their CSQ requirements:
        - Score related to item quality (from 1 to 10)
        - Score related to delivery on time (from 1 to 10)
        - Score related to item packaging (from 1 to 10)
        - Score related to pricing (from 1 to 10)

- The `Vendor Quality Card` must also display some financial data:
    - Invoiced for current year *N*
    - Invoiced for the year *N-1*
    - Invoiced for the year *N-2*
    - Amount due for this vendor
    - Amount to pay (not already due) for this vendor
- The assigned scores determine a vendor rating (a numeric value) based on an algorithm.
- The purchase office cannot release a purchase order if the vendor does not meet standard company requirements (the vendor rating).
- The application's behavior could be extended in the future.

These customizations will be developed as a single extension by using the per-tenant range (50.000 – 99.999). We will use AppSource rules and we'll use the **PKT** tag (registered with Microsoft as our AppSource prefix/suffix) to target all of our objects. The project's `.al` files will be named according to the AppSource naming conventions.

We start our development tasks by opening Visual Studio Code and creating a new extension project (**View | Command Palette | AL:GO!**), selecting the Wave 2 release as the target.

We set the extension's manifest file (`app.json`) as follows:

```json
{
  "id": "dd03d28e-4dfe-48d9-9520-c875595362b6",
  "name": "PacktDemoExtension",
  "publisher": "SD",
  "brief": "Customer Category, Gift Campaigns and Vendor Quality
Management",
  "description": "Customer Category, Gift Campaigns and Vendor Quality
Management",
  "version": "1.0.0.0",
  "privacyStatement": "",
  "EULA": "",
  "help": "",
  "url": "http://www.demiliani.com",
  "logo": "./Logo/ExtLogo.png",
  "dependencies": [
    {
```

```
      "appId": "63ca2fa4-4f03-4f2b-a480-172fef340d3f",
      "publisher": "Microsoft",
      "name": "System Application",
      "version": "1.0.0.0"
    },
    {
      "appId": "437dbf0e-84ff-417a-965d-ed2bb9650972",
      "publisher": "Microsoft",
      "name": "Base Application",
      "version": "15.0.0.0"
    }
  ],
  "screenshots": [],
  "platform": "15.0.0.0",
  "features": [
    "TranslationFile"
  ],
  "idRanges": [
    {
      "from": 50100,
      "to": 50149
    }
  ],
  "contextSensitiveHelpUrl": "https://PacktDemoExtension.com/help/",
  "runtime": "4.0"
}
```

Here, we set the extension details, such as the name, publisher, version, description, the path of the logo image, the admitted object range IDs (from 50100 to 50149), and the supported runtime version.

We also set the following option:

```
"features": [
    "TranslationFile"
  ]
```

The `TranslationFile` feature means that we want to have an XLIFF translation file that handles the multilanguage capabilities of this extension.

We want to organize our project structure with subfolders for functionalities and then for object types. Our base project structure will be as follows:

Here, we have an `Src` folder, and inside that, we have three main folders for functionalities:

- `CustomerCategory`: This contains the implementation of the `Customer Category` requirements.
- `Gifts`: This contains the implementation of the gift campaign requirements.
- `VendorQuality`: This contains the implementation of the vendor quality requirements.

Inside each of these folders, we have subfolders organized into object types.

Let's start working on each of these three modules.

Customer Category implementations

To handle the customer category management requirements, we need to do the following:

1. Define the Customer Category table.
2. Create the pages (user interface) that will handle the Customer Category entity (the List and Card pages).
3. Add a new Customer Category field to the standard Customer table.
4. Add the new field to the standard Customer Card page and add some actions to the Customer pages to handle some tasks.
5. Create the business logic to handle the requirements.

In the next sections, we'll see the definitions and implementations of the various objects in detail.

Tables definition

By using the ttable snippet, we define the Customer Category table as follows:

```
table 50100 "Customer Category_PKT"
{
    DrillDownPageId = "Customer Category List_PKT";
    LookupPageId = "Customer Category List_PKT";
    Caption = 'Customer Category';

    fields
    {
        field(1; Code; Code[20])
        {
            DataClassification = CustomerContent;
            Caption = 'No.';
        }
        field(2; Description; Text[50])
        {
            DataClassification = CustomerContent;
            Caption = 'Description';
        }
        field(3; Default; Boolean)
        {
            DataClassification = CustomerContent;
            Caption = 'Default';
        }
        field(4; EnableNewsletter; Enum NewsletterType)
```

```
            {
                Caption = 'Enable Newsletter';
                DataClassification = CustomerContent;
            }
            field(5; FreeGiftsAvailable; Boolean)
            {
                DataClassification = CustomerContent;
                Caption = 'Free Gifts Available';
            }
            field(6; Blocked; Boolean)
            {
                DataClassification = CustomerContent;
                Caption = 'Blocked';
            }
            field(10; TotalCustomersForCategory; Integer)
            {
                FieldClass = FlowField;
                CalcFormula = count (Customer where ("Customer Category
Code_PKT" = field (Code)));
                Caption = 'No. of associated customers';
            }
        }
    keys
    {
        key(PK; Code)
        {
            Clustered = true;
        }
        key(K2; Description)
        {
            Unique = true;
        }
    }

procedure GetSalesAmount(): Decimal
var
    CustomerCategoryMgt: Codeunit "Customer Category Mgt_PKT";
    begin
        exit(CustomerCategoryMgt.GetSalesAmount(Rec.Code));
    end;
}
```

The name of the object has the registered _PKT suffix (to be unique across the application).

In this table definition, we have defined the following fields:

- `Code`: This is the code of the category (the `key` field).
- `Description`: This is the description of the category.
- `Default`: This is a `Boolean` field used to set the default category.
- `FreeGiftsAvailable`: This is a `Boolean` field used to set whether the category can be used with gift campaigns.
- `Blocked`: This is a `Boolean` field used to set the category as blocked (cannot be used).
- `EnableNewsletter`: This is an option field used to select the newsletter type to send for this category (commercial purposes). This field is of the `enum` type. As described in the previous chapter, the `enum` type allows us to have an extendable option field.
- `TotalCustomersForCategory`: This is a calculated field (`flowfield`) used to automatically calculate the number of customers associated with the selected category.

This table's definition has a keys section, where we have defined a primary key (the `No` field) and a secondary key with the `Description` field. This secondary key is defined with the `Unique` property set to `true`, and this ensures that you cannot have records in this table with the same value as this field:

```
key(K2; Description)
{
    Unique = true;
}
```

The `NewsletterType` enum is defined as follows:

```
enum 50100 NewsletterType
{
  Extensible = true;
  value(0; None)
  {
      Caption = 'None';
  }
  value(1; Full)
  {
      Caption = 'Full';
  }
```

```
value(2; Limited)
{
    Caption = 'Limited';
}
}
```

As a generic programming rule, a table acts like a class and, in the table definition, we want to expose the methods related to that class. This is why we have defined a method (procedure) here called `GetSalesAmount` (which is used to return the total sales amount for the selected category).

The method's implementation will be on an external codeunit (which will contain our business logic).

We've also defined a setup table for this extension (the `Packt Extension Setup` table, which we'll use also in the next sections) to handle all of the variable parameters needed for the company's business configuration.

This setup table is defined as follows:

```
table 50103 "Packt Extension Setup"
{
 DataClassification = CustomerContent;
 Caption = 'Packt Extension Setup';

 fields
 {
     field(1; "Primary Key"; Code[10])
     {
         DataClassification = CustomerContent;
     }
     field(2; "Minimum Accepted Vendor Rate"; Decimal)
     {
         Caption = 'Minimum Accepted Vendor Rate for Purchases';
         DataClassification = CustomerContent;
     }
     field(3; "Gift Tolerance Qty"; Decimal)
     {
         Caption = 'Gift Tolerance Quantity for Sales';
         DataClassification = CustomerContent;
     }
 }
 keys
 {
     key(PK; "Primary Key")
     {
         Clustered = true;
```

```
        }
    }
}
```

Having a dedicated setup table for an extension is a best practice because it permits you to consolidate the settings in a single place. If possible, please avoid adding setup settings to different standard Dynamics 365 Business Central setup tables.

Pages definition

To handle the Customer Category records (insert, modify, delete, and select), we need to have a list page and a card page.

By using the tpage snippet, we have defined a card page (PageType = Card) and a list page (PageType = List).

The list page (Customer Category List_PKT) has an action for creating a default Customer Category record (it calls a method defined in an external codeunit because we don't want business logic on pages).

The code for the list page definition is as follows:

```
page 50100 "Customer Category List_PKT"
{
 PageType = List;
 SourceTable = "Customer Category_PKT";
 UsageCategory = Lists;
 ApplicationArea = All;
 CardPageId = CustomerCategoryCard_PKT;
 Caption = 'Customer Category List';
 AdditionalSearchTerms = 'ranking, categorization';

 layout
 {
     area(content)
     {
         repeater(Group)
         {
             field(Code; Code)
             {
                 ApplicationArea = All;
             }
             field(Description; Description)
             {
                 ApplicationArea = All;
             }
```

```
            field(Default; Default)
            {
                ApplicationArea = All;
            }
            field(TotalCustomersForCategory;
TotalCustomersForCategory)
            {
                ApplicationArea = All;
                ToolTip = 'Total Customers for Category';
            }
        }
    }
}
actions
{
    area(processing)
    {
        action("Create Default Category")
        {
            Image = CreateForm;
            Promoted = true;
            PromotedCategory = Process;
            PromotedIsBig = true;
            ApplicationArea = All;
            ToolTip = 'Create default category';
            Caption = 'Create default category';

            trigger OnAction();
            var
                CustManagement: Codeunit "Customer Category Mgt_PKT";
            begin
                CustManagement.CreateDefaultCategory();
            end;
        }
    }
}
}
```

As a best practice, to improve the search experience and help users to easily find the correct page by using the search feature of Dynamics 365 Business Central, we have also defined the AdditionalSearchTerms property. These terms will be used in addition to the Caption page property to find the page via the search engine.

The **CUSTOMER CATEGORY LIST** page appears as follows:

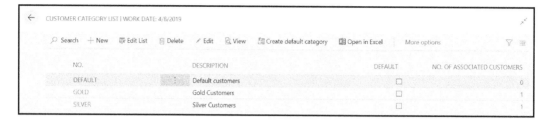

The card page (CustomerCategoryCard_PKT) has different groups for displaying data on separate FastTabs. In the OnAfterGetRecord trigger, we calculate the total sales amount for the category, we assign that value to a global decimal field (called TotalSalesAmount), and we display this variable as a page field. The code is as follows:

```
page 50101 CustomerCategoryCard_PKT
{
 PageType = Card;
 ApplicationArea = All;
 UsageCategory = Documents;
 SourceTable = "Customer Category_PKT";
 Caption = 'Customer Category Card';

 layout
 {
     area(Content)
     {
         group(General)
         {
             Caption = 'General';
             field(Code; Code)
             {
                 ApplicationArea = All;
             }
             field(Description; Description)
             {
                 ApplicationArea = All;
             }
             field(Default; Default)
             {
                 ApplicationArea = All;
             }
             field(EnableNewsletter; EnableNewsletter)
             {
                 ApplicationArea = All;
```

```
            }
            field(FreeGiftsAvailable; FreeGiftsAvailable)
            {
                ApplicationArea = All;
            }
        }
        group(Administration)
        {
            Caption = 'Administration';
            field(Blocked; Blocked)
            {
                ApplicationArea = All;
            }
        }
        group(Statistics)
        {
            Caption = 'Statistics';
            field(TotalCustomersForCategory;
TotalCustomersForCategory)
            {
                ApplicationArea = All;
                Editable = false;
            }
            field(TotalSalesAmount; TotalSalesAmount)
            {
                ApplicationArea = All;
                Caption = 'Total Sales Order Amount';
                Editable = false;
                Style = Strong;
            }
        }
    }
}
var
    TotalSalesAmount: Decimal;
trigger OnAfterGetRecord()
begin
    TotalSalesAmount := Rec.GetSalesAmount();
end;
}
```

The ...**CUSTOMER CATEGORY CARD** page looks like this:

We've also created a page for the extension setup (called `Packt Extension Setup`), defined as follows:

```
table 50103 "Packt Extension Setup"
{
 DataClassification = CustomerContent;
 Caption = 'Packt Extension Setup';

 fields
 {
     field(1; "Primary Key"; Code[10])
     {
         DataClassification = CustomerContent;
     }
     field(2; "Minimum Accepted Vendor Rate"; Decimal)
     {
         Caption = 'Minimum Accepted Vendor Rate for Purchases';
         DataClassification = CustomerContent;
     }
     field(3; "Gift Tolerance Qty"; Decimal)
     {
```

```
            Caption = 'Gift Tolerance Quantity for Sales';
            DataClassification = CustomerContent;
        }
    }

    keys
    {
        key(PK; "Primary Key")
        {
            Clustered = true;
        }
    }
}
```

This page looks like this:

This will permit the users to handle the settings for our extension.

The tableextension definition

We need to create a new field in the Customer table to handle the Customer Category assignment and, in order to do that, we need to create a tableextension object. This can be done in AL by using the ttableext snippet.

The tableextension object for the Customer table is defined as follows:

```
tableextension 50100 "CustomerTableExtensions_PKT" extends Customer
//18
{
 fields
 {
     field(50100; "Customer Category Code_PKT"; Code[20])
     {
         TableRelation = "Customer Category_PKT".No;
         Caption = 'Customer Category Code';
```

```
        DataClassification = CustomerContent;

        trigger OnValidate()
        var
            CustomerCategory: Record "Customer Category_PKT";
            ErrBlocked: Label 'This category is Blocked.';
        begin
            CustomerCategory.Get("Customer Category Code_PKT");
            if CustomerCategory.Blocked then
                Error(ErrBlocked);
        end;
    }
}

keys
{
    key(CustomerCategory; "Customer Category Code_PKT")
    {
    }
}
}
```

Here, we've also handled the `OnValidate` trigger for this field to avoid the insertion of a blocked category.

We've also created a new secondary key on the `Customer` table based on this new field:

```
keys
{
    key(CustomerCategory; "Customer Category_PKT")
    {
    }
}
```

One of the requirements for this is to also add the `Customer Category Code` field to the `Item Ledger Entry` table (this must be written during posting for reporting purposes), so we have also defined the following `tableextension` object:

```
tableextension 50101 "ItemLedgerEntryExtension_PKT" extends "Item Ledger Entry"
{
    fields
    {
        field(50100; "Customer Category Code_PKT"; Code[20])
        {
            TableRelation = "Customer Category_PKT".No;
```

```
                Caption = 'Customer Category';
                DataClassification = CustomerContent;
            }
        }

    keys
    {
        key(FK; "Customer Category Code_PKT")
        {
        }
    }
}
```

This new custom field will be used for statistical purposes.

The pageextension definition

This newly created Customer Category field must be visible on the Customer Card and Customer List pages.

To do that, we have defined two pageextension objects (by using the tpageext snippet). The following is the definition of the pageextension object for the Customer Card page:

```
pageextension 50102 "CustomerCardExtension_PKT" extends "Customer
Card"
{
    layout
    {
        addlast(General)
        {
            field("Customer Category PKT"; "Customer Category
Code_PKT")
            {
                ToolTip = 'Customer Category';
                ApplicationArea = All;
            }
        }
    }

    actions
    {
        addlast("Functions")
        {
            action("Assign default category")
            {
```

```
                    Image = ChangeCustomer;
                    Promoted = true;
                    PromotedCategory = Process;
                    PromotedIsBig = true;
                    ApplicationArea = All;
                    Caption = 'Assign Default Category';
                    ToolTip = 'Assigns Default Category to the current
Customer';
                    trigger OnAction();
                    var
                        CustomerCategoryMgt: Codeunit "Customer Category
Mgt_PKT";
                    begin
CustomerCategoryMgt.AssignDefaultCategory(Rec."No.");
                    end;
                }
            }
        }
    }
}
```

This is the `pageextension` **object definition for the** `Customer List` **page:**

```
pageextension 50103 CustomerListExtension_PKT extends "Customer List"
{
    actions
    {
        addlast(Processing)
        {
            action("Assign Default Category")
            {
                Image = ChangeCustomer;
                Promoted = true;
                PromotedCategory = Process;
                PromotedIsBig = true;
                ApplicationArea = All;
                Caption = 'Assign Default Category to all Customers';
                ToolTip = 'Assigns the Default Category to all
Customers';
                trigger OnAction();
                var
                    CustomerCategoryMgt: Codeunit "Customer Category
Mgt_PKT";
                begin
                    CustomerCategoryMgt.AssignDefaultCategory();
                end;
            }
        }
    }
```

```
views
{
    addlast
    {
        view(CustomersWithoutCategory)
        {
            Caption = 'Customers without Category assigned';
            Filters = where ("Customer Category Code_PKT" =
filter (''));
        }
    }
}
}
```

Here, on the Customer List page, we've added an action to assign the category set as default to all customers. On Customer Card, the same action works on the currently selected record.

You can see here that these two functions call a method on an external codeunit called AssignDefaultCategory. This method has two implementations (it is overloaded), which we'll look at later in this chapter.

The standard Customer List page now looks like this:

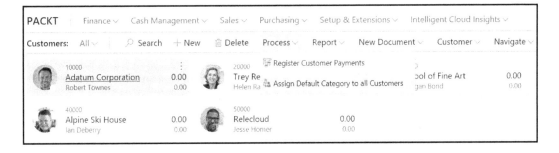

`Customer Card` **looks like this:**

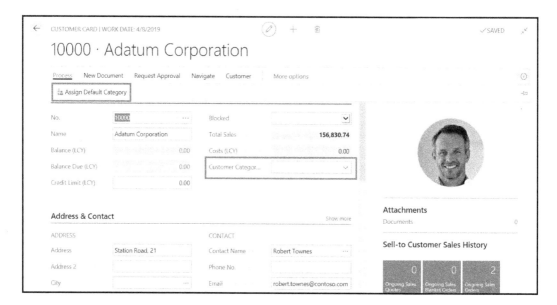

Here, we have the newly added `Customer Category` field and the new action for assigning `Customer Category`.

Codeunit definition

To handle the `Customer Category` business requirements that our customer has, all of the required business logic is defined in a dedicated codeunit called `Customer Category Mgt_PKT`.

The codeunit is defined as follows:

```
codeunit 50100 "Customer Category Mgt_PKT"
{
 procedure CreateDefaultCategory()
 var
     CustomerCategory: Record "Customer Category_PKT";
 begin
     CustomerCategory.Code := 'DEFAULT';
     CustomerCategory.Description := 'Default Customer Category';
     CustomerCategory.Default := true;
     if CustomerCategory.Insert then;
 end;
```

```
procedure AssignDefaultCategory(CustomerCode: Code[20])
var
    Customer: Record Customer;
    CustomerCategory: Record "Customer Category_PKT";
begin
    //Set default category for a Customer
    Customer.Get(CustomerCode);
    CustomerCategory.SetRange(Default, true);
    if CustomerCategory.FindFirst() then begin
        Customer."Customer Category Code_PKT" :=
CustomerCategory.Code;
        Customer.Modify();
    end;
end;

procedure AssignDefaultCategory()
var
    Customer: Record Customer;
    CustomerCategory: Record "Customer Category_PKT";
begin
    //Set default category for ALL Customer
    CustomerCategory.SetRange(Default, true);
    if CustomerCategory.FindFirst() then begin
        Customer.SetFilter("Customer Category Code_PKT", '%1', '');
        Customer.ModifyAll("Customer Category Code_PKT",
CustomerCategory.Code, true);
    end;
end;

//Returns the number of Customers without an assigned Customer
Category
procedure GetTotalCustomersWithoutCategory(): Integer
var
    Customer: record Customer;
begin
    Customer.SetRange("Customer Category Code_PKT", '');
    exit(customer.Count());
end;

procedure GetSalesAmount(CustomerCategoryCode: Code[20]): Decimal
var
    SalesLine: Record "Sales Line";
    Customer: record Customer;
    TotalAmount: Decimal;
begin
    Customer.SetCurrentKey("Customer Category Code_PKT");
    Customer.SetRange("Customer Category Code_PKT",
CustomerCategoryCode);
```

```
      if Customer.FindSet() then
      repeat
          SalesLine.SetRange("Document Type", SalesLine."Document
Type"::Order);
          SalesLine.SetRange("Sell-to Customer No.", Customer."No.");
          if SalesLine.FindSet() then
          repeat
              TotalAmount += SalesLine."Line Amount";
          until SalesLine.Next() = 0;
      until Customer.Next() = 0;
      exit(TotalAmount);
  end;
}
```

Here, we have the following functions:

- `CreateDefaultCategory`: This creates an entry in the `Customer Category` table with a predefined code and with the `Default` flag set to true.
- `AssignDefaultCategory`: This assigns the default category to customers. Here, we use overloading (supported in AL) and we have the same function with the following two different implementations (one without parameters and one with a `Code[20]` parameter):
  - `AssignDefaultCategory(CustomerCode: Code[20])`: Works on the current customer
  - `AssignDefaultCategory()`: Works on all customers
- `GetTotalCustomersWithoutCategory`: This returns the number of customers without a category assigned.
- `GetSalesAmount`: This returns the total amount of the sales order for the `Customer Category` selected.

After this, we move on to implementing the gift campaign's business requirements.

Gift campaign implementations

To handle the gift campaign requirements, we need to do the following:

- Define the Gift Campaign table. This table must be able to store data as follows:

Customer Category	Item	Start Date	End Date	Minimum Quantity Ordered	Gift Quantity
GOLD	ITEM1	01/01/2019	30/03/2019	5	1
GOLD	ITEM2	01/01/2019	30/03/2019	10	2
SILVER	ITEM1	01/01/2019	30/03/2019	7	1

- Create the page (user interface) for handling the gift campaign data (a list page).
- Handling the business logic for assigning gifts to a sales order is based on Customer Category and the active campaign for this category. This will be done in an external codeunit.
- Add a new function to the Sales Order page interface in order to permit the sales operator to automatically insert a gift line when the sales order is finished.
- When the sales operator inserts the Quantity in a sales order line, we want to check the active campaigns and alert the user if the ordered quantity is near to an active promotion.

Table definition

By using the ttable snippet, we define the Gift Campaign table as follows:

```
table 50101 "GiftCampaign_PKT"
{
 DataClassification = CustomerContent;
 DrillDownPageId = "Gift Campaign List_PKT";
 LookupPageId = "Gift Campaign List_PKT";
 Caption = 'Gift Campaign';

 fields
 {
     field(1; CustomerCategoryCode; Code[20])
     {
         DataClassification = CustomerContent;
         TableRelation = "Customer Category_PKT";
         Caption = 'Customer Category Code';
         trigger OnValidate()
```

```
        var
            CustomerCategory: Record "Customer Category_PKT";
            ErrNoGifts: Label 'This category is not enabled for Gift
Campaigns.';
            ErrBlocked: Label 'This category is blocked.';
        begin
            CustomerCategory.Get(CustomerCategoryCode);
            if CustomerCategory.Blocked then
                Error(ErrBlocked);
            if not CustomerCategory.FreeGiftsAvailable then
                Error(ErrNoGifts);
        end;
    }
    field(2; ItemNo; Code[20])
    {
        DataClassification = CustomerContent;
        TableRelation = Item;
        Caption = 'Item No.';
    }
    field(3; StartingDate; Date)
    {
        DataClassification = CustomerContent;
        Caption = 'Starting Date';
    }
    field(4; EndingDate; Date)
    {
        DataClassification = CustomerContent;
        Caption = 'Ending Date';
    }
    field(5; MinimumOrderQuantity; Decimal)
    {
        DataClassification = CustomerContent;
        Caption = 'Minimum Order Quantity';
    }
    field(6; GiftQuantity; Decimal)
    {
        DataClassification = CustomerContent;
        Caption = 'Free Gift Quantity';
    }
    field(7; Inactive; Boolean)
    {
        DataClassification = CustomerContent;
        Caption = 'Inactive';
    }
}

keys
{
```

```
    key(PK; CustomerCategoryCode, ItemNo, StartingDate, EndingDate)
    {
        Clustered = true;
    }
  }
}
```

The primary key for this table is a composite key, defined as follows:

```
keys
    {
        key(PK; CustomerCategoryCode, ItemNo, StartingDate,
EndingDate)
        {
            Clustered = true;
        }
    }
```

Here, we've handled the `OnValidate` trigger of the `CustomerCategoryCode` field, which performs some validations:

- If the `Customer Category` selected is blocked, an error is thrown.
- If the `Customer Category` selected is not available for gift promotions (`FreeGiftsAvailable = false`), then an error is thrown.

Page definition

By using the `tpage` snippet, we define the `Gift Campaign List` page as follows:

```
page 50103 "Gift Campaign List_PKT"
{
    PageType = List;
    SourceTable = GiftCampaign_PKT;
    UsageCategory = Lists;
    Caption = 'Gift Campaigns';
    ApplicationArea = All;
    AdditionalSearchTerms = 'promotions, marketing';

    layout
    {
        area(content)
        {
            repeater(Group)
            {
                field(CustomerCategoryCode; CustomerCategoryCode)
                {
```

```
                ApplicationArea = All;
            }
            field(ItemNo; ItemNo)
            {
                ApplicationArea = All;
            }
            field(StartingDate; StartingDate)
            {
                ApplicationArea = All;
            }
            field(EndingDate; EndingDate)
            {
                ApplicationArea = All;
            }
            field(MinimumOrderQuantity; MinimumOrderQuantity)
            {
                ApplicationArea = All;
                Style = Strong;
            }
            field(GiftQuantity; GiftQuantity)
            {
                ApplicationArea = All;
                Style = Strong;
            }
            field(Inactive; Inactive)
            {
                ApplicationArea = All;
            }
        }
    }
}

views
{
    view(ActiveCampaigns)
    {
        Caption = 'Active Gift Campaigns';
        Filters = where (Inactive = const (false));
    }
    view(InactiveCampaigns)
    {
        Caption = 'Inactive Gift Campaigns';
        Filters = where (Inactive = const (true));
    }
}
}
```

When published, the page appears as follows:

To handle the gift assignment logic in a sales order, by creating a `pageextension` object, we have added a new action to the `Sales Order` page, and from this action, we call the `AddGifts` method defined in a codeunit in the next section.

The `pageextension` object is defined as follows:

```
pageextension 50100 SalesOrderExt_PKT extends "Sales Order"
{
    actions
    {
        addlast(Processing)
        {
            action(AddFreeGifts)
            {
                Caption = 'Add Free Gifts';
                ToolTip = 'Adds Free Gifts to the current Sales Order
based on active Campaigns';
                ApplicationArea = All;
                Image = Add;
                Promoted = true;
                PromotedCategory = Process;
                PromotedIsBig = true;
                trigger OnAction()
                begin
                    GiftManagement.AddGifts(Rec);
                end;
            }
        }
    }

    var
        GiftManagement: Codeunit GiftManagement_PKT;
}
```

The `Sales Order` page (with the new action) now looks like this:

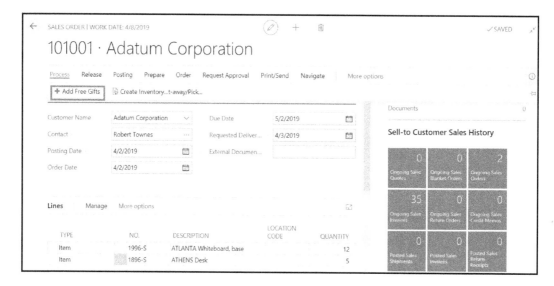

Codeunit definition

All of the business logic for handling the requirements is defined in a `GiftManagement` codeunit, as follows:

```
codeunit 50101 "GiftManagement_PKT"
{
 procedure AddGifts(var SalesHeader: Record "Sales Header")
 var
     SalesLine: record "Sales Line";
 Handled: Boolean;
 begin
     SalesLine.SetRange("Document Type", SalesHeader."Document Type");
     SalesLine.SetRange("Document No.", SalesHeader."No.");
     SalesLine.SetRange(Type, SalesLine.Type::Item);
     //We exclude the generated gifts lines in order to avoid loops
     SalesLine.SetFilter("Line Discount %", '<>100');
     if SalesLine.FindSet() then
     repeat
         //Integration event raised
         OnBeforeFreeGiftSalesLineAdded(SalesLine, Handled);
         AddFreeGiftSalesLine(SalesLine, Handled);
         //Integration Event raised
         OnAfterFreeGiftSalesLineAdded(SalesLine);
     until SalesLine.Next() = 0;
```

```
end;

 local procedure AddFreeGiftSalesLine(var SalesLine: Record "Sales
Line"; var Handled: Boolean)
 var
     GiftCampaign: Record GiftCampaign_PKT;
     SalesHeader: record "Sales Header";
     Customer: Record Customer;
     SalesLineGift: Record "Sales Line";
     LineNo: Integer;
 begin
     if Handled then
         exit;
     SalesHeader.Get(SalesLine."Document Type", SalesLine."Document
No.");
     Customer.Get(SalesLine."Sell-to Customer No.");
     GiftCampaign.SetRange(CustomerCategoryCode, Customer."Customer
Category Code_PKT");
     GiftCampaign.SetRange(ItemNo, SalesLine."No.");
     GiftCampaign.SetFilter(StartingDate, '<=%1', SalesHeader."Order
Date");
     GiftCampaign.SetFilter(EndingDate, '>=%1', SalesHeader."Order
Date");
     GiftCampaign.SetRange(Inactive, false);
     GiftCampaign.SetFilter(MinimumOrderQuantity, '<= %1',
SalesLine.Quantity);
     if GiftCampaign.FindFirst() then begin
         //Active promo found. We need to insert a new Sales Line
         LineNo := GetLastSalesDocumentLineNo(SalesHeader);
         SalesLineGift.init;
         SalesLineGift.TransferFields(SalesLine);
         SalesLineGift."Line No." := LineNo + 10000;
         SalesLineGift.Validate(Quantity, GiftCampaign.GiftQuantity);
         SalesLineGift.Validate("Line Discount %", 100);
         if SalesLineGift.Insert() then;
     end;
 end;

 local procedure GetLastSalesDocumentLineNo(SalesHeader: Record "Sales
Header"): Integer
 var
     SalesLine: Record "Sales Line";
 begin
     SalesLine.SetRange("Document Type", SalesHeader."Document Type");
     SalesLine.SetRange("Document No.", SalesHeader."No.");
     if SalesLine.FindLast() then
         exit(SalesLine."Line No.")
     else
```

```
            exit(0);
    end;

    [EventSubscriber(ObjectType::Table, Database::"Sales Line",
    'OnAfterValidateEvent', 'Quantity', false, false)]
    local procedure CheckGiftEligibility(var Rec: Record "Sales Line")
    var
        GiftCampaign: Record GiftCampaign_PKT;
        Customer: Record Customer;
        SalesHeader: Record "Sales Header";
        Handled: Boolean;
    begin
        if (Rec.Type = Rec.Type::Item) and (Customer.Get(Rec."Sell-to
    Customer No.")) then begin
        SalesHeader.Get(Rec."Document Type", Rec."Document No.");
        GiftCampaign.SetRange(CustomerCategoryCode, Customer."Customer
    Category Code_PKT");
        GiftCampaign.SetRange(ItemNo, Rec."No.");
        GiftCampaign.SetFilter(StartingDate, '<=%1', SalesHeader."Order
    Date");
        GiftCampaign.SetFilter(EndingDate, '>=%1', SalesHeader."Order
    Date");
        GiftCampaign.SetRange(Inactive, false);
    GiftCampaign.SetFilter(MinimumOrderQuantity, '> %1',
    Rec.Quantity);
        if GiftCampaign.FindFirst() then begin
            //Integration event raised
            OnBeforeFreeGiftAlert(Rec, Handled);
            DoGiftCheck(Rec, GiftCampaign, Handled);
            //Integration Event raised
            OnAfterFreeGiftAlert(Rec);
        end;
    end;
    end;

    local procedure DoGiftCheck(var SalesLine: Record "Sales Line"; var
    GiftCampaign: Record GiftCampaign_PKT; var Handled: Boolean)
    var
        PacktSetup: record "Packt Extension Setup";
        GiftAlert: Label 'Attention: there is an active promotion for
    item %1. if you buy %2 you can have a gift of %3';
    begin
        if Handled then
            exit;
        PacktSetup.Get();
        if (SalesLine.Quantity < GiftCampaign.MinimumOrderQuantity) and
    (GiftCampaign.MinimumOrderQuantity - SalesLine.Quantity <=
    PacktSetup."Gift Tolerance Qty") then
```

```
            Message(GiftAlert, SalesLine."No.",
    Format(GiftCampaign.MinimumOrderQuantity),
    Format(GiftCampaign.GiftQuantity));
        end;
```

Here, we have some procedures, some event subscribers, and some event publishers. The main procedure is called `AddGifts` and it adds the gift lines (promotions) to the sales order passed as the argument. It raises some integration events, and the main code is handled by the `AddFreeGiftSalesLine` procedure.

The integration events defined in this codeunit are as follows:

```
[IntegrationEvent(true, false)]
 local procedure OnBeforeFreeGiftSalesLineAdded(var Rec: Record "Sales
Line"; var Handled: Boolean)
 begin
 end;

 [IntegrationEvent(true, false)]
 local procedure OnAfterFreeGiftSalesLineAdded(var Rec: Record "Sales
Line")
 begin
 end;

 [IntegrationEvent(true, false)]
 local procedure OnBeforeFreeGiftAlert(var Rec: Record "Sales Line";
var Handled: Boolean)
 begin
 end;

 [IntegrationEvent(true, false)]
 local procedure OnAfterFreeGiftAlert(var Rec: Record "Sales Line")
 begin
 end;

 [EventSubscriber(ObjectType::Table, Database::"Item Ledger Entry",
'OnAfterInsertEvent', '', false, false)]
 local procedure OnAfterItemLedgerEntryInsert(var Rec: Record "Item
Ledger Entry")
 var
     Customer: Record Customer;
 begin
     if rec."Entry Type" = rec."Entry Type"::Sale then begin
         if Customer.Get(Rec."Source No.") then begin
             Rec."Customer Category Code_PKT" := Customer."Customer
Category Code_PKT";
             Rec.Modify();
         end;
```

```
        end;
    end;
  }
```

Here, we've implemented the `Handled` pattern (to guarantee extensibility). In this way, a dependent extension can change the gift assignment logic as needed without modifying the base code of the main extension.

The `Handled` pattern implementation is as follows:

```
OnBeforeFreeGiftSalesLineAdded(SalesLine, Handled);
AddFreeGiftSalesLine(SalesLine, Handled);
OnAfterFreeGiftSalesLineAdded(SalesLine);
```

In this code, we have the following:

- We have a global variable called `Handled` set to `false`.
- We raise an integration event called `OnBeforeFreeGiftSalesLineAdded` by passing the sales line we're working on and the `Handled` variable.
- We implement the business logic in a procedure called `AddFreeGiftSalesLine`. In this procedure, if the event is handled, we skip the standard logic:

  ```
  if Handled then
      exit;
  ```

- At the end of the process, we raise an integration event called `OnAfterFreeGiftSalesLineAdded`.

So, why does this pattern guarantee extensibility? This is because, in a dependent extension, you can subscribe to the `OnBeforeFreeGiftSalesLineAdded` event and set the `Handled` variable to `true` and implement your new business logic for adding gifts. Then, the standard business logic (`AddFreeGiftSalesLine`) is skipped.

After this, you can subscribe to the `OnAfterFreeGiftSalesLineAdded` event and implement other custom business logic that must be executed after the process of adding gifts. We'll see an example of a dependent extension that alters the standard business logic of our extension in the *Understanding dependent extensions* section of this chapter.

In this codeunit, we've also created a procedure called `CheckGiftEligibility`, which is an event subscriber of the `OnAfterValidateEvent` event of the `Quantity` field of the `Sales Line` table. The following code shows this:

```
[EventSubscriber(ObjectType::Table, Database::"Sales Line",
'OnAfterValidateEvent', 'Quantity', false, false)]
    local procedure CheckGiftEligibility(var Rec: Record "Sales Line")
```

In this function, we handle the business logic for the alert that must be triggered when the sales operator inserts the quantity in a sales line. As you can see in the preceding code, we've implemented the `Handled` pattern again here to provide extensibility.

In this codeunit, we've also handled the event subscriber for the `OnAfterInsertEvent` event of the `Item Ledger Entry` table to transfer the `Customer Category` data to the `Item Ledger Entry` field (this was one of the requested requirements):

```
[EventSubscriber(ObjectType::Table, Database::"Item Ledger Entry",
'OnAfterInsertEvent', '', false, false)]
    local procedure OnAfterItemLedgerEntryInsert(var Rec: Record "Item
Ledger Entry")
```

What happens when, from a sales order, you trigger the **Add Free Gifts** action? Refer to the following screenshot:

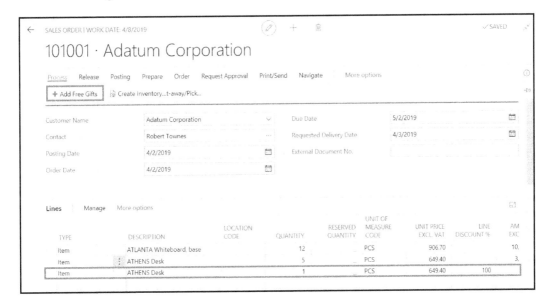

We can see that the events are raised, the `AddGifts` function is executed, and the gift promotions (if any) are inserted in the `Sales Line` table (a new line with the **LINE DISCOUNT** % field value set to `100`).

We've now implemented all of the business requirements needed to manage the customer's gift campaigns. Now, let's move on to the vendor quality implementation details.

Vendor quality implementations

To handle the vendor quality management requirements, we need to do the following:

- Define a `Vendor Quality` table (related to the standard `Vendor` table) that will contain details about the quality scores for vendor and quality-related financial data.
- Define the relevant card page and attach it to the vendor card (this will be the quality detail card for a vendor as per our requirements).
- Add a new action to the standard `Vendor` card page to open `Vendor Quality card`.
- Define a codeunit that handles all of the business logic related to this implementation

In the following sections, we'll see the various object implementations in detail.

Table definition

By using the `ttable` snippet, we define the `Vendor Quality` table as follows:

```
table 50102 "Vendor Quality_PKT"
{
 Caption = 'Vendor Quality';
 DataClassification = CustomerContent;

 fields
 {
     field(1; "Vendor No."; Code[20])
     {
         Caption = 'Vendor No.';
         DataClassification = CustomerContent;
         TableRelation = Vendor;
     }
```

```
    field(2; "Vendor Name"; Text[50])
    {
        Caption = 'Vendor Name';
        FieldClass = FlowField;
        CalcFormula = lookup (Vendor.Name where ("No." = field
("Vendor No.")));
    }
    field(3; "Vendor Activity Description"; Text[250])
    {
        Caption = 'Vendor Activity Description';
        DataClassification = CustomerContent;
    }
    field(4; ScoreItemQuality; Integer)
    {
        Caption = 'Item Quality Score';
        DataClassification = CustomerContent;
        MinValue = 1;
        MaxValue = 10;
        trigger OnValidate()
        begin
            UpdateVendorRate();
        end;
    }
    field(5; ScoreDelivery; Integer)
    {
        Caption = 'Delivery On Time Score';
        DataClassification = CustomerContent;
        MinValue = 1;
        MaxValue = 10;
        trigger OnValidate()
        begin
            UpdateVendorRate();
        end;
    }
    field(6; ScorePackaging; Integer)
    {
        Caption = 'Packaging Score';
        DataClassification = CustomerContent;
        MinValue = 1;
        MaxValue = 10;
        trigger OnValidate()
        begin
            UpdateVendorRate();
        end;
    }
    field(7; ScorePricing; Integer)
    {
        Caption = 'Pricing Score';
```

```
            DataClassification = CustomerContent;
            MinValue = 1;
            MaxValue = 10;
            trigger OnValidate()
            begin
                UpdateVendorRate();
            end;
        }
        field(8; Rate; Decimal)
        {
            Caption = 'Vendor Rate';
            DataClassification = CustomerContent;
        }
        field(10; UpdateDate; DateTime)
        {
            Caption = 'Update Date';
            DataClassification = CustomerContent;
        }
        field(11; InvoicedYearN; Decimal)
        {
            Caption = 'Invoiced for current year (N)';
            DataClassification = CustomerContent;
        }
        field(12; InvoicedYearN1; Decimal)
        {
            Caption = 'Invoiced for year N-1';
            DataClassification = CustomerContent;
        }
        field(13; InvoicedYearN2; Decimal)
        {
            Caption = 'Invoiced for year N-2';
            DataClassification = CustomerContent;
        }
        field(14; DueAmount; Decimal)
        {
            Caption = 'Due Amount';
            DataClassification = CustomerContent;
        }
        field(15; AmountNotDue; Decimal)
        {
            Caption = 'Amount to pay (not due)';
            DataClassification = CustomerContent;
        }
    }

    keys
    {
        key(PK; "Vendor No.")
```

```
    {
        Clustered = true;
    }
}

trigger OnInsert()
begin
    UpdateDate := CurrentDateTime();
end;
trigger OnModify()
begin
    UpdateDate := CurrentDateTime();
end;
local procedure UpdateVendorRate()
var
    VendorQualityMgt: Codeunit VendorQualityMgt_PKT;
begin
    VendorQualityMgt.CalculateVendorRate(Rec);
end;
}
```

In this table, we have the definitions of the required score fields (rating) and the required financial fields.

For the score rates, we handle the OnValidate trigger to dynamically update the rate calculation when the user inserts values in the fields (this is done by calling the UpdateVendorRate function defined in the table (as a class method) but implemented in the external codeunit that we'll see later.

We've also handled the table's OnInsert and OnModify triggers to save the insertion or modification date of the record (business requirements).

Page definition

For our business requirements, we need to create a Vendor Quality card page. We create a new page of the Card type by using the tpage snippet, as follows:

```
page 50102 "Vendor Quality Card_PKT"
{
    PageType = Card;
    ApplicationArea = All;
    UsageCategory = Administration;
    SourceTable = "Vendor Quality_PKT";
    Caption = 'Vendor Quality Card';
    InsertAllowed = false;
```

```
    layout
    {
        area(Content)
        {
            group(General)
            {
                Caption = 'General';
                field("Vendor No."; "Vendor No.")
                {
                    ApplicationArea = All;
                    Editable = false;
                }
                field("Vendor Name"; "Vendor Name")
                {
                    ApplicationArea = All;
                    Editable = false;
                }
                field("Vendor Activity Description"; "Vendor Activity
Description")
                {
                    ApplicationArea = All;
                }
                field(Rate; Rate)
                {
                    ApplicationArea = All;
                    Editable = false;
                    Style = Strong;
                }
                field(UpdateDate; UpdateDate)
                {
                    ApplicationArea = All;
                    Editable = false;
                }
            }
            group(Scoring)
            {
                Caption = 'Score';
                field(ScoreItemQuality; ScoreItemQuality)
                {
                    ApplicationArea = All;
                }
                field(ScoreDelivery; ScoreDelivery)
                {
                    ApplicationArea = All;
                }
                field(ScorePackaging; ScorePackaging)
                {
                    ApplicationArea = All;
```

```
            }
            field(ScorePricing; ScorePricing)
            {
                ApplicationArea = All;
            }
        }
        group(Financials)
        {
            Caption = 'Financials';
            field(InvoicedYearN; InvoicedYearN)
            {
                ApplicationArea = All;
                Editable = false;
            }
            field(InvoicedYearN1; InvoicedYearN1)
            {
                ApplicationArea = All;
                Editable = false;
            }
            field(InvoicedYearN2; InvoicedYearN2)
            {
                ApplicationArea = All;
                Editable = false;
            }
            field(DueAmount; DueAmount)
            {
                ApplicationArea = All;
                Editable = false;
                Style = Attention;
            }
            field(AmountNotDue; AmountNotDue)
            {
                ApplicationArea = All;
                Editable = false;
            }
        }
    }
}

trigger OnOpenPage()
begin
    if not Insert() then;
end;

trigger OnAfterGetRecord()
var
    VendorQualityMgt: Codeunit VendorQualityMgt_PKT;
begin
```

```
            VendorQualityMgt.UpdateVendorQualityStatistics(Rec);
        end;
    }
```

This page is designed by creating different groups (`FastTabs` in the UI):

- `General`: Contains the general quality classification of the selected vendor, such as the name, a description of the activity, and the calculation rate
- `Scoring`: Contains the quality scores (as assigned by the company's quality manager)
- `Financials`: Contains the financial data required from the quality requirements

This page has the `InsertAllowed` property set to `true` because the record here is inserted automatically when the page is opened from `Vendor card` (we handle the `OnOpenPage` trigger here) and the user can't directly insert new records from this page.

We also handle the `OnAfterGetRecord` page trigger, and from here, we call a function that refreshes the financial statistics.

The pageextension definition

We need a `pageextension` object to create the action of opening the previously created `Vendor Quality card` page from the standard `Vendor Card` page. By using the `tpageext` snippet, we create the following object:

```
pageextension 50101 VendorCardExt_PKT extends "Vendor Card"
{
    actions
    {
        addafter("Comments")
        {
            action(QualityClassification)
            {
                Caption = 'Quality Classification';
                ApplicationArea = All;
                Image = QualificationOverview;
                Promoted = true;
                PromotedCategory = Process;
                PromotedIsBig = true;
                RunObject = Page "Vendor Quality Card_PKT";
                RunPageLink = "Vendor No." = field ("No.");
            }
```

```
            }
        }
    }
```

Here, we have defined a `QualityClassification` action, which opens the `Vendor Quality card` page for the selected `Vendor` record (by using the `RunPageLink` property).

The page action appears as follows:

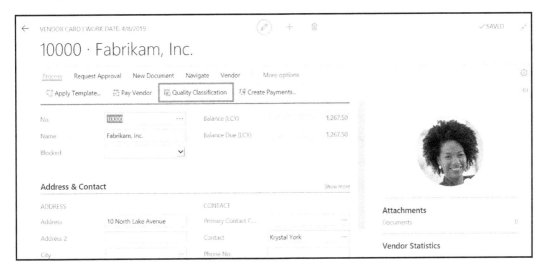

When triggering the action, the `Vendor Quality Card` is opened and looks like this:

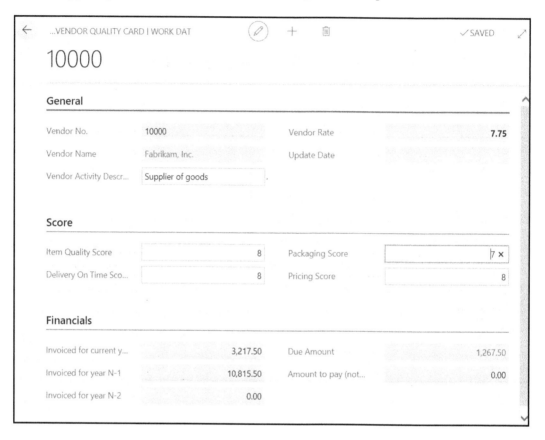

When the quality manager inserts score values, the `Vendor Rate` value is automatically calculated. Financial statistics are automatically calculated when opening the page (in real time).

Codeunit definition

As usual, we define all of our business logic in an external codeunit called `VendorQualityMgt` using the `tcodeunit` snippet, defined as follows:

```
codeunit 50102 VendorQualityMgt_PKT
{
    procedure CalculateVendorRate(var VendorQuality: Record "Vendor
Quality_PKT")
    var
```

```
        Handled: Boolean;
    begin
        OnBeforeCalculateVendorRate(VendorQuality, Handled);
        //This is the company's criteria to assign the Vendor rate.
        VendorRateCalculation(VendorQuality, Handled);
        OnAfterCalculateVendorRate(VendorQuality);
    end;

    local procedure VendorRateCalculation(var VendorQuality: Record
"Vendor Quality_PKT"; var          Handled: Boolean)
    begin
        if Handled then
            exit;
        VendorQuality.Rate := (VendorQuality.ScoreDelivery +
VendorQuality.ScoreItemQuality +
        VendorQuality.ScorePackaging + VendorQuality.ScorePricing) /
4;
    end;

    procedure UpdateVendorQualityStatistics(var VendorQuality: Record
"Vendor Quality_PKT")
    var
        Year: Integer;
        DW: Dialog;
        DialogMessage: Label 'Calculating Vendor statistics...';
    begin
        DW.OPEN(DialogMessage);
        Year := DATE2DMY(TODAY, 3);
        VendorQuality.InvoicedYearN :=
GetInvoicedAmount(VendorQuality."Vendor No.", DMY2DATE(1, 1,
Year), TODAY);
        VendorQuality.InvoicedYearN1 :=
GetInvoicedAmount(VendorQuality."Vendor No.", DMY2DATE(1, 1,
Year - 1), DMY2DATE(31, 12, Year - 1));
        VendorQuality.InvoicedYearN2 :=
GetInvoicedAmount(VendorQuality."Vendor No.", DMY2DATE(1, 1,
Year - 2), DMY2DATE(31, 12, Year - 2));
        VendorQuality.DueAmount := GetDueAmount(VendorQuality."Vendor
No.", TRUE);
        VendorQuality.AmountNotDue :=
GetDueAmount(VendorQuality."Vendor No.", FALSE);
        DW.CLOSE;
    end;

    local procedure GetInvoicedAmount(VendorNo: Code[20]; StartDate:
Date; EndDate: Date): Decimal
    var
        VendorLedgerEntry: Record "Vendor Ledger Entry";
```

```
        Total: Decimal;
    begin
        VendorLedgerEntry.SETRANGE("Vendor No.", VendorNo);
        VendorLedgerEntry.SETFILTER("Document Date", '%1..%2',
StartDate, EndDate);
        if VendorLedgerEntry.FINDSET then
        repeat
            Total += VendorLedgerEntry."Purchase (LCY)";
        until VendorLedgerEntry.NEXT = 0;
        exit(Total * (-1));
    end;

    local procedure GetDueAmount(VendorNo: Code[20]; Due: Boolean):
Decimal
    var
        VendorLedgerEntry: Record "Vendor Ledger Entry";
        Total: Decimal;
    begin
        VendorLedgerEntry.SETRANGE("Vendor No.", VendorNo);
        VendorLedgerEntry.SETRANGE(Open, TRUE);
        if Due then
            VendorLedgerEntry.SETFILTER("Due Date", '< %1', TODAY)
        else
            VendorLedgerEntry.SETFILTER("Due Date", '> %1', TODAY);
VendorLedgerEntry.SETAUTOCALCFIELDS(VendorLedgerEntry."Remaining Amt.
(LCY)");
        if VendorLedgerEntry.FINDSET then
        repeat
            Total += VendorLedgerEntry."Remaining Amt. (LCY)";
        until VendorLedgerEntry.NEXT = 0;
        exit(Total * (-1));
    end;
}
```

Here, we have defined the following functions:

- CalculateVendorRate: This is the function that calculates the vendor rate based on the quality scores assigned by the quality manager. We want this function to be extendable to be able to change the standard rate algorithm as needed in the future. To do that, we use the HANDLE pattern:
    - We raise an OnBeforeCalculateVendorRate event with the current Vendor Quality record and the Handled Boolean variable as event parameters.

- We perform the standard rate calculation in the VendorRateCalculation function by checking the Handled parameter, and we exit from the function if we want to skip the standard calculation (by setting Handled = true).
  - We raise an OnAfterCalculateVendorRate event for handling post calculation operations or for handling a totally new calculation.
- UpdateVendorQualityStatistics: This function calculates the financial statistics required by the quality manager:
  - GetInvoicedAmount: For a given Vendor No. field and date period (start/end date), it calculates the invoiced amount by checking the Vendor Ledger Entry table (the Purchase (LCY) field). The returned result is –1 because we want the absolute value.
  - GetDueAmount: For a given Vendor No. field, it calculates the due amount (the Due parameter is set to true) or the amount to pay (the Due parameter is set to false) by checking the Vendor Ledger Entry table (the Remaining Amt. (LCY) field). The returned result is multiplied by –1 because we want the absolute value.

The codeunits events are defined as follows:

```
[IntegrationEvent(true, false)]
    local procedure OnBeforeCalculateVendorRate(var VendorQuality:
Record "Vendor Quality_PKT"; var          Handled: Boolean)
    begin
    end;

    [IntegrationEvent(true, false)]
    local procedure OnAfterCalculateVendorRate(var VendorQuality:
Record "Vendor Quality_PKT")
    begin
    end;
```

In this codeunit, we've also defined an event subscriber (the teventsub snippet) for the OnBeforeManualReleasePurchaseDoc standard event defined in Microsoft's Release Purchase Document codeunit, which is defined as follows:

```
[EventSubscriber(ObjectType::Codeunit, Codeunit::"Release Purchase
Document", 'OnBeforeManualReleasePurchaseDoc', '', false, false)]
```

We use this event to raise an error during the order release phase if the vendor does not meet the company's rate criteria (that is, the minimum acceptable rate) defined in the extension's setup table.

The event subscriber implementation is as follows:

```
[EventSubscriber(ObjectType::Codeunit, Codeunit::"Release Purchase
Document",        'OnBeforeManualReleasePurchaseDoc', '', false,
false)]
    local procedure QualityCheckForReleasingPurchaseDoc(var
PurchaseHeader: Record "Purchase                 Header")
    var
        VendorQuality: Record "Vendor Quality_PKT";
        PacktSetup: Record "Packt Extension Setup";
        ErrNoMinimumRate: Label 'Vendor %1 has a rate of %2 and it''s
under the required minimum                value (%3)';
    begin
        PacktSetup.Get();
        if VendorQuality.Get(PurchaseHeader."Buy-from Vendor No.")
then begin
            if VendorQuality.Rate < PacktSetup."Minimum Accepted
Vendor Rate" then
                Error(ErrNoMinimumRate, PurchaseHeader."Buy-from
Vendor No.",
                Format(VendorQuality.Rate), Format(PacktSetup."Minimum
Accepted Vendor Rate"));
        end;
    end;
```

All of the customer's business requirements are now handled by our extension.

In the next section, we'll see how to enhance the customer's user experience by creating customized page views in Dynamics 365 Business Central.

Creating page views

Since the fall 2019 release of Dynamics 365 Business Central, you can create customized views for your list pages. These customized views can be used in a dedicated section of the Dynamics 365 Business Central user interface to immediately apply filters to the list.

You can create a view definition in a page object by using the `tview` snippet. In the previously created `Gift Campaign List` page, we have defined the following `view` objects:

```
views
{
    view(ActiveCampaigns)
    {
        Caption = 'Active Gift Campaigns';
        Filters = where (Inactive = const (false));
    }
    view(InactiveCampaigns)
    {
        Caption = 'Inactive Gift Campaigns';
        Filters = where (Inactive = const (true));
    }
}
```

The first view (called `ActiveCampaigns`) shows all of the active gift campaigns (the `Inactive` field is set to `false`), while the second view (called `InactiveCampaigns`) shows all of the inactive gift campaigns (the `Inactive` field is set to `true`).

These views in the Dynamics 365 Business Central user interface look like this:

If you select the **Active Gift Campaigns** view, the list is filtered accordingly (`Inactive` is set to `false`):

If you select the `Inactive Gift Campaigns` view, the list is automatically filtered by `Inactive` being set to `true`:

We have also added a view to the `Customer List` page to show all of the customers who do not have an associated category.

The view definition in the `Customer List pageextension` object is defined as follows:

```
views
{
    addlast
    {
        view(CustomersWithoutCategory)
        {
            Caption = 'Customers without Category assigned';
            Filters = where ("Customer Category_PKT" = filter (''));
        }
    }
}
```

We have placed this newly created view as the last of the available views for the page:

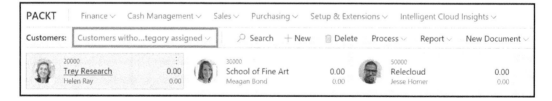

As shown in the preceding screenshot, this view appears in the user interface of the application and, when selected, it automatically filters all of the customers without an associated category (so `Customer Category = Blank`). In this way, our customers can immediately filter records by selecting a pre-defined view (just a click) and without reinserting the required filters.

After this, let's move on and see how installing and upgrading codeunits works.

Installing and upgrading codeunits

When you create an extension, you need to check some conditions for the installation to be successful, or you need to initiate some setup tables or pre-populate other tables. To do this, you need to create **Install codeunit**.

The extension's install logic must be written in a codeunit with the `SubType` property set to `Install`. This logic is triggered when the following is true:

- You're installing the extension for the first time.
- You have uninstalled the extension and then you're installing it again.

An `Install` codeunit supports the following system triggers:

- `OnInstallAppPerCompany()`: The code inside this trigger runs once for each company in the Dynamics 365 Business Central database.
- `OnInstallAppPerDatabase()`: The code inside this trigger runs once for the entire install process.

The same logic occurs when upgrading the extension. If you need to create a new version of your extension (the version number in the `app.json` file must be greater than the previous version number) and this version involves data modifications from previous versions, you need to create **Upgrade codeunit**.

The extension's upgrade logic must be written in a codeunit with the `SubType` property set to `Upgrade`.

An `Upgrade` codeunit supports the following system triggers:

- `OnCheckPreconditionsPerCompany()`: The code inside this trigger is used to check the preconditions for the upgrade process. This code runs once for each company in the database.
- `OnCheckPreconditionsPerDatabase()`: The code inside this trigger is used to check the preconditions for the upgrade process. This code runs once for the entire upgrade process.
- `OnUpgradePerCompany()`: The code inside this trigger contains the upgrade logic. This code runs once for each company in the database.
- `OnUpgradePerDatabase()`: The code inside this trigger contains the upgrade logic. This code runs once for the entire upgrade process.

- `OnValidateUpgradePerCompany()`: The code inside this trigger is used to check the results of the upgrade process. This code runs once for each company in the database.
- `OnValidateUpgradePerDatabase()`: The code inside this trigger is used to check the results of the upgrade process. This code runs once for the entire upgrade process.

For our extension, we have created an `Install` codeunit as follows:

```
codeunit 50105 CustomerCategoryInstall_PKT
{
    Subtype = Install;
    trigger OnInstallAppPerCompany();
    var
        archivedVersion: Text;
        CustomerCategory: Record "Customer Category_PKT";
        PacktSetup: Record "Packt Extension Setup";
    begin
        archivedVersion := NavApp.GetArchiveVersion;
        if archivedVersion = '1.0.0.0' then begin
            NavApp.RestoreArchiveData(Database::"Customer
Category_PKT");
            NavApp.RestoreArchiveData(Database::Customer);
            NavApp.RestoreArchiveData(Database::"Packt Extension
Setup");
            NavApp.RestoreArchiveData(Database::GiftCampaign_PKT);
            NavApp.RestoreArchiveData(Database::"Vendor Quality_PKT");
            NavApp.DeleteArchiveData(Database::"Customer
Category_PKT");
            NavApp.DeleteArchiveData(Database::Customer);
            NavApp.DeleteArchiveData(Database::"Packt Extension
Setup");
            NavApp.DeleteArchiveData(Database::GiftCampaign_PKT);
            NavApp.DeleteArchiveData(Database::"Vendor Quality_PKT");
        end;
        if CustomerCategory.IsEmpty() then
            InsertDefaultCustomerCategory();
        if PacktSetup.IsEmpty() then
            InsertDefaultSetup();
    end;

    // Insert the GOLD, SILVER, BRONZE reward levels
    local procedure InsertDefaultCustomerCategory();
    begin
        InsertCustomerCategory('TOP', 'Top Customer', false);
        InsertCustomerCategory('MEDIUM', 'Standard Customer', true);
        InsertCustomerCategory('BAD', 'Bad Customer', false);
```

```
    end;

    // Create and insert a Customer Category record
    local procedure InsertCustomerCategory(ID: Code[30]; Description:
Text[250]; Default: Boolean);
    var
        CustomerCategory: Record "Customer Category_PKT";
    begin
        CustomerCategory.Init();
        CustomerCategory.Code := ID;
        CustomerCategory.Description := Description;
        CustomerCategory.Default := Default;
        CustomerCategory.Insert();
    end;

    local procedure InsertDefaultSetup()
    var
        PacktSetup: Record "Packt Extension Setup";
    begin
        PacktSetup.Init();
        PacktSetup."Minimum Accepted Vendor Rate" := 6;
        PacktSetup."Gift Tolerance Qty" := 2;
        PacktSetup.Insert();
    end;
}
```

In the `OnInstallAppPerCompany` trigger, we check whether there's an archived version of our extension (this could happen if someone has uninstalled the extension):

```
    archivedVersion := NavApp.GetArchiveVersion;
```

If so, we restore the archived data from the `NavApp` system table (so the user has their old data retrieved automatically).

If there's nothing restored, we initialize the `Customer Category` table and the extension's setup table (`Packt Extension Setup` table) with default data.

More information about the `Install` and `Upgrade` codeunits can be found in `Chapter 9`, *Debugging*, of this book and at the following links: `https://docs.microsoft.com/en-us/dynamics365/business-central/dev-itpro/developer/devenv-extension-install-code` and `https://docs.microsoft.com/en-us/dynamics365/business-central/dev-itpro/developer/devenv-upgrading-extensions`.

When published from Visual Studio Code on Dynamics 365 Business Central, our extension appears as *installed* on the **EXTENSION MANAGEMENT** page:

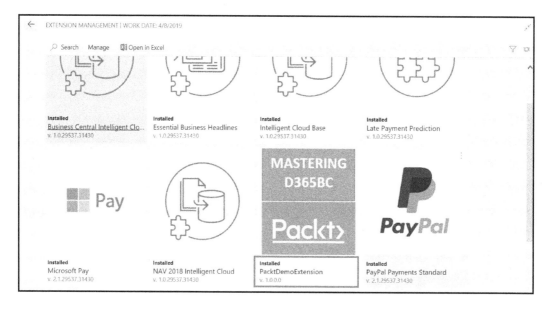

We have now learned how to handle the install and upgrade operations required when publishing an extension in Dynamics 365 Business Central.

In the next section, we'll explore the concept of dependent extensions and learn how to use a dependency to make customizations to our previously deployed application.

Understanding a dependent extension

In the previous sections, we developed our extension and deployed it.

Imagine now that you've deployed this extension to a customer tenant and now the customer asks you for some customization:

- They want to add the `Certification No.` field to the **Vendor Quality** table.
- They want to change the gift assignment logic by always assigning a fixed gift quantity of 2.

To create a customization for your customer, you should *never* directly modify your standard extension code, but instead, you should create a new extension that will be *dependent* on your base extension.

To do this, we create a new extension project in Visual Studio Code called `PacktDemoDependencyExtension`. This new extension must be dependent on our previously created `PacktDemoExtension`; otherwise, we won't be able to see the objects defined in that extension.

First, we need to retrieve the `appId`, `name`, `publisher`, and `version` of the base extension. Then, we have to open the `app.json` file of our new extension, go to the `dependencies` block, and insert the details of the dependent extension as follows:

```
"dependencies": [
    {
        "appId": "63ca2fa4-4f03-4f2b-a480-172fef340d3f",
        "publisher": "Microsoft",
        "name": "System Application",
        "version": "1.0.0.0"
    },
    {
        "appId": "437dbf0e-84ff-417a-965d-ed2bb9650972",
        "publisher": "Microsoft",
        "name": "Base Application",
        "version": "15.0.0.0"
    },
    {
        "appId": "dd03d28e-4dfe-48d9-9520-c875595362b6",
        "name": "PacktDemoExtension",
        "publisher": "SD",
        "version": "1.0.0.0"
    }
],
```

Now, if we download the symbols (`AL:Download Symbols`), you will see that the symbols of our dependent extension are downloaded into the `.alpackages` folder in our project:

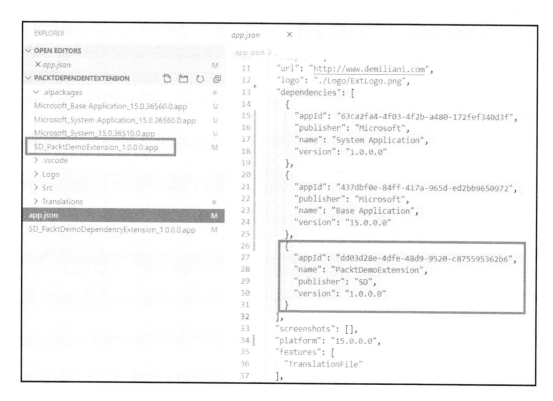

We're now ready to create our new extension.

To add the `Certification No.` field to `Vendor Quality Card`, we need to do the following:

- Extend the `Vendor Quality` table by adding a new field.
- Extend the `Vendor Quality Card` page to add the new field to the UI.

We can do that because we have the symbols downloaded; otherwise, it's impossible to see the objects defined in another extension.

The `tableextension` object code that extends the `Vendor Quality` table is defined as follows:

```
tableextension 50120 VendorQualityExt_PKN extends "Vendor Quality_PKT"
{
    fields
    {
        field(50120; "Certification No."; Text[50])
        {
            Caption = 'Classification No.';
            DataClassification = CustomerContent;
        }
    }
}
```

The `pageextension` object that extends the `Vendor Quality Card` page is defined as follows:

```
pageextension 50120 VendorQualityCardExt_PKN extends "Vendor Quality
Card_PKT"
{
    layout
    {
        addlast(General)
        {
            field("Certification No."; "Certification No.")
            {
                ApplicationArea = All;
            }
        }
    }
}
```

The second requirement is to customize a standard business process defined in the base extension (`PacktDemoExtension`) that creates the gifts line on a sales order if there's an active campaign (in the standard business process, the gift quantity is the quantity defined in the `Gift Campaign` table).

You can do that **only** if the base extension has events to subscribe because you cannot directly modify the code of another extension.

To handle extensibility, we used the `Handled` pattern in our base extension. In the `PacktDemoExtension` extension, we have the `AddGifts` procedure defined as follows:

```
procedure AddGifts(var SalesHeader: record "Sales Header")
    var
        SalesLine: record "Sales Line";
        Handled: Boolean;
    begin
        SalesLine.SetRange("Document Type", SalesHeader."Document
Type");
        SalesLine.SetRange("Document No.", SalesHeader."No.");
        SalesLine.SetRange(Type, SalesLine.Type::Item);
        if SalesLine.FindSet() then
            repeat
                //Integration event raised
                OnBeforeFreeGiftSalesLineAdded(SalesLine, Handled);
                AddFreeGiftSalesLine(SalesLine, Handled);
                //Integration Event raised
                OnAfterFreeGiftSalesLineAdded(SalesLine);
            until SalesLine.Next() = 0;
    end;
```

To skip the standard business process (`AddFreeGiftSalesLine`) and add a new custom gift assignment process, we do the following:

1. We subscribe to the `OnBeforeFreeGiftSalesLineAdded` event, and we set the `Handled` parameter to `true`. This ensures that the standard business logic will be skipped because, in the `AddFreeGiftSalesLine` procedure, we have used the following code as the first line:

```
if Handled then
    exit;
```

2. We call our custom business logic from this event subscriber.

All of this logic is defined in a codeunit object as follows:

```
codeunit 50120 CustomGiftLogic_PKN
{
    [EventSubscriber(ObjectType::Codeunit,
Codeunit::GiftManagement_PKT,
'OnBeforeFreeGiftSalesLineAdded', '', false, false)]
    local procedure HideDefaultBehaviour(var Rec: Record "Sales Line";
var Handled: Boolean)
    begin
        Handled := true;
```

```
        //Here we create a custom gift line with a fixed quantity
        //(override of standard behavior)
        CreateCustomGiftLine(Rec);
    end;

    local procedure CreateCustomGiftLine(var SalesLine: Record "Sales
Line")
    var
        SalesHeader: Record "Sales Header";
        SalesLineGift: Record "Sales Line";
        LineNo: Integer;
        FixedQty: Decimal;
    begin
        FixedQty := 2;
        SalesHeader.Get(SalesLine."Document Type", SalesLine."Document
No.");
        LineNo := GetLastSalesDocumentLineNo(SalesHeader);
        SalesLineGift.init;
        SalesLineGift.TransferFields(SalesLine);
        SalesLineGift."Line No." := LineNo + 10000;
        SalesLineGift.Validate(Quantity, FixedQty);
        SalesLineGift.Validate("Line Discount %", 100);
        if SalesLineGift.Insert() then;
    end;

    local procedure GetLastSalesDocumentLineNo(SalesHeader: Record
"Sales Header"): Integer
    var
        SalesLine: Record "Sales Line";
    begin
        SalesLine.SetRange("Document Type", SalesHeader."Document
Type");
        SalesLine.SetRange("Document No.", SalesHeader."No.");
        if SalesLine.FindLast() then
            exit(SalesLine."Line No.")
        else
            exit(0);
    end;
}
```

When published, we now have two extensions installed (the standard extension and the new customization extension):

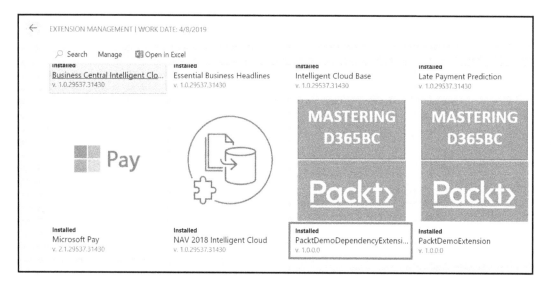

To test whether our customization works, we create a new sales order with an item that has an associated gift campaign, and then we start the gift assignment process:

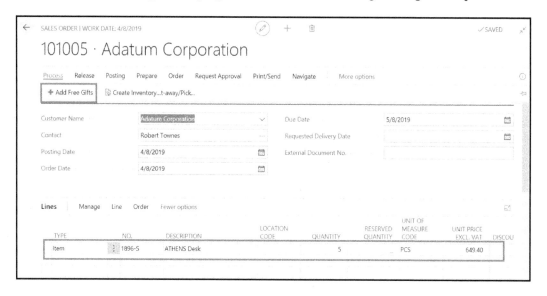

So, what happens now? The `OnBeforeFreeGiftSalesLineAdded` event is raised, we skip the standard event (`Handled = true`), and then our new custom function (`CreateCustomGiftLine`) is triggered:

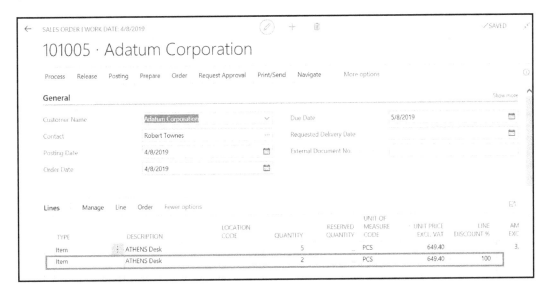

As we can see in the preceding screenshot, a new gift line with a fixed quantity of 2 and a discount of 100% is inserted in our sales order.

We have customized our gift campaign business logic without modifying the base code (our base extension), but instead by creating a new dependent extension. This should be the mandatory model to use with Dynamics 365 Business Central.

Summary

In this chapter, we saw the implementation of a real-world extension for Dynamics 365 Business Central. We defined the backend of our solution (tables) and we created the pages (the user interface) and the required business logic (codeunits and events) according to the initial needs of the business. We saw how to make our code extensible by using the `Handled` pattern and how to create installation and upgrade code.

In the last part of this chapter, we created a new extension that modifies the standard behavior of our base extension, and we looked at the concept of dependency between extensions.

You have also learned how to create extensions with objects and events, how to use coding rules, and how to create customizations without modifying the base code of your application.

In the next chapter, we'll see how to handle some advanced topics with AL and the extension model, such as files, media, XML and JSON objects, web services, and asynchronous programming.

Advanced AL Development

6

In the previous chapter, we developed a complete extension for Dynamics 365 Business Central, and during development, we looked at many aspects of AL programming.

In this chapter, we'll focus on other development topics that you need to manage when developing real-world solutions for Dynamics 365 Business Central. These topics are important and useful, especially for improving the user experience and when you need to handle integrations with external services from AL.

This chapter will cover the following topics:

- Understanding immutable keys
- Handling files with AL
- Handling BLOBs
- Handling XMLports
- Handling XML and JSON objects with AL
- Creating and extending Role Centers and headlines
- Consuming web services and APIs from AL code
- Using Azure functions from AL code
- Using Isolated Storage to handle sensitive data
- Creating control add-ins for Dynamics 365 Business Central
- Handling notifications
- Page background tasks and asynchronous programming

Understanding immutable keys

With the Dynamics 365 Business Central wave 2 release, all tables now have a (unique) immutable key (a GUID field) that can be used for integration scenarios and for replacing the old RECORDID property. This new field is called SystemId and it's a GUID data type field that specifies a unique, immutable (read-only) identifier for records in a table.

The new SystemId field (identified with the field number 2000000000 on every table object) has the following characteristics:

- It has a value for every record in a table.
- You can assign a value at insert time; otherwise, the platform automatically assigns one.
- Once SystemId has been set, it cannot be changed.
- There is always a unique secondary key in the SystemId field.

As a platform rule, modifying SystemId of an existing record is not allowed. The INSERT function now has a new override:

```
Record.Insert([RunTrigger: Boolean[, InsertWithSystemId: Boolean]])
```

SystemId can be manually specified when inserting a new record, as in the following example:

```
myRec.SystemId := '{B6667654-F4B2-B945-8567-006DD6B6775E}';
myRec.Insert(true,true);
```

You can now use the GetBySystemId function to retrieve a record via its SystemId, as in the following example:

```
var
    Customer: Record Customer;
    Text000: Label 'Customer was found.';
    begin
    if Customer.GetBySystemId('{B6667654-F4B2-
B945-8567-006DD6B6775E}') then
        Message(Text000);
end;
```

You can also set table relations by using the new `SystemId` field, as in the following code:

```
field(1; EntryID; GUID)
{
    DataClassification = CustomerContent;
    TableRelation = Item.SystemId;
}
```

The `Integration Record` table before version 15 has GUIDs for records. The upgrade process to Dynamics 365 Business Central version 15 will use these values to initialize the new `SystemId` field. In the future, the `Integration Record` table will be declared obsolete. The `SystemID` field is also useful on API pages.

In the next section, we'll see how to handle files with AL in an **software as a service (SaaS)** environment.

Handling files with AL

Working with files is one of the tricky points with Dynamics 365 Business Central. While in the on-premises version you have full access to your local resources and a filesystem, in the SaaS version of Dynamics 365 Business Central, things are different. Here, you don't have a filesystem and you don't have access to local resources (all processes runs in Microsoft's data centers).

If you create a function, you declare a `File` variable and then you invoke one of the common file management methods (such as `Create`, which creates and opens an ASCII or binary file), and this is the error that Visual Studio Code spits out:

```
     0 references
37      procedure TestFiles()
38      var
39          MyFile: File;
40      begin
41          MyFile.Create()
42      end;
43
```

PROBLEMS 1   OUTPUT   DEBUG CONSOLE   TERMINAL   Filter. Eg: text, **/*.ts, !*...

▲   MyCodeunit2.al SRC\Functionality2\codeunit 1

    ❌ [AL] The type or method 'Create' cannot be used for 'Extension' development. [AL0296] (41, 16)

This error occurs because the extension you're trying to create targets the Dynamics 365 Business Central SaaS environment by default (`"target"`: `"Extension"` in the `app.json` file).

If you add `"target"`: `"Internal"` to your `app.json` file (in this way, you're declaring that your extension is for the on-premise world only), then the error disappears and you can use the classic `File` object methods, as follows:

```
     0 references
37   procedure TestFiles()
38   var
39       MyFile: File;
40   begin
41       MyFile.Create('C:\TestFolder\packt.txt',TextEncoding::MSDos);
42   end;
43
44
45
```

```
PROBLEMS    OUTPUT    DEBUG CONSOLE    TERMINAL              Filter. Eg: text, **/*.ts, !**/n...

No problems have been detected in the workspace so far.
```

The same thing happens if you use the `File Management` codeunit to handle files. Some of its methods cannot be used in an SaaS extension:

```
     0 references
37   procedure TestFiles()
38   var
39       MyFile: File;
40       FileManagement: Codeunit "File Management";
41   begin
42       FileManagement.CreateClientFile();
43   end;
44
45
46
47
48
```

```
PROBLEMS  1   OUTPUT    DEBUG CONSOLE    TERMINAL              Filter. Eg: text, **/*.ts, !*...

  MyCodeunit2.al  SRC\Functionality2\codeunit  1
      ⊗ [AL] The type or method 'CreateClientFile' cannot be used for 'Extension' development. [AL0296] (42, 24)
```

To handle files in the cloud environment, you need to use **Streams** (the InStream and OutStream objects).

The InStream and OutStream data types are generic stream objects used for reading from or writing to files and BLOBs.

> More information about these objects can be found at the following links:
>
> - https://docs.microsoft.com/en-us/dynamics365/
>   business-central/dev-itpro/developer/methods-auto/
>   instream/instream-data-type
> - https://docs.microsoft.com/en-us/dynamics365/
>   business-central/dev-itpro/developer/methods-auto/
>   outstream/outstream-data-type

To upload a file from the client computer to a server-side stream object, you need to call the UploadIntoStream method:

```
[Ok := ]  File.UploadIntoStream(DialogTitle: String, FromFolder:
String, FromFilter: String, var FromFile: Text, var InStream:
InStream)
```

The method's parameters are the following:

- DialogTitle (string): This is the text displayed in the title bar of the file selection dialog box. This parameter is not supported by the web client (the title is determined by the user's browser).
- FromFolder (string): This is the path of the folder that is displayed in the file selection dialog box. This is the default folder, but the user can browse to any available location. This parameter is not supported by the web client (by default, the browser uses the folder that was last accessed).
- FromFilter (string): This is the type of file that can be uploaded to the server. In the Windows client, the type is displayed in the upload dialog box, so the user can only select files of the specified type. For the web client, this filter is not supported in the user interface. The user can try to upload any file type but an error occurs if the file is not as the specified type.
- FromFile (text): This is the default file to upload to the service. The user can change the file. This parameter is not supported by the web client.
- InStream: This is the InStream object to load data in.

More details about the method can be found at `https://docs.microsoft.com/en-us/dynamics365/business-central/dev-itpro/developer/methods-auto/file/file-uploadintostream-method`.

As an example, this is a function that loads an image file from the client side (using an InStream object and UploadIntoStream to load the client file into the InStream object) and adds it as an Item object:

```
procedure ImportItemPicture(Item: Record Item)
    var
        FileInstream: InStream;
        FileName: Text;
    begin
        if UploadIntoStream('', '', '', FileName, FileInstream) then
        begin
            Clear(Item.Picture);
            Item.Picture.ImportStream(FileInstream,FileName);
            Item.Modify(true);
        end;
    end;
```

As another example, this is a function that reads a CSV file that contains Item details into an InStream object, loads its content into the CSV Buffer table, and then updates the Item fields accordingly:

```
local procedure UploadCSV()
   var
        CSVInStream : InStream;
        UploadResult : Boolean;
        TempBlob : Codeunit "Temp Blob";
        DialogCaption : Text;
        CSVFileName : Text;
        CSVBuffer: Record "CSV Buffer";
        Item: Record Item;
   begin
        UploadResult :=
UploadIntoStream(DialogCaption,'','',CSVFileName,CSVInStream);
        CSVBuffer.DeleteAll;
        CSVBuffer.LoadDataFromStream(CSVInStream,';');
        if CSVBuffer.FindSet() then
        repeat
         if (CSVBuffer."Field No." = 1) then
            Item.Init();
            case CSVBuffer."Field No." of
                1: Item.Validate("No.",CSVBuffer.Value);
                2: Item.Validate(Description,CSVBuffer.Value);
```

```
            3: Item.Validate("Item Category
Code",CSVBuffer.Value);
            4: if not Item.Insert() then Item.Modify();
        end;
    until CSVBuffer.Next()=0;
end;
```

To download a file from the server side (the SaaS environment) to the client side (the user machine), you need to use the DownloadFromStream method:

```
[Ok := ]  File.DownloadFromStream(InStream: InStream, DialogTitle:
String, ToFolder: String, ToFilter: String, var ToFile: Text)
```

The method's parameters are as follows:

- InStream object (https://docs.microsoft.com/en-us/dynamics365/business-central/dev-itpro/developer/methods-auto/instream/instream-data-type) contains the file data.

- DialogTitle string (https://docs.microsoft.com/en-us/dynamics365/business-central/dev-itpro/developer/methods-auto/string/string-data-type): This is the title that you want to display in the dialog box for downloading the file. This parameter is not supported by the web client (here, the title is determined by the end user's browser).

- ToFolder string (https://docs.microsoft.com/en-us/dynamics365/business-central/dev-itpro/developer/methods-auto/string/string-data-type): This is the default folder in which to save the downloaded file. The folder name is displayed in the dialog box for the download, and the folder can be changed by the user. This parameter is not supported by the web client (because default files are saved to the default download location that is configured in the end user's browser).

- ToFilter string (https://docs.microsoft.com/en-us/dynamics365/business-central/dev-itpro/developer/methods-auto/string/string-data-type): This is the type of file that can be downloaded to the client. The type is displayed in the dialog box for downloading the file. This parameter is not supported by the web client.

- ToFile text (https://docs.microsoft.com/en-us/dynamics365/business-central/dev-itpro/developer/methods-auto/text/text-data-type): This is the name assigned to the downloaded file. This value can be changed by the user.

More information about this method can be found at https://docs. microsoft.com/en-us/dynamics365/business-central/dev-itpro/ developer/methods-auto/file/file-downloadfromstream-method.

As an example, this code exports the images associated with an Item card as the MediaSet type. It uses DownloadFromStream to download the file to the client. The images are retrieved from the Tenant Media table and saved with a filename made up of Item Number, the image index, and the image extension (the GetImageExtension function retrieves the image file extension according to its Mime Type):

```
procedure ExportItemPicture(Item: Record Item)
    var
        FileInStream: InStream;
        FileName: Text;
        i: Integer;
        TenantMedia: Record "Tenant Media";
        ErrMsg: Label 'No images stored for the selected item.';
    begin
        if Item.Picture.Count() = 0 then
            Error(ErrMsg);
        for i := 1 to Item.Picture.Count() do begin
            if TenantMedia.Get(Item.Picture.MediaId()) then begin
                TenantMedia.CalcFields(Content);
                if TenantMedia.Content.HasValue() then begin
                    FileName := Item."No." + '_' + Format(i) +
GetImageExtension(TenantMedia);
                    TenantMedia.Content.CreateInStream(FileInStream);
                    DownloadFromStream(FileInStream, '', '', '',
FileName);
                end;
            end;
        end;
    end;

    procedure GetImageExtension(var TenantMedia: record "Tenant
Media"): Text
    begin
        case TenantMedia."Mime Type" of
        'image/jpeg': exit('.jpg');
        'image/bmp': exit('.bmp');
        'image/png': exit('.png');
        'image/gif': exit('.gif');
        'image/tiff': exit('.tiff');
        'image/wmf': exit('.wmf');
```

```
        end
    end;
```

If you need to create a file from Dynamics 365 Business Central, you need to create it on the server side using the new `Temp Blob` codeunit defined in the `System Application` and `OutStream` objects.

This is an example of an AL function that receives a filename as input, creates a text file with three lines, and downloads it to the client side:

```
procedure CreateTextFile(FileName: Text)
var
    InStr: InStream;
    OutStr: OutStream;
    TempBlob: Codeunit "Temp Blob";
    CR: char;
    LF: char;
begin
    CR := 13;
    LF := 10;
    TempBlob.CreateOutStream(OutStr);
    OutStr.WriteText('First line'+ CR + LF);
    OutStr.WriteText('Second line'+ CR + LF);
    OutStr.WriteText('Third line'+ CR + LF);
    TempBlob.CreateInStream(InStr);
    DownloadFromStream(InStr, '', '', '', FileName);
end;
```

With Dynamics 365 Business Central, you cannot directly save a file to a local folder (a local machine or network folder). To perform this action, you need to use something different, such as Azure Functions (we'll see that later in this chapter).

 With the Dynamics 365 Business Central wave 2 release, the old `TempBlob` table is deprecated and has been replaced by some system codeunits (`Temp Blob`, `Persistent Blob`, and `Temp Blob List`).

In this section, you saw how to use streams to handle files in Dynamics 365 Business Central. In the next section, we'll see how to handle attachments to documents and entities in Dynamics 365 Business Central.

Handling attachments

Attachments are files that you can link to entities or documents in Dynamics 365 Business Central. Two main tables are used to store attachments:

- Document attachment (ID = 1173)
- Attachment (ID = 5062)

To store an attachment in these tables and then download an attachment from these tables, you need to use the previously mentioned UploadIntoStream and DownloadFromStream methods and load the BLOB field by using Streams.

An example of a function that uploads a file to the Attachment table is as follows:

```
procedure UploadAttachment()
    var
        Attachment: Record Attachment;
        outStr: OutStream;
        inStr: InStream;
        tempfilename: text;
        FileMgt: Codeunit "File Management";
        DialogTitle: Label 'Please select a File...';
    begin
        if UploadIntoStream(DialogTitle, '', 'All Files (*.*)|*.*',
tempfilename, inStr) then
        begin
            Attachment.Init();
            Attachment.Insert(true);
            Attachment."Storage Type" := Attachment."Storage
Type"::Embedded;
            Attachment."Storage Pointer" := '';
            Attachment."File Extension" :=
FileMgt.GetExtension(tempfilename);
            Attachment."Attachment File".CreateOutStream(outStr);
            CopyStream(outStr, inStr);
            Attachment.Modify(true);
        end;
    end;
```

An example of a function that downloads a file from the `Attachment` table is as follows:

```
procedure OpenAttachment(AttachmentEntryNo: Integer)
    var
        Attachment: record Attachment;
        inStr: InStream;
        tempfilename: text;
        ErrorAttachment: Label 'File not available.';
    begin
        if Attachment.get(AttachmentEntryNo) then
            if Attachment."Attachment File".HasValue then begin
                Attachment.CalcFields("Attachment File");
                Attachment."Attachment File".CreateInStream(inStr);
                tempfilename := CreateGuid() + '.' + Attachment."File
Extension";
                DOWNLOADFROMSTREAM(inStr, 'Save file', '', 'All Files
(*.*)|*.*',
                    tempfilename);
            end
            else
                Error(ErrorAttachment);
    end;
```

We can use the same process for the `Document Attachment` table; you've only to add the reference to the `attachment` record to the document itself.

We've seen how to handle attachments (a useful feature to add to your extensions). In the next section, we'll see how to read and write data to and from BLOB fields.

Reading and writing text data to and from BLOB fields

To read data from and write text data to a BLOB field, you need to use the `InStreams` and `OutStreams` objects as previously described.

The two methods in the following code read and write text data from and to a BLOB field defined in a custom table:

```
table 50120 MyBlobTable
{
    DataClassification = CustomerContent;
    fields
    {
        field(1;ID; Integer)
        {
            DataClassification = CustomerContent;
        }

        field(2; BlobField; Blob)
        {
            DataClassification = CustomerContent;
        }
    }
    keys
    {
        key(PK; ID)
        {
            Clustered = true;
        }
    }
    procedure SetBlobValue(value: Text)
    var
        outStr: OutStream;
    begin
        BlobField.CreateOutStream(outStr);
        outStr.WriteText(value);
    end;

    procedure GetBlobValue(value: Text)
    var
        inStr: InStream;
    begin
        CalcFields(BlobField);
        if BlobField.HasValue() then
        begin
            BlobField.CreateInStream(inStr);
            inStr.ReadText(value);
        end
        else
            value := 'No value on the BLOB field';
    end;
}
```

Here, we have defined a table with a BLOB field and we have created two methods for reading and writing data to this BLOB field:

- The `SetBlobValue` function writes data (passed as input) to a BLOB field.
- The `GetBlobValue` function reads data from a BLOB field.

With these two methods, we've achieved the goal to read and write text to our BLOB field. In the next section, we'll see how to use XMLports from AL.

Using XMLports in AL code

As we said in `Chapter 2`, *Mastering a Modern Development Environment*, **XMLports** are objects used to import and export data between Dynamics 365 Business Central and external data sources (this is managed by the `Direction` property, which can be set to `Import`, `Export`, or `Both`). Data can be imported or exported in XML or CSV (text) format (the `Format` property can be set to `Xml`, `Variable Text`, or `Fixed Text`).

XMLport properties are detailed at `https://docs.microsoft.com/en-us/dynamics-nav/xmlport-properties`.

XMLport triggers are detailed at `https://docs.microsoft.com/en-us/dynamics-nav/xmlport-triggers`.

Now, consider the sample XMLport defined in `Chapter 4`, *Extension Development Fundamentals*:

```
xmlport 50100 MyXmlportImportCustomer
{
    Direction = Import;
    Format = VariableText;
    FieldSeparator = ';';
    RecordSeparator = '<LF>';
    schema
    {
        textelement(NodeName1)
        {
            tableelement(Customer; Customer)
            {
                fieldattribute(No; Customer."No.")
                {
                }
                fieldattribute(Name; Customer.Name)
                {
                }
```

```
                          fieldattribute(Address;Customer.Address)
                          {
                          }
                          fieldattribute(City;Customer.City)
                          {
                          }
                          fieldattribute(Country;Customer."Country/Region Code")
                          {
                               trigger OnAfterAssignField()
                               begin
                                 //Executed after a field has been assigned a
       value and before it is validated and imported.
                               end;
                          }
                      }
                  }
              }
          }
```

To execute an XMLport in Dynamics 365 Business Central, you need to run it from a page or a codeunit object (you cannot directly run it). XMLport request pages (used to set filters or insert parameters) in the Dynamics 365 Business Central web client are not supported.

To execute an XMLport in Dynamics 365 Business Central to import data from a file, you need to use the following code:

```
procedure RunXMLportImport()
    var
        FileInstream: InStream;
        FileName: Text;
    begin
        UploadIntoStream('','','',FileName,FileInstream);
        Xmlport.Import(Xmlport::MyXmlportImportCustomer,FileInStream);
        Message('Import Done successfully.');
    end;
```

Here, the file is loaded into an InStream object and then the XMLport is executed by passing the InStream object as input.

To execute an XMLport in Dynamics 365 Business Central to export data to a file, you need to use the following code:

```
procedure RunXMLportExport()
    var
        TempBlob: Codeunit "Temp Blob";
        FileName: Text;
        FileOutStream: OutStream;
        FileInStream: InStream;
        outputFileName: Text;
    begin
        TempBlob.CREATEOUTSTREAM(FileOutStream);
        Xmlport.Export(Xmlport::MyXmlportImportCustomer,
FileOutStream);
        TempBlob.CREATEINSTREAM(FileInStream);
        outputFileName := 'MyOutputFile.xml';
        DownloadFromStream(FileInStream,'','','',outputFileName);
        //The output is saved in the default browser's Download folder
    end;
```

Here, we have seen how to use XMLports from AL code to import or export data. In the next section, we'll see how to create and extend Role Centers in Dynamics 365 Business Central.

Creating and extending Role Centers

When a user logs in to Dynamics 365 Business Central, they are presented with a page that shows information and actions tailored to their role inside the company. This page is called a **Role Center**, and it's an integral part of the role-tailored experience of the application.

Dynamics 365 Business Central offers about 20 Role Centers out of the box (as standard) that you can extend and customize, and you can create new Role Centers.

A Role Center is a page that has the `PageType` property set to `RoleCenter`. The page structure is as follows:

In the structure diagram, the sections are as follows:

- Section 1 is the **Navigation Menu** area (one or more items that, when clicked, show other sub-menus). This is used to provide access to the relevant entities for the role to which this Role Center page is assigned.
- Section 2 is the **Navigation Bar** area, which displays a list of links to other pages that will be opened in the Content area. This is normally used to add links to the user's most useful entities for their business role.

- Section 3 is the **Action** area, used to add links for running the most important tasks for this role (links to pages, reports, or codeunits).
- Section 4 is the **Headline** area, used to display dynamically generated information about the business. We'll see more details about this area in the *Customizing the Headline* section of this chapter.
- Section 5 is the **Wide Cue** area, a set of cues that display numerical values about the business. This area is created with a cuegroup control on a page with PageType = CardPart and with the Layout property set to wide.
- Section 6 is the **Data Cue** area, used to provide a visual representation of aggregated business data (such as KPIs). This part is created with a cuegroup control on a page with PageType = CardPart.
- Section 7 is the Action Cue area, which shows tiles that link to some business tasks. This area is created with a cuegroup control on a page with PageType = CardPart.
- Section 8 is the **Chart** area, used to show information as charts (custom business chart control add-ins or embedded Power BI reports).
- Section 9 is the **CardPart or ListPart page** area, used to display data from the application with a card or a list layout.
- Section 10 is the **Control add-in** area, used for displaying custom content using HTML-based control add-ins (written in JavaScript).

A Role Center page can be created in AL using the following code:

```
page 50101 "My Role Center"
{
    PageType = RoleCenter;
    layout
    {
        area(rolecenter)
        {
            part(SalesPerformance; "Sales Performance")
            {
                ApplicationArea = All;
                Visible = true;
            }

            part(MyCustomers; "My Customers")
            {
                ApplicationArea = All;
                Visible = true;
            }

            part(News;"Headline RC Business Manager")
```

```
        {
            ApplicationArea = All;
            Visible = true;
        }
    }
  }
}
```

Here, we have created a Role Center page with three **parts** (sub-pages).

You can customize an existing Role Center page by creating a pageextension object:

```
pageextension 50100 SalesManagerRoleCenterExt_SD extends "Sales
Manager Role Center"
{
    layout
    {
        addlast(Content)
        {
            part(MyNews; MyRoleCenterHeadline)
            {
                ApplicationArea = All;
                Visible = true;
            }
        }
    }
    actions
    {
        addlast(Sections)
        {
            group("My Customers")
            {
                action("Customer Ledger Entries")
                {
                    RunObject = page "Customer Ledger Entries";
                    ApplicationArea = All;
                }
            }
        }
    }
}
```

Here, we have extended the Sales Manager Role Center page by adding a new custom headline part to the content and a new action to open the Customer Ledger Entries page.

Customizing or creating Role Centers is important because it gives your users a better user experience.

In the next section, we'll see how we can customize the Headline part of a Role Center.

Customizing the Headline

As described earlier, the **Headline** is a new part introduced with the Dynamics 365 Business Central web client that's used to dynamically display important information about your business. Consider the following screenshot:

This is an important part of the Dynamics 365 Business Central role-tailored user experience, and it's recommended to use and customize it to give your users a better experience.

A Headline is essentially a page that contains one or more fields (each field is a headline line) and with `PageType` set as `HeadlinePart`. This page is only visible inside a Role Center page.

Dynamics 365 Business Central has nine standard headlines available:

- Headline RC Business Manager
- Headline RC Order Processor
- Headline RC Accountant
- Headline RC Project Manager

- Headline RC Relationship Management
- Headline RC Administrator
- Headline RC Team Member
- Headline RC Production Planner
- Headline RC Service Dispatcher

You can also create your own Headlines by using AL and Visual Studio Code.

A Headline page can be defined in AL as follows:

```
page 50100 "MyRoleCenterHeadline"
{
    PageType = HeadLinePart;
    layout
    {
        area(content)
        {
            field(Headline1; text001)
            {
                ApplicationArea = all;
            }

            field(Headline2; text002)
            {
                ApplicationArea = all;
                trigger OnDrillDown()
                var
                    DrillDownURL: Label 'http://www.demiliani.com';
                begin
                    Hyperlink(DrillDownURL)
                end;
            }

            field(Headline3; text003)
            {
                ApplicationArea = all;
            }

            field(Headline4; text004)
            {
                ApplicationArea = all;
                // Determines visibility while the page is open
(custom criteria)
                Visible=showHeadline4;
            }
        }
    }
```

```
var
    text001: Label 'This is Headline 1';
    text002: Label 'This is Headline 2 (click for details)';
    text003: Label 'This is Headline 3';
    text004: Label 'This is Headline 4';
    showHeadline4: Boolean;

    trigger OnOpenPage()
    var
        myInt: Integer;
    begin
        showHeadline4 := true;
    end;
}
```

Here, we have defined a Headline page with four text fields that appears in the Dynamics 365 Business Central UI with the appropriate text.

In the second headline, we have handled the `OnDrillDown` event, and if you click on the second headline in this example, you're redirected to a URL. By handling this event, you can have a clickable headline that shows business details (for example, it can open a Dynamics 365 Business Central detail page). A headline page can also be hidden and visibility can be programmatically set by code (as in Headline 4 in the previous example).

The text displayed on a headline page can be formatted according to the following `Expression` property:

Expression TAG	Description
`<qualifier></qualifier>`	This specifies the title that appears above the headline. If it's not present, the text HEADLINE will be used by default.
`<payload></payload>`	This specifies the displayed headline text.
`<emphasize></emphasize>`	The text on this tag is displayed with the biggest size.

To modify an existing headline, you need to create a `pageextension` object and extend it. As an example, here we are modifying the standard `Headline RC Business Manager` page by adding a new headline panel with dynamically created content:

```
pageextension 50101 MyNewBCHeadline extends "Headline RC Business
Manager"
{
    layout
```

```
    {
        addafter(Control4)
        {
            field(newHeadlineText;newHeadlineText)
            {
                ApplicationArea = all;
            }
        }
    }
    var
        newHeadlineText: Text;

        trigger OnOpenPage()
        var
            HeadlineMgt : Codeunit "Headline Management";
        begin
            //Set Headline text
            newHeadlineText := 'This is my new Business Central
Headline for ' + HeadlineMgt.Emphasize('Packt Publishing');
        end;
}
```

Here, we've added a new field called newHeadlineText, and this field is populated in the OnOpenPage trigger of the Headline page with the information that we want to display to our users.

This section has explained how to customize the Headline of a Role Center page and how to show relevant business information to our users.

Handling XML and JSON files with the AL language

The AL language extension has native support for handling XML and JSON documents.

An XML document is represented by using the XmlDocument data type, as explained at https://docs.microsoft.com/en-us/dynamics365/business-central/dev-itpro/developer/methods-auto/xmldocument/xmldocument-data-type.

The following code shows how you can import an XML file and load it into an
`XmlDocument` object:

```
local procedure ImportXML()
    var
        TempBlob : Codeunit "Temp Blob";
        TargetXmlDoc : XmlDocument;
        XmlDec : XmlDeclaration;
        Instr: InStream;
        filename: Text;
    begin
        // Create the Xml Document
        TargetXmlDoc := XmlDocument.Create;
        xmlDec := xmlDeclaration.Create('1.0','UTF-8','');
        TargetXmlDoc.SetDeclaration(xmlDec);

        // Create an Instream object & upload the XML file into it
        TempBlob.CreateInStream(Instr);
        filename := 'data.xml';
        UploadIntoStream('Import XML','','',filename,Instr);

        // Read stream into new xml document
        Xmldocument.ReadFrom(Instr, TargetXmlDoc);
    end;
```

Here, we have created an `XmlDocument` object with an XML declaration, then we
have created an `InStream` object to load the XML file, and we have read the
`InStream` content into the `XmlDocument` object.

If you reference the `TargetXmlDoc` object, you see all of the available methods for
handling and manipulating the XML file:

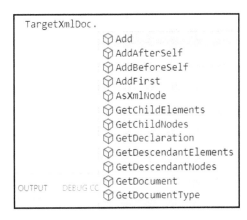

To create an XML document directly from AL code, you can use the `XmlDocument` and `XmlElement` classes:

```
local procedure XMLDocumentCreation()
    var
        xmldoc: XmlDocument;
        xmlDec: XmlDeclaration;
        node1: XmlElement;
        node2: XmlElement;
    begin
        xmldoc := XmlDocument.Create();
        xmlDec := xmlDeclaration.Create('1.0','UTF-8','');
        xmlDoc.SetDeclaration(xmlDec);
        node1:= XmlElement.Create('node1');
        xmldoc.Add(node1);
        node2 := XmlElement.Create('node2');
        node2.SetAttribute('ID','3');
        node1.Add(node2);
    end;
```

This code creates an XML document with a root node (called `node1`) and a child node (called `node2`) with an ID attribute that has a value of 3 (`<node2 ID="3">`).

Native support for JSON documents is provided by using the `JsonObject` and `JsonArray` data types. Each of these data types contains the methods for handling a JSON file (both reading and writing) and for manipulating the JSON data (tokens).

 A detailed explanation of all of the available methods for these data types can be found at the following links:
https://docs.microsoft.com/en-us/dynamics365/business-central/dev-itpro/developer/methods-auto/jsonobject/jsonobject-data-type
https://docs.microsoft.com/en-us/dynamics365/business-central/dev-itpro/developer/methods-auto/jsonarray/jsonarray-data-type

The following code shows an example of how to create a JSON representation of a sales order document:

```
procedure CreateJsonOrder(OrderNo: Code[20])
    var
        JsonObjectHeader: JsonObject;
        JsonObjectLines: JsonObject;
        JsonOrderArray: JsonArray;
        JsonArrayLines: JsonArray;
        SalesHeader: Record "Sales Header";
        SalesLines: Record "Sales Line";
```

```
    begin
        //Retrieves the Sales Header
        SalesHeader.Get(SalesHeader."Document Type"::Order,OrderNo);
        //Creates the JSON header details
        JsonObjectHeader.Add('sales_order_no', SalesHeader."No.");
        JsonObjectHeader.Add(' bill_to_customer_no',
SalesHeader."Bill-to Customer No.");
        JsonObjectHeader.Add('bill_to_name', SalesHeader."Bill-to
Name");
        JsonObjectHeader.Add('order_date', SalesHeader."Order Date");
        JsonOrderArray.Add(JsonObjectHeader);

        //Retrieves the Sales Lines
        SalesLines.SetRange("Document Type", SalesLines."Document
Type"::Order);
        SalesLines.SetRange("Document No.", SalesHeader."No.");
        if SalesLines.FindSet then
        // JsonObject Init
        JsonObjectLines.Add('line_no', '');
        JsonObjectLines.Add('item_no', '');
        JsonObjectLines.Add('description', '');
        JsonObjectLines.Add('location_code', '');
        JsonObjectLines.Add('quantity', '');
        repeat
            JsonObjectLines.Replace('line_no', SalesLines."Line No.");
            JsonObjectLines.Replace('item_no', SalesLines."No.");
            JsonObjectLines.Replace('description',
SalesLines.Description);
            JsonObjectLines.Replace('location_code',
SalesLines."Location Code");
            JsonObjectLines.Replace('quantity', SalesLines.Quantity);
            JsonArrayLines.Add(JsonObjectLines);
        until SalesLines.Next() = 0;
        JsonOrderArray.Add(JsonArrayLines);
    end;
```

This procedure receives an order number as input, retrieves the Sales Header and Sales Line details, and creates a JSON representation. The final result is as follows:

```
[
    {
        "sales_order_no": "SO1900027",
        "bill_to_customer_no": "C001435",
        "bill_to_name": "Packt Publishing",
        "order_date": "2019-03-23"
    },
    [
        {
```

```
                    "line_no": "10000",
                    "item_no": "IT00256",
                    "description": "Dynamics 365 Business Central Development
        Guide",
                    "location_code": "MAIN",
                    "quantity": 30
            },
            {
                    "line_no": "20000",
                    "item_no": "IT03465",
                    "description": "Mastering Dynamics 365 Business Central",
                    "location_code":"MAIN",
                    "quantity": 27
            }
        ]
    ]
```

Obviously, you can also receive a JSON representation as input (for example, as a response from an API call) and handle it using the same data types.

Here, we have seen how to handle JSON documents in AL by using the native JSON types.

In the next section, we'll see a complete example on how to call an API, receive a JSON response, parse it, and save data to a Dynamics 365 Business Central entity.

Consuming web services and APIs from AL

The AL HttpClient object provides a base class for handling HTTP requests and responses from web resources (identified by a URI). With the HttpClient class, you can send GET, DELETE, POST, and PUT HTTP request messages (HttpRequestMessage with HttpHeaders and HttpContent) and receive an HttpResponseMessage object as a result of this request (including the status code and the response data).

You can find more details about all of the exposed methods at the following link: https://docs.microsoft.com/en-us/dynamics365/business-central/dev-itpro/developer/methods-auto/httpclient/httpclient-data-type.

As an example, in the following code, we create an extension that permits you to pull customers' address details by calling a service called Fullcontact (https://www. fullcontact.com). When you are registered for the free account, Fullcontact gives you an API with an access key that you can use to retrieve customer details by providing the customer's name.

What we want is the following: if you insert the domain name of a company in the Name field of the Customer Card (for example, packt.com), the system must call the API and retrieve the customer' details for this domain name.

We create a pageextension object by extending the Customer Card, and in the OnAfterValidate trigger of the Name field, we call a custom method (called LookupAddressInfo and defined in a codeunit called TranslationManagement) to handle the data retrieval logic:

```
pageextension 50100 CustomerCardExt extends "Customer Card"
{
    layout
    {
        modify(Name)
        {
            trigger OnAfterValidate()
            var
                TranslationManagement: Codeunit TranslationManagement;
            begin
                if Name.EndsWith('.com') then begin
                    if Confirm('Do you want to retrieve company
details?', false) then
                        TranslationManagement.LookupAddressInfo(Name,
Rec);
                end;
            end;
        }
    }
}
```

The TranslationManagement codeunit is defined as follows:

```
codeunit 50100 TranslationManagement
{
    procedure LookupAddressInfo(Name: Text; var Customer: Record
    Customer)
    var
        Client: HttpClient;
        Content: HttpContent;
        ResponseMessage: HttpResponseMessage;
```

```
    Result: Text;
    JContent: JsonObject;
    JDetails: JsonObject;
    JLocations: JsonArray;
    JLocation: JsonObject;
    JPhones: JsonArray;
    JPhone: JsonObject;
begin
    Content.WriteFrom('{domain":"' + Name + '"}');
    Client.DefaultRequestHeaders().Add('Authorization', 'Bearer
    <YOUR KEY>');
    Client.Post('https://api.fullcontact.com/v3/company.enrich',
    Content, ResponseMessage);
    if not ResponseMessage.IsSuccessStatusCode() then
        Error('Error connecting to the Web Service.');
    ResponseMessage.Content().ReadAs(Result);
    if not JContent.ReadFrom(Result) then
        Error('Invalid response from Web Service');
    JDetails := GetTokenAsObject(JContent, 'details', 'Invalid
    response from Web Service');
    JLocations := GetTokenAsArray(JDetails, 'locations', 'No
    locations available');
    JLocation := GetArrayElementAsObject(JLocations, 0, 'Location
    not available');
    JPhones := GetTokenAsArray(JDetails, 'phones', '');
    JPhone := GetArrayElementAsObject(JPhones, 0, '');
    Customer.Name := GetTokenAsText(JContent, 'name', '');
    Customer.Address := GetTokenAsText(JLocation, 'addressLine1',
    '');
    Customer.City := GetTokenAsText(JLocation, 'city', '');
    Customer."Post Code" := GetTokenAsText(JLocation,
    'postalCode', '');
    Customer."Country/Region Code" := GetTokenAsText(JLocation,
    'countryCode', '');
    Customer.County := GetTokenAsText(JLocation, 'country', '');
    Customer."Phone No." := GetTokenAsText(JPhone, 'value', '');
end;

procedure GetTokenAsText(JsonObject: JsonObject; TokenKey: Text;
Error: Text): Text;
var
    JsonToken: JsonToken;
begin
    if not JsonObject.Get(TokenKey, JsonToken) then begin
        if Error <> '' then
            Error(Error);
        exit('');
    end;
```

```
        exit(JsonToken.AsValue.AsText);
    end;

    procedure GetTokenAsObject(JsonObject: JsonObject; TokenKey: Text;
    Error: Text): JsonObject;
    var
        JsonToken: JsonToken;
    begin
        if not JsonObject.Get(TokenKey, JsonToken) then
            if Error <> '' then
                Error(Error);
        exit(JsonToken.AsObject());
    end;

    procedure GetTokenAsArray(JsonObject: JsonObject; TokenKey: Text;
    Error: Text): JsonArray;
    var
        JsonToken: JsonToken;
    begin
        if not JsonObject.Get(TokenKey, JsonToken) then
            if Error <> '' then
                Error(Error);
        exit(JsonToken.AsArray());
    end;

    procedure GetArrayElementAsObject(JsonArray: JsonArray; Index:
    Integer; Error: Text): JsonObject;
    var
        JsonToken: JsonToken;
    begin
        if not JsonArray.Get(Index, JsonToken) then
            if Error <> '' then
                Error(Error);
        exit(JsonToken.AsObject());
    end;
}
```

Here, the LookupAddressInfo procedure calls the Fullcontact API (with an authorization header that contains the key provided by the API registration) by using the HttpClient object and sending a POST request to the provided URL by passing the HttpContent to the call (this content contains the name to check in the format as per API specifications).

The HTTP request returns an `HttpResponseMessage` object that contains the response message. If the HTTP response is successful, we read the content of the HTTP response message (which is a JSON string). Then, we parse this JSON string by using some helper methods (which you can see defined in the previous code) that permit us to read JSON tokens and retrieve their values in a specified format (or return an error string or a default value if the token data is not available).

With the `HttpClient` class, you can handle authentication to your web service or the API that you want to call. For example, this is how you can use basic authentication with `HttpClient`:

```
var
   RequestMessage : HttpRequestMessage;
   Headers : HttpHeaders;
   base64Convert: Codeunit "Base64 Convert";
   AuthenticationString: Text;
begin
   RequestMessage.GetHeaders(Headers);
   AuthenticationString :=
StrSubstNo('%1:%2',YOURUSERNAME,YOURPASSWORD);
   Headers.Add('Authorization', StrSubstNo('Basic
%1',base64Convert.ToBase64(AuthenticationString)));
end
```

In this section, we saw how to consume web services and APIs from AL and how to handle requests, responses, and authentication. In the next section, we'll see how to automatically publish objects as web services in Dynamics 365 Business Central when installing an extension.

Publishing Dynamics 365 Business Central objects as web services from AL

When developing extensions, you may need to automatically publish a Dynamics 365 Business Central object as a web service instance for external applications.

There are essentially two different ways to automate this process:

- Create an `Install` codeunit and, in this codeunit, create the web service instance by inserting a record in the `Tenant Web Service` table via AL code.
- Create an XML file with a `TenantWebService` definition.

With the first method, you define an `Install` codeunit, and (for example, in the `OnInstallAppPerCompany` trigger) you can create the web service definition by creating a new entry in the `Tenant Web Service` table, as follows:

```
codeunit 50104 TestInstallCodeunit
{
    Subtype = Install;
    trigger OnInstallAppPerCompany()

    var
        TenantWebService: Record "Tenant Web Service";
    begin
        TenantWebService.Init();
        TenantWebService."Object Type" := TenantWebService."Object
Type"::Page;
        TenantWebService."Object ID" := 26;  //Vendor Card
        TenantWebService."Service Name" := 'VendorCardWS';
        TenantWebService.Published := true;
        TenantWebService.Insert(true);
    end;
}
```

Here, we have published the `Vendor Card` page as a web service with a **SERVICE NAME** of `VendorCardWS`. This web service will be visible in the `Web Services` page in Dynamics 365 Business Central, as follows:

With the second method, you can use the `twebservices` snippet to create a `TenantWebService` XML definition file. The following screenshot shows this:

With the XML definition file, to publish the `Vendor Card` page as a web service, you have to write the following in a new XML file:

```xml
<?xml version="1.0" encoding="UTF-8"?>
<ExportedData>
    <TenantWebServiceCollection>
        <TenantWebService>
            <ObjectType>Page</ObjectType>
            <ServiceName>VendorCardWS</ServiceName>
            <ObjectID>26</ObjectID>
            <Published>true</Published>
        </TenantWebService>
    </TenantWebServiceCollection>
</ExportedData>
```

This XML definition file will be part of your AL project extension's code.

The two methods described here have the same effect when installing the extension: your web service will be published and visible on the `Web Services` page in Dynamics 365 Business Central. But what happens when you uninstall the extension?

When you uninstall the extension, if the web service is published using the XML definition file, it is automatically removed from the `Tenant Web Service` table, while if the web service is published directly via AL code, it's not removed from that table. If you need to automatically publish a web service from an extension at the installation phase, it's recommended to use the `TenantWebService` XML definition file.

In the next section, we'll see how to use Azure Functions to execute serverless processes in the cloud and to replace standard .NET code.

Using Azure Functions to replace .NET code

With Dynamics 365 Business Central, usage of .NET assemblies (the `DotNet` variable type) is supported only in an on-premise scenario. With Dynamics 365 Business Central in the cloud (SaaS), you cannot use DotNet objects (for security reasons) and the official way to replace a `DotNet` variable is by using an HTTP call to an **Azure function**.

Azure Functions is a serverless compute service offered by the Azure platform that permits you to run code in the cloud without managing the infrastructure. We'll talk about Azure Functions in more depth in `Chapter 14`, *Monitoring, Scaling, and CI/CD with Azure Functions,* so here we'll not see how to create an Azure function from scratch, but only how to call it from your extension's code.

Now, imagine having an Azure function called `PostCodeValidator` that validates post codes. This function (of the `HttpTrigger` function type) receives a post code via a query string, validates it, and the function returns a JSON response with a Boolean value that indicates whether the post code is valid or not.

The Azure function can be called via a query string with the following URL:

```
http://postcodevalidator.azurewebsites.net/api/postcodevalidator?code=
POSTCODE
```

Here, `POSTCODE` is the post code to validate.

The JSON response message from the Azure function is as follows:

```
{"Isvalid":false}
```

For this example, we want to call this function in the `OnAfterValidate` event of the `Post Code` field of the `Customer` table:

The code to call the Azure function from AL is as follows:

```
[EventSubscriber(ObjectType::Table, Database::Customer,
'OnAfterValidateEvent', 'Post Code', false, false)]
    local procedure ValidatePostCodeViaAzureFunction(var Rec: Record
Customer)
    var
        Client: HttpClient;
        Response: HttpResponseMessage;
        json: Text;
        jsonObj: JsonObject;
        token: JsonToken;
        FunctionURL: Label
'http://postcodevalidator.azurewebsites.net/api/postcodevalidator?code
=';
        InvalidResponseError: Label 'Invalid Response from Azure
Function.';
        InvalidCodeError: Label 'Invalid Post Code. Please reinsert.';
        TokenNotFoundError: Label 'Token not found in Json.';

    begin
        client.Get(FunctionURL + rec."Post Code", Response);
        //Reads the response content from the Azure Function
        Response.Content().ReadAs(json);
        if not jsonObj.ReadFrom(json) then
            Error(InvalidResponseError);
        //Retrieves the JSon token from the response
        if not jsonObj.Get('IsValid',token) then
            Error(TokenNotFoundError);
        //Convert the Json token to a Boolean value. is TRUE the post
code is valid.
        if not token.AsValue().AsBoolean() then
            Error(InvalidCodeError);
    end;
```

Here, by using the `HttpClient` object, we send an HTTP GET request to the Azure function URI by passing the requested code function's parameter with the value of the `Post Code` field to validate. Then, we read the `HttpResponseMessage` content returned by the Azure function (which is a JSON object) with the following:

```
Response.Content().ReadAs(json);
```

This method loads the `json` text variable from the HTTP response content. After that, we search for the `IsValid` token in the JSON object:

```
jsonObj.Get('IsValid',token)
```

If the token is found, its value is saved into the `token` variable. We read its Boolean value and if it's false, an error is raised (`InvalidCodeError`).

We have seen how to call an Azure function and then how to read and handle its response. We'll talk in more depth about Azure Functions in `Chapter 13`, *Serverless Business Processes with Business Central and Azure*.

In the next section, we'll see how to use the Isolated Storage feature to handle and secure sensitive data from a Dynamics 365 Business Central extension.

Understanding Isolated Storage

Isolated Storage is key-value-based storage that provides data isolation between extensions. Isolated Storage can be used to store data that must be preserved inside the extension scope, and this data is accessible via AL code. The `DataScope` option type identifies the scope of stored data in Isolated Storage.

`DataScope` is an optional parameter and the default value is `Module`. All possible values are listed in the following table:

Member	Description
`Module`	It indicates that the record is available in the scope of the app context.
`Company`	It indicates that the record is available in the scope of the company within the app context.
`User`	It indicates that the record is available for a user within the app context.
`CompanyAndUser`	It indicates that the record is available for a user and specific company within the app context.

To manage data in Isolated Storage, you have the following methods:

Method	Description
`[Ok := ] IsolatedStorage.Set(Key: String, Value: String, [DataScope: DataScope])`	This sets the value associated with the specified key within the extension. The optional `DataScope` parameter is the scope of the stored data.
`[Ok := ] IsolatedStorage.Get(Key: String, [DataScope: DataScope], var Value: Text)`	This gets the value associated with the specified key within the extension. The optional `DataScope` parameter is the scope of the data to retrieve.
`HasValue := IsolatedStorage.Contains(Key: String, [DataScope: DataScope])`	This determines whether the storage contains a value with the specified key within the extension. The optional `DataScope` parameter is the scope to check for the existence of the value with the given key.
`[Ok := ] IsolatedStorage.Delete(Key: String, [DataScope: DataScope])`	This deletes the value with the specified key from the Isolated Storage within the extension. The optional `DataScope` parameter is the scope to remove the value with the given key.

Isolated Storage is useful for storing sensitive data, user options, and license keys.

Let's consider the following example:

```
local procedure IsolatedStorageTest()
    var
        keyValue: Text;
    begin
        IsolatedStorage.Set('mykey','myvalue',DataScope::Company);
        if IsolatedStorage.Contains('mykey',DataScope::Company) then
        begin
            IsolatedStorage.Get('mykey',DataScope::Company,keyValue);
            Message('Key value retrieved is %1', keyValue);
        end;
        IsolatedStorage.Delete('mykey',DataScope::Company);
    end;
```

From the preceding code, we get the following:

1. `IsolatedStorage.Set`: In the first step, we save, in Isolated Storage, a key called `mykey` with a value of `myvalue` and `DataScope` set to `Company`. The key is visible in the scope of the company within the app context, so no other extensions can access this key.

2. `IsolatedStorage.Get`: In the second step, we check whether a key called `mykey` is saved in Isolated Storage with `DataScope` set to `Company`. If a match is found (key and scope), the key is retrieved (with the `Get` method) and the value is returned in the `keyValue` text variable.

3. `IsolatedStorage.Delete`: In the last step, we delete the key for this `DataScope`.

As previously said, you could also use Isolated Storage to save license keys or license details for your extension. The following code shows how to export the records of a table called `License` to JSON, then how to encrypt the JSON value, and finally how to store the encrypted text in Isolated Storage:

```
local procedure StoreLicense()
    var
        StorageKey: Text;
        LicenseText: Text;
        EncryptManagement: Codeunit "Cryptography Management";
        License: Record License temporary;

    begin
        StorageKey := GetStorageKey();
        LicenseText := License.WriteLicenseToJson();
        if EncryptManagement.IsEncryptionEnabled() and
EncryptManagement.IsEncryptionPossible() then
            LicenseText := EncryptManagement.Encrypt(LicenseText);
        if IsolatedStorage.Contains(StorageKey, DataScope::Module)
then
            IsolatedStorage.Delete(StorageKey);
        IsolatedStorage.Set(StorageKey, LicenseText,
DataScope::Module);
    end;

    local procedure GetStorageKey(): Text
    var
        //Returns a GUID
        StorageKeyTxt: Label 'dd03d28e-4acb-48d9-9520-c854495362b6',
Locked = true;
    begin
        exit(StorageKeyTxt);
```

```
        end;

    local procedure ReadLicense()
    var
        StorageKey: Text;
        LicenseText: Text;
        EncryptManagement: Codeunit "Cryptography Management";
        License: Record License temporary;
    begin
        StorageKey := GetStorageKey();
        if IsolatedStorage.Contains(StorageKey, DataScope::Module)
then
            IsolatedStorage.Get(StorageKey, DataScope::Module,
LicenseText);
        if EncryptManagement.IsEncryptionEnabled() and
EncryptManagement.IsEncryptionPossible() then
            LicenseText := EncryptManagement.Decrypt(LicenseText);
        License.ReadLicenseFromJson(LicenseText);
    end;
```

Here, the `License` table is declared as a temporary table. In this way, the data is isolated into the calling codeunit.

With the Dynamics 365 Business Central wave 2 release, there are some changes related to secret management with Isolated Storage. Here are the details:

- In Dynamics 365 Business Central SaaS, sensitive data stored in Isolated Storage is always encrypted.
- In Dynamics 365 Business Central on-premise, encryption is controlled by the end user (via the **Data Encryption Management** page):
    - If encryption is turned on, a secret stored in the Isolated Storage is automatically encrypted.
    - A secret that was inserted while encryption was turned off will remain unencrypted if encryption is turned on.
    - If you turn off encryption, the secret will be decrypted.

According to these changes, if you have an extension that works for Dynamics 365 Business Central SaaS and on-premise and you're using Isolated Storage to store secrets, you need to check whether encryption is enabled (which is always true for SaaS) and then save the secret accordingly.

So, a function that saves a license key to Isolated Storage and that works for Dynamics 365 Business Central SaaS and on-premise will be as follows:

```
local procedure StoreLicense()
var
    licenseKeyValue: Text;
begin
    if not EncryptionEnabled() then
IsolatedStorage.Set('LicenseKey',licenseKeyValue,DataScope::Module)
    else
IsolatedStorage.SetEncrypted('LicenseKey',licenseKeyValue,DataScope::M
odule)
end;
```

With the `SetEncrypted` method, you can now automatically save a secret by using encryption (no more calls to the `Cryptography Management` codeunit).

We have seen how to use Isolated Storage to improve data security in our extensions. In the next section, we'll see how to create control add-ins.

Working with control add-ins

Control add-in objects are a way to add custom functionalities (functions or UI customizations) to the Dynamics 365 Business Central client. A control add-in can interact with Dynamics 365 Business Central events and can raise events for your AL code.

A control add-in can be defined in AL code by using the `tcontroladdin` snippet, which has the following structure:

```
controladdin MyControlAddIn
{
    RequestedHeight = 300;
    MinimumHeight = 300;
    MaximumHeight = 300;
    RequestedWidth = 700;
    MinimumWidth = 700;
    MaximumWidth = 700;
    VerticalStretch = true;
    VerticalShrink = true;
    HorizontalStretch = true;
    HorizontalShrink = true;
    Scripts =
        'script1.js',
        'script2.js';
```

```
        StyleSheets =
            'style.css';
        StartupScript = 'startupScript.js';
        RecreateScript = 'recreateScript.js';
        RefreshScript = 'refreshScript.js';
        Images =
            'image1.png',
            'image2.png';
        event MyEvent()
        procedure MyProcedure()
    }
```

As you can see from the code snippet, when you define a `controladdin` object, you need to set the `Scripts` property to include the scripts of your control add-in (in a JavaScript file). These scripts can be local `.js` files or external files referenced via HTTP or HTTPS.

The `StartupScript` property permits you to call a script that must be executed when the page that hosts the `controladdin` object is loaded. You can style your `controladdin` object by using the `StyleSheet` property (which permits you to reference a CSS file) and the `Images` property (which permits you to load images into your add-in).

 When defining the style of a `controladdin` object in Dynamics 365 Business Central, please always refer to the *Control Add-in Style Guide* at the following link: https://docs.microsoft.com/en-us/ dynamics365/business-central/dev-itpro/developer/devenv-control-addin-style.

As a basic example, here we create a control add-in object that will be placed in a Dynamics 365 Business Central page (specifically, an Item Card).

The `controladdin` object is composed of two JavaScript files:

- `Start.js`, which contains the startup script and is loaded when the Dynamics 365 Business Central object that contains the add-in starts
- `Main.js`, which contains the add-in business logic

The `Start.js` JavaScript file is defined as follows:

```
init();
var controlAddin = document.getElementById('controlAddIn');
controlAddin.innerHTML = 'This is our D365BC control addin';
Microsoft.Dynamics.NAV.InvokeExtensibilityMethod("ControlReady", []);
```

Here, we initialize the add-in object, we print some HTML text inside the add-in, and we use the `InvokeExtensibilityMethod` method to invoke the AL trigger on the page that contains the add-in.

 More information about the `InvokeExtensibilityMethod` method can be found at https://docs.microsoft.com/en-us/ dynamics365/business-central/dev-itpro/developer/methods/ devenv-invokeextensibility-method.

The `Main.js` JavaScript file is defined as follows:

```
function init()
{
    window.alert('INIT');
}

function HelloWorld()
{
    window.alert('HELLO WORLD FROM D365BC ADDIN');
}
```

Now, in Visual Studio Code, we create the `controladdin` object, as follows:

```
controladdin DemoD365BCAddin
{
    RequestedHeight = 300;
    MinimumHeight = 300;
    MaximumHeight = 300;
    RequestedWidth = 700;
    MinimumWidth = 250;
    MaximumWidth = 700;
    VerticalStretch = true;
    VerticalShrink = true;
    HorizontalStretch = true;
    HorizontalShrink = true;
    Scripts = 'Scripts/main.js';
    StyleSheets = 'CSS/stylesheet.css';
    StartupScript = 'Scripts/start.js';
    Images = 'Images/Avatar.png';
    event ControlReady()
    procedure HelloWorld()
}
```

In the preceding code, we can see the following:

- `VerticalStretch` specifies that the add-in can be enlarged vertically.
- `VerticalShrink` specifies that the add-in can be made smaller vertically.
- `HorizontalStretch` specifies that the add-in can be enlarged horizontally.
- `HorizontalShrink` specifies that the add-in can be made smaller horizontally.
- `MinimumHeight/MaximumHeight` specifies the minimum/maximum height that the control add-in can be shrunk or stretched to.
- `MinimumWidth/MaximumWidth` specifies the minimum/maximum width that the control add-in can be shrunk or stretched to.
- `RequestedHeight` and `RequestedWidth` specify the height and width of the add-in control inside the page.

The `controladdin` object references the previously described scripts, and it can reference a stylesheet (CSS) file, where you can handle the appearance of the add-in. In this example, we have used a simple stylesheet:

```
#controlAddIn
{
    width: 300px;
    margin-top: 25px;
    border: 2px;
    background-color: lightcoral;
    box-sizing: border-box;
    border: 2px solid red;
}
```

To add the `controladdin` object to the Item Card page, we create a `pageextension` object, and here we add a `usercontrol` field as follows:

```
pageextension 50100 ItemCardExt extends "Item Card"
{
    layout
    {
        addlast(Item)
        {
            group(AddinGroup)
            {
                Caption = 'Control Add-in';
                usercontrol(DemoAddin; DemoD365BCAddin)
                {
                    ApplicationArea = All;
```

```
trigger ControlReady()
begin
    CurrPage.DemoAddin.HelloWorld();
end;
            }
        }
    }
  }
}
```

The `usercontrol` field triggers the `ControlReady` event, and from this event, we call the `HelloWord` method (defined in the `main.js` file).

The final result is the following. When the page is loaded, the `INIT` method is triggered:

This is the HTML of the Dynamics 365 Business Central page, where you can see the control add-in in the `div` element:

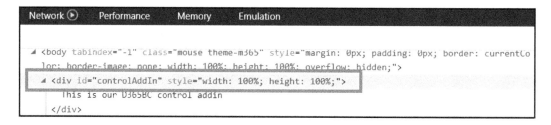

Then, the add-in triggers the `ControlReady` event and our JavaScript `HelloWorld` function is executed:

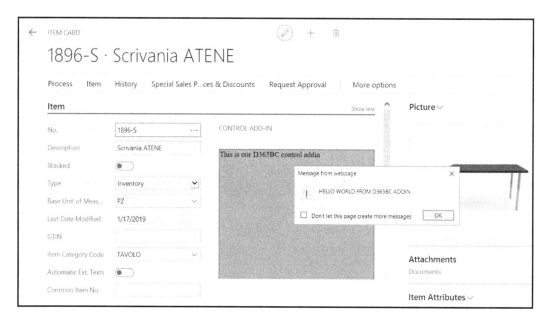

We have seen how to create visual control add-ins and how to use them inside a Dynamics 365 Business Central page. In the next section, we'll see how to create and use a timer-based control add-in.

Creating a timer-based control add-in

Control add-ins are useful also for creating timer-based logic inside a Dynamics 365 Business Central page (which is called **ping-pong** logic) to execute business logic every *N* times.

In our AL project, we define our `controladdin` object as follows:

```
controladdin D365BCPingPong
{
    Scripts = 'Scripts/pingpong.js';
    StartupScript = 'Scripts/start.js';
    HorizontalShrink = true;
    HorizontalStretch = true;
    MinimumHeight = 1;
    MinimumWidth = 1;
    RequestedHeight = 1;
    RequestedWidth = 1;
    VerticalShrink = true;
    VerticalStretch = true;

    procedure SetTimerInterval(milliSeconds: Integer);
    procedure StartTimer();
    procedure StopTimer();

    event ControlAddInReady();
    event PingPongError();
    event TimerElapsed();
}
```

The `start.js` file contains the add-in initialization:

```
$(document).ready(function()
{
    initializeControlAddIn('controlAddIn');
});
```

The `pingpong.js` file contains the JavaScript business logic of our add-in:

```
"use strict"
var timerInterval;
var timerObject;
function initializeControlAddIn(id) {
    var controlAddIn = document.getElementById(id);
    controlAddIn.innerHTML =
        '<div id="ping-pong">' +
        '</div>';
    pageLoaded();
```

```
Microsoft.Dynamics.NAV.InvokeExtensibilityMethod('ControlAddInReady',
null);
}

function pageLoaded() {
}

function SetTimerInterval(milliSeconds) {
    timerInterval = milliSeconds;
}

function StartTimer() {
    if (timerInterval == 0 || timerInterval == null) {
Microsoft.Dynamics.NAV.InvokeExtensibilityMethod('PingPongError', ['No
timer interval was set.']);
        return;
    }
    timerObject = window.setInterval(ExecuteTimer, timerInterval);
}

function StopTimer() {
    clearInterval(timerObject);
}

function ExecuteTimer() {
    Microsoft.Dynamics.NAV.InvokeExtensibilityMethod('TimerElapsed',
null);
}
```

We can now insert our add-in object to a Dynamics 365 Business Central page (for example, the Item Card) and from here, we can call the add-in methods, as follows:

```
pageextension 50100 ItemCardExt extends "Item Card"
{
    layout
    {
        addlast(Item)
        {
            group(userControlTimer)
            {
                usercontrol(D365BCPingPong; D365BCPingPong)
                {
                    ApplicationArea = All;

                    trigger TimerElapsed()
                    begin
                        //Stops the timer when the timer has elapsed
                        CurrPage.D365BCPingPong.StopTimer();
```

```
                        //Here you can have your code that must be
executed every tick
                        Message('Run your timer-based code here');
                        CurrPage.D365BCPingPong.StartTimer();
                    end;
                }
            }
        }
    }

    trigger OnAfterGetCurrRecord()
    begin
        //Sets a timer interval every 10 seconds
        CurrPage.D365BCPingPong.SetTimerInterval(10000);
        CurrPage.D365BCPingPong.StartTimer();
    end;
}
```

Here, we set a timer interval (for example, 10 seconds) and start the timer. When the timer tick has elapsed, the `TimerElapsed` trigger is called and your custom business logic is executed. When the `TimerElapsed` trigger is raised, it's important to stop the timer to avoid raising a new event while the message is still displayed (as you can see, we stop the timer, run the custom code, and then restart the timer).

 More information about **control add-in** objects and properties can be found at `https://docs.microsoft.com/en-us/dynamics365/business-central/dev-itpro/developer/devenv-control-addin-object`.

A timer-based add-in is useful for executing timer-based operations or refreshing pages.

In the next section, we'll see how to use notifications in Dynamics 365 Business Central to better handle errors and messages in the standard UI.

Notifications inside Dynamics 365 Business Central

Dynamics 365 Business Central permits you to programmatically send non-intrusive notifications to your users inside the web client user interface to display information, messages, or error notifications. These notifications are non-modal, so they don't require your users to stop working and perform some action on the notification message immediately. They can also be dismissed if necessary.

Notifications appear in the **notification bar** at the top of the page in which the user is currently working. The application can send multiple notifications to the user, and they will all appear in the notification bar in chronological order. They will remain in the notification bar until the user takes action on them, dismisses them or for the duration of the page instance.

As a developer, you can programmatically create notifications by using the `Notification` and `NotificationScope` AL objects.

As an example of how to use `Notifications` inside Dynamics 365 Business Central, we will create a notification in the `Purchase Order` page that appears if the selected `Vendor` has a balance due.

The `pageextension` object is defined as follows:

```
pageextension 50100 PurchaseOrderExt extends "Purchase Order"
{
    trigger OnOpenPage()
    var
        Vendor: Record Vendor;
        VendorNotification: Notification;
        OpenVendor: Text;
        TextNotification: Label 'This Vendor has a Balance due. Please
check before sending orders.';
        TextNotificationAction: Label 'Check balance due';
    begin
        Vendor.Get("Buy-from Vendor No.");
        Vendor.CalcFields("Balance Due");
        if Vendor."Balance Due" > 0 then begin
            VendorNotification.Message(TextNotification);
            VendorNotification.Scope := NotificationScope::LocalScope;
            VendorNotification.SetData('VendorNo', Vendor."No.");
            VendorNotification.AddAction(TextNotificationAction,
Codeunit::ActionHandler, 'OpenVendor');
            VendorNotification.Send();
```

```
            end;
        end;
    }
```

We are checking whether the vendor has a balance due. If so, a Notification object is created. A Notification object has a Message property (that defines the content of the notification that will appear in the UI) and Scope. Now, Scope defines where the message will appear to the user, and it could be one of the following:

- LocalScope (default): The notification will appear on the user's current page.
- GlobalScope (not currently supported): The notification will appear regardless of which page the user is working on.

When defining the Notification object, we use the SetData method to set a data property value to the notification (in this case, the Vendor number) and we use the AddAction method to add an action to the notification message (we want an action that immediately opens the Vendor Card page). The AddAction method starts a method called OpenVendor, defined in a codeunit called ActionHandler.

The codeunit object for this is defined as follows:

```
codeunit 50100 ActionHandler
{
    procedure OpenVendor(VendorNotification: Notification)
    var
        VendorCode: Text;
        Vendor: Record Vendor;
        VendorCard: Page "Vendor Card";
    begin
        VendorCode := VendorNotification.GetData('VendorNo');
        if Vendor.Get(VendorCode) then begin
            VendorCard.SetRecord(Vendor);
            VendorCard.Run();
        end;
    end;
}
```

Here, when the action inside the notification is clicked, the code retrieves the VendorNo parameter from the Notification object, retrieves the Vendor record, and opens the Vendor Card by passing the retrieved record.

When you open a Purchase Order from Dynamics 365 Business Central and the selected vendor has a balance due, you will now see the following notification:

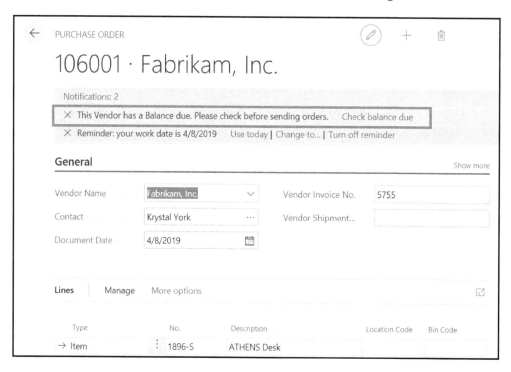

If you click on the **Check balance due** action inside the notification, the `Vendor Card` page with the selected vendor record is opened and the user can act accordingly.

Notifications are extremely important to use when you create extensions for Dynamics 365 Business Central because they will permit you to give a better experience to your users.

In the next section, we'll see how to use asynchronous programming inside Dynamics 365 Business Central.

Understanding page background tasks

Dynamics 365 Business Central version 15 introduces a new feature to handle asynchronous programming called **page background tasks**.

Page background tasks permit you to define a read-only and long-running process on a page that can be executed asynchronously in a background thread (isolated from the parent session). You can start the task and continue working on the page without waiting for the task to complete. The following diagram (provided by Microsoft) shows the flow of a background task:

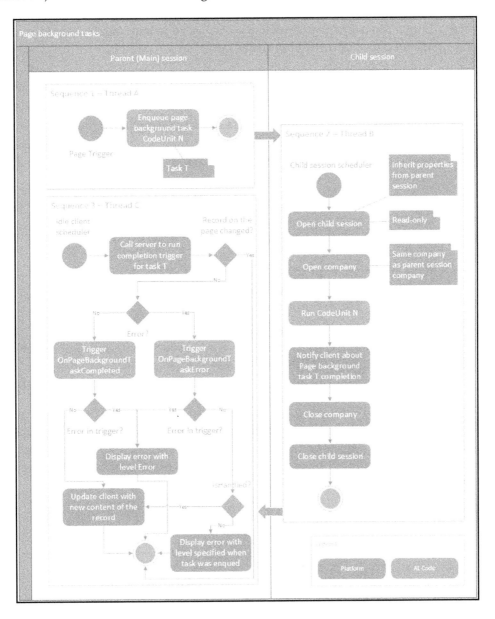

A page background task has the following properties:

- It's a read-only session (it cannot write or lock the database).
- It can be canceled and it has a default and maximum timeout.
- Its lifetime is controlled by the current record (it is canceled when the current record is changed, the page is closed, or the session ends).
- Completion triggers are invoked on the page session (such as updating page records and refreshing the UI).
- It can be queued up.
- The parameters passed to and returned from page background tasks are in the form of a `Dictionary<string, string>` object.
- The callback triggers cannot execute operations on the UI, except notifications and control updates.
- There is a limit on the number of background tasks per session (if the limit is reached, the tasks are queued).

To create a page background task, the basic steps are as follows:

- Create a codeunit that contains the business logic to execute in the background.
- On the page where the task must be started, do the following:
    - Add code that creates the background task (`EnqueueBackgroundTask`).
    - Handle the task completion results by using the `OnPageBackgroundTaskCompleted` trigger (this is where you can update the page UI).
    - You can also use the `OnPageBackgroundTaskError` trigger to handle possible task errors.

Here is an example of how to implement the preceding logic. In the Customer Card, we want to execute a background task that calculates some sales statistics values for the selected customer without blocking the UI (in a more complex scenario, imagine retrieving this data from an external service).

Our calling page (Customer Card) passes a Dictionary<string,string> object (a key-value pair) to the background task with the key set to CustomerNo and the value set to the No. field of our selected **Customer** record. The task codeunit retrieves the CustomerNo value, calculates the total sales amount for this customer, the number of items sold, and the number of items shipped and returns a Dictionary<string><string> object with the key set to TotalSales and a value that is the calculated sales amount.

The task codeunit is defined as follows:

```
codeunit 50105 TaskCodeunit
{
    trigger OnRun()
    var
        Result: Dictionary of [Text, Text];
        CustomerNo: Code[20];
        CustomerSalesValue: Text;
        NoOfSalesValue: Text;
        NoOfItemsShippedValue: Text;
    begin
        CustomerNo :=
Page.GetBackgroundParameters().Get('CustomerNo');
        if CustomerNo = '' then
            Error('Invalid parameter CustomerNo');
        if CustomerNo <> '' then begin
            CustomerSalesValue :=
Format(GetCustomerSalesAmount(CustomerNo));
            NoOfSalesValue := Format(GetNoOfItemsSales(CustomerNo));
            NoOfItemsShippedValue :=
Format(GetNoOfItemsShipped(CustomerNo));
            //sleep for demo purposes
            Sleep((Random(5)) * 1000);
        end;
        Result.Add('TotalSales', CustomerSalesValue);
        Result.Add('NoOfSales', NoOfSalesValue);
        Result.Add('NoOfItemsShipped', NoOfItemsShippedValue);
        Page.SetBackgroundTaskResult(Result);
    end;

    local procedure GetCustomerSalesAmount(CustomerNo: Code[20]):
Decimal
    var
        SalesLine: Record "Sales Line";
        amount: Decimal;
    begin
        SalesLine.SetRange("Document Type", SalesLine."Document
Type"::Order);
```

```
    SalesLine.SetRange("Sell-to Customer No.", CustomerNo);
    if SalesLine.FindSet() then
        repeat
            amount += SalesLine."Line Amount";
        until SalesLine.Next() = 0;
    exit(amount);
end;

local procedure GetNoOfItemsSales(CustomerNo: Code[20]): Decimal
var
    SalesLine: Record "Sales Line";
    total: Decimal;
begin
    SalesLine.SetRange("Document Type", SalesLine."Document
Type"::Order);
    SalesLine.SetRange("Sell-to Customer No.", CustomerNo);
    SalesLine.SetRange(Type, SalesLine.Type::Item);
    if SalesLine.FindSet() then
        repeat
            total += SalesLine.Quantity;
        until SalesLine.Next() = 0;
    exit(total);
end;

local procedure GetNoOfItemsShipped(CustomerNo: Code[20]): Decimal
var
    SalesShiptmentLine: Record "Sales Shipment Line";
    total: Decimal;
begin
    SalesShiptmentLine.SetRange("Sell-to Customer No.",
CustomerNo);
    SalesShiptmentLine.SetRange(Type,
SalesShiptmentLine.Type::Item);
    if SalesShiptmentLine.FindSet() then
    repeat
        total += SalesShiptmentLine.Quantity
    until SalesShiptmentLine.Next() = 0;
    exit(total);
end;
}
```

Then, we create a `pageextension` object to extend the Customer Card to add the new `SalesAmount`, `NoOfSales`, and `NoOfItemsShipped` fields (calculated by the background task) and to add code to start the task and read the results. The `pageextension` object is defined as follows:

```
pageextension 50105 CustomerCardExt extends "Customer Card"
{
    layout
    {
        addlast(General)
        {
            field(SalesAmount; SalesAmount)
            {
                ApplicationArea = All;
                Caption = 'Sales Amount';
                Editable = false;
            }
            field(NoOfSales; NoOfSales)
            {
                ApplicationArea = All;
                Caption = 'No. of Sales';
                Editable = false;
            }
            field(NoOfItemsShipped; NoOfItemsShipped)
            {
                ApplicationArea = All;
                Caption = 'Total of Items Shipped';
                Editable = false;
            }
        }
    }
    var
        // Global variable used for the TaskID
        TaskSalesId: Integer;
        // Variables for the sales amount field (calculated from the
background task)
        SalesAmount: Decimal;
        NoOfSales: Decimal;
        NoOfItemsShipped: Decimal;

    trigger OnAfterGetCurrRecord()
    var
        TaskParameters: Dictionary of [Text, Text];
    begin
        TaskParameters.Add('CustomerNo', Rec."No.");
        CurrPage.EnqueueBackgroundTask(TaskSalesId, 50105,
TaskParameters, 20000, PageBackgroundTaskErrorLevel::Warning);
```

```
    end;

    trigger OnPageBackgroundTaskCompleted(TaskId: Integer; Results:
Dictionary of [Text, Text])
    var
        PBTNotification: Notification;
    begin
        if (TaskId = TaskSalesId) then begin
            Evaluate(SalesAmount, Results.Get('TotalSales'));
            Evaluate(NoOfSales, Results.Get('NoOfSales'));
            Evaluate(NoOfItemsShipped,
Results.Get('NoOfItemsShipped'));
            PBTNotification.Message('Sales Statistics updated.');
            PBTNotification.Send();
        end;
    end;

    trigger OnPageBackgroundTaskError(TaskId: Integer; ErrorCode:
Text; ErrorText: Text; ErrorCallStack: Text; var IsHandled: Boolean)
    var
        PBTErrorNotification: Notification;
    begin
        if (ErrorText = 'Invalid parameter CustomerNo') then begin
            IsHandled := true;
            PBTErrorNotification.Message('Something went wrong.
Invalid parameter CustomerNo.');
            PBTErrorNotification.Send();
        end
        else
            if (ErrorText = 'Child Session task was terminated because
of a timeout.') then begin
                IsHandled := true;
                PBTErrorNotification.Message('It took to long to get
results. Try again.');
                PBTErrorNotification.Send();
            end
    end;
}
```

In the OnAfterGetCurrRecord trigger, we add the parameters required to start our background task and call the EnqueueBackgroundTask method. The EnqueueBackgroundTask method creates and queues a background task that runs the specified codeunit (without a UI) in a read-only child session of the page session. If the task completes successfully, the OnPageBackgroundTaskCompleted trigger is invoked. If an error occurs, the OnPageBackgroundTaskError trigger is invoked. If the page is closed before the task completes, or the page record ID on the task changed, the task is canceled.

In the `OnPageBackgroundTaskCompleted` trigger, we retrieve the `TotalSales` parameter from the dictionary and the UI (the relative field on the page) is updated accordingly.

We have seen how to use the new asynchronous programming features inside Dynamics 365 Business Central pages. This is an important feature that improves general application performance in many scenarios.

Summary

In this chapter, we covered a lot of advanced topics and saw some tricks for implementing particular tasks with the AL language extension, especially how to handle files and pictures, using XMLports, creating and extending Role Centers and headlines, handling XML and JSON serializations, consuming web services and APIs via AL code, and publishing a web service from an extension. Apart from this, we can use Isolated Storage to store sensitive data in an extension and we learned how to create control add-ins, how to handle notifications, and how to use asynchronous programming features (page background tasks) in your extensions.

After reading this chapter, you're now able to create advanced customizations to improve general user experience and to handle different business tasks.

In the next chapter, we'll see how to customize, develop, and publish reports for Dynamics 365 Business Central.

Report Development with AL 7

In this book, we have been introduced to and analyzed a vast variety of AL language objects, and we've seen how to develop simple to complex extensions with them.

In this chapter, we will deep dive into a specific object and look at its properties, triggers, and methods and how to use it proficiently. This object is **the report object**.

An overview, with pros and cons, will be provided regarding which tool to use to design and develop datasets and layouts, such as Microsoft Word for Word layouts and Microsoft Report Builder for **Report Definition Language** (**RDL**) layouts. We will discuss the main shortcuts, tips, and tricks related to dataset development with Visual Studio Code and both Word and RDL layouts.

In this chapter, we aspire to provide you with the confidence you need to develop Dynamics 365 Business Central report extensions, explain how to make them perform to their best, and help you troubleshoot the most common issues in this area.

In this chapter, we will cover the following topics:

- Anatomy of the AL report object
- Tools to use for Word and RDL layouts
- Converting an existing C/AL report into AL
- Feature limitation when developing an RDL or Word layout report
- Understanding report performance considerations

Anatomy of the AL report object

Requests for new reports come from every department and in many different forms. Most of the time, users have an idea in mind of how they would like the data to be shown.

Nevertheless, a report developer should always keep in mind some important points. Everything is related to data:

- **Retrieval**: A good report developer should have a good knowledge of the business process (how data is created, modified, and deleted) and data topology (where data is stored). Data can be retrieved from heterogenous resources that cannot be directly stored in Dynamics 365 Business Central tables. As an example, you might want to run an HTTP call to a web service to gather some data outside the database and store it in a physical or temporary table before processing it.
- **Processing**: Some of the data that's presented could be the result of data aggregation, could be calculated from different fields, or could even be the results from a concatenation of values from different tables. The result of data retrieval and processing generates the dataset.
- **Presentation**: Datasets are sent from the application to the Report Viewer component, which takes care of data rendering and presentation. Together with the dataset, a report definition file (`Report.rdlc`) is sent to the Report Viewer to build up the content of the report. The report definition file contains the metadata structure and rules to render the report. Despite its extension (`.rdlc`), this is actually an XML-formatted flat file. Tools such as the Report Builder or Visual Studio can digest the XML file and create a presentation of the report structure in a more human-readable way. Every action that's taken in this designer has the consequence of editing and changing the XML file.

With Dynamics 365 Business Central, it is also possible to design reports to perform only data retrieval and processing, typically committing changes in tables as a result of the process. No data is presented to the users, hence no layout is needed, and no dataset will be created.

Reports can be grouped into two main categories: processing only and dataset-based.

Reports that are processing only do not have any layout. They also typically do not have any columns defined in the dataset and are only used to process data. Quite often, the same result could be achieved using codeunit objects instead since these are just simple code repositories and do not have any graphical or **User Interface** (**UI**) interaction. To give you a simple example, you could create a processing-only report with a data item that loops all the customer records and prints a flat JSON file with the customer number, name, and email. The same could be achieved by implementing a codeunit with a function that declares an `IF CustomerRec FINDSET THEN REPEAT UNTIL NEXT=0` loop. Within this loop, it is possible to write a flat JSON file with exactly the same information.

The pros and cons of using a processing-only report or a codeunit have been tabulated here:

	Processing Only Report	Codeunit
Easy to Implement	It's faster. The data item looping construct is predefined.	There's more development activity to build a loop.
Flexibility	It's limited to data item triggers.	It's more flexible.
Performance	It has worse performance.	It has better performance.

A report object has the following tree structure:

- **Request Page**:
    - **Columns**:
        - **Groups**:
            - **Fields**

    - **Actions**
- **Dataset**:
    - **Data items**:
        - **Properties**
        - **Triggers**
        - **Columns**:
            - **Properties**
            - **Triggers**

    - **Labels**:
        - **Properties**
    - **Layout**:
        - **RDL**
        - **Word**

After installing the standard **AL Language extension** and **CRS AL Language extension tool**, we could use a `treport` or `treport` (CRS) snippet to create a prototype of a report and inspect all the different items related to the main content areas: the dataset and the request page. Layouts are just references to the corresponding output (an RDL and/or Word file) within the report objects, and these are created with tools other than Visual Studio Code. We will work with them later in this chapter.

After exploring the anatomy of a report object in AL, it is time to see the tools that are used in Word and RDL layouts.

Tools to use for Word and RDL layouts

Visual Studio Code does not have a valid extension—yet—that would replace the best-in-class RDL report editor, which is supported by the Dynamics 365 Business Central development team. With a release every six months, the application is always up to date and, at the time of writing, it deploys Report Viewer 2017 and the latest RDL 2016 schema-based syntax.

To develop an RDL layout report, you have two choices:

- **Report Builder for SQL Server 2016**: `https://www.microsoft.com/en-us/download/details.aspx?id=53613`
- **Visual Studio 2017 with the Microsoft RDLC Report Designer for the Visual Studio extension installed**: `https://marketplace.visualstudio.com/items?itemName=ProBITools.MicrosoftRdlcReportDesignerforVisualStudio-18001`

To find out more, please visit the following official reference and this useful blog:

- `https://docs.microsoft.com/en-us/dynamics365/business-central/dev-itpro/deployment/system-requirement-business-central`
- `https://thinkaboutit.be/2019/01/how-do-i-configure-my-rdlc-layout-designers-for-vscode/`

The Word layout feature is built around the latest Aspose.Words (`https://products.aspose.com/words`) component and is implemented in the application by the backend server team. Designing and editing must be done with a version of Microsoft Word that supports XML mappings. Minimum system requirements specify that we should use **Microsoft Word 2016** or later.

RDL and Word layout features

To explain and show some of the most important RDL and Word layout features supported by Dynamics 365 Business Central, we will go through a step-by-step example.

In `Chapter 5`, *Developing a Customized Solution for Dynamics 365 Business Central*, we extended the Item Ledger Entry table by creating the Customer Category field for statistics. It is now time to create a report that uses this extended field for sales analysis purposes. Create a new directory in your extension called `.\Src\CustomerCategory\report`. Let's learn how to do this.

Part 1 – Designing the dataset

The dataset is designed within the report by specifying the data item field's columns and their properties. They have a big influence from a qualitative perspective (in which format is data exported?) and from a quantitative perspective (how many rows are processed?). Both have a clear impact on report performance.

A short example is represented by decimal data types. When specifying a decimal data type in a dataset, two fields are always included: the decimal data and its formatting. This means that, together with the decimal field, you always have a repeated text variable tightly bound to it. This would increase the dimension of the dataset and, consequently, influence report performance.

What could be the definition of a Dynamics 365 Business Central dataset? Here's mine:

> *"A dataset is like a table in the client memory whose columns are made of all of the column fields defined in the dataset section and whose rows are all valid (not skipped) records that are processed in the DataItems."*

Let's design/create our report dataset:

1. Create a new file in the `.\Src\CustomerCategory\report` folder called `Rep50111.ItemLedegerEntryAnalysis.al`.

2. Type `treport` or `treport` (CRS) to enable the report snippet.

3. Add the following data item and columns:

```
report 50111 "Item Ledger Entry Analysis"
{
    Caption ='Item Ledger Entry Analysis';
```

```al
        UsageCategory=ReportsAndAnalysis;
        ApplicationArea = All;
    dataset
    {
        dataitem("Item Ledger Entry";"Item Ledger Entry")
        {
            column(ItemNo_ItemLedgerEntry;"Item Ledger
Entry"."Item No.")
            {
                IncludeCaption = true;
            }
            column(PostingDate_ItemLedgerEntry;"Item Ledger
Entry"."Posting Date")
            {
                IncludeCaption = true;
            }
            column(EntryType_ItemLedgerEntry;"Item Ledger
Entry"."Entry Type")
            {
                IncludeCaption = true;
            }
            column(CustCatPKT_ItemLedgerEntry;"Item Ledger
Entry"."Customer Category_PKT")
            {
                IncludeCaption = true;
            }
            column(DocumentNo_ItemLedgerEntry;"Item Ledger
Entry"."Document No.")
            {
                IncludeCaption = true;
            }
            column(Description_ItemLedgerEntry;"Item Ledger
Entry".Description)
            {
                IncludeCaption = true;
            }
            column(LocationCode_ItemLedgerEntry;"Item Ledger
Entry"."Location Code")
            {
                IncludeCaption = true;
            }
            column(Quantity_ItemLedgerEntry;"Item Ledger
Entry".Quantity)
            {
                IncludeCaption = true;
            }
            column(COMPANYNAME;CompanyName)
            {
```

```
            }
            column(includeLogo;includeLogo)
            {
            }
            column(CompanyInfo_Picture;CompanyInfo.Picture)
            {
            }
        }
    }
```

After this, we add the labels:

```
    labels
        {
            PageNo = 'Page';
            BCReportName ='Item Ledger Entry Analysis';
        }
        var
            CompanyInfo: Record "Company Information";
            includeLogo: Boolean;

    }
```

4. Build and publish the extension as is in your online or Docker-contained sandbox.
5. Go to **Report Layout Selection** and filter for your report's ID or name.
6. Select **Actions | Custom Layouts**.
7. Click **New**, select **Insert RDLC layout**, and click **OK**. This will add an empty RDL layout to the report and reference the dataset structure.
8. Choose **Process | Export Layout** and save the `Default.rdl` report in the `.\Src\CustomerCategory\report` folder. You might call the report layout `Rep50111.ItemLedgerEntryAnalysis.rdl`.
9. Bind the report to the RDL layout within the extension and make RDL the default layout by specifying the following parameter in the AL report object:

```
    report 50111 "Item Ledger Entry Analysis"
    {
        DefaultLayout = RDLC;
        RDLCLayout =
    './Src/CustomerCategory/report/Report50111.ItemLedgerEntryAnal
    ysis.rdl';
      Caption = 'Item Ledger Entry Analysis';
```

10. In Visual Studio Code, right-click the RDL file and choose **Open externally**. It will open in whichever program you selected to work with the `.rdl` file extension by default. In this example, we will work with **Microsoft SQL Server Report Builder 2016**.

11. If it's not already enabled, be sure to have the **Report Data** option checked in the **View | Show/Hide** ribbon menu in your Report Builder 2016 instance. In the **Report Data** pane, expand `Parameters` and `DataSets`.

You will notice that `Parameters` items are labels and field captions (specified by the `IncludeCaption=true` property in the dataset). `DataSet_Results` shows the entire dataset's definition transposed into the Report Builder IDE. Here is a screenshot of the Report Data pane:

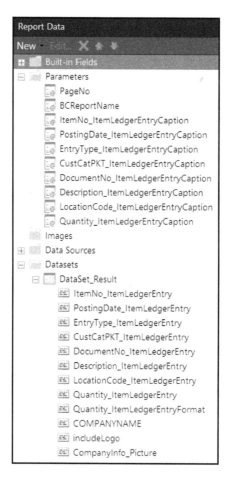

Part 2 – Creating a simple RDL layout

RDL layout development is one of the two layout design options you have for Dynamics 365 Business Central. Report layout design with Visual Studio 2017 (plus the Microsoft RDLC Report Designer for Visual Studio extension) has a fully-fledged development experience compared to Report Builder. An example is the Document Outline window, which shows a hierarchical view of the controls in the layout and lets you jump from one control to another quickly.

Specifically targeted at RDL layout development, you may find quite exhaustive official documentation from SQL Server Reporting Services, official courseware, or third-party books. This section contains some very good development references if you would like to completely master the RDL layout for Dynamics 365 Business Central. Even if they mostly come from earlier versions of Dynamics NAV or SQL Server Reporting Services, they still contain great hints, and you should spare them a spot in your personal library.

Here are some RDL layout development references:

Microsoft Dynamics NAV 2015 Professional Reporting	Renders (Packt)
Microsoft Dynamics NAV 2009: Professional Reporting	Renders (Packt)
Microsoft Dynamics NAV 2009 INSIDE Reporting	Gayer (Mbst)
Professional Microsoft SQL Server 2008 Reporting Services	Misner (Microsoft)

Part 2.1 – Creating the RDL report header

In this section, we will create the report header step by step:

1. In the **Report Builder**, let's set up the report properties: right-click anywhere in the gray development area and select **Report Properties**:

2. Change the **Page Setup** parameters, as follows:

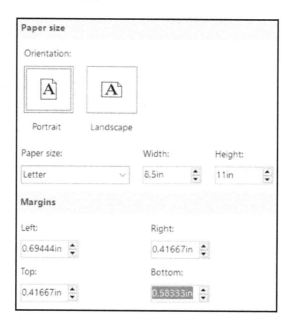

3. Let's add a page header: right-click anywhere in the gray development area and select **Add Page Header**.
4. Right-click anywhere in the page header and select **Header Properties**.
5. Edit **Page Header Properties** as follows:

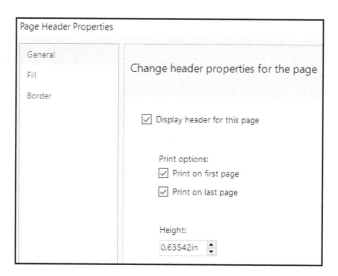

6. Click on the body section and change the body size property as follows:
   - **Width: 7.21205in**
   - **Height: 1.93403in**

7. Now, let's directly add some report item control to the header. Right-click anywhere in the report header and select **Insert | TextBox** in the page header. Perform this action six times.

8. Change the following properties for the textboxes:

Name	Value	Size	Location	Font	Padding	CanGrow	TextAlign	VerticalAlign
txtReportName	=Parameters!BCReportName.Value	7.5 cm; 0.423 cm	0 cm; 0.0005 cm	Arial; 8 pt; Default; Bold; Default	0 pt; 0 pt; 0 pt; 0 pt	False	Default	Middle
txtCompanyName	=Fields!COMPANYNAME.Value	7.5 cm; 0.423 cm	0 cm; 0.45878 cm	Arial; 7 pt; Default; Default; Default	0 pt; 0 pt; 0 pt; 0 pt	False	Default	Middle
txtExecutionTime	=Globals!ExecutionTime	3.15 cm; 0.423 cm	15 cm; 0.0005 cm	Arial; 7 pt; Default; Default; Default	0 pt; 0 pt; 0 pt; 0 pt	False	Right	Middle
txtPageNoLabel	=Parameters!PageNo.Value	1.25271 cm; 0.423 cm	16.44729 cm; 0.4235 cm	Arial; 7 pt; Default; Default; Default	0 pt; 0 pt; 0 pt; 0 pt	False	Left	Middle
txtPageNumber	=Globals!PageNumber	0.45 cm; 0.423 cm	17.7 cm; 0.45878 cm	Arial; 7 pt; Default; Default; Default	0 pt; 0 pt; 0 pt; 0 pt	False	Right	Middle
txtUserID	=User!UserID	3.15 cm; 0.423 cm	14.8868 cm; 0.91298 cm	Arial; 7 pt; Default; Default; Default	0 pt; 0 pt; 0 pt; 0 pt	False	Right	Middle

This is what it should look like in the report header section:

Part 2.2 – Adding a table control to the RDLC report body

In this section, we will add a table control in the report body to display data in a tabular format:

1. Right-click somewhere in the middle of the report body and choose **Insert**. Select the **Table** control from the menu. Keep the table small since we will need to add some extra columns and resize the width manually.
2. Select the last table column, right-click and select **Insert Column**, and choose **Right**:

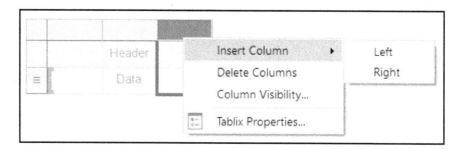

3. Repeat *step 2* three more times so that we have seven columns in total.
4. Keep the table aligned by changing the following table properties:
   - **Location: 0.02584 in; 0.18403in**
   - **Size: 7.06693 in; 0.48958in**

5. Change the column width property for each column, from left to right, as follows:

Column	1	2	3	4	5	6	7
Width (cm)	1,905	2,222	2,593	2,990	3,373	2,620	1,798

This should be the current layout result:

[@BCReportName]		[&ExecutionTime]
[COMPANYNAME]		[@PageNcber]
		[&UserID]
	Header	
	Data	

6. It is now time to set the table properties appropriately and bind them to the Dynamics 365 Business Central dataset. Select the table (once you have clicked on the table, a gray column/row area appears, and in a Microsoft Excel-like style, just click in the top left of this area to select the whole table).

7. In the **Properties** window, click the **Property Pages** button.

8. Change the values in the **General** tab as follows and click **OK**:
   - **Name:** tableItemLedgerEntry
   - **Dataset name:** Dataset_Result

Now, the table is bound to the appropriate dataset and it has a self-explanatory name. Giving an appropriate name to every single control in the RDL layout is useful because you can find out the purpose of the control and where it is located at a glance. Now, let's bind every table control to the dataset caption and field values.

9. For every single text box in the first row of the table (the table header row), open the **Property Pages** window and change the **Value** property of the first seven table header textboxes, as follows:

Name	Value
txtItemNoCap	=Parameters!ItemNo_ItemLedgerEntryCaption.Value
txtPostingDateCap	=Parameters!PostingDate_ItemLedgerEntryCaption.Value
txtCustCatPKTCap	=Parameters!CustCatPKT_ItemLedgerEntryCaption.Value
txtDocumentNoCap	=Parameters!DocumentNo_ItemLedgerEntryCaption.Value
txtDescriptionCap	=Parameters!Description_ItemLedgerEntryCaption.Value
txtLocationCodeCap	=Parameters!LocationCode_ItemLedgerEntryCaption.Value
txtQuantityCap	=Parameters!Quantity_ItemLedgerEntryCaption.Value

10. Let's bind table body text box controls to the dataset fields. For every text box in the second row of the table (the table body), open the **Property Pages** window and change the following properties:

Name	Value	Format
txtItemNo	=Fields!ItemNo_ItemLedgerEntry.Value	
txtPostingDate	=Fields!PostingDate_ItemLedgerEntry.Value	
txtCustCatPKT	=Fields!CustCatPKT_ItemLedgerEntry.Value	
txtDocumentNo	=Fields!DocumentNo_ItemLedgerEntry.Value	
txtDescription	=Fields!Description_ItemLedgerEntry.Value	
txtLocationCode	=Fields!LocationCode_ItemLedgerEntry.Value	
txtQuantity	=Fields!Quantity_ItemLedgerEntry.Value	=Fields!Quantity_ItemLedgerEntryFormat.Value

11. Create an alternate line color to make it easier to read. In the table details, select the seven textboxes mentioned in the previous table and add the following values to the following properties in each of these textboxes:
    - **Background Color**: =iif(RowNumber(Nothing) mod 2, "AliceBlue", "White")
    - **TextAlign**: **Right**

12. Conditionally format the **Color** property for the txtQuantity text box. Select txtQuantity and change the **Color** property as follows:
    - **Color**: =iif(Fields!Quantity_ItemLedgerEntry.Value <= 0, "Red", "Black")

13. Enable the ability to display the table header at the beginning of every page to improve report readability. Click on the small down arrow in **Column Groups** and enable **Advanced Mode**.

14. Select the **(Static)** group in **Row Groups**:

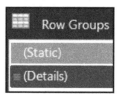

Change the properties for the **(Static)** group as follows:

- **KeepTogether**: True
- **RepeatOnNewPage**: True

Part 3 – Understanding grouping

With the term **grouping**, we mean the capacity of aggregate result sets based on one or more discriminant elements. Grouping is typically used to show totals per group and/or aggregate and calculate totals (typically using sum formulas). The grouping feature is used typically within controls that implement the data region scope, such as table, matrix, list, chart, and gauge.

In this section, we will create group totals for the table control of our report:

1. In the **Row Groups** section, right-click on the **(Details)** static row group and select **Add Group**. Choose **Parent Group...**.

2. A pop-up window should appear, asking you to provide a grouping element. Select the **[ItemNo_ItemLedgerEntry]** field value and choose to add both a group header and a group footer. Then, click **OK**:

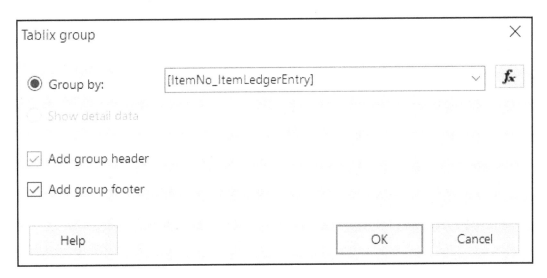

3. Select the group we've just created (typically named ItemNo_ItemLedgerEntry by default), right-click, and select **Group Properties...**.

4. In the **Group Properties** window, change the name to ItemNoGroup and click **OK**.

5. Select **ItemNoGroup**, right-click, and select **Add Group** and **Child Group....**.

6. A pop-up window appears, asking you to provide a grouping element. Select **CustCatPKT_ItemLedgerEntry**, choose to add just the group header (no group footer), and click **OK**.

7. Select the group we've just created, right-click, and select **Group Properties....**.

8. In the **Group Properties** window, change the **Name** to CustCatPKTNoGroup. Then, go to the **Advanced** tab and set **CustCatPKT_ItemLedgerEntry** in the **Recursive Parent** box. Click **OK** to confirm this:

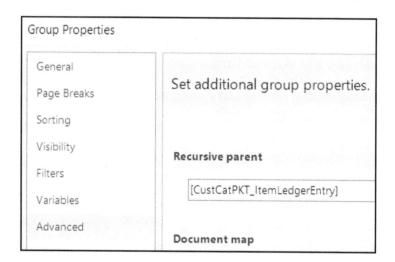

9. All of these operations should have created, by default, two extra unwanted columns in the table to display grouping elements. Select the first two columns and then right-click and choose **Delete Columns**.

10. The automatic action of adding two extra columns should have automatically enlarged the **Report Body**: bring this back to its original size. Set the following value:
    - **Size: 7.21205in; 1.93403in**

11. Let's add group caption labels. Select the first text box in the **ItemNoGroup** header row, as shown in the following screenshot:

Change its properties as follows:

- **Name**: txtItemNoGroup
- **Value**: =Fields!ItemNo_ItemLedgerEntry.Value
- **BackgroundColor**: LightBlue

12. Select the third text box in the SourceNoGroup header column and change its properties as follows:
    - **Name**: txtCustCatPKTGroup
    - **Value**: =Fields!CustCatPKT_ItemLedgerEntry.Value
    - **BackgroundColor**: LightSteelBlue

13. Select the last text box in the bottom right, in the ItemNoGroup footer row, and change its properties as follows:
    - **Name**: txtSumQuantity
    - **Value**: =Sum(Fields!Quantity_ItemLedgerEntry.Value)
    - **Color**:
      =iif(Sum(Fields!Quantity_ItemLedgerEntry.Value) <= 0,"Red","Black")
    - **Font**: Arial; 10pt; Default; Bold; Default
    - **Format**: =Fields!Quantity_ItemLedgerEntryFormat.Value

14. Now, for the rest of the textboxes in all the grouping rows (both headers and footers), remove the `BackgroundColor` formula, `=iif(RowNumber(Nothing) mod 2, "AliceBlue", "White")`, that has been automatically copied from the details group. When the formula is deleted from the **Properties** window, **BackGroundColor** will default to **No Color**.

15. We are almost finished with groupings. Let's add the last touch to the totals. Select the sixth text box in the **ItemNoGroup** footer row, click on the **Property Pages** pop-up window for this text box, and change the **Border** properties, as shown in the following screenshot:

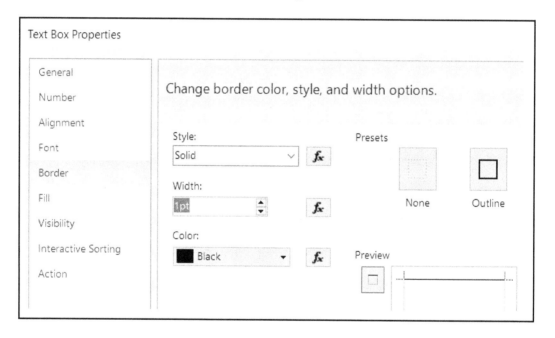

16. Repeat *step 15* for the seventh text box (`txtSumQuantity`).

17. Enable the ability to display the table header if there is more than one page to be rendered. Click on the small down arrow in **Column Groups** and enable **Advanced Mode**. Select the **(Static)** group in **Row Groups** and change the properties of the Static member, as follows:

    - **KeepTogether:** True
    - **KeepWithGroup:** After
    - **RepeatOnNewPage:** True

Part 4 – Building a simple request page

If report objects have been set with `UseRequestPage = true;` (the default value), then a request page will be shown to the user so that they can set filters, gather user information, and populate AL variables or parameters that influence the processing and output of the report.

Within a request page, you can also add actions to perform some extra activities before running the report. Typical examples include a shortcut to run a page to check for some specific setup or an action that performs preprocessing tasks before setting request page variables.

In Visual Studio Code, add (or change, if you have used the `treport` snippet) the `requestpage` section and the `OnPreReport()` trigger section. Consider the following code:

```
requestpage
{
    layout
    {
        area(content)
        {
            group(Options)
            {
                Caption = 'Options';
                field(includeLogo;includeLogo)
                {
                    Caption = 'Include company logo';
                }
            }
        }
    }
    actions
    {
    }
}
trigger OnPreReport()
begin
    if includeLogo then begin
    CompanyInfo.Get;  //Get Company Information record
    CompanyInfo.CalcFields(Picture);  //Retrieve company logo
    end;
end;
```

Part 5 – Adding database images

In this section, we will add the ability to display images at runtime to our report:

1. Go back to **Report Builder** and the RDL layout. In the center of the report header, right-click and select **Insert | Image**.
2. The **Image Properties** pop-up window will load. In the **General** tab, change the **Name** to imgCompanyLogo and input the parameters shown in the following screenshot:

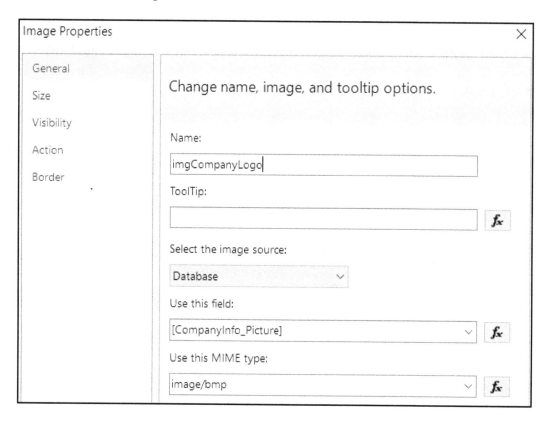

3. In the **Visibility** tab, change the display option to **Show or hide based on an expression** and add the following formula:

```
=iif(Fields!includeLogo.Value,iif(Len(Convert.ToString(Fields!
CompanyInfo_Picture.Value))>0,False,True),True)
```

This expression sets the visibility of the image control if the user has chosen to include the company logo and if the conversion from binary format into text returns values greater than 0 bytes (in short, if there is image data in the dataset).

4. Click **OK** to confirm the modifications you've made.
5. Set the image control's location and size as follows:
   - **Location: 3,29875in; 0in**
   - **Size: 2,42708in; 0,56578in**

The final report layout should now look like this:

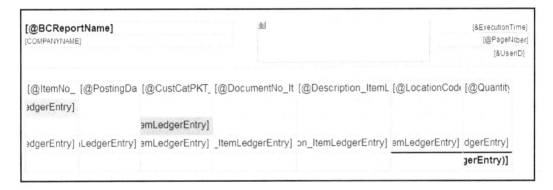

The RDL report and its layout are now ready to be deployed. Compile the extension (*Ctrl + Shift + B*) and deploy the package into your online or containerized sandbox (*F5*). Once the web client is loading, just search (*Alt + Q*) for the Item Ledger Entry Analysis report and fill in the request page if you want to include the company logo in the report's output:

If you click **Preview**, the output should look as follows:

Item No.	Posting Date	Customer Category	Document No.	Description	Location Code	Quantity
Item Ledger Entry Analysis						3/24/2019
CRONUS AG						Page 1
						EUROPE\DTACCONI
1000						
		MEDIUM				
1000	9/5/2020	MEDIUM	1011002			27
		TOP				
1000	9/4/2020	TOP	1011001			5
						32
1100						
		BAD				
1100	9/6/2020	BAD	1011003			-16
		MEDIUM				
1100	6/1/2019	MEDIUM	FERT-START			200
1100	9/4/2020	MEDIUM	1011001			-5
		TOP				
1100	9/5/2020	TOP	1011002			-27
						152

Part 6 – Adding a Word layout

In this section, together with the RDL layout, we will also add a Word layout to our report:

1. Go to **Report Layout Selection** and filter for report ID **50111**.
2. Select **Actions | Custom Layouts**.
3. Click **New**, select **Insert Word layout**, and click **OK**. This will add an empty Word layout to the report and reference the dataset structure as an XML mapping.
4. Choose **Process | Export Layout** and save the `Default.docx` report into the `.\Src\CustomerCategory\report` folder. You might call the report layout `Rep50111.ItemLedgerEntryAnalysis.docx`.
5. Bind the report to the RDL layout within the extension, change the default layout to Word, and change record sorting by specifying the following report properties in the AL report object. Consider the following code:

```
report 50111 "Item Ledger Entry Analysis"
{
DefaultLayout = Word;
RDLCLayout =
'./Src/CustomerCategory/report/Rep50111.ItemLedgerEntryAnalysi
s.rdl';
WordLayout =
'./Src/CustomerCategory/report/Rep50111.ItemLedgerEntryAnalysi
s.docx';
Caption = 'Item Ledger Entry Analysis';
UsageCategory = ReportsAndAnalysis;
ApplicationArea = All;
dataset
{
dataitem("Item Ledger Entry";"Item Ledger Entry")
{
  DataItemTableView=SORTING("Item No.") ORDER(Ascending);
```

6. In Visual Studio Code, right-click the DOCX file and choose **Open externally**. This will open Microsoft Word.

7. If you haven't already, be sure that you have the **Developer** tab enabled. Click on **File** | **Options** | **Customize Ribbon**. In the main tab, check the **Developer (custom)** ribbon option and click **OK**:

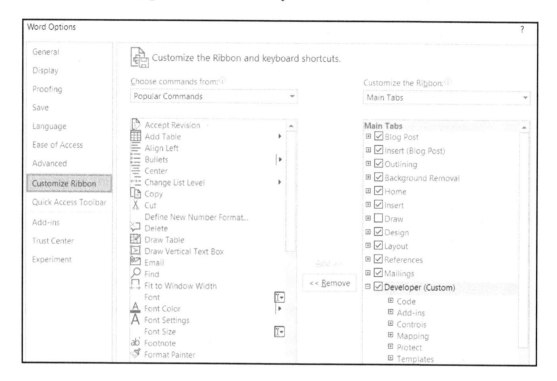

8. Back in the Word layout, select the **Developer** tab and click on the XML Mapping pane.

9. In the **Custom XML Part** box, select the last entry from the drop-down menu and expand the **Labels** and **Item_Ledger_Entry** nodes from the **NavWorldReportXMLPart** root.

It should look like this:

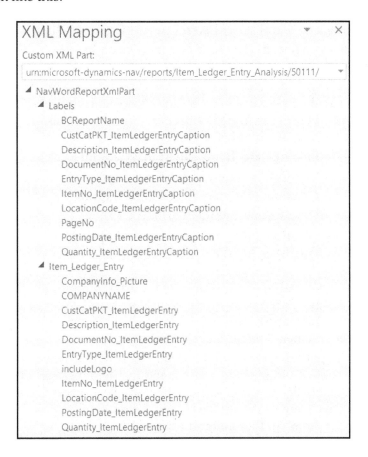

Let's add a Word layout list report to our extension:

1. Right-click in the **XML Mapping** pane, select **Item_Ledger_Entry** the drop-down menu, and choose **CompanyInformation_Picture**. Right-click on it and select **Insert Content Control | Picture**. This will add a placeholder for the company information logo in the Word layout.

2. Add an extra line. Right-click in the **XML Mapping** pane, select **Labels**, and choose **BCReportName.** Right-click on it and select **Insert Content Control | Plain Text**.

3. Add an extra line. Right-click in the **XML Mapping** pane, select the **Item_Ledger_Entry** drop-down menu, and choose **COMPANYNAME**. Right-click on it and select **Insert Content Control | Plain Text**.

4. Add an extra line. In the Word ribbon, click on **Insert | Table** and create a 7-row x 2-column table.

5. In the first row, for each cell, place the cursor in the **XML Mapping** pane, select **Labels**, right-click in each caption element, and select **Insert Content Control | Plain Text**. Here is a list of the column captions:
    - ItemNo_ItemLedgerEntryCaption
    - PostingDate_ItemLedgerEntryCaption
    - CustCatPKT_ItemLedgerEntryCaption
    - DocumentNo_ItemLedgerEntryCaption
    - Description_ItemLedgerEntryCaption
    - LocationCode_ItemLedgerEntryCaption
    - Quantity_ItemLedgerEntryCaption

6. Select the second row of the table. In the **XML Mapping** pane, select **Item_Ledger_Entry** element, right-click on it, and select **Insert Content Control | Repeating**. This will make the line elements repeat for every record in the Item Ledger Entry dataset.

7. In the second row, inside the repeater element, place the cursor in every cell in the **XML Mapping** pane, expand the **Item_Ledger_Entry** drop-down menu, right-click in the field element, and select **Insert Content Control | Plain Text**. Here is a list of the column fields:
    - ItemNo_ItemLedgerEntry
    - PostingDate_ItemLedgerEntry
    - CustCatPKT_ItemLedgerEntry
    - DocumentNo_ItemLedgerEntry
    - Description_ItemLedgerEntry
    - LocationCode_ItemLedgerEntry
    - Quantity_ItemLedgerEntry

This will be the result:

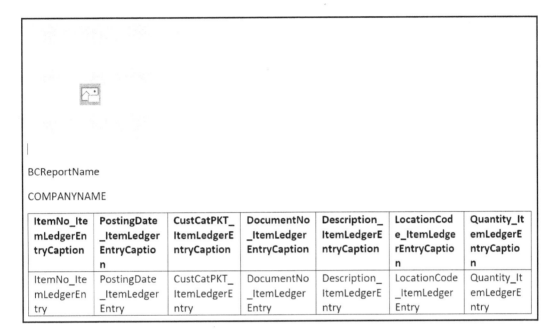

Save and close the Word file.

The Word layout is now ready to be deployed. Build the extension (*Ctrl + Shift + B*) and deploy the package into your online or containerized sandbox (*F5*). Once the web client is loading, search (*Alt + Q*) for **Report Layout Selection**, filter for the current report, and change the selected layout to **Word (built-in)**, as shown here:

REPORT ID ▼		REPORT NAME	SELECTED LAYOUT
50111	⋮	Item Ledger Entry Analysis	Word (built-in)

After searching for the **Item Ledger Entry Analysis** report, choose to include the company logo in the report output and print it to Microsoft Word. Here is the outcome:

cronus

Item Ledger Entry Analysis

CRONUS AG

Item No.	Posting Date	Customer Category	Document No.	Description	Location Code	Quantity
1000	10/09/2021 00:00:00	TOP	1011001			5
1000	11/09/2021 00:00:00	MEDIUM	1011002			27
1100	01/06/2020 00:00:00	TOP	FERT-START			200
1100	10/09/2021 00:00:00	TOP	1011001			-5
1100	11/09/2021 00:00:00	MEDIUM	1011002			-27

This concludes this section, where we created and beautified a report from scratch. In the next section, we will have a look at the most common task for a developer: copying and refactoring an existing report to cope with customer feature requirements.

Converting an existing C/AL report into AL

Making small modifications to an existing report is a very common task. Together with creating new pages and codeunits, this is probably one of the most repetitive and frequent jobs for a developer.

Let's say that we would like to make the following changes to the standard sales order report:

- Show the Customer Category field in the sales order header
- Print *GIFT* in the sales lines for item lines with 100% discount

The current version of the AL Language extension does not have any artifact such as the `ReportExtension` object that could be used to modify or merge existing reports. Therefore, it is always required to create a brand new report from scratch, even if we need to make very small modifications to the dataset and/or layout.

The easiest way to accomplish this task, then, is to copy and give a different ID to an existing report after converting it from C/AL into AL.

The first part of the task (copy an existing report) is pretty straightforward with the Dynamics 365 Business Central October 2019 update since all of the legacy C/AL reports have been transformed into their equivalent AL objects and included in the base application extension.

With the on-premises version, you can find them in the DVD installation folder in the `\Applications\BaseApp\Source` directory. Just unzip the file named `Base Application.Source.zip` and search for the standard report you need to make a copy of, together with its `.rdl` and `.docx` files.

If you are using a Docker-contained sandbox, you might think of using a powerful cmdlet implemented in the `NavContainerHelper` library that is specifically intended for the Dynamics 365 Business Central October 2019 update: `Create-AlProjectFolderFromBcContainer`. This cmdlet will unpack the base application source code in a local folder of your choice. Here is a very simple code snippet:

```
#Set local variables
#####################
$alFolder = 'C:\APP\BaseApp'
$existingContainerName = "BC15ITCU1"


#Extract Base Application into a folder of your choice
######################################################
Create-ALProjectFolderFromBcContainer -containerName
$existingContainerName `
-useBaseLine `
-useBaseAppProperties
```

In $alFolder, you can pick up the AL report items that you need and renumber and customize them.

With the Dynamics 365 Business Central April 2019 update or earlier, Microsoft provides a very useful—and powerful—command-line tool called txt2al.exe, which helps to convert C/AL objects into AL syntax. But there is more.

The New-NavContainer cmdlet contained in the NavContainerHelper PowerShell library, which we discussed in Chapter 3, *Online and Container-Based Sandboxes*, also implements a useful switch (-includeAL) that extracts all of the C/AL objects in TXT format from a container and converts them one by one using txt2.al.exe.

Since the Dynamics 365 Business Central October 2019 update, Microsoft discontinued the C/AL and CSIDE development environment, hence txt2al.exe is only present in deployments based on the Dynamics 365 Business Central April 2019 update or earlier versions.

Here is a very useful script that converts all of the standard base C/AL objects into their AL equivalents:

```
#Set local variables
####################
$mylicense = 'C:\DOCKER\LICENSE\BC14.flf'
$imageName = "mcr.microsoft.com/businesscentral/sandbox:1904"
$containerName = "BC14W1-LATEST"
#Create a Docker sandbox container with converted AL objects
###########################################################
New-NavContainer -accept_eula `
-imageName $imageName `
-containerName $containerName `
-licenseFile $mylicense `
-auth NavUserPassword `
-shortcuts None `
-includeAL
```

Here's a snippet of the PowerShell standard output that shows what is happening when the -includeAL switch is enabled:

```
...
Export Objects with filter 'Id=1..1999999999' (new syntax) to
C:\ProgramData\NavContainerHelper\Extensions\Original-14.1.33107.0-W1-
newsyntax\objects.txt (container path)
Split
C:\ProgramData\NavContainerHelper\Extensions\Original-14.1.33107.0-W1-
newsyntax\objects.txt to
```

```
C:\ProgramData\NavContainerHelper\Extensions\Original-14.1.33107.0-W1-
newsyntax (container paths)
Converting objects file from OEM(437) to UTF8 before splitting
Converting object files from UTF8 to OEM(437) after splitting
Converting files in
C:\ProgramData\NavContainerHelper\Extensions\Original-14.1.33107.0-W1-
newsyntax to .al files in
C:\ProgramData\NavContainerHelper\Extensions\Original-14.1.33107.0-W1-
al with startId 50100 (container paths)
Converting my delta files from OEM(437) to UTF8 before converting
txt2al.exe --
source="C:\ProgramData\NavContainerHelper\Extensions\Original-14.1.331
07.0-W1-newsyntax" --
target="C:\ProgramData\NavContainerHelper\Extensions\Original-14.1.331
07.0-W1-al" --rename --extensionStartId=50100 --
dotNetAddInsPackage="C:\ProgramData\NavContainerHelper\Extensions\BC14
W1-LATEST\coredotnetaddins.al"
Converting my delta files from UTF8 to OEM(437) after converting
Creating .net Assembly Reference Folder for VS Code
Copying DLLs from C:\Windows\assembly to assemblyProbingPath
Copying DLLs from C:\Program Files\Microsoft Dynamics NAV\140\Service
to assemblyProbingPath
Copying DLLs from C:\Program Files (x86)\Microsoft Dynamics
NAV\140\RoleTailored Client to assemblyProbingPath
Copying DLLs from C:\Program Files (x86)\Open XML SDK to
assemblyProbingPath
...
```

The output files are located in
the `C:\ProgramData\NavContainerHelper\Extensions\Original-`
`<ApplicationVersion>-<localization>-al` directory.

In this directory, we have to search for the converted AL standard object for order
confirmation. Just type `Standard Sales Order` into the file explorer search field
and three objects will be available to be copied and renamed:

- `Report 1305 - Standard Sales - Order Conf..al`
- `Standard Sales - Order Conf..docx`
- `Standard Sales - Order Conf..rdlc`

The following screenshot shows this:

Standard Sales - Order Conf..docx	C:\ProgramData\NavContainerHelper\Extensions\Ori...	Size: 46,2 KB	
Date modified: 10/07/2019 22:14			
Standard Sales - Order Conf..rdlc		Date modified: 10/07/2019 22:14	
C:\ProgramData\NavContainerHelper\Extensions\Ori... Type: RDLC File		Size: 472 KB	
Report 1305 - Standard Sales - Order Conf..al		Date modified: 10/07/2019 22:14	
C:\ProgramData\NavContainerHelper\Extensions\Ori... Type: AL File		Size: 40,0 KB	

Copy these files into the .\Src\CustomerCategory\report directory and rename
them as follows:

- Rep50115.PacktSalesOrderConf.al
- Rep50115.PacktSalesOrderConf.docx
- Rep50115.PacktSalesOrderConf.rdl

The next step is to renumber the AL report within the allowed customization range to
avoid duplicate object IDs and then change its properties to use the appropriate
.docx and .rdl files.

Edit Rep50115.PacktSalesOrderConf.al in Visual Studio Code and change the
name and properties, as shown in the following code:

```
report 50115 "Packt Sales - Order Conf."
{
    WordLayout =
'./Src/CustomerCategory/report/Rep50115.PacktSalesOrderConf.docx';
    RDLCLayout =
'./Src/CustomerCategory/report/Rep50115.PacktSalesOrderConf.rdl';
    Caption = 'Packt Sales-Confirmation';
    UsageCategory=ReportsAndAnalysis;
    ApplicationArea=All;
    AdditionalSearchTerms='Packt Sales Order report';

    DefaultLayout = Word;
    PreviewMode = PrintLayout;
    WordMergeDataItem = Header;
```

Now, we have to let the application understand that every time standard report 1305 is invoked, it should be substituted with custom report 50115 instead. This is easily done by subscribing to a specific event called `OnAfterSubstituteReport`, which is published through the `ReportManagement` codeunit.

Edit the `Cod50100.CustomerCategoryMgt_PKT.al` file, which is contained in `.\Src\CustomerCategory\codeunit`, and add the following code:

```
[EventSubscriber(ObjectType::Codeunit, Codeunit::ReportManagement,
'OnAfterSubstituteReport', '', false, false)]
local procedure OnAfterSubstituteReport(ReportId: Integer; var
NewReportId: Integer)
begin
    if ReportId = Report::"Standard Sales - Order Conf." then
        NewReportId := Report::"Packt Sales - Order Conf.";
    end;
```

 At this stage, if you build (*Ctrl + Shift + B*) and publish (*F5*) the extension, the whole (code and layouts) standard sales order report will automatically be replaced behind the scenes with the custom one.

Now, it is time to make the appropriate changes to the custom sales order report code and Word layout to print out the Customer Category field in the document header and print out GIFT for every item line that has a 100% discount.

Edit `Rep50115.PacktSalesOrderConf.al` in Visual Studio Code and add the following columns in the dataset section of the Header data item:

```
column(CustomerCategory_PKT;Cust."Customer Category_PKT")
{
}
column(CustomerCategory_PKT_Lbl;Cust.FIELDCAPTION("Customer
Category_PKT"))
{
}
```

Add a label for the gift description:

```
GiftLbl: Label 'GIFT';
```

Then, change the IF conditional statement related to the discount percentage in the `OnAfterGetRecord` trigger for the `Line` data item:

```
if "Line Discount %" = 0 then
    LineDiscountPctText := ''
else
    LineDiscountPctText := StrSubstNo('%1%',-Round("Line Discount
%",0.1));
Replace the preceding code with the following case statement:
case "Line Discount %" OF
    0    : LineDiscountPctText := '';
    100  : LineDiscountPctText := GiftLbl;
    ELSE
    LineDiscountPctText := StrSubstNo('%1%',-Round("Line Discount
%",0.1));
END;
```

Everything is now ready to work as expected. We simply need to display the Customer Category column in the report layout.

Just build the app (*Ctrl + Shift + B*) and publish (*F5*) it in the online sandbox.

Go to **Report Layout Selections**, filter the list for report **50115**, and click on **Custom Layouts**. The following screenshot shows the filtered report layout selections:

Create a new layout and choose **Insert Word layout**:

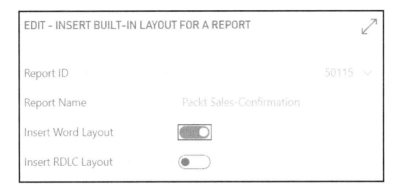

Export the custom Word layout we just created. In the Word layout, remove the `CustomerAddress8` field and instead, add the following:

- **CustomerCategory_PKT_Lbl** as plaintext
- A space, a colon (:), and another space
- **CustomerCategory_PKT** as plaintext

This is how it appears:

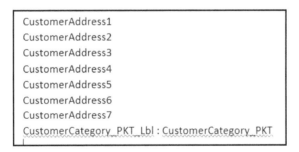

Save the layout and import it back into the customer layout record.

You could also use this Word layout in the standard extension and replace the original report 50115 `.docx` file with this one if you intend to use this version as part of your standard extension deployment.

Run any sales order that has a gift line and customer category assigned to inspect the result. It should look like this:

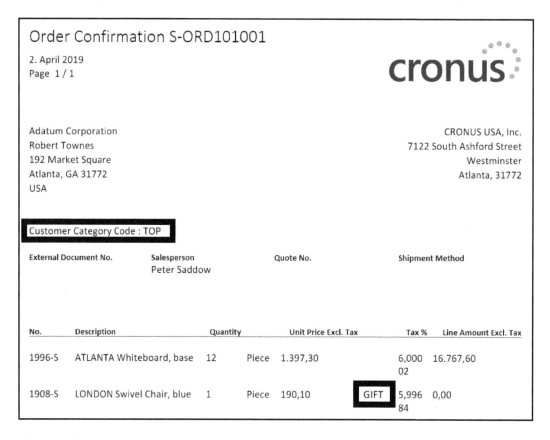

This concludes our section related to converting a C/AL report into AL. Next, let's learn how feature limitation works on RDL and Word reports.

Feature limitation when developing an RDL or Word layout report

Basically—and historically—professional report development could/should be done by developing RDL report layouts with Visual Studio and the RDLC report extension installed. The Word document layout has more limitations than RDL and its main advantage is that it is quite popular and easy to adopt by power users.

The major pain points you might find when developing layouts are typically related to documents. The most commonly known ones are as follows:

- **Header and footer space is always retained**: Report headers and footers have static content, and they have been engineered so that they are always displayed on every page if they are present. Nevertheless, with RDL, you could use the typical `SetData` function in the body and the `GetData` function in the header. An example of this trick can be found in the standard object 206 Sales Invoice RDL layout.

- **There's no easy way to mimic the `PlaceInBottom` property for a document report from the old classic client report**: When developing a document, you might be asked to generate an entire document, but the totals (VAT, totals per group, and so on) must be always printed at the bottom, always in the same place, only on the last page. This problem arises because a Dynamics 365 Business Central document report could be considered as *a batch of multiple documents and multiple copies* rather than a single report. This implies that the breakdown for renumbering pages must be done for every document number and copy number. An example is the *report 205 Sales Order*.

  In standard document reports, totals are never placed at the bottom of the page; they are printed right after the last document line. This means that they could be printed anywhere on a page, or even be on an extra page. There is no feasible way to print a batch of the document and the totals printed at the bottom of the last page for every document and copy.

- **Complexity in implementing running totals**: Typically, with documents, you would like to implement running totals at the bottom of the page that are reported at the top of the next page, such as **To be Continued** and **continue** labels when printing the ledger or some transactional entries. With the old classic client report designer, you could resolve this by adding a `transheader/transfooter`. These artifacts no longer exist with RDL or Word layout reports. With a Word layout report, there is no feasible solution. With RDL, you might implement running totals, but only with header and footer sections. This is an old but useful development reference: `https://blogs.msdn.microsoft.com/nav/2011/06/06/transfooter-and-transheader-functionality-in-rdlcssrs-reports-revisited/`.

Considering Word layouts only, the design limitations you might also frequently hit are as follows:

- **No conditional formatting**: If you need to set the visibility of a control, change a field value within the layout, or set any conditional formatting, this is not possible with Word. A typical example is when you need to print a blank character instead of zero. This must be done in the dataset, and values have to be sent to the document already formatted as strings (blank or with a numeric value).

- **No totaling formulas**: There is no equivalent to RDL =SUM functions or similar. Value calculations must be done through AL code and the result added to the dataset.

- **Having nested repeaters in the same table is a challenge**: Since it is not possible to conditionally trigger the visibility of a table line, there is a tradeoff between a good-looking layout and different data items in the same table. A typical example is comment lines under a sales line or an additional description/barcode line under a sales shipment line.
  These might be achieved by adding a nested table structure repeater within the lines repeater, which maps the extra additional information. The nested table structure can be freely defined, as long as it spans a set of merged cells in the outer table. When you develop this, be aware that if there is no extra additional information, at least one empty instance of the nested structure will be included.

 The best solution would be to use a buffer table in the dataset and create the exact line structure as it has to be printed in the layout.

If you come across one or more of these limitations, then probably the best and easiest solution is to develop an RDL layout report instead.

Understanding report performance considerations

With Dynamics 365 Business Central online, there are performance considerations that need to be taken into account.

Currently, both Word and RDL built-in layouts are rendered in the same application domain process when they run with `SAVEASPDF` or `SAVEAS` statements.

Since RDL layouts might enable some external code artifacts that may potentially affect data within the same application domain, it has been decided to run every custom RDL report layout in isolated mode. It's worth noticing that if you develop a report and declare `DefaultLayout` as RDL and the `RDLLayout` property, this is considered a built-in layout and should render in the same application domain.

Word layouts, no matter whether they are built-in or custom-made, do not run in isolation.

Enabling application domain isolation for custom RDL layouts provides a more secure and reliable processing environment. However, the drawback is that it could considerably increase the rendering time.

Whenever you develop RDL reports for Dynamics 365 Business Central online, you must also test performance with the `SAVEASPDF` or `SAVEAS` statements within an online sandbox or a Docker-contained sandbox with the `customsettings.config` file server parameter, **ReportAppDomainIsolation**, set to `true`.

Other performance considerations that are valid for both Word and RDL report layouts are based on dataset optimization.

These are the equations to keep in mind when developing the data structure of the AL report. Let's consider that the dataset is an in-memory table (`X axis = columns` and `Y axis = rows`):

```
Smaller Dataset = Better Performance
Smaller Dataset = Reduce X axis (columns) + Reduce Y axis (rows)
Better Performance = Optimize (reduce) the number of columns in
Dataset + Optimize (reduce) the number of records processed in
DataItems
```

You can use the following links to optimize standard reports or your own custom reports:

- https://blogs.msdn.microsoft.com/nav/2014/03/09/rdlc-report-and-performance-in-microsoft-dynamics-nav/
- https://blogs.msdn.microsoft.com/nav/2016/05/20/rdlc-report-and-performance-in-microsoft-dynamics-nav-2015-and-2016/
- https://blogs.msdn.microsoft.com/nav/2015/03/17/a-couple-of-rdlc-performance-optimization-tips/

Summary

In this chapter, we have learned which tools to use to develop reports with AL. We saw how to create RDL and Word layouts and which tools are supported. We got a better understanding of the creation of reports and how to use them. We have also explained how to use `txt2al.exe` to convert a C/AL report into an AL report and refactor it to be reused within the standard application with a practical example.

In the end, we learned that there are some reporting limitations, a few workarounds, and some performance considerations that can help you become a master in AL report development.

In the next chapter, we'll learn how to build an automated test for Dynamics 365 Business Central to check for application business process consistency and improve the robustness of our development solutions.

3
Section 3: Debugging, Testing, and Release Management (DevOps)

In this section, we will give you an in-depth overview of how you can debug extensions from Visual Studio Code and how you can handle the installation and upgrade processes. Then, you will learn how to write automated tests and how to handle source control management and CI/CD in your development processes.

This section comprises the following chapters:

- Chapter 8, *Installing and Upgrading Extensions*
- Chapter 9, *Debugging*
- Chapter 10, *Automated Test Development with AL*
- Chapter 11, *Source Control Management and DevOps with Business Central*

8
Installing and Upgrading Extensions

Acquiring the Installed status for an extension is a four-step procedure: publish, synchronize, upgrade (if and where needed), and install. In this chapter, we will cover each of these steps in detail.

Installing a simple or even a complex extension with the most exotic code artifacts might turn out to be an easy task compared to its maintenance. The maintenance of an extension is done through the upgrade process of the extension. An upgrade may be needed because of the introduction of a new feature, bug fixes or, quite frequently with SaaS, because of dependency changes from the base app.

Throughout this chapter, we will explore both basic extension installation and complex dependency upgrades in order to help AL developers have a better understanding of how to review their `SaaSified` private IPs.

With a continuous upgrade process that happens roughly every month, Dynamics 365 Business Central online is an ever-changing and evolutionary product. Therefore, partners and customers should be ready to upgrade their extensions to cope with the monthly update releases of both platforms and applications.

In this chapter, you will learn how to do the following:

- Deploy extensions in an online sandbox and production environment
- Check the status for published, synchronized, and installed extensions
- Handle install codeunits
- Handle breaking changes through upgrade codeunits
- Define app dependencies
- Work with a simple upgrade scenario
- Upgrade extensions with dependencies

Deploying extensions

Like in any other programming language, the terminology is very important. It is vital to clearly understand and distinguish the different deployment phases and statuses for the extension in order to target the appropriate troubleshooting, where necessary.

Depending on the development life cycle and deployment, extensions fall into two categories:

- **Per tenant extensions (PTE)**: This resembles the old-school development, tailored per customer. Development is typically performed per tenant in a sandbox that contains a copy of the production configuration and data. The CSP partner and/or its reseller, together with the customer, manage the development and deployment the life cycle.
  Despite the fact that this is, historically, the most common scenario for on-premises ERP development, partners are encouraged to create their own standard extension to be deployed and/or sold through the Dynamics 365 Business Central Marketplace.
- **AppSource extensions**: These are published on AppSource and their destiny is to be consumed by any/all tenants on a given system, acquired via the official Dynamics Marketplace. AppSource extensions follow a very strict process of technical and marketing validation before being approved and pushed as being worldwide (globally) available for production tenant deployments.
  Different from PTEs, AppSource-credited extensions are already published by Microsoft in every application database, ready to be installed per tenant on demand. This makes the extension deployment process faster, more reliable, and more professional.

PTEs can be deployed in two ways:

- Automatically
- Manually

Let's take a look at both of these deployments here.

Automatically

In Visual Studio Code, you have to set up `launch.json` to work against a specific target sandbox tenant environment (`"tenant": ""`) and provide the appropriate credentials to establish a connection.

Since you may have several sandboxes within the same environment, you can also specify which tenant you want to connect to download symbols and/or publish the extension (`"sandboxName": ""`).

 This is not possible in online production environments, only in sandboxes. This is only possible for PTEs. PTEs that are deployed in this way are often called developer extensions, since they can only target developer sandboxes.

By default, the deployment is executed by applying a synchronization to the existing schema (`"schemaUpdateMode": "Synchronize"`). The default option, then, is useful for preserving the data, just in case the developer has made some changes that do not involve any breaking changes. It is, however, possible to completely clean up any previous extension deployment and deploy it from scratch (`"schemaUpdateMode": "Recreate"`) or even force the synchronization (`"schemaUpdateMode": "ForceSync"`) to guarantee fast deployment and further tests to the extension.

 ForceSync has to be used with caution and should be avoided as much as possible. Even if we speed up deployment and tests, it will not work in a production environment where an upgrade codeunit job is required. Sometimes, lazy developers might use ForceSync and forget to handle the appropriate upgrade and synchronization in production.

Manually

The typical production deployment is done manually. It is also possible in online sandboxes since the April 2019 update, as follows:

1. Connect to your production or sandbox tenant.
2. Search (*Alt + Q*) for the **Extension Management** page.

3. In the **Extension Management** page, click on the **Manage** action group (you could pin it if you wanted to), choose **Upload Extension**, and pick up the extension (.app) you developed. The following screenshot shows the upload and deploy page:

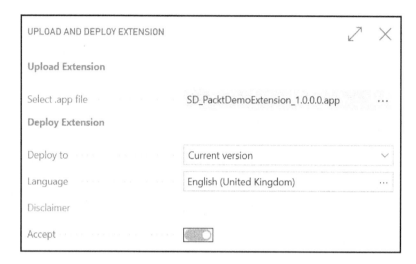

In the screenshot, we see that the **Deploy to** parameter is very important, because it triggers when the extension has to be deployed by the platform.

By specifying **Current version**, the deployment is performed immediately and the extension attempts to be synchronized. Developers can check whether the task has completed successfully, or if there have been failure errors in the **Deployment status** page.

Selecting **Next Minor Version** or **Next Major Version** defers the deployment to when the next minor or major update would happen.

To find out more about this topic, visit `https://demiliani.com/2019/04/29/dynamics-365-business-central-and-per-tenant-extensions-check-page-control-names-between-platform-upgrades/`.

Some deployment tips

Developers must have it etched on their mind that Dynamics 365 Business Central is a multitenant environment that declares the following paradigms:

- Applications and data are decoupled and stored in different databases.
- A single application database, bound to an application service, could serve hundreds of tenants (customer data databases). This is the pillar of the one-to-many concept of multitenancy.
- In the application, the database is stored as the extension manifests (records that store the definition of the extension as it appears in the app.json file).
- Mounting and synchronizing tenants in a service bound to an application database would expose these extensions to the tenants.
- Tenant extensions could then be chosen for installation by users.

Whenever a minor update (typically monthly) or major update (typically every six months) happens, the extensions will be uninstalled. Subsequently, the tenant will be dismounted from the old application service and mounted to another application service that is bound to the new application version.

Even if the new application service has not published the PTE, the tenant structure and its data will be totally preserved.

Whenever this operation happens, developers just have to publish and install the extension once again, to resynchronize everything. This is valid, as mentioned, for all online sandboxes.

PTEs that are deployed in the production environment have a more global scope, and extensions are automatically ported into the new application service. Within this context, if an extension is chosen to be deployed with the next minor/major version, when the upgrade happens, the new extension will be triggered for installation.

To get a deeper overview of this topic, visit https://demiliani.com/2019/01/24/ dynamics-365-business-central-tenant-upgrade-extensions-disappeared-in-sandbox-environment/.

PTEs must maintain their uniqueness across the ecosystem, and developers should not violate this principle. The uniqueness of a PTE, or any extension in general, is defined by the composition of the following values in the app.json file:

- **Package ID**: A new GUID assigned to the .app file every time the extension is built (*Ctrl + Shift + B*).
- **Application ID**: The unique GUID that defines the extension.
- **Name**
- **Publisher**
- **Version**: (in the form of x.x.x.x).

Whenever one of these values is changed, the extension is considered to be a new extension. If a developer is considering reusing a PTE for another customer tenant, then they have to deal with this uniqueness paradigm.

Trying to deploy the very same PTE in another tenant, or even redeploying the same after rebuilding the package, might lead to a failure with an error like the one shown here:

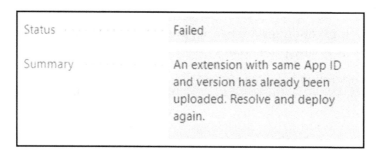

In this case, it might be necessary to simply increase (bump) the application version to make the deployment work smoothly.

If this happens in the tenant in which the PTE has never been installed before, then the root cause might be a duplicate within the same application service. To resolve the issue, the developer has to change the application ID and the name, and redeploy it in order to install the PTE successfully.

For a deeper overview of this issue, visit `https://demiliani.com/2019/03/14/` `dynamics-365-business-central-online-sandbox-makes-you-crazy-maybe-` `remember-these-points/`.

There are another two error messages that might typically arise when deploying extensions. These are:

- Cannot install the extension `<name>` by `<publisher>` because the tenant `<Tenant` Id> already uses a different version of it.

- The application extension with app id '`<Extension Id>`' is already configured for use by the global tenant.

The first error occurs because it has tried to publish a Per tenant extension with the same Application Id and Version parameters as another Per tenant extension which is present on the system, but with potentially different contents. The easiest solution to this error is to increase the version of the extension.

The second error occurs because it has tried to upload a Per tenant extension using the same Id as one assigned to an AppSource Extension or a standard Microsoft owned extension. In this case, the solution is quite straightforward: change the extension Id and republish.

In the next section, we'll see what happens under the hood when you deploy an extension.

Deployment under the hood

Deploying any type of extension in an online sandbox means the following:

- The extension is published in a specific application service with a specific application version.
- The same extension is synchronized (the Azure SQL database structure matches the object metadata definition) and installed in the sandbox tenant.

Extension deployment can be summarized in four phases:

- **Publish**: The extension is uploaded into the application database onto which the reference tenant is mounted during the publishing process. There are no changes in the physical structure of the tables in the tenant database.

  Publishing means a declaration of the object contents (metadata) and the database structure changes that need to be applied on demand by a specific tenant. These contents and relative changes are defined by the AL objects (such as tables, pages, and page extensions).

- **Synchronize**: The contents that are published might be transferred to the tenant as is (such as pages or codeunits) or they might require an extra action to be taken against the tenant data structure (such as a table or a table extension). The most important step in the synchronization process is to apply changes to the underlying database, typically a table structure as defined in the AL objects. This is the step where tables are created or new fields are added or modified inside the tenant database.

- **Data Upgrade**: If there are changes in the application version, then, after the synchronization, it must follow a data upgrade. When running the data upgrade, the application will search for upgrade codeunits and run the code inside them.

  A data upgrade is typically necessary when you have to handle breaking changes, such as changing a data type for a field, or when you are enhancing existing extension features that are already deployed.

- **Install**: When both metadata changes and data upgrades are performed successfully, everything is ready in the tenant to provide all the functionality to the users. This last operation changes the status of the extension to Installed, and the application is extended and is ready to be used with the new functionalities.

To demonstrate these phases in a prototype real-life development scenario, let's create a simple extension and double-check what's happening behind the scenes using a Docker-contained environment.

 At the time we are writing, Dynamics 365 Business Central Spring 2019 release is the latest version available, hence, what will follow is based on that major release.

We have a PowerShell script that will perform the following activities:

- Install or update the `NavContainerHelper` library to the latest version.
- Prompt you to provide a name and password for a user to be used inside the container.
- Generate a Docker-contained sandbox using the latest Dynamics 365 Business Central version and update.
- Create a folder in the desktop with the same name as the container and move all the relevant shortcuts created by the `New-NAVContainer` cmdlet in to there.

The script can be seen in the following code:

```
#Set local variables
####################
$imageName = "mcr.microsoft.com/businesscentral/sandbox:1904"
$containerName = "BC14MTW1"
$createDirectory = $true #move shortcuts into a directory
$checkHelper = $true #install navcontainerhelper
#Install or update NavContainerHelper
####################################
Clear-Host
if ($checkHelper)
{
Write-Host 'Installing navcontainerhelper module, please wait...'
install-module navcontainerhelper -force
    Write-Host 'Checking navcontainerhelper module updates, please
wait...'
    update-module navcontainerhelper -force
    Get-InstalledModule navcontainerhelper | Format-List -Property
name, version
}
#Create a new container
######################
New-NavContainer -accept_eula `
            -containerName $containerName `
```

```
                    -useBestContainerOS `
                    -imageName $imageName `
                    -auth NavUserPassword `
                    -alwaysPull `
                    -updateHosts `
                    -licenseFile $mylicense `
                    -assignPremiumPlan `
                    -doNotExportObjectsToText `
                    -multitenant `
                    -includeCSide
#Create a desktop directory and move all the shortcuts
#####################################################
if ($createDirectory)
{
    $desktop = [System.Environment]::GetFolderPath('Desktop')
    New-Item -Path $desktop -Name $containerName -ItemType 'directory'
-Force
    Get-ChildItem $desktop -Filter "$containerName*" -File | Move-Item
-Destination "$desktop\$containerName"
    $code = @'
[System.Runtime.InteropServices.DllImport("Shell32.dll")]
private static extern int SHChangeNotify(int eventId, int flags,
IntPtr item1, IntPtr item2);
public static void Refresh()  {
 SHChangeNotify(0x8000000, 0x1000, IntPtr.Zero, IntPtr.Zero);
}
'@
    Add-Type -MemberDefinition $code -Namespace WinAPI -Name Explorer
    [WinAPI.Explorer]::Refresh()
}
```

After running the script, there should be a new directory in the desktop named BC14MTW1, with six shortcuts inside, as follows:

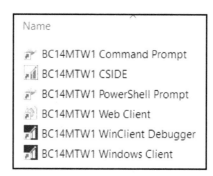

By running SQL Server Management Studio (SSMS – see `https://docs.microsoft.com/en-us/sql/ssms/download-sql-server-management-studio-ssms?view=sql-server-2017`), we can connect to the **BC14MTW1\SQLEXPRESS** server inside the container using SQL Server authentication. The following screenshot shows a list of the databases in the **BC14MTW1\SQLEXPRESS** instance:

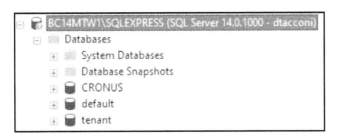

It's worth noticing that there are three databases allocated with a multitenancy Docker-contained environment:

- **CRONUS**: This is an application database. It contains all the system tables that are needed to manage the application objects (such as objects and object metadata) that are shared through customer tenants.
- **default** and **tenant**: **default** is the sandbox that is mounted against the **CRONUS** application. **tenant** is just a dismounted copy of default.

In this environment, we will now focus on the following deployments:

- The main extension, which contains a new table and a table extension
- The second extension, which depends on the main extension
- A new version of the main extension that contains a breaking change (a change that impacts the schema synchronization)
- A new version of the second extension to cope with the main extension breaking change

Understanding how to perform the aforementioned deployments is vital in order to master both simple and complex extension deployments.

To download symbols from this multitenant, on-premises, Docker-contained environment, we will use the following `launch.json` file parameters:

```json
{
  "version": "0.2.0",
  "configurations": [
    {
      "type": "al",
```

```
"request": "launch",
"name": "Your own server",
"server": "http://BC14MTW1",
"serverInstance": "NAV",
"authentication": "UserPassword",
"tenant": "default"
}
]
}
```

Using this very simple script, we have created our own Docker-contained multitenant environment to mimic a sandbox SaaS deployment. We are now ready to start our extension deployment journey, and analyze what is happening at the database level and in the application.

Deploying the main extension

To make it very simple, we will create a brand new table (Tab50105.NewTable.al) with a few fields in it:

```
table 50105 "NewTable"
{
    DataClassification = ToBeClassified;
    fields
    {
        field(1;"Entry No."; Integer)
        {
          DataClassification = ToBeClassified;
        }
        field(2;"Description"; Text [30] )
        {
            DataClassification = ToBeClassified;
        }
        field(3; "Posting Date"; Date)
        {
            DataClassification = ToBeClassified;
        }
        field(4; "Open"; Boolean)
        {
          DataClassification = ToBeClassified;
        }
    }
     keys
     {
        key(PK; "Entry No.")
```

```
        {
            Clustered = true;
        }
    }
}
```

Then, we create a table extension (`Tab-Ext50105.NewTableExtension.al`) that extends the standard `Item` table with a new field called `Catalogue No.`:

```
tableextension 50105 "New Table Extension" extends Item
{
    fields
        {
            field(50105;"Catalogue No.";Integer)
                {
                    DataClassification = ToBeClassified;
                }
        }
}
```

This will be the very first version of the extension, with the following parameters in the manifest file (`app.json`), which define the extension:

```
"id": "15ecd2e5-b7a8-4612-ae6f-d722af29c0c0",
"name": "MainExtension",
"publisher": "DTacconi Inc.",
"version": "1.0.0.0",
```

Typically (but it's not mandatory), extensions use a special codeunit called the installation codeunit. The installation codeunit is defined with `Subtype = Install`, and its execution is triggered every time the extension is installed. Its main purpose is to configure the extension during the installation by creating a record in a setup table, or by populating the table with default values.

In the following code example, we will design an installation codeunit (`Cod50100.MainExtensionInstall.al`):

1. We begin by creating a record in the new table:

```
codeunit 50100 "MainExtensionInstall"
{
    Subtype = Install;

    trigger OnInstallAppPerCompany();
    var
        NewTable : Record NewTable;
    begin
```

```
                    if NewTable.IsEmpty() then
                        InsertDefaultValues();
            end;

            local procedure InsertDefaultValues();
            begin
                InsertValue(1,'Activity Start',TODAY,false);
                InsertValue(2,'First Activity',TODAY,false);
                InsertValue(3,'Second Activity',TODAY,false);
            end;

            local procedure InsertValue(EntryNo : Integer; Desc :
        Text[30]; PostingDate :
            Date; isOpen : Boolean);
            var
                NewTable : Record NewTable;
            begin
                NewTable.Init();
                NewTable."Entry No." := EntryNo;
                NewTable.Description := Desc;
                NewTable."Posting Date" := PostingDate;
                NewTable.Open := isOpen;
                NewTable.Insert();
            end;
        }
```

Since you can install and uninstall the extension at will, and however many times you want, the key point here is to check whether `NewTable.IsEmpty()` performs the activity exactly in the first installation. That code snippet will make sure to populate the table with some default values, but only if it is needed.

 Uninstalling an extension with Dynamics 365 Business Central SaaS will always be performed while preserving the data. They are not cleaned up, but are simply made not visible as the extension uninstalls. Re-installing the extension will bring the old saved data back again. The cloud paradigm is to be conservative in all shapes, and no data will ever be deleted behind the scenes.

2. After building the extension (*Ctrl + Shift + B*), we are ready to deploy the app file using the following sequence of PowerShell cmdlets, which are contained in the `NavContainerHelper` PowerShell library:

   - `Publish-BCContainerApp`
   - `Sync-BCContainerApp`
   - `Start-BCContainerAppDataUpgrade`
   - `Install-BCContainerApp`

3. After the execution of each PowerShell cmdlet, we will check the content of the relevant system tables that are involved in the extension deployment, synchronization, and upgrade mechanism. We will use the following simple T-SQL script by swapping `[Name]` and `[Version Major]` in the `DECLARE` sections with the appropriate extension name and major version:

```
-- Application database
USE "CRONUS"
GO

DECLARE @PackageID uniqueidentifier
SELECT @PackageID = NavApp.[Package ID]
FROM [CRONUS].[dbo].[NAV App] NavApp
WHERE (([Name] = 'MainExtension') and ([Version Major] = 1))

SELECT * FROM [NAV App] WHERE [Package ID] = @PackageID
SELECT * FROM [NAV App Dependencies] WHERE [Package ID] =
@PackageID
SELECT * FROM [NAV App Object Metadata] WHERE [App Package ID]
= @PackageID
SELECT * FROM [NAV App Object Prerequisites] WHERE [Package
ID] = @PackageID
SELECT * FROM [NAV App Publish Reference] WHERE [App Package
ID] = @PackageID
SELECT * FROM [NAV App Resource] WHERE [Package ID] =
@PackageID
SELECT * FROM [NAV App Tenant App] WHERE [App Package ID] =
@PackageID

-- Tenant database
USE "default"
GO

DECLARE @AppID uniqueidentifier
DECLARE @PackageID uniqueidentifier
SELECT @AppID = NavApp.ID, @PackageID = NavApp.[Package ID]
FROM [CRONUS].[dbo].[NAV App] NavApp
WHERE (([Name] = 'MainExtension') and ([Version Major] = 1))
```

```
SELECT * FROM [$ndo$navappschemasnapshot] WHERE appid = @AppID
SELECT * FROM [$ndo$navappschematracking] WHERE appid = @AppID
SELECT * FROM [$ndo$navappuninstalledapp] WHERE appid = @AppID
SELECT * FROM [NAV App Data Archive] WHERE [App ID] = @AppID
SELECT * FROM [NAV App Installed App] WHERE ([App ID] =
@AppID) and ([Package ID] = @PackageID)
SELECT * FROM [NAV App Published App] WHERE ([App ID] =
@AppID) and ([Package ID] = @PackageID)
SELECT * FROM [NAV App Setting] WHERE [App ID] = @AppID
SELECT * FROM [NAV App Tenant Add-In] WHERE [App ID] = @AppID
```

4. Next, you will observe in the following code that the publish action will declare the extension manifest in the [NAV App] table with a specific package ID, and its application ID in the application database (which is called CRONUS):

```
Publish-BCContainerApp -containerName 'BC14MTW1' `
    -appFile 'C:\TEMP\UPGRADE\MainExtension\DTacconi
Inc._MainExtension_1.0.0.0.app' `
    -skipVerification
```

The source code for the Publish-BCContainerApp script is available here: https://github.com/Microsoft/ navcontainerhelper/blob/master/AppHandling/Publish-NavContainerApp.ps1

Then, the object that is contained in the extension is extracted and populates [NAV App Object Metadata], the table in the application database.

A metadata record is also created in the [NAV App Resource] table, and contains the permission object.

No action is performed in the tenant database (named default) at this stage. The following screenshot shows the relevant query result snippet after the main extension has been published:

5. After publishing the main extension, we need to synchronize its content and apply metadata changes to the database structure, if and where needed. Consider the following code:

```
Sync-BCContainerApp -containerName 'BC14MTW1' `
    -tenant 'default' `
    -appName 'MainExtension' `
    -Mode Add
```

The source code of the `Sync.BCContainerApp` script is available here: `https://github.com/microsoft/navcontainerhelper/blob/master/AppHandling/Sync-NavContainerApp.ps1`.

This action will synchronize the extension metadata content of the main extension in the application database (in this example, CRONUS) against a specific mounted tenant (in this example, default). Practically, it will create records in the tenant `[$ndo$navappschemasnapshot]` table for every object that has an impact on schema changes at the database level, such as tables and/or table extensions.

6. One record is also created in the `[$ndo$navappschematracking]` table to correlate the objects in the snapshot table with the extension ID, name, publisher, and version. The following screenshot shows the relevant query result snippet after the main app synchronizes:

When the extension is synchronized, the next step is to perform a data upgrade, if and where needed. Consider the following code:

```
Start-BCContainerAppDataUpgrade -containerName 'BC14MTW1' `
    -tenant 'default' `
    -appName 'MainExtension' `
    -appVersion '1.0.0.0'
```

The source code for the `Start-BCContainerAppDataUpgrade` script is available here: https://github.com/microsoft/navcontainerhelper/blob/master/AppHandling/Start-NavContainerAppDataUpgrade.ps1.

7. If you run the data upgrade now, this has no effect, since there is no previous extension from which to upgrade. The PowerShell cmdlet will return an error as shown here:

    ```
    "Cannot upgrade the extension 'MainExtension by DTacconi Inc.
    1.0.0.0' because no previous version was found."
    ```

8. The last step is installing the extension:

    ```
    Install-BCContainerApp –containerName 'BC14MTW1' `
    –tenant 'default' `
    –appName 'MainExtension' `
    –appVersion '1.0.0.0'
    ```

The source code for the `Install-BCContainerApp` script is available here: https://github.com/microsoft/navcontainerhelper/blob/master/AppHandling/Install-NavContainerApp.ps1.

During the installation task, one record is inserted in the application database [NAV App Tenant App] table in order to report and link the tenant ID (in this case, default) and the app package ID. The same is reflected in the tenant database where a record is inserted in the [NAV App Installed App] table, reporting the package ID and the app ID.

At this stage, the synchronization mechanism between the application database and the tenant database is completed and the metadata structure changes are also applied to the SQL Server database structure.

In this example, you will find the following in the tenant database:

- A new table called $item$<appID> that contains the new field, Catalogue No..
- A new table called $NewTable$<appID> that contains all the relevant fields that have been defined for that table in the AL table object.

The following screenshot shows the overview of the two new tables that were created during the installation process:

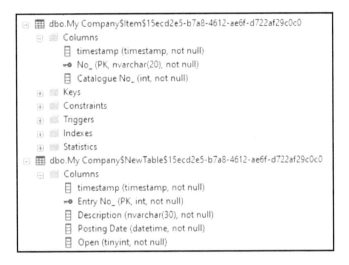

The installation process also executes the code that is contained in the installation codeunit and, in this example, populates New Table with three records. You can easily inspect the table's content by running the following code:

```
SELECT * FROM [My Company$NewTable$15ecd2e5-b7a8-4612-ae6f-
d722af29c0c0]
```

The output for this is as follows:

	timestamp	Entry No_	Description	Posting Date	Open
1	0x000000000001FBD5	1	Activity Start	2019-06-24 00:00:00.000	0
2	0x000000000001FBD6	2	First Activity	2019-06-24 00:00:00.000	0
3	0x000000000001FBD7	3	Second Activity	2019-06-24 00:00:00.000	0

Now that the main extension has been installed, let's move forward in our example, by creating and deploying another extension that has a dependency on the objects declared by the main extension.

Deploying a dependent extension

The dependency to the main extension is declared in the `app.json` file:

```
"id": "6d527590-711f-410c-b233-d267d192b13b",
"name": "SecondExtension",
"publisher": "DTacconi Inc.",
"version": "1.0.0.0",
"dependencies": [
    {
    "appId": "15ecd2e5-b7a8-4612-ae6f-d722af29c0c0",
    "name": "MainExtension",
    "publisher": "DTacconi Inc.",
    "version": "1.0.0.0"
    }
],
```

In the preceding code, we can see that the dependency must define four parameters: the application ID, name, publisher, and version. These are mandatory if we want to define a unique extension target.

 Once the dependency in the `app.json` file is defined, it is mandatory to download the appropriate symbols from the tenant. To perform this action, just run the command palette (*Ctrl + Shift + P*) and choose **AL: Download symbols**.

To make it very simple, we will create a second extension as follows:

1. The second extension will be with just a page extension object that is based on the table extension field implemented with the main extension (`PagExt50115.NewTablePageExtension.al`). Hence, the second extension must declare a dependency on the main extension. Consider the following code:

```
pageextension 50115 "New Table Page Extension" extends "Item
Card"
{
    layout
    {
        addafter(Description)
        {
            field("Catalogue No.";"Catalogue No.")
            {
                ApplicationArea = All;
            }
        }
```

```
    }
}
```

2. We are now ready to publish the second extension using the following PowerShell snippet:

```
Publish-BCContainerApp -containerName 'BC14MTW1' `
    -appFile 'C:\TEMP\UPGRADE\SecondExtension\DTacconi
Inc._SecondExtension_1.0.0.0.app' `
    -skipVerification
```

3. Like in the main extension, the publish action will declare the extension manifest in the [NAV App] table and the object contained in the extension is extracted into the [NAV App Object Metadata] table in the application database.

4. A record is also created in the [NAV App Resource] table of type metadata.

5. The significant change, compared to the previous extension, is a new record in the [NAV App Dependencies] table that links the second extension package ID with the main extension application ID, name, publisher, and version. The following screenshot shows the relevant query result snippet, after the dependent app is published:

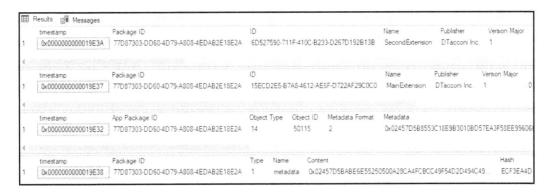

No action is performed; hence, there are no changes in the tenant database.

6. After publishing, we need to synchronize the second extension:

```
Sync-BCContainerApp -containerName 'BC14MTW1' `
    -tenant 'default' `
    -appName 'SecondExtension' `
    -Mode Add
```

This action will synchronize the extension metadata content of the second extension in the application database against a specific mounted tenant. In this case, since we have a page object in the extension and nothing more, no records will be created in the nav app schema snapshot table in the tenant database.

However, one record will be created in the [ndonavappschematracking] table, just to correlate the extension objects in the snapshot table with the extension ID, name, publisher, and version, no matter whether or not there are objects that need to be tracked. The following screenshot shows the relevant query result snippet after the main app has been synchronized:

	appid	version	name	publisher	baselineversion
1	6D527590-711F-410C-B233-D267D192B13B	1.0.0.0	SecondExtension	DTacconi Inc.	1.0.0.0

7. After synchronizing the second extension, we could check whether there is some data that needs to be upgraded. We could then use the following PowerShell script:

```
Start-BCContainerAppDataUpgrade -containerName 'BC14MTW1' `
    -tenant 'default' `
    -appName 'SecondExtension' `
    -appVersion '1.0.0.0'
```

As with the main extension, an error will be thrown, stating that there is nothing to upgrade.

8. The last step is to install the second extension:

```
Install-BCContainerApp -containerName 'BC14MTW1' `
-tenant 'default' `
-appName 'SecondExtension' `
-appVersion '1.0.0.0'
```

In this case, it will be a super-fast task, because we do not have any objects that will cause a schema change (we only have a page extension in the second extension).

One record is inserted in the application database's [NAV App Tenant App] table to report and link the tenant ID and the app package ID, and the same record is inserted in the tenant database's [NAV App Installed App] table, reporting the package ID and the app ID.

Everything is now ready to work in our solution (that is, a combination of two dependent extensions) and, in the BC14MTW1 folder, just run the BC14MTW1 Web Client shortcut.

After providing access credentials and creating a 30-day trial version, go to the **Item** list and create three items called **ITEM1**, **ITEM2**, and **ITEM3**, or whatever you like, and assign them **Catalogue No.** 111, 222, and 333, respectively. The following screenshot shows the **Item** card:

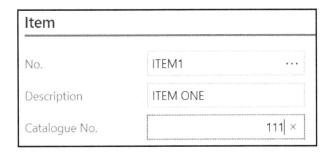

This will make sure that we now have some data to upgrade, as required in the next section.

Deploying a new version of the main extension

Again, in order to make it very simple, we will create a second version of the main extension where one field, Catalogue No., will change its data type from integer to text 30. This is a data type conversion that constitutes a breaking change in the data schema. The second version of the extension must then cope with the following:

- **Increase (bump) the extension version**: Change the app.json file version field as follows:

  ```
  "version": "2.0.0.0",
  ```

- **Table or table extension object changes**: We should declare the original Catalogue No. field with the ObsoleteState property set to Removed (for a definition of ObsoleteState and an overview of how it is used, please visit https://docs.microsoft.com/en-us/dynamics365/business-central/dev-itpro/developer/properties/devenv-obsoletestate-property). We should also declare a brand new field with the text 30 data type, and with the same Caption as the Catalogue No. field, in order to make these changes with a smooth transition. The following code shows this:

```
tableextension 50105 "New Table Extension" extends Item
{
    fields
    {
        field(50105;"Catalogue No.";Integer)
        {
            DataClassification = ToBeClassified;
            ObsoleteState = Removed;
        }
        field(50106;NewCatalogueNo;Text[30])
        {
            CaptionML=ENU='Catalogue No. 2';
            DataClassification = ToBeClassified;
        }
    }
}
```

- **Installation codeunit changes**: If there will be some code referencing the Catalogue No. and pre-populated values during the initial installation phase, these need to be changed according to the new data type in the installation codeunit. We do not have such cases in our example, but it might happen in real-life scenarios.
- **Upgrade codeunit**: The code changes that are declared in the table or table extension objects might involve data handling. A brand new codeunit with the Subtype property set to Upgrade is now needed to handle this data transit from the old field to the new one.

To find out more about upgrade codeunits, check out the online documentation at https://docs.microsoft.com/en-us/dynamics365/business-central/dev-itpro/developer/devenv-upgrading-extensions.

Within this codeunit and in a specific function, it is possible to write the upgrade code and check whether a specific version of an extension has been installed and performs actionable tasks based on this information. All of this information is retrieved in an upgrade codeunit using a combination of the `NavApp` and `ModuleInfo` data types.

This would make an upgrade codeunit very powerful and flexible.

In our case, we will retrieve the information of the currently installed version (`NavApp.GetCurrentModuleInfo(Module)`), and transform the existing integer value for the `Catalogue No.` field into text with the `C` as a prefix. Consider the following code:

```
codeunit 50105 "Upgrade Catalogue No."
{
    Subtype = Upgrade;


    trigger OnUpgradePerCompany();
    var
        ItemRec : Record Item;
        Module : ModuleInfo;
    begin


        NavApp.GetCurrentModuleInfo(Module);


        if (Module.DataVersion.Major = 1) then begin
            ItemRec.Reset();
            IF ItemRec.FindSet(true,false) then repeat
              if (ItemRec."Catalogue No." > 0) THEN begin
                ItemRec.NewCatalogueNo := 'C' +
                    FORMAT(ItemRec."Catalogue No.");
                ItemRec.Modify(true);
              end;
            until ItemRec.Next() = 0;
        end;
    end;
}
```

We are now able to publish the new version of the main extension:

```
Publish-BCContainerApp -containerName 'BC14MTW1' `
-appFile 'C:\TEMP\UPGRADE\MainExtensionV2\DTacconi
Inc._MainExtension_2.0.0.0.app' `
-skipVerification
```

The extension manifest for version 2 will be loaded in the [NAV App] table, and the object that is contained in the extension is extracted into the [NAV App Object Metadata] table in the application database. A metadata record is also created in the [NAV App Resource] table. The following screenshot shows the relevant query result snippet after the new version of the main extension has been published:

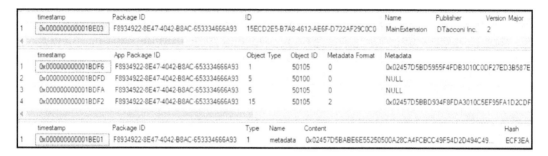

No action is performed in the tenant database.

Let's synchronize the new version of the main extension with the following PowerShell snippet:

```
Sync-BCContainerApp -containerName 'BC14MTW1' `
-tenant 'default' `
-appName 'MainExtension' `
-appVersion '2.0.0.0' `
-Mode Add
```

Records will be created in the tenant's [ndonavappschemasnapshot] table for every object that has an impact on schema changes at the database level.

The record that is created in the [ndonavappschematracking] table has been updated to correlate the objects in the snapshot table with the extension ID, name, publisher, and the new version. The record updates the version field to 2.0.0.0 and changes the baselineversion field to 1.0.0.0.

This is also the crucial stage at which metadata changes are applied. Let's run a simple query from SSMS as follows:

```
SELECT * FROM [default].[dbo].[My Company$Item$15ecd2e5-b7a8-4612-
ae6f-d722af29c0c0]
```

The preceding query will show that the new `NewCatalogueNo` field has been created. The following screenshot shows the result of the query in the extended item table:

	timestamp	No_	Catalogue No_	NewCatalogueNo
1	0x00000000000259C2	ITEM1	111	
2	0x00000000000259C6	ITEM2	222	
3	0x00000000000259CD	ITEM3	333	

It is worth noticing that users are still able to work seamlessly and without any problems, continuing to assign values to the old `Catalogue No.` field.

The next step in the deployment of version 2.x of the main extension is to perform the data upgrade:

```
Start-BCContainerAppDataUpgrade -containerName 'BC14MTW1' `
    -tenant 'default' `
    -appName 'MainExtension' `
    -appVersion '2.0.0.0'
```

The previous step synchronized the metadata structure at the database level and created the new field, leaving the old field with its values untouched.

It is in this step where all the upgrade magic happens and the data is moved into the new field. Run the following query again:

```
SELECT * FROM [default].[dbo].[My Company$Item$15ecd2e5-b7a8-4612-
ae6f-d722af29c0c0]
```

You will notice that the values in `NewCatalogueNo` have been updated according to the upgrade codeunit code. The following screenshot shows the result of the query in the extended item table:

	timestamp	No_	Catalogue No_	NewCatalogueNo
1	0x00000000000278D9	ITEM1	111	C111
2	0x00000000000278DC	ITEM2	222	C222
3	0x00000000000278DF	ITEM3	333	C333

The record in the application database's `[NAV App Tenant App]` table that linked the tenant ID and the app package ID is also updated with the version 2 package ID. This is also reflected in the tenant database by updating the relevant record in the `[NAV App Installed App]` table with the new package ID from version 2.

The dependent extension is, then, broken at this stage, because it is bound to a field that is effectively marked as removed; hence, the page text box control related to the old `Catalogue No.` field will not be shown in the client anymore. The following screenshot shows a snippet of the **Item** card after upgrading to the new version of the main extension:

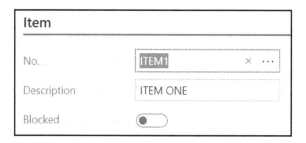

The last step to check is whether there are changes when installing the extension using the following PowerShell statement:

```
Install-BCContainerApp -containerName 'BC14MTW1' `
-tenant 'default' `
-appName 'MainExtension' `
-appVersion '2.0.0.0'
```

In this case, no action is performed, because the extension was already installed, and it has just been upgraded to another version.

We should, then, receive the following message when running the PowerShell cmdlet:

```
"WARNING: Cannot install extension MainExtension by DTacconi Inc.
2.0.0.0 for the tenant default because it is already installed."
```

After this, let's see how we can deploy to a new independent version.

Deploying a new version of the dependent extension

After performing the data upgrade of the main extension to a new version, we saw that the dependent extension has been broken. It is crucial at this stage to let the user read or update the new `NewCatalogueNo.` field from the client.

First things first. We must bump the `app.json` version of the dependent extension to 2.0.0.0, and also update the dependency to the appropriate version of the main extension. See the following updated snippet:

```
"version": "2.0.0.0",
"dependencies": [
    {
        "appId": "15ecd2e5-b7a8-4612-ae6f-d722af29c0c0",
        "name": "MainExtension",
        "publisher": "DTacconi Inc.",
        "version": "2.0.0.0"
    }
],
```

When the `app.json` file is updated, we must download the new symbols from our multitenant environment in order to have them set appropriately. The results of the `.alpackages` directory content, right after the downloading symbols, are shown in the following screenshot. This shows a list of symbols that are needed to build the new version for the dependent extension:

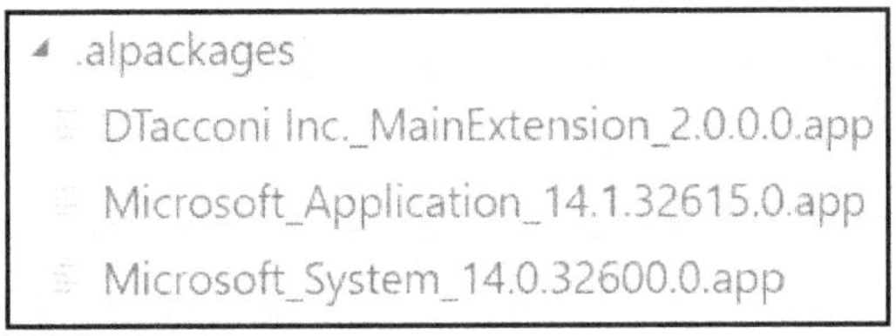

The updated page extension object will then have the appropriate reference to the new `NewCatalogueNo` field:

```
pageextension 50115 "New Table Page Extension" extends "Item Card"
{
    layout
    {
        addafter(Description)
        {
            field(NewCatalogueNo;NewCatalogueNo)
            {
                ApplicationArea = All;
            }
        }
    }
}
```

We could then publish the new version of the second extension using the following script:

```
Publish-BCContainerApp -containerName 'BC14MTW1' `
-appFile 'C:\TEMP\UPGRADE\DependentExtensionV2\DTacconi
Inc._SecondExtension_2.0.0.0.app' `
-skipVerification
```

As in version 2 of the main extension, the manifest will be loaded in the [NAV App] table, and the object contained in the extension is extracted into the [NAV App Object Metadata] table in the application database. A metadata record is also created in the [NAV App Resource] table, and also in the [NAV App Dependency] table, reflecting the dependency of the second extension version 2 on main extension version 2.

No action is performed in the tenant database.

We should, then, synchronize the app in the tenant using the following PowerShell script:

```
Sync-BCContainerApp -containerName 'BC14MTW1' `
    -tenant 'default' `
    -appName 'SecondExtension' `
    -appVersion '2.0.0.0' `
    -Mode Add
```

Once you run the synchronization, the original record that was created in the [ndonavappschematracking] table will be updated in order to correlate the objects in the snapshot table with the extension ID, name, publisher, and the new version.

The version field for the dependent extension will be 2.0.0.0, while the baselineversion field remains 1.0.0.0. The following screenshot shows the query result after the new version of the dependent extension has been synchronized:

	appid	version	name	publisher	baselineversion
1	6D527590-711F-410C-B233-D267D192B13B	2.0.0.0	SecondExtension	DTacconi Inc.	1.0.0.0

If we stop now, we have a hybrid half-deployment state, where schema synchronization is now enabled for the new version, but the installed version is still the old one.

It is now time to start the data upgrade for the second extension. See the following simple script:

```
Start-BCContainerAppDataUpgrade -containerName 'BC14MTW1' `
    -tenant 'default' `
    -appName 'SecondExtension' `
    -appVersion '2.0.0.0'
```

The record in the application database's [NAV App Tenant App] table that linked the tenant ID and the app package ID is updated with the new version's package ID. The same thing happened in the tenant database by updating the relevant record in the [NAV App Installed App] table with the new version's package ID.

The dependent extension is, then, consistent at this stage and the new page extension is used to read and update the NewCatalogueNo field. The following screenshot shows the **Item** card after upgrading to the new version of the dependent extension:

Just to be consistent in following the four deployment phases, we could also execute the installation statement:

```
Install-BCContainerApp -containerName 'BC14MTW1' `
    -tenant 'default' `
    -appName 'SecondExtension' `
    -appVersion '2.0.0.0'
```

It is trivial to say that we will receive the following message:

```
"WARNING: Cannot install extension SecondExtension by DTacconi Inc.
2.0.0.0 for the tenant default because it is already installed."
```

This concludes the life cycle of our simple extension that covers complex upgrade scenarios. It is left to you, as an exercise, to deploy all four extensions manually in an online Dynamics 365 Business Central production environment, and see whether there are any differences.

In the end, you could filter the extension that is deployed online, and you might notice that you will find all of them in the extension management list: two installed (version 2) and two not installed (version 1). The following screenshot explains the situation:

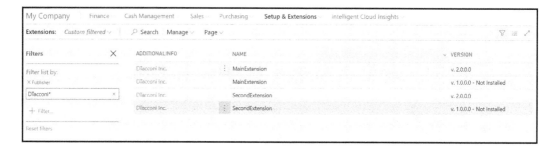

Handling installation and upgrade operations are two important steps that you need to handle with your applications. Upgrading in particular is mandatory if you want to upgrade an extension without data loss.

Summary

In this chapter, we took a close look at the various options for deploying an extension targeted at Dynamics 365 Business Central sandbox or production. We have also covered all four stages of extension deployment in detail: publish, synchronize, data upgrade, and installation.

This chapter closes the development section, and now you're ready to start working with extensions on real-world projects (you know how to create extensions, how to deploy them, and how to extend them).

In the next chapter, we'll begin a brand new section that looks at debugging and testing extensions. The final chapter relates to source code management and its life cycle.

9
Debugging

Dynamics 365 Business Central AL Language extension provides a debugger to help developers check, correct, or modify code so that custom extensions can build successfully, deploy smoothly, and act as expected.

Another way to track potential logical errors is to write test codeunits, but this will be a topic for another chapter. For now, we will see how to debug an extension and create tests for reports with ease.

This chapter will cover the following topics:

- Running the AL Language extension in debug mode
- Defining specific non-debuggable functions or variables
- Mastering debugger and code editor issues (*debugging the debugger*)
- Working with code analyzers
- Using Event Recorder to track information about event availability

Running in debug mode

The basic concept behind debugging is the *breakpoint*, which is a mark that you can set on a statement. When the program flow hits the statement, the debugger is kicked in and suspends execution (technically, it breaks) until instructed to continue. Without any breakpoints, the code would run just fine as long as the debugger is active.

The debugger will automatically stop the execution of the code only when it encounters an error, or if it has been instructed in the `launch.json` file to break on record changes.

A developer could also use the debugger to find potential logic errors since the debugger enables them to execute AL code syntax, one statement at a time, while inspecting the contents of variables at each runtime step. In this way, the developer can check and match what is expected when they have designed the application extension.

You can run the debugger from Visual Studio Code in three ways:

- Click **Debug** | **Start Debugging**.
- Press the *F5* shortcut key.
- Go to DEBUG view (*Ctrl* + *Shift* + *D*) and press the green right arrow in the top bar. The top bar also shows the debugger session name specified in the `launch.json` file. It will open that file if you press the gear icon. The last icon on the right enables and shows the debug console, which typically shows contextual debugging information. The following screenshot depicts the debugger top bar:

These actions will result in building your extension (equivalent to *Ctrl* + *Shift* + *B*), if this has not already been done, and then publishing the extension in the target online sandbox tenant.

Since the release of Dynamics 365 Business Central Spring 2019, it is now possible to run a debugger session without the need to build and publish the extension over and over again. This helps reduce the debug cycle and increases development productivity. To try this, in Visual Studio Code just hit *Ctrl* + *Shift* + *F5*, or run the Command Palette (*Ctrl* + *P*) and search for `AL: Debug without publishing`.

The `launch.json` file contains some elements that influence the debugging behavior and its target. The following is a list of them and what they do:

- `BreakOnError`: Specifies whether the debugger should stop when it hits an error.
- `BreakOnRecordWrite`: Specifies whether the debugger should stop on record changes (typically record create or update).
- `Tenant`: Specifies the **Azure Active Directory** (**AAD**) tenant in which to create the debugger session.
- `SandboxName`: With the April 2019 update, it is possible to have multiple sandbox tenants. This parameter will let the developer specify the name of the sandbox to which to connect the debugger session.

Also, the `app.json` file contains a parameter that is vital for the debugger to work against specific extension code: `ShowMyCode`.

If you publish and debug the extension as-is, it does not need to have this value set: it would work as implicitly set to `true`.

Nevertheless, if the code needs to be debugged from other extensions (and different Visual Studio Code sessions), since the default value for `ShowMyCode` is `false`, this parameter must be explicitly declared and set to `true`.

 Be careful when handling the `ShowMyCode` parameter, since it not only lets you debug code, but also enables users to download the source code for the extension. This parameter enables or disables the **download source code** action from the **Extension management** menu in the client.

Visual Studio Code debugger sections

The **DEBUG** view provides several sections and output windows to inspect, step by step, what's currently executing, the variable assignment status, and the code process flow. Additionally, since the release of Dynamics 365 Business Central Spring 2019, it is also possible to have some insight into code performance by gathering the longest-running database queries.

Consider the following screenshot:

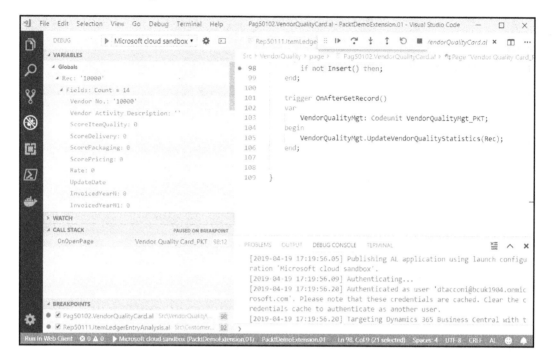

The debugger is basically divided into four sections: sidebar, toolbar, editor, and output windows. The editor window will highlight where the code is currently stopped. This is typically marked in yellow. The debug console, in the output window section, will show debugging information.

In the next sections we'll look into the debugging features with AL and Visual Studio Code.

Debugger sidebar

The sidebar is enabled by default and is located on the left side of the debugger. It is possible to switch the position with the editor (right-click in one of the sections and select **Move SideBar Right**), hide it (*Ctrl + B*), or even just hide some of the sections (right-click in one of the sections and uncheck the section(s) that you need to keep hidden).

The sidebar is divided into four sections, which are used to provide information related to the current code flow. Let's go through them here.

Variables

The **VARIABLES** section provides an overview of global and local variable assignments:

In the **Locals** section, it is also possible to check performance counters that are related to code execution:

In particular, it is possible to measure the following:

- Current SQL latency (ms): When the debugger hits a breakpoint, the Dynamics 365 Business Central Server service will send a probing SQL statement to the Azure SQL database and keep track of how long it takes to receive an answer. This information is helpful if the sandbox node for the tenant has healthy latency or there are infrastructure issues.
- Number of SQL executes: The total number of SQL statements executed in the session since the debugger was started.
- Number of SQL row reads: The total number of database rows read since the debugger was started.
- Top-10 long-running queries: Expanding the Last Executed SQL Statements section, you might observe up to 10 SQL Server statement entries (numbered from 0 to 9). The statements represent the 10 least performant queries, in terms of duration, that have been executed since the session started up, to the first breakpoint hit. These are defined by the following elements:
  - **Statement**: The T-SQL statement executed.
  - **Execution time (UTC)**: A timestamp defining when the SQL statement was executed.
  - **Duration (ms)**: The duration of the total execution time of the SQL statement. It's useful to analyze this if there are some missing indexes when developing extensions.
  - **Rows read**: Shows the approximate number of rows read by the SQL statement. It might be useful when looking for missing filters when developing extensions.

Watch

The *Watch* section is used to monitor variables of particular interest while debugging. It is possible to right-click on the name of the variable that you want to watch from the `Variables` window or in the code editor while debugging: this will display the value of the watched variable. In this window, you can also insert the names of the variables that you want to monitor into the watch list while debugging.

Callstack

Variable values and expression evaluations are relative to the selected stack frame. This will report a cascade/stack of objects in descending execution order.

Breakpoints

This shows a list of available breakpoints that could be enabled, disabled, or reapplied at will. Breakpoints can be toggled in the Visual Studio Code editor window by clicking in the left margin or by pressing *F9* in a selected line. Breakpoints that are displayed in the editor margin are shown as red-filled circles. Disabled breakpoints have a filled gray circle.

 Breakpoints that cannot be assigned to any code in the debugger session are shown with a gray hollow circle.

Debugger toolbar

The toolbar contains commands that pause, stop, restart, or control the debugging process. The following screenshot shows a debugger toolbar:

Possible actions are as follows:

- Continue (*F5*).
- Pause (*F6*).
- Restart (*Shift* + *F11*): Depicted by the green circular arrow in.
- Stop (*Shift* + *F5*): Depicted by the red square: The debugger toolbar commands allow you to continue (*F5*) the process until it comes to an end. In this way, developers can continue with their iterative process and start the operation again without running a new web client session in debug mode. The process could also be paused (*F6*)—the debugger session is still alive; restarted (*Shift* + *F11*)—it will create a new debugger session; or definitively stopped (*Shift* + *F5*)—the debugger session is closed.

- Step Over (*F10*): All statements are executed one at a time. If this command is used, when a function call is reached, the function is executed without the debugger stepping through the function instructions. If there is a breakpoint in one of the functions that it has been instructed to step over, the debugger will break at that breakpoint in any case.
- Step Into (*F11*): All statements are executed one at a time. If this command is used, when a function call is reached, the debugger will step through all the function's instructions.

- Step Out (*Shift + F11*): It will skip the current function and jump into the next one.

Debugging in attach mode

With the Dynamics 365 Business Central October 2019 update, the ability to debug, not only by launching a new debug session, but also by attaching the debugger to the next new session that is created by the application) has been introduced.

This capability currently has some limitations, and the following table explains its support scenario:

Deployment type	Web client	Web service	Background session
On-premises	Supported	Supported	Supported
Online sandbox	Not supported	Supported	Not supported

To enable the attach process, it is mandatory to add a new configuration parameter set to the extensions `launch.json` file.

The key parameters that need to be specified are as follows:

- `"request": "attach"`: In a typical debugging scenario, this parameter is set to default its value: `launch`.
- `"breakOnNext" : "WebServiceClient"` : With online sandboxes, the only option allowed is `"WebServiceClient"`, while with on-premise and Docker-based sandboxes, it is also possible to attach the debugger to the `"WebClient"` or `"Background"` sessions.

 To find out more about how to attach the debugger, visit `https://demiliani.com/2019/10/25/dynamics-365-business-central-debugging-the-base-application/`.

Non-debuggable items

Typically, developers would like to have a full debugging experience on every extension line of code. There are some circumstances where a specific variable or function should not show its current value. These circumstances are typically related to variables that store private information, or functions that return private values (such as user passwords or license checks).

When developing extensions, there is a special attribute that can be used with functions and/or variables that stop them from being processed (the debugger cannot step into them) or visible (variables and/or function output values are not shown) within the debugger. Writing the [NonDebuggable] statement before the declaration of a function or a variable would mean that they are not inspectable, and no breakpoints could be set against them.

In Report 50111 Item Ledger Entry Analysis, created in Chapter 7, *Report Development with AL*, add a breakpoint in the OnPreReport trigger in the very first statement, if includeLogo then begin, as follows:

```
90        trigger OnPreReport()
91        begin
92            if includeLogo then begin
93                CompanyInfo.Get;   //Get Company Information record
```

And after that, just publish the extension (*F5*).

When the client loads, search for packt report, and when the Item Ledger Entry Analysis report record is shown, click on it, choose to include the logo in the request page, and click **Preview**.

The debugger will stop precisely in the OnPreReport breakpoint that was just added.

Now, press *F11* twice to move the code execution down to run the Get statement in the Company Information table:

```
Src ▸ CustomerCategory ▸ report ▸    RepS  ⠿  I▶  ⌐  ↓  ↑  ↺  ■  Report "Item Ledger
90        trigger OnPreReport()
91        begin
92            if includeLogo then begin
93                CompanyInfo.Get;   //Get Company Information record
94                CompanyInfo.CalcFields(Picture);   //Retrieve company logo
95            end;
96        end;
```

If you expand the **VARIABLES** section in the debugger activity pane, you might notice that the Company Information (named CompanyInfo) record can be expanded, and you can see all its values:

```
◢ VARIABLES
  ◢ Globals
      Rec: <Uninitialized>
      xRec: <Uninitialized>
    ◢ CompanyInfo: ''
      ◢ Fields: Count = 73
          Primary Key: ''
          Name: 'CRONUS UK Ltd.'
          Name 2: ''
          Address: '7122 South Ashford Street'
          Address 2: 'Westminster'
          City: 'London'
```

Stop the debugger (*Shift* + *F5*) and add the non-debuggable attribute before the Company Information global variable, as follows:

```
. . .
    var
        [NonDebuggable]
        CompanyInfo: Record "Company Information";
        includeLogo: Boolean;
. . .
```

Publish the extension (*F5*) again.

When the client loads, search for packt report and perform the same action as before to preview the report: the debugger will stop once again in the same place.

Press *F11* twice to move the code execution down to run the Get statement in the Company Information table and retrieve the record data. Now, if you expand the **VARIABLES** section, you might notice that the Company Information record is not even shown:

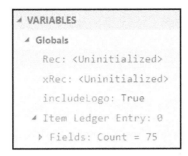

Hovering the mouse in any `CompanyInfo` statement in the code editor will result in an `<Out of Scope>` message, due to the presence of the `[NonDebuggable]` attribute in the runtime action.

Mastering debugger issues

In some real-world scenarios, it might be that, for some reason, the debugger will not start and it will report an unhandled error message in the output window; or you might simply need to keep track of the debugger service process. In other words, you might need to debug the debugger. After all, the debugger is just another software artifact.

To gain more insight and verbose diagnostics, there is an undocumented feature that you need to enable by entering a specific parameter in the `settings.json` file in order to use:

```
"al.editorServicesLogLevel": "Debug".
```

Once it's enabled, you need to restart Visual Studio Code to make the changes effective across the application.

This parameter will instruct the AL Language extension to create a verbose logging activity for the code editor (`EditorServices.log`), and the debugger (`DebuggerServices.log`) in the following `C:\Users\<USER>\.vscode\extensions\ms-dynamics-smb.al-3.0.121490\bin` directory.

 `ms-dynamics-smb.al-3.0.121490` represents the AL Language extension name and version that are registered in the current Visual Studio Code session.

The following is a snippet of the logged activity for the debugger service showing its processing:

```
. . .
04/19/2019 16:53:15 [/6] Process:
 launch
04/19/2019 16:53:24 [/14] Process:
 setBreakpoints
04/19/2019 16:53:24 [/14] Parsing Report 50111 "Item Ledger Entry
Analysis".
04/19/2019 16:53:25 [/14] Parsing Codeunit 50100 "Customer Category
Mgt_PKT".
04/19/2019 16:53:25 [/14] Parsing Page 50100 "Customer Category
List_PKT".
. . .
```

In the next section, we'll see how you can use code analyzers when developing with AL.

Understanding code analyzers

The AL language proactive debugging experience is greatly enhanced by code analyzers. Code analyzers are part of the standard AL Language extension, and are a set of contextual rules that are applied to extension development. These rules can generate an error or a warning when you're developing an extension.

Code analyzers can be enabled and disabled at will, both per workspace and globally.

To enable code analyzers, perform the following steps:

Go to **File** | **Preferences** | **Settings (Workspace settings)** | **Extension** | **AL language extension** and choose to edit the settings.json file.

You could also choose to edit the settings.json file by choosing user settings. However, since you might develop per-tenant extensions and also AppSource apps in the same environment, it would make more sense to have these enabled per workspace instead of per user settings.

In the `settings.json` file, it is possible to specify the following parameters:

`al.enableCodeAnalysis` (default: `false`)

Changing this parameter to `true` enables the analyzers that are specified in the JSON array parameter, `al.codeAnalyzers`. If no analyzers are specified, or there is no `al.codeAnalyzers` entry, it is assumed that all analyzers are enabled.

al.codeAnalyzers[]

The `al.codeAnalyzers[]` parameter represents an array of code analyzers. Currently, the supported values and the official links to the appropriate rules, ordered by ID, are as follows:

- `"${AppSourceCop}"`: This must be enabled when developing apps targeted for the AppSource marketplace. To find out more, visit `https://docs.microsoft.com/en-us/dynamics365/business-central/dev-itpro/developer/analyzers/appsourcecop`.

- `"${CodeCop}"`: This strengthens the standard AL Language development guidelines, and it is recommended that it is enabled for every kind of development target. To find out more, visit `https://docs.microsoft.com/en-us/dynamics365/business-central/dev-itpro/developer/analyzers/codecop`.

- `"${PerTenantExtensionCop}"`: Together with `CodeCop`, it should be enabled on every online development target, except when developing extensions for the AppSource marketplace, where `AppSourceCop` should be used. To find out more, visit `https://docs.microsoft.com/en-us/dynamics365/business-central/dev-itpro/developer/analyzers/pertenantextensioncop`.

- `"${UICop}"`: This is the last addition to the code analyzers, and it checks that the code matches the features that are supported by modern clients, and avoids hitting user interface limitations. To find out more, visit `https://docs.microsoft.com/en-us/dynamics365/business-central/dev-itpro/developer/analyzers/uicop`.

al.ruleSetPath

This is the path for a ruleset file that contains changes to the rules that are provided through standard code analyzers.

A ruleset file is written in JSON notation, and has a reference to an existing ruleset item ID that is implemented in the standard AL Language extension. This file is typically edited to redefine the importance of the rules within a specific extension project or workspace.

If we implement code analyzers in the demo extension project that we have created, it will help us to find out more info about our code style, and whether there are improvements to be applied. Let's enable the relevant analyzers for our extension project by changing the `settings.json` file in our `workspace` settings as follows:

```json
{
    "al.enableCodeAnalysis": true,
    "al.codeAnalyzers": [
        "${CodeCop}",
        "${PerTenantExtensionCop}",
        "${UICop}"
    ]
}
```

In the **PROBLEMS** window, there might now be a bunch of records with errors, warnings, and information. Considering only those that are related to `Report 50111 ItemLedgerEntryAnalysis.al`, there should be one error, two warnings, and one piece of useful information. Take a look at the following screenshot:

Looking at the error, this is pretty clear: the `includeLogo` column definition does not have its `ApplicationArea` property defined. For this reason, it will not be visible within the application, because the `ApplicationArea` property must be explicitly declared.

Just click on the error line in the **PROBLEM** window, the one marked by ID AL(PTE0008). This action will result in placing the focus of the cursor in the `includeLogo` field definition within the code editor.

Add the `ApplicationArea` property for the `includelogo` column in the request page as follows:

```
field(includeLogo;includeLogo)
{
Caption = 'Include company logo';
ApplicationArea = All;
}
```

You might notice that the error in the **PROBLEMS** window suddenly disappears. Moreover, the report is moved down in the object stack in the **PROBLEMS** window:

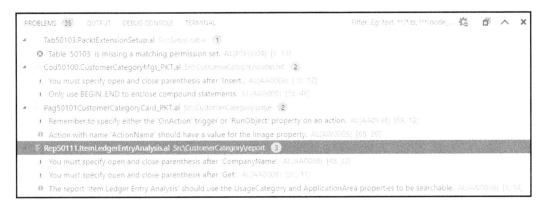

This happened because the problems record stack is ordered by descending priority, hence `Table 50103 Packt Extension Setup`, which contains an error, is moved to the top of the object list to be reviewed first, before warnings and info.

A rule's importance value can be changed at will by creating a JSON file that contains the IDs of the rules that need to be changed and how they have to be set according to your company's development rules.

Let's create a directory in the extension's main folder called `.ruleset`, and create a file called `demo.ruleset.json`:

Open `demo.ruleset.json`, and invoke the `truleset` standard snippet to write the following:

```
{
    "name": "PacktDemoExtensionRuleSet",
    "description": "Rule Set for Packt Demo Extension (PTE)",
    "rules": [
        {
            "id": "AA0008",
            "action": "Hidden",
            "justification": "Open and Close parenthesis warning is
kept hidden"
        }
    ]
}
```

In this way, we would like to instruct the AL Language code analyzer to avoid adding a warning record in the problems window for the rule whose ID is AA008. Word for word, the rule is *"Function calls should have parentheses even if they do not have any parameters."*

The last step to make it work is to assign the `.alRuleSetPath` parameter to point to the newly created file:

```
{
    "al.enableCodeAnalysis": true,
        "al.codeAnalyzers": [
            "${CodeCop}",
            "${PerTenantExtensionCop}",
            "${UICop}"
        ],
        "al.ruleSetPath": "././.ruleset/demo.ruleset.json"
}
```

 When you assign the path to a ruleset file, it is recommended that you save all files and close and reopen Visual Studio Code, in order to be sure that there are no permission errors, and access the ruleset file by the current process.

Once the ruleset file is in place, there should not be any warnings in the **PROBLEMS** window related to opened and closed parentheses, and the number of records shown in the problems should be reduced. This can be seen in the following screenshot:

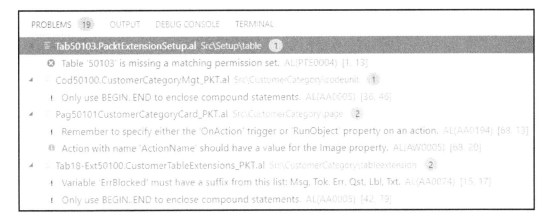

There are still 19 elements that need to be evaluated in order to be compliant with the AL best coding practice. Takeaways at this stage are that they should make good use of these rules in their own company and discuss what needs to be promoted higher, maintained as-is, or be completely turned off.

Be careful when enabling code analyzers, since they might increase memory consumption (RAM) in the development machine.

We saw here how to improve the quality of your code by activating AL code analyzers. In the next section, we'll see how you can use *Event Recorder* when developing extensions with Dynamics 365 Business Central.

Understanding Event Recorder

We all know that Dynamics 365 Business Central online development can only be done through extensions. Accessing code base extensibility is guaranteed by subscribing to standard event publishers.

Considering that there are several thousands of standard event publishers all over the application and the number is growing with every online update, finding the right spot to hook up a standard publisher is sometimes as hard as trying to find the proverbial needle in the haystack.

The recommended way to find out the appropriate entry point at which to subscribe is to use the Event Recorder.

This application feature is a must if you do not know what standard objects are, or you do not have access to the third-party source code in order to look at publisher definitions (in the event the code you subscribe to is part of a third-party extension or a private IP).

There are two ways to enable this feature:

- From Visual Studio Code: Open an extension source code project that defines a suitable sandbox connection in the `launch.json` file. Run the Command Palette (*Ctrl + Shift + P*) and then select **AL: Open Events Recorder**.

- Connect to your production or sandbox tenant and search for `Event Recorder`: The Event Recorder page offers a very simple action menu called **Record Events** with a **Start** and **Stop** button.

By simply pressing **Start**, the Event Recorder is activated and is ready to track the code processing flow.

It is crucial to understand that the Event Recorder session will capture absolutely everything that the code is executing; therefore it is recommended you opt for one of the following actions:

- Go to the Event Recorder page in one browser tab (let's call it TAB 1) and then create a new tab (TAB 2) where you browse to the page where you would like to start recording events. Then, start the Event Recorder in TAB 1 and start performing the actions that are needed to track the business process flow in TAB 2. When finished, go back to TAB 1 and stop the Event Recorder.
- Browse to the page where you would like to start recording events (TAB 1,) and in a new tab (TAB 2) go to the Event Recorder page and start it. Back in TAB 1, perform the actions that are needed to track the process and, when you're finished, stop event recording in TAB 2.

The page will refresh and display the records inserted in a temporary table in order of code execution, as follows:

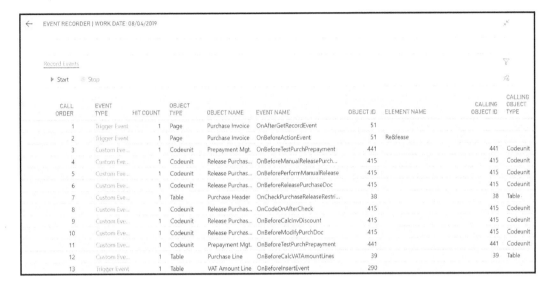

CALL ORDER	EVENT TYPE	HIT COUNT	OBJECT TYPE	OBJECT NAME	EVENT NAME	OBJECT ID	ELEMENT NAME	CALLING OBJECT ID	CALLING OBJECT TYPE
1	Trigger Event	1	Page	Purchase Invoice	OnAfterGetRecordEvent	51			
2	Trigger Event	1	Page	Purchase Invoice	OnBeforeActionEvent	51	Re&lease		
3	Custom Eve...	1	Codeunit	Prepayment Mgt.	OnBeforeTestPurchPrepayment	441		441	Codeunit
4	Custom Eve...	1	Codeunit	Release Purchas...	OnBeforeManualReleasePurch...	415		415	Codeunit
5	Custom Eve...	1	Codeunit	Release Purchas...	OnBeforePerformManualRelease	415		415	Codeunit
6	Custom Eve...	1	Codeunit	Release Purchas...	OnBeforeReleasePurchaseDoc	415		415	Codeunit
7	Custom Eve...	1	Table	Purchase Header	OnCheckPurchaseReleaseRestri...	38		38	Table
8	Custom Eve...	1	Codeunit	Release Purchas...	OnCodeOnAfterCheck	415		415	Codeunit
9	Custom Eve...	1	Codeunit	Release Purchas...	OnBeforeCalcInvDiscount	415		415	Codeunit
10	Custom Eve...	1	Codeunit	Release Purchas...	OnBeforeModifyPurchDoc	415		415	Codeunit
11	Custom Eve...	1	Codeunit	Prepayment Mgt.	OnBeforeTestPurchPrepayment	441		441	Codeunit
12	Custom Eve...	1	Table	Purchase Line	OnBeforeCalcVATamountLines	39		39	Table
13	Trigger Event	1	Table	VAT Amount Line	OnBeforeInsertEvent	290			

Event Recorder in action

Since these are records stored in a temporary table, they are volatile in memory and are not stored in the database. You now have the full list of events that were triggered during your business process, and from here you can find the right entry points to use for your customizations.

Summary

In this chapter, we have learned how to run the debugger and master its interface. We have also seen how to pin non-debuggable functions and variables in order to avoid showing private data when needed. We also inspected cool standard features that make our debugging and development life easier: code analyzers and Event Recorder.

Now you're ready to debug extensions, to inspect events, and to analyze your AL code.

In this chapter, we have also saw how to catch runtime errors while inspecting code flow. In the next chapter, we will master how to detect logic issues (bugs) in application code through the development of automated tests.

10
Automated Test Development with AL

In the previous chapter, we saw how to debug AL extensions with Visual Studio Code.

In this chapter, we will have a look at how to write automated tests for an extension in AL. We need to do this in order to have a modern development life cycle, and it's mandatory if you want to publish your extensions on AppSource.

Using the demo extension that was developed in `Chapter 5`, *Developing a Customized Solution for Dynamics 365 Business Central*, we will cover the following topics:

- Designing tests using the Acceptance Test-Driven Development pattern
- Setting up a test extension
- The technique behind testing code
- Implementing test code

Test automation and testing design principles

Application testing is not rocket science. Neither is automated application testing. It's just another learnable skill. From a developer's perspective, however, you need a change of mindset to write code with a totally different purpose than you're used to do. It's common knowledge that developers should never test their own code, as they, consciously or unconsciously, know how to use the software and how to evade issues. They write code to make something work.

Testing, however, is not about *how to make it*; rather, it's about *how to break it*. But this knowledge applies to manual, exploratory testing, where tests are executed based on knowledge and experience, not to scripts. And automatic tests are scripts.

To code these scripts into automated tests, we'll need developers. And more often than not, it will be the same developer that did the application coding.

In order for developers to code automated tests, they need to be provided with well-defined scripts. If there is **no design**, there will be **no test**. And that's the approach we will take in this chapter—we will first design tests and then show you how to code them.

Designing tests with ATDD

In his book, *Automated Testing in Microsoft Dynamics 365 Business Central,* Luc van Vugt delves into how to design and implement your tests. Based on the so-called **Acceptance Test-Driven Development** (ATDD) methodology, he shows how to write your requirements like a test design using the ATDD pattern. This pattern introduces five tags:

- FEATURE: Defines what feature(s) the test or collection of test cases is testing.
- SCENARIO: Defines the scenario being tested for a single test.
- GIVEN: Defines what data setup is needed; a test case can have multiple GIVEN tags when the data setup is more complex.
- WHEN: Defines the action under test; each test case should have only one WHEN tag.
- THEN: Defines the result of the action, or more specifically, the verification of the result. If multiple results apply, multiple THEN tags will be needed.

The following is what a ATDD scenario would look like for our customer category feature:

- **[FEATURE]** Customer Category
- **[SCENARIO #0002]** Assign blocked customer category to customer
- **[GIVEN]** A blocked customer category
- **[GIVEN]** A customer
- **[WHEN]** Set customer category on customer
- **[THEN]** Blocked category error thrown

You can acquire Luc's book at
`https://www.packtpub.com/automated-testing-in-microsoft-`
`dynamics-365-business-central.`

After learning how to design, we will now look at how to prepare the environment.

Preparing the environment

In order to start writing automated tests on your AL extension, you need to import *Microsoft Test Framework* into your Dynamics 365 Business Central environment. If you're working with Dynamics 365 Business Central on-premise (standalone installation), you can import it from the product DVD. If you are using a Docker-based development sandbox, you can import the Test Toolkit automatically with the `navcontainerhelper` module by adding the `-includeTestToolkit` switch parameter to the `New-BcContainer` cmdlet.

If you have an already-running Docker container with Dynamics 365 Business Central, you can import the Test Toolkit by using the following cmdlets:

```
Import-TestToolkitToBcContainer -containerName d365bcdev
Generate-SymbolsInNavContainer -containerName d365bcdev
```

The Test Toolkit Test Libraries consist of the following five apps (included in the latest Docker images in the `C:\Applications folder`):

- `Microsoft_Any.app`
- `Microsoft_Library Assert.app`
- `Microsoft_System Application Test Library.app`
- `Microsoft_Tests-TestLibraries.app`
- `Microsoft_Test Runner.app`

Your environment now contains all that you need to write and execute automatic tests. In the next section, we'll see how to set up tests for your extensions.

Setting up test development for extensions

If we take the most restrictive requirement for extensions (the requirement that Microsoft considers mandatory for approving your extension for release to AppSource), app and test code should be placed in separate extensions. As such, the test extension should have a dependency on the app extension.

This separation, however, might restrict the parallel development of the app and test code, since any change to an app extension results in its redeployment. This potentially also results in an update and redeployment of the test extension.

Before you realize it, you are continuously juggling your extensions, thereby reducing the productivity of the development team. The best course of action, while developing, is to have the app and test code placed in the same extension. Once it's ready, you can split up the code and create the two mandatory extensions by means of an automated build script or a specific merging strategy.

If your extension is not to be put on AppSource, I still strongly advise you not to release the test code in the app extension, in order to prevent automated tests from being run in a production environment.

In the specific case of our demo extension, where the app code is already completed, we can set up our test in a separate, dependent extension. In the next section, we'll see how to do that in practice.

Setting up our Visual Studio Code test project

To set up a new project for our test automation, perform the operation we carried out in Chapter 5, *Developing a Customized Solution for Dynamics 365 Business Central*, when we started our demo extension. Make sure that the app.json of our new test project is updated as follows:

```
{
  "id": "7737ab78-c872-4bca-b9f8-2de788818c21",
  "name": "TestPacktDemoExtension",
  "publisher": "fluxxus.nl",
  "brief": "Tests for Customer Category, Gift Campaigns and Vendor
  Quality Management",
  "description": "Tests for Customer Category, Gift Campaigns and
  Vendor Quality Management",
  "version": "1.0.0.0",
```

```
"privacyStatement": "",
"EULA": "",
"help":
"https://www.packtpub.com/business/automated-testing-microsoft-dynamic
s-365-business-central",
"url": "http://www.fluxxus.nl",
"logo": "./Logo/ExtLogo.png",
"dependencies": [
    {
      "appId": "63ca2fa4-4f03-4f2b-a480-172fef340d3f",
      "publisher": "Microsoft",
      "name": "System Application",
      "version": "1.0.0.0"
    },
    {
      "appId": "437dbf0e-84ff-417a-965d-ed2bb9650972",
      "publisher": "Microsoft",
      "name": "Base Application",
      "version": "15.0.0.0"
    },
    {
      "appId": "dd03d28e-4dfe-48d9-9520-c875595362b6",
      "name": "PacktDemoExtension",
      "publisher": "SD",
      "version": "1.0.0.0"
    },
    {
      "appId": "dd0be2ea-f733-4d65-bb34-a28f4624fb14",
      "publisher": "Microsoft",
      "name": "Library Assert",
      "version": "15.0.36560.0"
    },
    {
      "appId": "e7320ebb-08b3-4406-b1ec-b4927d3e280b",
      "publisher": "Microsoft",
      "name": "Any",
      "version": "15.0.36560.0"
    },
    {
      "appId": "9856ae4f-d1a7-46ef-89bb-6ef056398228",
      "publisher": "Microsoft",
      "name": "System Application Test Library",
      "version": "15.0.36560.0"
    },
    {
      "appId": "5d86850b-0d76-4eca-bd7b-951ad998e997",
      "publisher": "Microsoft",
       "name": "Tests-TestLibraries",
```

```
        "version": "15.0.36560.0"
     }
  ],
  "screenshots": [],
  "platform": "15.0.0.0",
  "idRanges": [
  {
     "from": 60100,
     "to": 60150
  }],
  "runtime":"4.0",
  "showMyCode": true
}
```

As you can see, we have added the dependencies from the extension to the test, and from all the *Test Toolkit Libraries* apps that are needed for testing.

Learning about the technique behind test code

Before we start coding tests, we need to learn a couple of things about the technique behind test code, the so-called **testability framework**.

Since NAV 2009 Service Pack 1, Microsoft has allowed the platform to let you build test suites by means of *test functions* in *test codeunits*. When executing a test codeunit, the platform will do the following:

- Run the OnRun trigger and each test function that resides in the test codeunit, from top to bottom
- Record the result of each test function

This is what Luc van Vugt calls the **first pillar** of the testability framework. Our first test example will implement this.

The **second pillar** allows you to create so-called *positive–negative*, or *rainy-path*, tests, in which we test the circumstances that led to failure. To achieve this, we use the AL asserterror keyword, which should be applied in front of the calling statement to catch the error and let the test pass:

```
asserterror <calling statement>
```

Our second scenario, which was used in a previous example, will make use of this testability feature.

In various parts of our code, we will interact with the user, asking them, for example, to confirm a certain action, or by simply displaying a message. When automating tests, we need to be able to handle these user interactions.

For this, the **third pillar**, the **user interface** (**UI**) *handler functions*, has been conceived. *Handler functions* are a special type of function that can only be created in test codeunits, and aim to handle UI interactions that exist in the code under test. They enable us to fully automate tests without the need for a real user to interact with them. Our third test example will show us how to do this.

The **fourth pillar** is the *test runner*. This is a specific codeunit that can do the following:

- Run tests that are stored in multiple codeunits, control their execution, and collect and secure the results
- Do this run in isolation so that write transactions, in the end, do not alter the database that we run the test on, and so that each rerun of a test is done using the same initial data setup

When running the test that we are going to build, we will make use of the standard test runner that resides in Dynamics 365 Business Central.

The initial trigger for adding the testability framework to the platform was implemented to get away from testing the business logic through the UI. As such, the testability framework is enabled headless, and thus there is faster testing of the business logic and it is not possible to test the UI.

Moving ahead, it became clear that sole headless tests excluded too much. How do we test business logic that typically resides on pages, such as a product configurator, in which options are displayed or hidden depending on the values entered by the user? So, later, Microsoft added a **fifth pillar** to the testability framework: the *test page*.

A test page is a logical representation of a page and is strictly handled in memory, displaying no UI. It adds methods that allow you to code the behavior of the user when accessing a page and its subparts, reading and changing data on it, and performing its actions. The fourth test example (in the *UI handlers – test example 4* section) will include a test page. So, let's see how we go about testing.

Find out more details of the five pillars of the testability framework in Luc's book at `https://www.packtpub.com/business/automated-testing-microsoft-dynamics-365-business-central`.

Designing our test scenarios

As we've already mentioned, we will illustrate four of the five pillars of testability in a test example:

- Test codeunit and test function
- `asserterror`
- Test page
- UI handlers

We need to have designed each scenario to enable us to code a test efficiently and effectively. This is what we will do first in the following section.

 In his book, Luc shows extensively how to get from requirements to an automated test, or as he calls it *From customer wish to test automation*.

Test codeunit and test function – test example 1

As test codeunits and test functions are the basis of test coding in AL, we could take any scenario as an example. But let's keep it simple and start with the basic requirement of our demo extension: the company wants to classify customers based on custom categories that they can define over time, and that can change in the future.

This has been implemented by adding a new table called *Customer Category* with a related page, and a new field in the *Customer* table called *Customer Category Code*.

A first test scenario when testing a basic part of this requirement would be as follows:

- **[FEATURE]** Customer Category
- **[SCENARIO #0001]** Assign non-blocked customer category to customer
- **[GIVEN]** A non-blocked customer category
- **[GIVEN]** A customer
- **[WHEN]** Set customer category on customer
- **[THEN]** Customer has customer category code field populated

As each scenario should be self-explanatory, we are not going to elaborate on each of the tags.

asserterror – test example 2

We can easily illustrate the usage of the asserterror keyword with the scenario discussed previously:

- **[FEATURE]** Customer Category
- **[SCENARIO #0002]** Assign blocked customer category to customer
- **[GIVEN]** A blocked customer category
- **[GIVEN]** A customer
- **[WHEN]** Set customer category on customer
- **[THEN]** Blocked category error thrown

This tests the same feature that was defined by the requirement to classify customers. However, even though the blocked pattern that was applied to the *Customer Category* was not mentioned in the requirements, it has been implemented in the extension, throwing an error when assigning a blocked customer category to a customer, and therefore it needs to be tested.

Test page – test example 3

According to the business requirements described in `Chapter 5`, *Developing a Customized Solution for Dynamics 365 Business Central*, the user must be *"able to create a default customer category and assign this default value to a customer automatically."*

This perfectly illustrates the use of a test page using the following scenario:

- **[FEATURE]** Customer Category UI
- **[SCENARIO #0007]** Assign default category to customer from customer card
- **[GIVEN]** A non-blocked default customer category
- **[GIVEN]** A customer with customer category not equal to default customer category
- **[WHEN]** Select **Assign Default Category** action on customer card
- **[THEN]** Customer has default customer category

It should be noted that we have *UI* in the [FEATURE] tag, which denotes that the feature is tested by making use of the UI. Preferably, test automation is about creating so-called *headless* tests; that is, tests that do not make use of the UI, as UI tests are 5 to 10 times slower than headless tests and non-UI tests. This is demonstrated by Luc in his book with the following screenshot, which compares a similar headless test and a UI test:

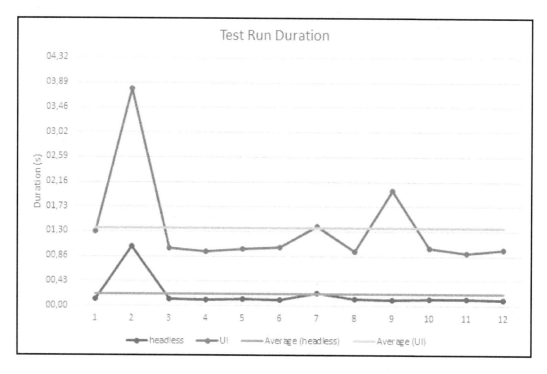

The average execution duration for UI tests is 1.35 s, while the headless average is almost seven times faster: 0.20 s.

UI handlers – test example 4

You might have already inspected all the application code of our demo extension on GitHub, and as such you might have seen that few UI elements triggered by code need a handler function. Actually, there is only one to be found in the `DoGiftCheck` function of the `50101 GiftManagement_PKT` codeunit:

```
if (SalesLine.Quantity < GiftCampaign.MinimumOrderQuantity) and
    (GiftCampaign.MinimumOrderQuantity - SalesLine.Quantity <=
        PacktSetup."Gift Tolerance Qty")
then
    Message(
        GiftAlert, SalesLine."No.",
        Format(GiftCampaign.MinimumOrderQuantity),
        Format(GiftCampaign.GiftQuantity));
```

Getting it triggered is not as simple as the other examples, as a lot of conditions need to be met. For that reason, it appears here the fourth, and last, example.

As you can see, the scenario is indeed somewhat more extensive:

- **[Feature]** Gifts
- **[Scenario #0010]** Assign quantity on sales line to trigger active promotion message
- **[Given]** Packt setup with **Gift Tolerance Qty** set
- **[Given]** Customer with non-blocked customer category with **Free Gifts Available**
- **[Given]** Item
- **[Given]** Gift campaign for item and customer category with **Minimum Order Quantity** set
- **[Given]** Sales invoice for customer with line for item
- **[When]** Set quantity on invoice line smaller than **Minimum Order Quantity** and within **Gift Tolerance Qty**
- **[Then]** Active promotion message is displayed

Here, we have designed our required test scenarios. In the next section, we'll see how to implement them effectively.

Implementing our test scenarios

Given an ATDD scenario, we can effectively implement test code using the following four steps:

1. Create a test codeunit with a name based on the [FEATURE] tag.
2. Embed the requirement into a test function with a name based on the [SCENARIO] tag.
3. Write the test story based on the [GIVEN], [WHEN], and [THEN] tags.
4. Construct the real code.

Test codeunit and test function – test example 1

Let's perform this four-step recipe for our first test example with the following ATDD scenario:

- **[FEATURE]** Customer Category
- **[SCENARIO #0001]** Assign non-blocked customer category to customer
- **[GIVEN]** A non-blocked customer category
- **[GIVEN]** A customer
- **[WHEN]** Set customer category on customer
- **[THEN]** Customer has customer category code field populated

Create a test codeunit

Using the [FEATURE] tag and applying the unique suffix for our extension is the basic structure of our codeunit, and will look as follows:

```
codeunit 60100 "Customer Category PKT"
{
    // [FEATURE] Customer Category
    SubType = Test;
}
```

As you can see, a test codeunit is defined by setting its SubType to Test.

Embed the requirement

Now, we create a test function with a name based on the SCENARIO description and embed the scenario, the GIVEN-WHEN-THEN part, in this function. I call this embedding green, as it's the commented-out GIVEN-WHEN-THEN sentences, before you start programming the .al test code.

Look at what the codeunit has now become:

```
codeunit 60100 "Customer Category PKT"
{
    // [FEATURE] Customer Category
    SubType = Test;
    [Test]
    procedure AssignNonBlockedCustomerCategoryToCustomer()
    // [FEATURE] Customer Category
    begin
        // [SCENARIO #0001] Assign non-blocked customer category
        //                   to customer
        // [GIVEN] A non-blocked customer category
        // [GIVEN] A customer
        // [WHEN] Set customer category on customer
        // [THEN] Customer has customer category code field
        //        populated
    end;
}
```

A test function is denoted by the [Test] tag. If you forget to add this tag to a function, it will be a normal function.

Writing the test story

Writing the first black parts is about writing pseudo-English, defining what needs to be achieved with a test. It makes a test readable by any non-technical peer in the project, and in the event their support is needed, the threshold for them to read the test is substantially lower than if the code had been written as technical code. And, maybe an even stronger argument is that the code will be embedded in reusable helper functions.

So, here we go; let's write the `black` parts:

```
codeunit 60100 "Customer Category PKT"
{
    // [FEATURE] Customer Category
    SubType = Test;
    [Test]
    procedure AssignNonBlockedCustomerCategoryToCustomer()
    begin
        // [SCENARIO #0001] Assign non-blocked customer category
        //                      to customer
        // [GIVEN] A non-blocked customer category
        CreateNonBlockedCustomerCategory();
        // [GIVEN] A customer
        CreateCustomer();
        // [WHEN] Set customer category on customer
        SetCustomerCategoryOnCustomer();
        // [THEN] Customer category on customer
        VerifyCustomerCategoryOnCustomer();
    end;
}
```

This `story` sets up four helper functions in which the content will be constructed in the next step. Note how close the names of the helper functions are to the descriptions of the tags that they belong to, and that no arguments or return values have been defined yet.

Constructing the real code

Writing the test story showed us that we need four helper functions, as follows:

- CreateNonBlockedCustomerCategory
- CreateCustomer
- SetCustomerCategoryOnCustomer
- VerifyCustomerCategoryOnCustomer

Let's construct and discuss them.

CreateNonBlockedCustomerCategory

CreateNonBlockedCustomerCategory is a manifold reusable helper function that creates a pseudo-random Customer Category record. At a later stage, we could promote this to become a library codeunit. The implementation is as follows:

```
local procedure CreateNonBlockedCustomerCategory(): Code[20]
var
    CustomerCategory: Record "Customer Category_PKT";
begin
    with CustomerCategory do begin
        Init();
        Validate(
            Code,
            LibraryUtility.GenerateRandomCode(FIELDNO(Code),
            Database::"Customer Category_PKT"));
        Validate(Description, Code);
        Insert();
        exit(Code);
    end;
end;
```

To populate the primary key field, we make use of the GenerateRandomCode function from the standard test library's LibraryUtility codeunit (131000). The LibraryUtility variable is declared globally as Microsoft does in their test codeunits, making it reusable in other helper functions.

We can observe the following from the preceding code:

- Pseudo-random means that whenever our test is executed in the same context, the GenerateRandomCode function will yield the same value, contributing to a reproducible test.
- The Description field is populated by the same value as the Code field, as the specific value of Description has no meaning, and this way it's most effective.
- Using the with-do construct in helper functions allows easy reuse of the code for similar purposes, but is applied to other tables as it only needs a change in the record variable (and the table it is referencing).

CreateCustomer

Using the `CreateCustomer` function in the standard library's `LibrarySales` codeunit (`130509`), our `CreateCustomer` creates a useable customer record and makes this helper function a straightforward exercise. Have a look at the following code:

```
local procedure CreateCustomer(var Customer: record Customer)
begin
    LibrarySales.CreateCustomer(Customer);
end;
```

As with the `LibraryUtility` variable, we will declare the `LibrarySales` variable globally.

You might wonder why we create a helper function that only has one statement line. As we've already mentioned, using helper functions makes the test readable for non-technical peers, and makes it reusable. What we haven't mentioned is that it also makes it more maintainable/extendable. If we need to update the customer record created by the `CreateCustomer` function in the `Library - Sales` codeunit, we only need to add that to our local `CreateCustomer` function.

SetCustomerCategoryOnCustomer

Have a look at the implementation of `SetLookupValueOnCustomer`:

```
local procedure SetCustomerCategoryOnCustomer(
        var Customer: record Customer;
        CustomerCategoryCode: Code[10])
begin
    with Customer do begin
        Validate(
            "Customer Category Code_PKT",
            CustomerCategoryCode);
        Modify();
    end;
end;
```

Calling Validate is essential here. SetLookupValueOnCustomer is not just about assigning a value to the Customer Category Code_PKT field, but also about making sure it is validated against existing values in the Customer Category table. Note that the OnValidate trigger of the Customer Category Code_PKT field does not contain code.

VerifyCustomerCategoryOnCustomer

Each test needs to verify its outcome. Put bluntly, a test without verification is not a test. And for the current test, we need to verify that the customer category code that is assigned to the Customer Category Code_PKT field of the customer record is indeed the value that was created in the Customer Category table. We therefore retrieve the record from the database and verify the content of the Customer Category Code_PKT field as follows:

```
local procedure VerifyCustomerCategoryOnCustomer(
        CustomerNo: Code[20]; CustomerCategoryCode: Code[20])
var
    Customer: Record Customer;
    FieldOnTableTxt: Label '%1 on %2';
begin
    with Customer do begin
        Get(CustomerNo);
        Assert.AreEqual(
            CustomerCategoryCode,
            "Customer Category Code_PKT",
            StrSubstNo(
                FieldOnTableTxt,
                FieldCaption("Customer Category Code_PKT"),
                TableCaption())
        );
    end;
end;
```

To verify that the expected value (first argument) and the actual value (second argument) are equal, we make use of the AreEqual function in the standard library Assert codeunit (130000). Of course, we could build our own verification logic using the error system function, and that's what AreEqual is doing too. Have a look at the following code:

```
[External] procedure AreEqual(Expected: Variant;
    Actual: Variant;Msg: Text)
  begin
    if not Equal(Expected,Actual) then
        Error(
```

```
            AreEqualFailedMsg,
            Expected,
            TypeNameOf(Expected),
            Actual,
            TypeNameOf(Actual),
            Msg)
    end;
```

By using the `AreEqual` function, however, we ensure that we get a standardized error message in case the expected and actual values are not equal. Over time, when reading the error of any failing test, you will be able to easily recognize the kind of error that occurred, given that your verification helper functions make use of the `Assert` library.

The completed test function would look like the following code, which is ready for execution:

```
[Test]
procedure AssignNonBlockedCustomerCategoryToCustomer()
// [FEATURE] Customer Category
var
    Customer: Record Customer;
    CustomerCategoryCode: Code[20];
begin
    // [SCENARIO #0001] Assign non-blocked customer category to
    //                  customer
    // [GIVEN] A non-blocked customer category
    CustomerCategoryCode := CreateNonBlockedCustomerCategory();
    // [GIVEN] A customer
    CreateCustomer(Customer);
    // [WHEN] Set customer category on customer
    SetCustomerCategoryOnCustomer(Customer, CustomerCategoryCode);
    // [THEN] Customer has customer category code field populated
    VerifyCustomerCategoryOnCustomer(
        Customer."No.",
        CustomerCategoryCode);
end;
```

Notice the variables and arguments that have been added to the test codeunit and functions.

Go to the GitHub repository for this book to have a look at the full implementation of the test codeunit: `https://github.com/PacktPublishing/Mastering-Microsoft-Dynamics-365-Business-Central/tree/master/Chapter%2010/TestPacktDemoExtension/Src/testcodeunit`.

Running the test

The proof of the pudding is in the eating, as they say, so let's run our test. The easiest and most instructive way to do this is by making use of the **Test Tool** in the application. You can easily access the Test Tool using the **Tell Me...** feature in Dynamics 365 Business Central:

When in a clean database, or at least a database or company where the **Test Tool** has not been used yet, this is what the Test Tool looks like, a suite called **DEFAULT** with no records in it, as shown here:

To add our test to the suite, follow these steps:

1. Select the **Get Test Codeunits** action.
2. In the dialog that opens, you have two options:
   1. **Select Test Codeunits**: This will open a page with a list showing all test codeunits that are present in the database, from which you can select specific test codeunits; once you have selected them and clicked **OK**, these codeunits will be added to the suite.
   2. **All Test Codeunits**: This will add all test codeunits that exist in the database to the test suite.

Let's select the first option, **Select Test Codeunits**. This will open the **CAL TEST GET CODEUNITS** page. It shows the test codeunit that we have just created and a bunch of tests that reside in the database, mainly due to standard extensions:

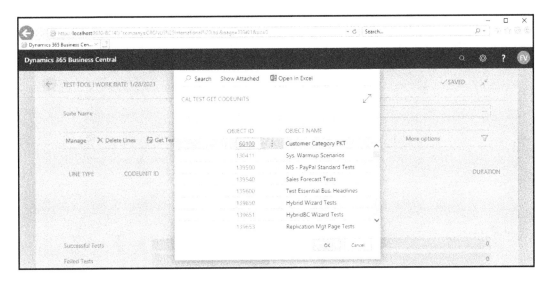

3. Select the test codeunit and click **OK**. The suite now shows for each test codeunit, a line with `Codeunit` in the Line Type column, and linked to this line (and indented), all its test functions (with `Function` in the Line Type column).

4. To run the tests, select the **Run** action in the dialog that opens, with the **Active Codeunit** and **All** options. Since we have only one codeunit in the DEFAULT test suite, it does not matter which option we choose, so click **OK**. Now our test codeunit will be run, and each test will yield a Success result:

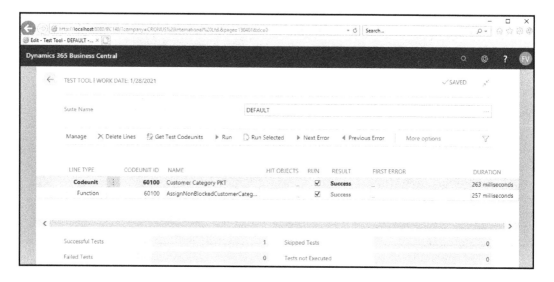

Had we selected the **Active Codeunit** option, only the selected codeunit would have been executed.

For each failure, the **First Error** field will display the error that caused the failure. As you can see, **First Error** is FlowField. If you drill down into it, the **CAL Test Result** window opens. This displays the whole test run history for a specific test.

Running the test by clicking on **Run** will call the standard test runner codeunit, **CAL Test Runner (130400)**, and will make sure that tests run from the Test Tool will be run in isolation, and the results of each test function will be logged.

asserterror – test example 2

As mentioned earlier, we will illustrate the use of *asserterror* with scenario #0002:

- **[FEATURE]** Customer Category
- **[SCENARIO #0002]** Assign blocked customer category to customer
- **[GIVEN]** A blocked customer category
- **[GIVEN]** A customer
- **[WHEN]** Set customer category on customer
- **[THEN]** Blocked category error thrown

Creating a test codeunit

Sharing the same [FEATURE] tag value as test example 1, our new test case will also share the same test codeunit, that is, 60100 Customer Category PKT.

Embedding the requirement

According to the previous requirements, we need to create the following new test function in the 60100 codeunit:

```
procedure AssignBlockedCustomerCategoryToCustomer()
// [FEATURE] Customer Category
begin
    // [SCENARIO #0002] Assign blocked customer category to
    //                  customer
    // [GIVEN] A blocked customer category
    // [GIVEN] A customer
    // [WHEN] Set customer category on customer
    // [THEN] Blocked category error thrown
end;
```

Writing the test story

Given test example 1, writing the test story isn't a difficult exercise. Have a look at the following code:

```
procedure AssignBlockedCustomerCategoryToCustomer()
// [FEATURE] Customer Category
var
    Customer: Record Customer;
    CustomerCategoryCode: Code[20];
begin
    // [SCENARIO #0002] Assign blocked customer category to
    //                  customer
    // [GIVEN] A blocked customer category
    CustomerCategoryCode := CreateBlockedCustomerCategory();
    // [GIVEN] A customer
    CreateCustomer(Customer);
    // [WHEN] Set customer category on customer
    asserterror SetCustomerCategoryOnCustomer(
                Customer,
                CustomerCategoryCode);
    // [THEN] Blocked category error thrown
    VerifyBlockedCategoryErrorThrown();
end;
```

First of all, note how `asserterror` has been applied – in front of the call to the `SetCustomerCategoryOnCustomer` helper function. This ensures that the platform will expect `SetCustomerCategoryOnCustomer` to throw an error. `asserterror` enables the test to continue with the next statement and it will not check the error, as such. So, it is up to us to verify that the expected did occur. If there is no verification of the specific error following `asserterror`, any error will make your test pass.

Next, note that, based on test example 1, the required variables have already been provided.

Constructing the real code

If we reuse the `CreateCustomer` and `SetCustomerCategoryOnCustomer` functions from test example 1, we only need to create two new helper functions:

- `CreateBlockedCustomerCategory`
- `VerifyBlockedCategoryErrorThrown`

Let's learn more about them both next.

CreateBlockedCustomerCategory

With the goal of `CreateBlockedCustomerCategory` being very similar to the `CreateNonBlockedCustomerCategory` helper function from test example 1, its construction is as simple, as follows:

```
local procedure CreateBlockedCustomerCategory(): Code[20]
var
    CustomerCategory: Record "Customer Category_PKT";
begin
    with CustomerCategory do begin
        Get(CreateNonBlockedCustomerCategory());
        Blocked := true;
        Modify();
        exit(Code);
    end;
end;
```

VerifyBlockedCategoryErrorThrown

Earlier, it was noted that, when `asserterror` enables the test to continue with the next statement, it will not check the error as such. And that is what this helper function needs to do, as shown in the following code:

```
local procedure VerifyBlockedCategoryErrorThrown()
var
    CategoryIsBlockedTxt: Label 'This category is blocked.';
begin
    Assert.ExpectedError(CategoryIsBlockedTxt);
end;
```

Running the test

Let's redeploy our extension and add the second test to the Test Tool by selecting **Actions | Functions | Get Test Methods**. **Get Test Methods** will update the selected test codeunit by adding all current test functions in the codeunit as lines in the Test Tool. Note that the **RESULT** column will be cleared. Now, run the test codeunit and see that both tests are successful.

Consider the next screenshot, which shows the results of the tests:

Running the test codeunit will show that both tests have been executed successfully.

Testing the test

How do we verify that success is a real success? We can do this in a simple way – by providing a different expected value to the verification function of our test case. So let's do it:

```
Assert.ExpectedError('Testing the test.');
```

Running our second test will now yield a failure with the next error text:

```
Assert.ExpectedError failed. Expected: Testing the test. Actual: This
category is blocked.
```

The *actual error*, indeed, is the one that should occur. After this, we move on to test example 3.

Test page – test example 3

We'll illustrate the usage of a test page in the next scenario:

- **[FEATURE]** Customer Category
- **[SCENARIO #0007]** Assign default category to customer from customer card
- **[GIVEN]** A non-blocked default customer category
- **[GIVEN]** A customer with customer category not equal to default customer category
- **[WHEN]** Select **Assign Default Category** action on customer card
- **[THEN]** Customer has default customer category

As you should now know the first steps in the four-step recipe, let's go faster and *create*, *embed*, and *write* in one fell swoop.

Creating a test codeunit

Sharing the same [FEATURE] tag value as test examples 1 and 2, our new test case will share the same test codeunit, which is 60100 Customer Category PKT.

Embedding and writing

In the already-existing `60100 Customer Category PKT` codeunit, we embed the requirements and write the test story, which leads us to the following test function:

```
[Test]
procedure AssignDefaultCategoryToCustomerFromCustomerCard()
// [FEATURE] Customer Category UI
var
    Customer: Record Customer;
    CustomerCategoryCode: Code[20];


begin
    // [SCENARIO #0007] Assign default category to customer from
    //                  customer card
    // [GIVEN] A non-blocked default customer category
    CustomerCategoryCode :=
        CreateNonBlockedDefaultCustomerCategory();
    // [GIVEN] A customer with customer category not equal to
    //         default customer category
    CreateCustomerWithCustomerCategoryNotEqualToDefault(Customer);
    // [WHEN] Select "Assign Default Category" action on customer
    //        card
    SelectAssignDefaultCategoryActionOnCustomerCard(
        Customer."No.");
    // [THEN] Customer has default customer category
    VerifyCustomerHasDefaultCustomerCategory(
        Customer."No.",
 CustomerCategoryCode);
end;
```

Constructing the real code

In order to have the `#0007` scenario working properly, we need to create these four helper functions:

- `CreateNonBlockedDefaultCustomerCategory`
- `CreateCustomerWithCustomerCategoryNotEqualToDefault`
- `SelectAssignDefaultCategoryActionOnCustomerCard`
- `VerifyCustomerHasDefaultCustomerCategory`

But, as you will see, and as you will also experience when writing more tests, the majority of these helper functions are easy to construct by making use of previously developed helper functions.

CreateNonBlockedDefaultCustomerCategory

`CreateNonBlockedDefaultCustomerCategory` resembles the `CreateBlockedCustomerCategory` helper function that was created for test example 2. We can use the same approach that was used there. Have a look at the following code:

```
local procedure
    CreateNonBlockedDefaultCustomerCategory(): Code[20]
var
    CustomerCategory: Record "Customer Category_PKT";
begin
    with CustomerCategory do begin
            SetRange(Default, true);
            if not FindFirst() then begin
              Get(CreateNonBlockedCustomerCategory());
              Default := true;
              Modify();
          end;
          exit(Code);
      end;
end;
```

Note that the `FindFirst` construction has been added to guarantee that only one default customer category will be added.

CreateCustomerWithCustomerCategoryNotEqualToDefault

Calling the `CreateCustomer` helper function suffices as the customer record that is created will have an empty `Customer Category Code` field. This makes the construction of this helper function a very easy exercise, as you can see in the following code:

```
local procedure
    CreateCustomerWithCustomerCategoryNotEqualToDefault(
        var Customer: Record Customer)
begin
    CreateCustomer(Customer);
end;
```

SelectAssignDefaultCategoryActionOnCustomerCard

With the helper function, we touch on the core of this test example – making use of a test page to achieve #0007, that is, testing that the user can assign a default customer category to a specific customer. The following is what the helper function looks like:

```
local procedure
    SelectAssignDefaultCategoryActionOnCustomerCard(
        CustomerNo: Code[20])
var
    CustomerCard: TestPage "Customer Card";
begin
    CustomerCard.OpenView();
    CustomerCard.GoToKey(CustomerNo);
    CustomerCard."Assign default category".Invoke();
end;
```

Note that I did not use a `with-do` construct to unambiguously show that the three statements in the function are referencing methods that you will only find on test page objects, and not on **normal** pages:

- `OpenView`: Opens the test page in view mode
- `GoToKey`: Finds the row in a dataset that is identified by the specified values
- `Invoke`: Invokes an action on a test page

For a complete listing of all test page methods, take a look at the following URLs:

- `TestPage`: https://docs.microsoft.com/en-us/dynamics365/business-central/dev-itpro/developer/methods-auto/testpage/testpage-data-type
- `TestField`: https://docs.microsoft.com/en-us/dynamics365/business-central/dev-itpro/developer/methods-auto/testfield/testfield-data-type
- `TestAction`: https://docs.microsoft.com/en-us/dynamics365/business-central/dev-itpro/developer/methods-auto/testaction/testaction-data-type

You can find more details on test pages in Luc's book at https://www.packtpub.com/business/automated-testing-microsoft-dynamics-365-business-central.

VerifyCustomerHasDefaultCustomerCategory

As the code for the default customer category is stored in the local `CustomerCategoryCode` variable in test example 4, verifying that the `CustomerCategoryCode` field on the customer record has indeed been populated with the default customer category is just a case of calling the already-existing `VerifyCustomerCategoryOnCustomer` helper function, as shown in the following code:

```
local procedure
    VerifyCustomerHasDefaultCustomerCategory(
        CustomerNo: Code[20];
        DefaultCustomerCategoryCode: Code[20])
begin
    VerifyCustomerCategoryOnCustomer(
        CustomerNo,
        DefaultCustomerCategoryCode)
end;
```

Running the test

Running both test codeunits will show that all tests are executed successfully.

More examples for the Customer Category feature

In the GitHub repository for this book, you will find an extra number of test scenarios regarding the Customer Category feature. Go there and study them, and see how various helper functions have to be reused, showing that building up a bigger test suite often involves the reuse of existing elements. You might have wondered why the test examples weren't consecutively numbered. Inspecting the other scenarios on GitHub will show you why.

UI handler – test example 4

In order to show you how to implement a `UI handler` function, we are going to have a go at the following scenario:

- **[Feature]** Gifts
- **[Scenario #0010]** Assign quantity on sales line to trigger active promotion message

- **[Given]** Packt setup with **Gift Tolerance Qty** set
- **[Given]** Customer with non-blocked customer category with **Free Gifts Available**
- **[Given]** Item
- **[Given]** Gift campaign for item and customer category with **Minimum Order Quantity** set
- **[Given]** Sales invoice for customer with line for item
- **[When]** Set quantity on invoice line smaller than **Minimum Order Quantity** and within **Gift Tolerance Qty**
- **[Then]** Active promotion message is displayed

As this is quite an extensive scenario, you will also explore and learn from a somewhat more complex test code sample.

Creating a test codeunit

Typically, a test codeunit can be viewed as a test suite that tests a feature. As this feature, `Gifts`, is different from the one addressed in the previous test examples, we should contain this test in a new test codeunit, as follows:

```
codeunit 60101 "Gifts PKT"
{
    // [FEATURE] Gifts
    SubType = Test;
}
```

Embedding and writing

Embedding and writing would now lead to a test function with the following pseudo-code:

```
codeunit 60101 "Gifts PKT"
{
    // [FEATURE] Gifts
    SubType = Test;

    [Test]
    procedure AssignQuantityOnSalesLineToTriggerActive
            PromotionMessage()
    // [FEATURE] Gifts
    begin
        // [SCENARIO #0010] Assign quantity on sales line
```

```
//[GIVEN] Packt setup with "Gift Tolerance Qty" set
CreatePacktSetupWithGiftToleranceQty();
// [GIVEN] Customer with non-blocked customer category
//         with "Free Gifts Available"
CreateCustomerWithNonBlockedCustomerCategoryWith
    FreeGiftsAvailable();
// [GIVEN] Item
CreateItem();
// [GIVEN] Gift campaign for item and customer category
//          with "Minimum Order Quantity" set
CreateGiftCampaignForItemAndCustomerCategory
    WithMinimumOrderQuantity();
// [GIVEN] Sales invoice for customer with line for item
CreateSalesInvoiceForCustomerWithLineForItem();
// [WHEN] Set quantity on invoice line smaller than
//        "Minimum Order Quantity" and within
//        "Gift Tolerance Qty"
SetQuantityOnInvoiceLineSmallerThanMinimumOrderQuantity
    AndWithinGiftToleranceQty();
// [THEN] Active promotion message is displayed
VerifyActivePromotionMessageIsDisplayed();
    end;
}
```

This is the pseudo-code that describes the process for assigning gifts. In the next section, we'll see the real implementation.

Note that, due to their length, some function names have been cut into two and spread over two lines.

Constructing the real code

Given the *written story* (in the previous section), we now need to create the following seven helper functions in order to implement real test code effectively:

- `CreatePacktSetupWithGiftToleranceQty`
- `CreateCustomerWithNonBlockedCustomerCategoryWith`
  `FreeGiftsAvailable`
- `CreateItem`

- CreateGiftCampaignForItemAndCustomerCategory
  WithMinimumOrderQuantity
- CreateSalesInvoiceForCustomerWithLineForItem
- AssignQuantityOnInvoiceLineSmallerThanMinimumOrderQuantity
  AndWithinGiftToleranceQty
- VerifyActivePromotionMessageIsDisplayed

Let's jump through the *real code* and take a look at a couple of specifics.

CreatePacktSetupWithGiftToleranceQty

The CreatePacktSetupWithGiftToleranceQty helper function's main purpose is to set GiftToleranceQty on the extension setup, and is given by the following code:

```
local procedure
    CreatePacktSetupWithGiftToleranceQty(
        GiftToleranceQtySet: Decimal)
var
    PacktExtensionSetup: Record "Packt Extension Setup";
begin
    with PacktExtensionSetup do begin
        if not Get() then
            Insert();
        Validate("Gift Tolerance Qty", GiftToleranceQtySet);
        Modify();
    end;
end;
```

The CreateCustomerWithNonBlockedCustomerCategoryWithFreeGiftsAvailable helper function

CreateCustomerWithNonBlockedCustomerCategoryWithFreeGiftsAvailable is a helper function that creates a customer with a non-blocking customer category set, and it's implemented as follows:

```
local procedure
    CreateCustomerWithNonBlockedCustomerCategory
        WithFreeGiftsAvailable(var Customer: record Customer)
begin
    LibrarySales.CreateCustomer(Customer);
    with Customer do begin
        Validate(
            "Customer Category Code_PKT",
```

```
        CreateNonBlockedCustomerCategory
            WithFreeGiftsAvailable());
        Modify();
    end;
end;
```

Note that, like our previous helper function, `CreateCustomer` (see test examples 1 and 2), this test function also makes use of the standard `CreateCustomer` function in the standard library `LibrarySales` codeunit (`130509`).

CreateItem

`CreateItem` is a similar construction to the `CreateCustomer` function, as it makes use of the `CreateItem` function in the standard library `LibraryInventory` codeunit (`132201`). As a matter of fact, it's just a wrapper around it, as seen in the following code:

```
local procedure CreateItem(var Item: Record Item)
begin
    LibraryInventory.CreateItem(Item);
end;
```

CreateGiftCampaignForItemAndCustomerCategoryWithMinimumOr derQuantity

`CreateGiftCampaignForItemAndCustomerCategoryWithMinimumOrderQuanti ty` has to create a gift campaign record that combines the item that has just been created and the customer category that is linked to the newly created customer, and defines the period of time within the campaign will be valid and active. Have a look at what the functions look like:

```
local procedure CreateGiftCampaignForItemAndCustomerCategoryWith
    MinimumOrderQuantity(
        NewItemNo: Code[20]; NewCustomerCategoryCode: code[20];
        NewMinimumOrderQuantity: Decimal; NewGiftQuantity: Decimal)
var
    GiftCampaign: Record GiftCampaign_PKT;
begin
    with GiftCampaign do begin
        Init();
        Validate(CustomerCategoryCode, NewCustomerCategoryCode);
        Validate(ItemNo, NewItemNo);
        Validate(MinimumOrderQuantity, NewMinimumOrderQuantity);
        Validate(EndingDate, DMY2Date(31, 12, 9999));
        Validate(GiftQuantity, NewGiftQuantity);
```

```
            Insert();
        end;
    end;
end;
```

CreateSalesInvoiceForCustomerWithLineForItem

When provided with the numbers of our item and customer, the
CreateSalesInvoiceForCustomerWithLineForItem helper function has to create
a new sales invoice with one line, making use of the
CreateSalesDocumentWithItem helper function from the standard library
Library – Sales codeunit (130509). The following is what its implementation
looks like:

```
local procedure CreateSalesInvoiceForCustomerWithLineForItem(
        CustomerNo: Code[20]; ItemNo: Code[20]): Code[20]
var
    SalesHeader: Record "Sales Header";
    SalesLine: Record "Sales Line";
begin
    with SalesHeader do begin
        LibrarySales.CreateSalesDocumentWithItem(
            SalesHeader,
            SalesLine,
            "Document Type"::Invoice,
            CustomerNo,
            ItemNo,
            0,
            '',
            0D);
        exit("No.");
    end;
end;
```

Note that no quantity is yet set on the line, as per the sixth parameter in the call to
CreateSalesDocumentWithItem. The last two parameters of
CreateSalesDocumentWithItem denote an undefined location and shipment date.

SetQuantityOnInvoiceLineSmallerThanMinimumOrderQuantityAnd WithinGiftToleranceQty

The main purpose of this helper function is to set and validate the quantity on the
sales invoice line, so that, when it is smaller than the minimum order quantity on the
gift campaign and everything is within the gift tolerance as defined in the setup,
calling Validate will trigger the message.

Have a look at the following code:

```
local procedure
    SetQuantityOnInvoiceLineSmallerThanMinimumOrderQuantity
        AndWithinGiftToleranceQty(
            SalesInvoiceNo: Code[20]; NewQuantity: Decimal)
var
    SalesLine: Record "Sales Line";
begin
    with SalesLine do begin
        SetRange("Document Type", "Document Type"::Invoice);
        SetRange("Document No.", SalesInvoiceNo);
        if FindFirst() then begin
            Validate(Quantity, NewQuantity);
            Modify();
        end;
    end;
end;
```

A very useful exercise before coding the [THEN] part is to run the test. In the case of this test, it will show us something that's very relevant. But before we do, we need to update the last details in our test function, as we haven't specified the various parameters when calling the helper functions. So, the following is what the new test codeunit has become:

```
codeunit 60101 "Gifts PKT"
{
    // [FEATURE] Gifts
    SubType = Test;

    [Test]
    procedure AssignQuantityOnSalesLineToTriggerActive
            PromotionMessage()
    // [FEATURE] Gifts
    var
        Customer: Record Customer;
        Item: Record Item;
        SalesInvoiceNo: Code[20];
    begin
        // [SCENARIO #0010] Assign quantity on sales line
        // [GIVEN] Packt setup with "Gift Tolerance Qty" set
        CreatePacktSetupWithGiftToleranceQty(6);
        // [GIVEN] Customer with non-blocked customer category
        //         with "Free Gifts Available"
        CreateCustomerWithNonBlockedCustomerCategoryWith
            FreeGiftsAvailable(Customer);
        // [GIVEN] Item
```

```
        CreateItem(Item);
        // [GIVEN] Gift campaign for item and customer category
        /          with "Minimum Order Quantity" set
        CreateGiftCampaignForItemAndCustomerCategory
            WithMinimumOrderQuantity (
                Item."No.", Customer."Customer Category Code_PKT",
                10, 3);
        // [GIVEN] Sales invoice for customer with line for item
        SalesInvoiceNo :=
            CreateSalesInvoiceForCustomerWithLineForItem(
                Customer."No.", Item."No.");
        // [WHEN] Set quantity on invoice line smaller than
        //        "Minimum Order Quantity" and within
        //        "Gift Tolerance Qty"
        SetQuantityOnInvoiceLineSmallerThanMinimumOrderQuantity
            AndWithinGiftToleranceQty(SalesInvoiceNo, 5);
        // [THEN] Active promotion message is displayed
        //VerifyActivePromotionMessageIsDisplayed();
    end;
}
```

Running the test

So, let's run the test, even though it's not ready yet. As the screenshot demonstrates, there is an unhandled UI element, Message:

If we read the error message more closely, we see that it's the message that we wanted to evoke:

```
Attention: there is an active promotion for item GL00000001. if you
buy 10 you can have a gift of 3
```

This shows us two things:

- We have successfully evoked the message.
- We need to implement a so-called MessageHandler function.

The following is what the simplest MessageHandler function looks like:

```
[MessageHandler]
procedure MessageHandler(Msg: Text[1024])
begin
end;
```

This will handle the message; that is, it will mimic a user pressing the **OK** button on the message dialog. Note that the name of this function doesn't need to be MessageHandler.

Having a MessageHandler function is not sufficient. It also needs to be bound to the test function that is triggering the message. This is done by setting the HandlerFunctions property of the test function as follows:

```
[Test]
[HandlerFunctions('MessageHandler')]
procedure AssignQuantityOnSalesLineToTriggerActive
        PromotionMessage()
// [FEATURE] Gifts
```

Running the test again demonstrates that it is successful now, but remember: *a test with no verification is no test*. The MessageHandler function could be triggered by any message. The last helper function we have to tackle, VerifyActivePromotionMessageIsDisplayed, needs to verify that our test did indeed evoke the right message.

VerifyActivePromotionMessageIsDisplayed

Let's leave something for you to discover. Go to GitHub and have a look at how this is implemented.

In this section, we have learned how to create automatic tests for your extensions according to your business scenarios. Automatic testing is absolutely a must-have with Dynamics 365 Business Central (it's mandatory for AppSource apps, but it's also a best practice to follow in general).

Summary

In this chapter, we have discussed the basics of how to create automated tests in Dynamics 365 Business Central.

We utilized the ATDD test case pattern in order to design each test, and then used it as a base structure in our four-step recipe to create a test codeunit, embed the customer choice into a test, write a test story, and finally construct your real code. You should now be comfortable with writing tests for your extensions according to your business needs.

In the next chapter, we'll explore another important aspect to master when developing solutions for Dynamics 365 Business Central: source code management and DevOps practices.

11
Source Control Management and DevOps with Business Central

Developing applications without using source code management is like driving without wearing a seat belt. Creating an app that must be supported for years and will be extended and modified to fit new requirements without knowing who wrote which code and why it was written is like going to the wilderness without a map and compass. Maybe you will manage to get through one day, but there will be nobody left with you.

By using Visual Studio Code to develop our app, we have all of the tools we need. The tools are **Git** for source code management and **Azure DevOps** for managing your app development, which will tighten cooperation between development and operation.

In this chapter, we will cover the following topics:

- Understanding Azure DevOps and what it offers
- Managing tasks, sprints, and boards in Azure DevOps
- Creating a repository for your code
- Managing repositories
- Branching policies
- Branching strategies
- Understanding Git merge strategies
- Exploring Git with Visual Studio Code
- Understanding Azure DevOps Pipelines
- Understanding the YAML pipeline

Understanding Azure DevOps and what it offers

Perhaps you have heard terms such as *Team Foundation Server*, *Team Foundation Service*, *TFS*, or *Visual Studio Team Services*—all of this is now **Azure DevOps**. You can find all that you need to develop your software in a team in Azure DevOps, such as the following:

- **Azure Pipelines**: This provides CI/CD for any language, platform, and cloud. It looks like this:

- **Azure Boards**: This is the area where you can track your project activities by using Kanban boards, backlogs, team dashboards, and reporting. It looks like this:

- **Azure Artifacts**: This is a tool for saving and distributing packages. It looks like this:

- **Azure Repos**: This has cloud-hosted private and public Git repositories. It looks like this:

- **Azure Test Plans**: This has tools for planned and exploratory testing. It looks like this:

Of course, you do not need to use all of the available tools. You can begin with Azure Repos, then add Azure Pipelines and connect all of this to Azure Boards.

Since you get five users for free, there is no cost associated with using these tools. And if your developers have MSDN subscriptions, they already have the license for Azure DevOps included. If this is not enough for you, you can buy additional licenses (from $6 per user per month—see `https://azure.microsoft.com/en-us/pricing/details/devops/`).

If your company domain is connected to **Azure Active Directory** (**AAD**), you can manage access to Azure DevOps by using these accounts and groups. It means your users do not need another account just to work with all of this.

Creating an Azure DevOps account and project

On **Azure DevOps**, you can have multiple accounts. On each account, you can have multiple projects. When you create a new project with Azure DevOps, the resulting project URL will look like the following:

`https://dev.azure.com/myaccount/myproject`

Let's begin by creating a new account on Azure DevOps. You can choose whether you will use Microsoft accounts to access Azure DevOps or use your company's AAD accounts.

If you use a personal account to create the Azure DevOps, you can transfer ownership to the company account later.

To create a new Azure DevOps account, follow these steps:

1. Go to `https://go.microsoft.com/fwlink/?LinkId=307137` and sign in with your Microsoft or AAD account.
2. Read through and accept the Terms of Service, Privacy Statement, and Code of Conduct. Click **Continue**.
3. If you have already used your account with Azure DevOps, you can create a new organization with the **New Organization** button.
4. Enter the name of your organization and select the location to host your projects.
5. Now, you can create your first project. Select if it will be **Public** (accessible by anyone) or **Private** (accessible only by users you give access to).
6. You are now the owner of a new Azure DevOps account and project; congratulations! The following screenshot shows this:

If you have access to multiple Azure DevOps accounts, you can freely switch between them and create projects in them, if you have permission.

By default, the new project will be using a **Git** repository and an **Agile** work item process template. You can change the process to **Scrum** if you prefer product backlog items to user stories and impediments to issues (among other differences, which are described at `https://docs.microsoft.com/en-us/azure/devops/boards/work-items/guidance/choose-process`).

You can create a project per product/customer, or you can use one project for everything and use other tools to group things together per product/customer. It depends on whether there are separate groups working on the projects or you are sharing resources between projects.

I recommend starting with one project where you have one backlog (queue) for prioritizing the work for the team. If you have two queues or two separate teams, you can use separate projects.

Managing tasks, sprints, and boards in Azure DevOps

Azure DevOps is an essential tool for managing Dynamics 365 Business Central projects, starting from the very early stages of the project. By using the **Boards** feature, you can start managing your project's tasks, features, bugs, and general activities in a centralized way.

In your Azure DevOps project, if you click on **Boards**, you get the following options:

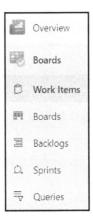

Here is a brief description of the available options (we'll see them in detail later):

- **Work Items**: Here, you can manage the list of your activities (activities that are assigned to you or that you follow, or your team's activities).
- **Boards**: Here, you can access your Board view.
- **Backlogs**: Here, you can access your product backlogs are a list of work items that a project team plans to develop and deliver.
- **Sprints**: Here, you can manage your project's iterations (in Scrum methodology, a sprint is normally defined as a period of not more than three weeks where tasks are grouped and must be completed).
- **Queries**: This is an area where you can set up your queries to find and list work items.

As a project manager, the first thing you can do is to select **Backlogs** and create a product backlog for your project (a product backlog corresponds to your project plan—the roadmap that your team plans to deliver).

Here, you can create phases and work items (tasks, bugs, and so on) and assign tasks to your team's users. The following screenshot shows this:

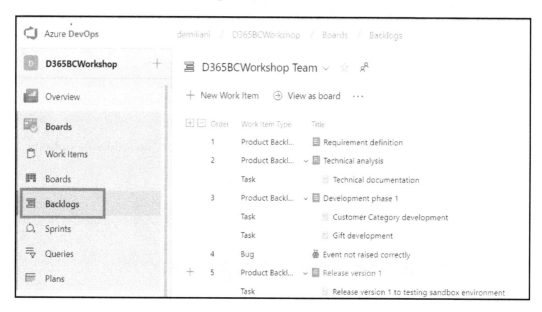

In the following screenshot, we have defined some work items whose type is **Product Backlog Item**. These items correspond to a group of activities. Under each of these **Product Backlog Items**, we have the corresponding tasks. Each task has its own **state** (**To Do**, **In Progress**, or **Done**), a description, and an associated priority:

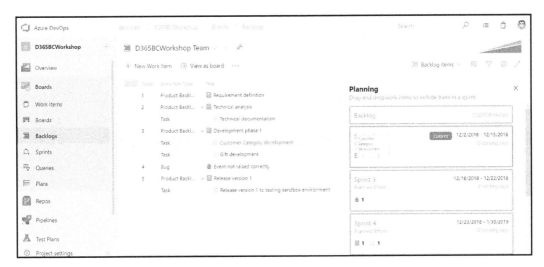

On the right-hand side of the **Backlog** page, you have the **Sprint** panel.

According to the Scrum methodology, teams plan and track work at regular time intervals, referred to as a *sprint cadence*. You can define sprints to correspond to the cadence your team uses for your project.

In Azure DevOps, you can select a **sprint**, define the start and end date, and then assign activities from **Backlog** to a specific sprint by dragging the activities (in the preceding screenshot, for example, I assigned the **Customer Category Development** activity to **Sprint 2**).

After scheduling activities and sprints for your project, there are also some other interesting views available. If you click on **Work Items**, you can see the work items status (such as the work items assigned to you, all work items, and recently created work items):

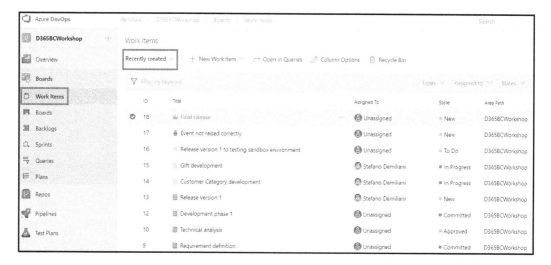

If you click on **Boards**, you can have a board of your project (a view of your project's tasks as a card ordered by status; you can drag and drop tasks to change their status):

If you select **Sprints**, you can see details of every sprint (iteration path) defined in your project. Here, you can have a **Taskboard** view and you can see the sprint backlog and capacity:

From here, you can monitor the progress of every sprint and the activities associated with every task.

On the **Queries** page, you can define custom queries to retrieve work items. Here, I've defined a query to immediately see all tasks declared as completed in my project:

When executed, the query returns the desired results (which can be viewed in different formats):

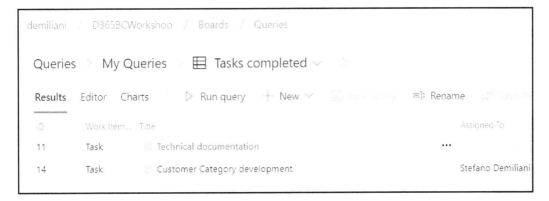

Another interesting feature is what is called the **Delivery Plans**. **Delivery Plans** display work items as cards along with a timeline or calendar view. It is very useful to see expected release dates or delivery dates for your team's activities.

Delivery Plans is not a standard feature, and to get it, you need to download and install an Azure DevOps extension from the Marketplace (click on the bag icon in the top-right corner of your page). The extension is shown here:

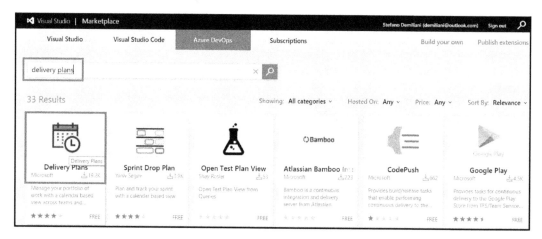

When it's installed, you have a new menu called **Plans** on the left and, if you click on it, you can see your project delivery plan in a timeline:

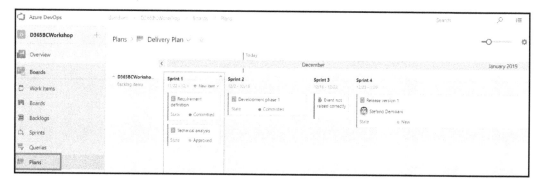

The coolest part is that all of these project management features are available in a single tool and are totally integrated with the development tools you use every day (such as Visual Studio Code). In Visual Studio Code you can, for example, commit your code and attach the commit to a task assigned to you. In this way, you have a complete product life cycle and a project manager can check what code modifications have been made to develop or solve a particular task or problem.

For example, if we select the completed **Customer Category development** task and click on **Links**, we can see all of the task's details. In particular, with the **History** link, we can see the entire history of the tasks:

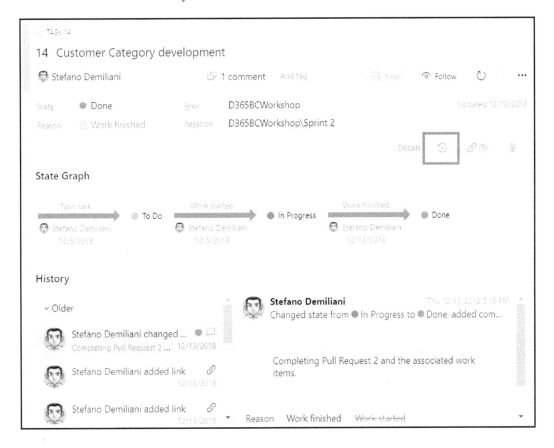

If we click on **Links**, we can see all of the commits related to this task. Here, we can see that, for this task, we have three commits and a pull request:

If you select a particular commit, you can see the details of the code modifications:

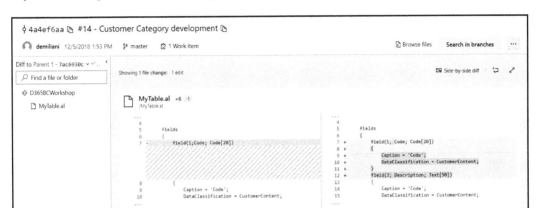

As you can see, you have complete control over all of the aspects of your project from a single portal and a unified interface.

Creating a repository for your code

Repositories are there to keep your source code safe, secure, and available when needed. Azure DevOps offers unlimited repositories. Having this secure store with unlimited space for free is a great way to calm your nerves if a notebook is stolen or hardware breaks. And you can access it from everywhere; no is VPN needed. Additionally, you can easily connect the changes to requirements (work items) to find out why something was done and by whom.

To create a new repository, follow these steps:

1. Go to the **Repos** section of Azure DevOps.
2. Expand the repository selection at the top (you can manage existing repositories, import repositories, or create a new one).
3. Select **New Repository**.
4. Enter a name.
5. Click **Create**.

In a while, your new repository is available, and the main page gives you all of the information you need to fill the repository with your code. The following screenshot shows this:

In the main page of the repository we've just created, you have links for the following features:

- Clone to your computer: You can use the project's URL with Git to clone the repository, or click **Clone in VS Code** to open Visual Studio Code (or some other supported development tool), select the target folder, and let Visual Studio Code clone the repository to your local disk. Then, you can fill it with your source code as you wish.
- Push an existing repository from the command line: Copy the commands, go to your local repository, and run the commands, and your local repository will be connected to this new Azure DevOps repository and will be pushed into it.

- Import a repository: If you have a Git repository somewhere else and you want to import it, just enter the URL and the current state will be imported.
- Initialize with README or gitignore: If you want, just create README with a project description or just a .gitignore file and you will fill the repository later with something else.

Next, let's see how to manage repositories.

Managing repositories

In each repository you create, you can set multiple settings. We will go through the most interesting ones. You can manage repositories by clicking on **Project Settings | Repos | Repositories**:

On the repository's settings page, we can manage the main settings, which we'll see in the following sections.

Security

You can assign groups and set permissions for all repositories and refine them for each repository and even per branch or tag as needed. I recommend to check which users can do the following:

- Delete the repository
- Force push (this could rewrite the history in the repository)
- Create a repository
- Bypass policies

If you set the right settings, you can prevent the loss of your code.

Options

On all Git repositories and each separate repository, you can set the following things:

- **Cross-platform compatibility**: This ensures that the settings are set to prevent problems with file/folder names that differ only by case. Git is case-sensitive and will allow the developer to add `File.txt` and `file.txt` as two separate files. But Windows and iOS are case-insensitive and will have problems in this regard. A best practice is to be consistent in naming and not to create such a file. Enabling the options in the repository will force developers to keep the names unique. And because even tags and branches are files internally in Git, the conflict could exist even in tag and branch names.
- **Forks**: If you do not want to allow users to create forks from the repository, you can disable this function. A fork is a copy of the repository that maintains a connection to the original repository. A developer can create a pull request to transfer changes from one repository to another, using forks. It is using the fact that Git is a distributed system and one repository can exist in multiple places (multiple servers or multiple repositories on one server—it doesn't matter).
- **Work item management (per repository)**: Keep this enabled to be able to connect your commit to existing work items. In this way, you will have information about what was done for each requirement, and you will even be able to say which changes are part of each build or release of your application. This could help you to create a change log for each version.
- **Code search branches (per repository)**: You can select up to five branches per repository to be indexed for code search. The files from these branches will be searchable by the search function of Azure DevOps. Just enter the text you want to search for and Azure DevOps will quickly find it in all your repositories. It's a very handy tool.
- **Branching Policies (per branch)**: See the *Branching policies* section.

Let's see these branching policies in the next section.

Branching policies

To maintain the quality of your app, you can define policies that must be met before changes from the developer can be integrated into the selected branch.

Mostly, the policy is defined on the *master* branch, but it could be any branch you want to keep healthy. If you define the policy for a branch, changes cannot be pushed into this branch directly, but only through Pull Requests (PRs). See the *Pull request* section for more details. In this way, each change is checked and tested, and if the policy is not met, the change will not make it into the branch. You can define the following in the policy:

- **The minimum number of reviewers**: This is how many reviewers must approve the PR to be accepted.
- **Check for linked work items**: This forces developers to associate the PR with work items to have links between requirements and changes.
- **Check for comment resolution**: If the reviewer wrote some comment, the comment must be resolved before the PR is accepted.
- **Enforce a merge strategy**: You can prohibit a fast-forward merge (you lose some detail but gain simplicity) or enforce a squash merge, which will condense all commits from the developer into one new commit on the target branch.
- **Build validation**: You can define a build pipeline that will be used to build and test the changes. If the build succeeds, the PR could be accepted. Failing the build may prevent the PR from being accepted (optional behavior). In this way, you can keep the branch healthy.
- **Automatically include code reviewers**: This defines user groups or users that will be used as reviewers by default. Reviewers could be chosen by specific changes, for example, when a script file or the settings of the app are changed, the responsible person will be added as a reviewer automatically.

Some developers tend to view branching policies as just additional hurdles in their way, but it is a great opportunity to grow your team and improve the quality through the reviews. It gives the team a chance to learn from each other and teach themselves new things. And additional eyes on the code are always good.

Branching strategies

We have set the policies for branches to make rules and technical checks, but the question is, how swap use branches in Git to support your work? Which strategy should you use? When should you create a new branch? When should you merge branches?

There are plenty of strategies you can use, and there is no silver-bullet solution. The best strategy for your team could be different for another team, or you may have one strategy for your **AppSource** app and another for your **PerTenant** app.

Before you decide which way you will go, think about the **KISS principle** (**Keep It Simple, Stupid**).

In all of the examples in this chapter, we will consider the master branch the most stable one, the one that represents the app as it is released to production. You can decide to name this branch differently and it has no impact on the strategies themselves. You just need to define the name and make it consistent through the team. Let's go through the branches in the following sections.

Only a master branch

Having one branch is the simplest strategy you can use. If you have only one developer working on the app, there is no need to create a branch. Even when there are more developers, they could still work on one branch, merging their changes into it each time they conflict. But it is hard to keep the product stable because half-done changes could be pushed into the branch:

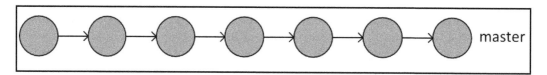

To stabilize the app, you will need to pause development. Still, you can change the strategy to something else later, when you see the need for it.

Feature/developer branches

To isolate changes for one feature or one developer, you can create a branch for each feature or developer. In this way, the developers are working on their own branches, with no conflicts with others until they hit a point when their work is done, and they then integrate the changes back into the master branch.

After the feature is finished and integrated back to the master branch, the feature branch can be deleted. If the branch is per developer, you can expect that the branch will live a long time. This could be a problem from a long-term point of view. The following diagram depicts this:

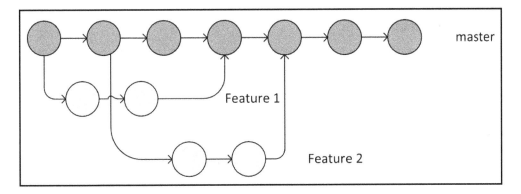

Using one branch per developer will mix different changes for different features together, and it could be a problem to release only selected features later in the process.

Using branches per feature gives you the possibility to release only selected features or cancel feature development for no cost (before it is integrated back into the master branch).

Release branching

The next strategy is to create a branch for each release you are preparing. It gives you the ability to stabilize the product before release and isolate it from ongoing development:

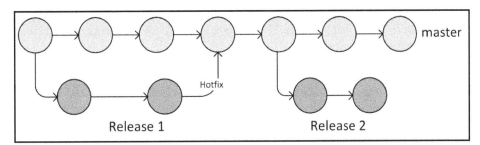

As we can see in the preceding diagram, it is good for apps going to AppSource because you can fix issues based on the AppSource validation procedure and the app will not be affected by new development in between. The fixes could be integrated back to the master branch at any time.

Other strategies

You can create a new branch even for servicing (if support for the released version is done by another team and is long-term, for example, when creating service packs), or per hotfix, when creating the hotfix takes a long time and you need to isolate it from the release and development.

As you can see, the only purpose of the branch is to isolate changes in it from other changes done for a different purpose in case you need to keep it isolated for a long time.

Every strategy can be combined with the others, and in this way, you can create your own strategies based on your needs. One of these combinations is named `Git flow`, and we will explore it next.

Git flow

Git flow is a workflow that uses feature branching together with bug and release branching. It is widely used, and you can even find tools that support this flow by automating different parts of it. In Git flow, the master branch represents the released versions, that is, each commit in it represents a released version of the product.

The second branch is the development branch, and it serves as the integration branch for feature branches that are created from it for each feature that is developed.

When a new release is prepared, a new release branch is created from the development branch. On the release branch, stabilization and fine-tuning is done until the version is ready for release. The release is finished by merging the release branch with the master branch.

If there is a bug in the released version, a new bug fix branch is created from the master branch. All fixes are made in this branch, and it is then integrated back into the master branch (creating a new fixed version of the app) and into the development branch (to keep the bug fix for the next releases).

The following diagram depicts this:

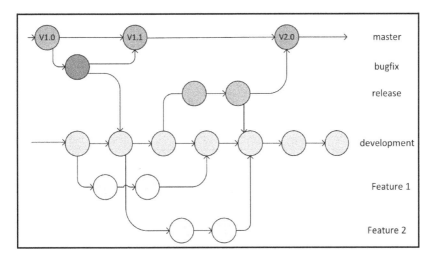

This flow is suitable for developing apps for AppSource because the release can be isolated and you can support multiple versions of the app easily.

GitHub flow

GitHub flow is a workflow used for development on GitHub. It is based on two rules:

- Everything in the master branch is releasable at any time.
- Release could be done at any time, even multiple times per day.

It is basically feature branching. Bug fixing is done like with the development of any other feature:

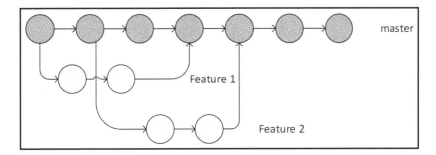

As we can see in the preceding diagram, it requires an automated release of the product, and hence, it could be applicable only for PerTenant or OnPrem apps in Business Central. AppSource has a long release time, and hence the flow is not suitable for it. It even assumes that only one version of the product is released, which is not true in the case of AppSource.

Branching considerations

You can use multiple branching strategies in your company because each one is suitable for a different situation. But do not forget KISS! Having a complicated strategy that brings nothing to the team only leads to shortcuts and teams not sticking to the rules. Having one branch is a strategy too. Start with it and add other branches as needed. The strategy can grow with your team.

For AppSource development, you can use any strategy, but the most suitable is Git flow because it allows you to separate each release and support multiple versions. Do not forget that apps on customer tenants are only automatically updated on major releases or when needed because of the presence of a critical bug (this occurs after a partner's request). It means multiple versions can live in the cloud together.

For PerTenant app development, because in this case, you have only one version of the product released to the customer tenant, you can use any strategy, including GitHub flow.

Understanding Git merge strategies

We will not go deep into all of the possibilities of the `git merge` command, but we will explain some of the terms used in connection with Git and merging.

Fast-forward merge

When you merge two branches in Git, and one branch is a subset of the commits of the other, the result will be a **fast-forward merge**, where no merge is done at all. Consider the following diagram:

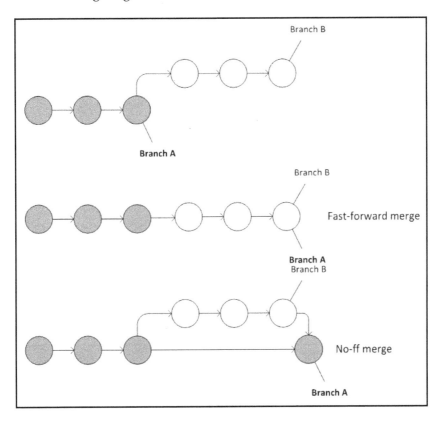

The branch will reset to a new position.

Squash commit

Using **squash commit** can help you to keep the branch clean and simple. When you want to merge one branch to another, by using squash commit, you can join the commits in the branch into new one commit, with a new commit message, and connect this new commit to the target branch. The following diagram shows this:

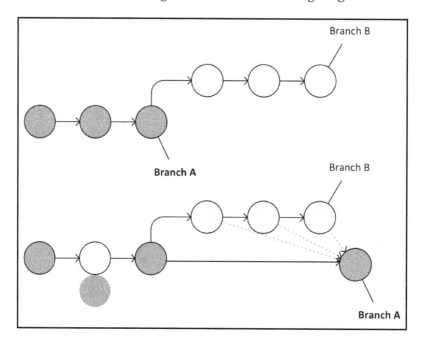

There will be no real merge between the branches. You just throw away the old branch because all changes are now committed to the target. You will lose detail but gain simplicity. It depends on what your priority is.

Rebase

Instead of `merge`, you can use the `rebase` command. As the name suggests, you take the branch, cut it from the tree, and rebase it on another commit. In this way, you can base your changes on the new version without merging. The following diagram shows this:

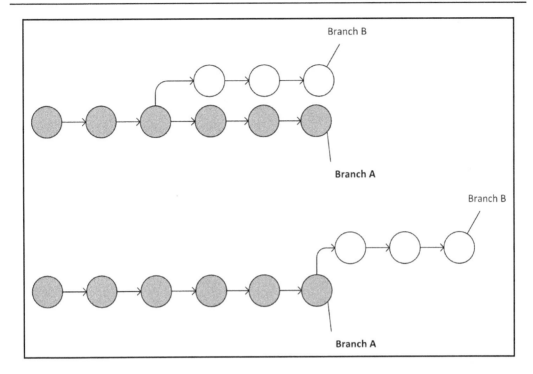

All of the commits between the original base and the branch head (the starting point of a branch) will be taken and reapplied to the new base. Again, you gain simplicity, but you lose reality because you are influencing the history.

Git merge considerations

When you need to integrate the changes back to the target branch, you can choose whether you will use fast-forward merges, merge or rebase, or use squash commit. By combining the techniques, you can have a simple history in Git, but you can lose the required detail. But again, do not be afraid of having choices. Just start with the simplest way, and you can change the rules later if you think that it will help.

Next, let's move on to see how we can use Git from Visual Studio Code.

Exploring Git with Visual Studio Code

Git is the default SCM system for Visual Studio Code, and you can execute the basic Git tasks (such as push, pull, fetch, and clone) from the Visual Studio Code GUI. You can also benefit from installing extensions that will enrich the integration.

I recommend these extensions:

- **Azure Repos**: Connects to the Azure DevOps repository, including work items and build pipelines
- **GitLens**: Adds different views to Git history, such as blame functionality

Let's see what Git has to offer.

Visual Studio Code GUI for Git

Visual Studio Code offers a totally integrated experience with Git and SCM. Here's the Visual Studio Code interface:

The numbers on the left-hand side of the screenshot represent the following details:

1. Current branch: If you click on this, you can create a new branch or check out another existing branch.

2. Status of the repository: We are in sync with the remote repository. If not, you can see the number of incoming and outgoing commits of the current branch. By clicking on them, you will perform synchronization, that is, fetch and merge with the remote repository.

3. The name of the project in Azure DevOps (Azure Repo extension): Clicking this will open the Azure DevOps portal.

4. The number of pull requests (Azure Repo extension): Clicking on this allows you to select and browse pull requests.

5. Last build status (Azure Repo extension): Clicking on this opens the last build for the repository.

6. The number of work items (Azure Repo extensions): Clicking on this allows you to browse the work items and open them in the web portal.

7. Source control activity bar: You can see the number of changed files. You can switch the activity to source control, where you can commit the changes.

8. Commit message textbox: Enter the commit message before you commit the changes.

9. List of changes: You can select which changes you want to undo or stage for committing. If you double-click on this, you can open the diff window, which shows you the differences between the current and the last committed state.

10. **Source Control** menu: You will find more commands regarding source control here.

After this, let's explore the Git/Visual Studio Code workflow.

Workflow with Git

When working with Visual Studio Code and Git, this is the common workflow you have:

1. The first step is to get the repository in which you want to work into your local system.

2. If you want to work on existing code, you need to have the URL of the remote repository. Then, you can use the `Git: Clone` command, enter the URL, and select the folder where the repository will be cloned (it will be cloned into a subfolder with the name of the repository).

3. If you are creating a new app, you can first create the folder, open it in Visual Studio Code, create the basic structure (using `AL: GO!` or another command), and then use `Git: Initialize Repository` to make the folder into a Git repository. Later, you can connect the local repository to some new remote one by using Command Prompt. See the *How to create a repository for your code* section.

4. Check out existing branches or create a new branch on which you want to do your development. You can do this by clicking the branch button at the bottom. Do not forget to check that you are working on the correct branch.

5. After you make some changes, go to the **Source Control Activity Bar** (press *Ctrl + Shift + G* for Git), write a meaningful message (such as `My first commit`), and commit the changes (click on the checkmark over the message or press *Ctrl + Enter*). If you haven't staged some changes (selected a changed file in the changes list and moved it into staged changes), Visual Studio Code will ask you whether you want to commit all changes instead. I recommend going through the changes and manually checking and staging them, because fixing something that has already been committed is not simple or nice. By staging changes, you can select a subset of all of the modifications that will be committed. You can stage/unstage even on the line level if you open the diff window, right-click on the lines, and select **Stage/Unstage Selected Ranges**. In this way, you can split your changes to separate commits if they, for example, are related to different requirements.

6. If you want to undo the changes, just click **Discard Changes** in the changed line.

7. After you have committed the changes and you want to make them available for others, you can click on the **Synchronize** button at the bottom of the window and it will push the commit to the remote repository (and pull changes from the remote repository if there are any). This is what the button looks like:

8. If you want to merge your changes into the development branch (or any other branch you are not responsible for), create a pull request in the Azure DevOps portal. You can go there through the **Browse your pull request** option when you click on the **Pull Request** button in the status bar (number 4 in the *Visual Studio Code GUI for Git* section). If you need to fix something, for example, because there is conflict during the pull request, just make the change, commit, and push, and the pull request will be updated with the new commit automatically.

9. If everything is in the remote repository and a change is merged, you can just delete the folder on your disk if you do not need it anymore.

It is a good practice to make some rules about what the commit message should look like, to be consistent through the company. Mastering the skill of writing good commit messages should be part of every developer's continuous improvement. You can refer to work items by writing #1234, where 1234 is the ID of the work item. You can find some examples and rules on the internet about how to write good Git commit messages. Here's an example:

```
Fix error "Value is incorrect" in Sales posting
Error text was changed to give more context to user and
in some cases, solved by finding correct value automatically.
Fix bug #1234
Related to #1258
```

You can create a new branch directly from a work item in Azure DevOps by clicking on **Create a new branch**:

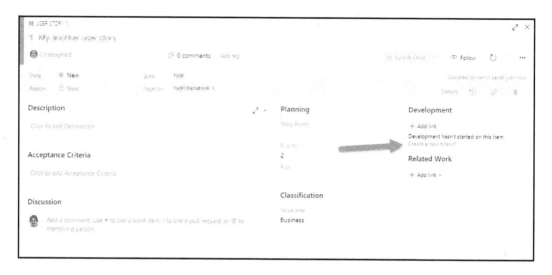

In this way, the branch will be connected to the work item and everybody will know where the changes are developed. It is good when you are using the feature branching strategy.

Merges

In some cases, you will need to merge changes from the remote repository with your local changes. In this case, after you sync your repository, you will have a new section named **MERGE CHANGES** in the Source Control section (during normal development work there are **CHANGES** and **STAGED CHANGES** sections).

When you click on each line/file, Visual Studio Code will open an editor window with the changes, and you can accept the changes or manually correct them. After all of the conflicts are resolved, stage the changes and commit them into a new merge commit and synchronize (push) the changes to the remote repository.

After learning about Git, let's see how Azure DevOps Pipelines work.

Understanding Azure DevOps Pipelines

Because the life cycle of business case apps is short and the cadence with which you are deploying new versions should be much higher than in the past (before the AL era), you cannot build, test, and deploy the app manually.

To automate this part of the life cycle, you can use Azure DevOps Pipelines, which will build, test, and deploy for you. You feed the pipeline on one side with the source code you are producing, and at the other end, you have a tested application, which can be even automatically delivered or deployed. Right now, there are two types of pipeline:

- **Build** pipeline: The input is the source code, and the output is the application and other artifacts.
- **Release** pipeline: The input is the output produced by the build pipeline, and the output is a tested application delivered or deployed to selected places.

The plan is that there will be one multi-stage pipeline instead that will cover the whole process. Consider the following diagram:

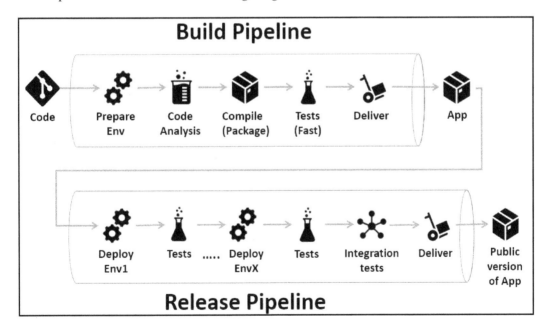

During the build stage, you are working with the source code and producing the product/application and testing it. In general, running tests on an application doesn't require the application to be deployed somewhere. For Dynamics 365 Business Central, it differs, and you need to deploy the app to a server to be able to test it—whether you use containers for this or not doesn't matter.

In the release pipeline, you are trying to deliver or deploy the application to different environments (the current version, the next version, different localizations, a new environment, or an environment with the previous version to test upgrades of the data, for example), test it in the environment, and carry out other steps that you need to deliver/deploy the app. This allows you to be able to deliver or deploy the application any time you want with as little manual input as possible.

Everything related to the work items you put into your commits or pull requests is transferred through the pipelines and, on each release, you can see all of the work items related to the release. This helps you to identify and describe the changes that are part of the specific version of your application, and the list could be automatically delivered with the application.

Agents

Pipelines that you create must be executed somewhere. Execution is done by an application called an **agent**.

You can use hosted agents, which are maintained by Microsoft in Azure and run on different operating systems with different additional software (such as macOS, Ubuntu, and Windows 2019 with Visual Studio 2019). For these hosted agents, you have some free minutes that you can use for your Azure DevOps organization (you can see the amount in the **Organization Settings** in the **Billing** section). But the use of these hosted agents is limited because you cannot install additional software.

You can use your own agents if you want. This means that you can install and configure a small application somewhere on your own server. This application will connect through a RESTful API to Azure DevOps and will execute the tasks from the pipelines on your server. How to install the agent is described on the web portal when you click on the **Download the agent** button in the **Agent Pool** section in **Settings**, as shown here:

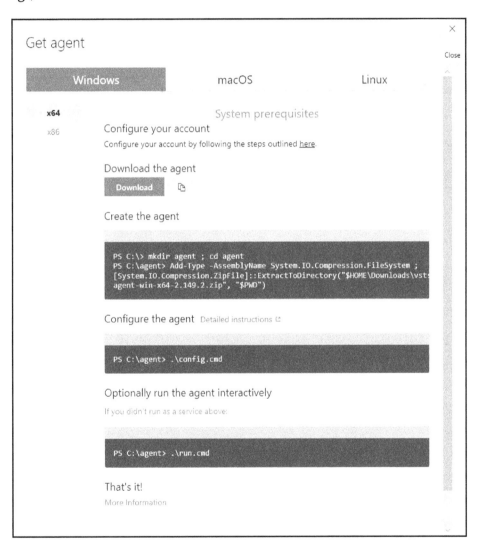

Details on how to configure the agent and get the access token needed to authenticate the agent can be found if you click on **Detailed instructions** on the **Download agent page** (`http://go.microsoft.com/fwlink/?LinkID=825113`). Do not forget to run the agent as an administrator to be able to do what is needed when running tasks for Dynamics 365 Business Central.

Which agent will be used for executing the pipeline is determined by the Agent's capabilities (which you can set in the Agent Pools section) and by the required agent task capabilities (that you can set later on the agent tasks in the pipeline definition). It means that each run of the pipeline can be processed by another agent if there are multiple agents available with the same capabilities. After this, let's see how to create a build pipeline.

Creating a build pipeline

To create your first build pipeline, open the **Pipelines** section of your Azure DevOps portal and click **New pipeline**:

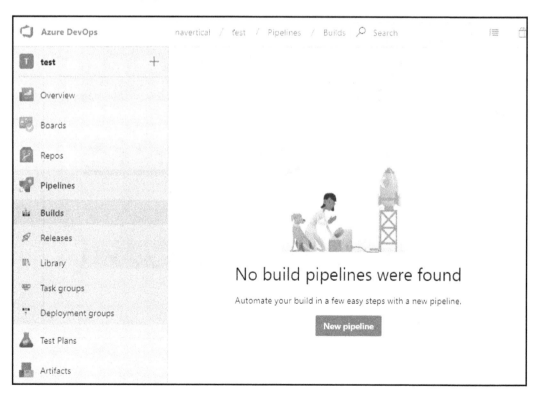

Now you can choose the source of your code to build. To start with, we will use the **Classic Editor**, which means we will create the pipeline manually, just to look at the different parts of the pipeline settings. Later, we will use **Azure Repos Git** to create the whole pipeline in one step from a YAML file.

After you click **Use the classic editor**, you can select the source of the code (select **Azure Repos Git | Team project**, then select the **Repository** for the source code and the **branch** from the repository itself). Select the correct values and click **Continue**.

Because there are no predefined pipeline templates for Dynamics 365 Business Central, we need to start with an empty job:

Now you are in the pipeline editor, where you can add pipeline agent jobs, which represent separate steps of the pipeline you need to execute to build and test the application. On the right, you can see the parameters of the actual steps you select on the left.

In the parameters, you can use variables, which can be defined in the **Variables** tab or can be defined by the system. You can find a detailed explanation of the variables in the documentation for Azure DevOps.

To use a variable in the parameters of the task, use the `$(variablename)` syntax. To use it inside your PowerShell script, use the `$env:VARIABLENAME` syntax. All of the variables that are accessible as environment variables are in uppercase, with dots replaced with underscores.

Note the **View YAML** button. It will be handy when we investigate YAML build pipelines.

When building applications for Business Central, you will mostly use the PowerShell task that can run existing scripts (for example, if they are part of the source code) or run inline defined scripts.

After you have defined all of the tasks you need, you can define the triggers for your new build pipeline. You can choose from the following:

- **Continuous integration**: This will run each time a new commit is pushed to the server. Check the branch filter to only run the build for branches where you want to save computing time. You can even specify a filter for paths inside the repository, which must be changed to trigger your pipeline (for example, to not trigger it when `readme.md` is changed).
- **Scheduled**: The pipeline will be triggered automatically at a set time. You can choose to trigger it only when something changed from last time.
- **Build completion**: This triggers the pipeline when another pipeline completes. It can be handy when you have dependencies between apps to run builds of the app when the dependency was built.

When all is ready and set, save the pipeline and try to run it. In most cases, you will need multiple runs and modifications before you get your first successful build.

Common build tasks will have these steps:

1. Prepare the build environment (install scripts, download tools, create a Docker container, and so on).
2. Compile the app (download symbols, use `ALC.exe` to compile the app, and so on).
3. Install the app (publish and install it into the Docker container).

4. Run tests for the app and download the results.

5. Publish the test results (should be done even when the tests fail).

6. Publish the artifacts (push the app to the Azure DevOps store or a shared folder).

7. Clean up the environment (drop the Docker container, for example; this should be done regardless of whether failing steps exist in the pipeline).

Variable groups and secure files

When creating your pipelines, you mostly need to define values that are shared between builds (such as usernames, passwords, keys, and so on). For this, you can create **Variable group**. To define a new **Variable group**, open the **Library**:

When creating the variable group, define the name and description. For better security, you can store your variables in an Azure key vault if you want, or you can just create variable name/value pairs and, on the password, just use the lock icon to hide the value. Additionally, you can define security for each variable group.

To be able to use the variables from a variable group, you need to link the group to your pipeline. Just open the editor, go to the **Variables** tab and select variable groups, and use the **Link variable group** button. After the group is linked, you can use the variables in your tasks.

If you need to use a certificate or another file in your build pipeline, you can store it in the library as a secure file. You can download such a file using the **Download Secure File** task in your pipeline. In this way, the users do not need to have access to the file and the file does not need to be able to access network resources to be used. The process will download the file from Azure DevOps storage where it is secured.

Next, let's see what the YAML pipeline is.

Understanding the YAML pipeline

In the previous section, we used the classic editor to create a pipeline to show you the different parts of the pipeline and to give you an idea of what the pipeline is. But creating a pipeline in the editor is not very convenient, and you cannot version the definition. This is why **YAML pipelines** exist. They have the same properties and parts as the classic pipelines but are defined by a YAML file as part of your source code. This means you can define *Pipelines as Code* (you can directly code a pipeline) and you can use all of the tools you are using to work with your code.

First, here's some information about **YAML**. YAML is a file syntax like XML and JSON, but it is primarily focused to be read by humans (XML and JSON are defined to be read by computers). This means that the syntax is easily understandable. Instead of artificial marks to give meaning, it uses indentation and symbols such as – for list items and : to separate names and values:

```
 1   receipt:      Oz-Ware Purchase Invoice
 2   date:         2012-08-06
 3   customer:
 4       first_name:   Dorothy
 5       family_name:  Gale
 6
 7   items:
 8       - part_no:   A4786
 9         descrip:   Water Bucket (Filled)
10         price:     1.47
11         quantity:  4
12
13       - part_no:   E1628
14         descrip:   High Heeled "Ruby" Slippers
15         size:      8
16         price:     133.7
17         quantity:  1
18
19   specialDelivery:  >
20       Follow the Yellow Brick
21       Road to the Emerald City.
22       Pay no attention to the
23       man behind the curtain.
24
```

If you look at the example, you should be able to recognize the properties (the format is `name: value`), objects with properties (for example, `customer` in the preceding screenshot), and lists (`items` in the preceding screenshot) with objects.

By using YAML, you can define all of the parts of the pipeline you saw in the pipeline editor:

- Jobs and tasks with parameters and properties
- Variables, including variable groups
- Triggers

If you created some pipeline in the editor, you can use the **View YAML** button in the editor to see the YAML that defines the same thing as you have in the editor. In this way, you can start creating your YAML pipeline. Just create an `azure-pipelines.yaml` file in your project, put the pipeline description into it, and commit the file into your repository.

When you want to change something in the pipeline, change the YAML file, commit, and push. The pipeline will change automatically.

Creating a YAML pipeline

To create a pipeline based on a YAML file, go to the **Pipelines | Builds** section and do the following:

1. Click on **New Pipeline**.
2. Select **Azure Repos Git (YAML)**.
3. Select the repository.
4. Azure DevOps will autodetect the YAML pipeline file in the repository and open it.
5. Click on **Run**.

You are done. Your new pipeline was created! Wasn't it easy?

YAML pipeline templates

To make it more generic, you can use templates in your YAML pipeline. This means that you store the YAML file definitions for each task as separate files in a repository and you can refer to these templates from your YAML pipeline. The definitions are shared with all of the apps using them in their YAML pipeline, and if you need to fix something in the definition, you will fix it in one place. Of course, in this way, you can screw up all of your pipelines from one place. Be warned!

This is how you create the pipeline:

1. Create a new repository for your templates.
2. Put the YAML files with the definitions of the tasks into it:

```
# File: TestALAppInContainer.yml

parameters:
  XUnitFile: '.\\TEST-Result.xml'
  testSuite: 'DEFAULT'
  pwd: 'pass@word1'

steps:
- powershell: |
    Import-Module NVRAppDevOps -DisableNameChecking
    Import-Module navcontainerhelper -DisableNameChecking
    $Config = Read-ALConfiguration -Path .\
    $FullPath = [System.IO.Path]::GetFullPath($env:XUnitFile)
    $Config | Run-AlTestInContainer -XUnitResultFileName $FullPath -testSuite $env:testSuite -AzureDevOps error -detailed

  displayName: 'Run Tests in container'
  env:
    XUnitFile: ${{ parameters.XUnitFile }}
    testSuite: ${{ parameters.testSuite }}
    USER_PWD: ${{ parameters.pwd }}
```

3. Add a reference to the repository to the YAML pipeline file:

```
resources:
  repositories:
  - repository: MSDYN365BC_Yaml
    type: github
    name: kine/MSDYN365BC_Yaml
    ref: 'refs/heads/master'
    endpoint: GitHub
```

The reference parameters are as follows:

- **Repository**: The name as it is used in the YAML pipeline file
- **Type**: The source repository type
- **Name**: The repository name
- **Ref**: The branch or a reference to the version of templates to be used
- **Endpoint**: The name of the endpoint defined in the Azure DevOps Service connections section

4. Add a service connection with the same name as your repository into Azure DevOps **Service connections**:

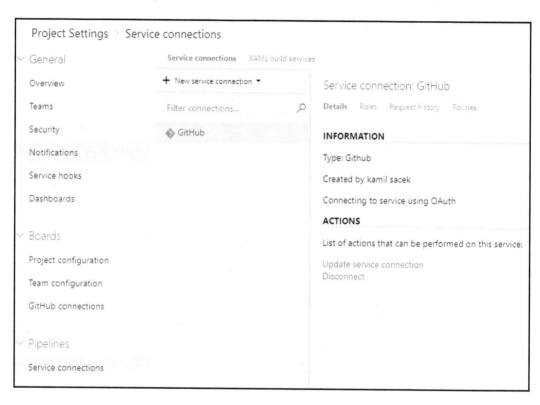

5. Change the YAML file to reference these templates as the steps:

```
- template: Templates/TestALAppInContainer.yml@MSDYN365BC_Yaml
  parameters:
    XUnitFile: 'TEST-Result.xml'
    testSuite: 'DEFAULT'
    pwd: $(UserPwd)
```

In the YAML file, we have these references:

- **Template**: The path and name of the file in the `@MSDYN365BC_Yaml` repository
- **Parameters**: The parameter values for the task

All repository-specific settings should stay in your YAML pipeline file. All shared things such as step definitions should be in the template repository.

You can find the example for the template and pipeline file at `https://github.com/kine/MSDYN365BC_Yaml`.

To swap a new app using this template, you can clone the app as a template at `https://github.com/kine/MSDyn365BC_AppTemplate`.

Just for future reference, as a generic YAML pipeline for Dynamics 365 Business Central, you can also refer to the following YAML definition:

```
variables:
 build.clean: all
 platform: x64

trigger: none

steps:
- task: PowerShell@2
  displayName: 'Install NAVContainerHelper module'
  inputs:
    targetType: filePath
    filePath: 'BuildScripts\InstallNAVContainerHelper.ps1'

- task: PowerShell@2
  displayName: 'Create a Docker Container for the build'
  inputs:
    targetType: filePath
    filePath: 'BuildScripts\CreateDockerContainer.ps1'
    arguments: '-credential
```

```
    ([PSCredential]::new("$(DockerContainerUsername)", (ConvertTo-
    SecureString -String "$(DockerContainerPassword)" -AsPlainText -
    Force)))'

  - task: PowerShell@2
    displayName: 'Copy Files to Docker Container'
    inputs:
      targetType: filePath
      filePath: 'BuildScripts\CopyFilesToDockerContainer.ps1'

  - task: PowerShell@2
    displayName: 'Compile extension stored in the repository'
    inputs:
      targetType: filePath
      filePath: 'BuildScripts\CompileApp.ps1'
      arguments: '-Credential
    ([PSCredential]::new("$(DockerContainerUsername)", (ConvertTo-
    SecureString -String "$(DockerContainerPassword)" -AsPlainText -
    Force))) -BuildFolder "$(Build.Repository.LocalPath)" -
    BuildArtifactFolder "$(Build.ArtifactStagingDirectory)"'
      failOnStderr: true

  - task: PowerShell@2
    displayName: 'Publish extension'
    inputs:
      targetType: filePath
      filePath: 'BuildScripts\PublishApp.ps1'
      arguments: '-Credential
    ([PSCredential]::new("$(DockerContainerUsername)", (ConvertTo-
    SecureString -String "$(DockerContainerPassword)" -AsPlainText -
    Force))) -BuildArtifactFolder "$(Build.ArtifactStagingDirectory)"'
      failOnStderr: true

  - task: PublishBuildArtifacts@1
    displayName: 'Publish Artifacts'
    inputs:
      PathtoPublish: '$(Build.ArtifactStagingDirectory)'
      ArtifactName: FinalApp
```

This pipeline model uses a set of PowerShell scripts that you can store in your repository in a folder called BuildScripts. This can be stored together with your extension's files, as shown in the following screenshot:

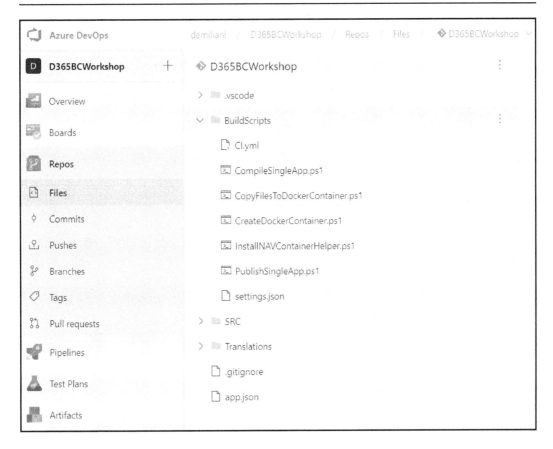

If successfully executed, this pipeline publishes the final `.app` file for your Dynamics 365 Business Central extension as an **Artifact** (output of the pipeline), which you can download from the build summary page.

Release pipeline

After the **build** pipeline finishes, you can use the **release** pipeline to deliver or deploy the build artifacts or do other actions that you want. To create a new release pipeline, go to the **Release** section and click on **New Release pipeline**. Because there is no template for Business Central release pipelines, begin with an empty job.

Each release pipeline is created with the following:

- **Artifacts**: This could be the output of the build pipeline, an Azure DevOps Git repository, a GitHub repository, a TFVC repository, an Azure artifact, an Azure container, a Docker Hub repository, or a Jenkins job.
- **Stages**: Each stage is a separate process that can be executed on different agents and can be triggered by different events.
- **Variables**: These are the same as in build pipelines.

For each **artifact**, you can define triggers to start the pipeline. It could be each time the artifact is updated (continuous deployment) or on a given schedule (such as nightly releases).

At each stage, you can set pre-deployment conditions and post-deployment conditions:

- Pre-deployment conditions: These include the following:
    - After release: This triggers when the selected artifact is deployed or on a given schedule.
    - After stage: This triggers when another stage is finished.
    - Manual only: Someone must trigger the deployment in the portal.
    - Pre-deployment approvals: Selected users must approve the deployment to this stage.
    - Gates: These are automated processes that can approve the deployment according to certain conditions (for example, when there are no errors after release to the previous stage).
- Post-deployment conditions: These include the following:
    - Post-deployment approvals: Selected users must approve that the release stage succeeded and that the release can continue.
    - Gates: Automated processes can approve the stage release.
    - Auto-redeploy trigger: You can trigger redeployment when needed; for example, after the stage fails, you can redeploy the last successful deployment. This could be useful for restoring to the last known working version.

Here's an example of a **release pipeline** for Dynamics 365 Business Central:

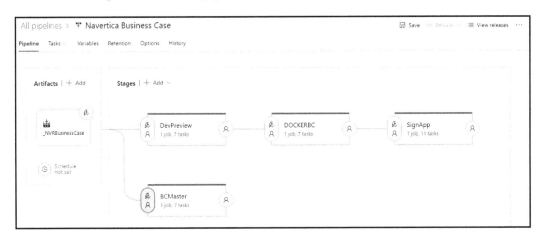

Each stage is deploying the app (and running tests) to a different version of the Business Central sandbox (the current version, the future version, and the master version). If everything is OK, the app is deployed to the QA environment for user testing. If the tests succeed, the app is signed by a certificate and stored on the server for later use (to be sent to AppSource) or is deployed to the target environment (a per-tenant app). This is what the YAML pipeline is about.

Summary

In this chapter, we learned what Azure DevOps is and what it provides, then created our account on Azure DevOps. We looked at how to manage and plan our work using Azure DevOps. We created a repository for our code and learned what we can set up to support our development cycle.

In the *Branching strategies* section, we learned how to use branches in our project to make the development stable and traceable. In the *Git merge strategies* and *Git in Visual Studio Code* sections, we looked at some specific aspects related to Git source control and how to use Git SCM from Visual Studio Code to keep our code safe.

We learned about Azure DevOps Pipelines, how to use them, and how to create them through the classic designer. In the last section, we looked at YAML files and how to use them to define our pipeline as part of our code.

In the next chapter, we'll go in depth into Dynamics 365 Business Central APIs and we'll explore how to create new APIs and use existing APIs to perform integrations.

4

Section 4: Advanced Integrations with Dynamics 365 Business Central

In this section, we will introduce the Dynamics 365 Business Central API framework. We will describe how to create real-world business processes by using Dynamics 365 Business Central and different Azure services. We will also cover the usage of Dynamics 365 Business Central in combination with the Dynamics 365 Power Platform. Finally, we'll build a real-world application using the Power Platform with Dynamics 365 Business Central.

This section comprises the following chapters:

- Chapter 12, *Dynamics 365 Business Central APIs*
- Chapter 13, *Serverless Business Processes with Business Central and Azure*
- Chapter 14, *Monitoring, Scaling, and CI/CD with Azure Functions*
- Chapter 15, *Business Central and Integration with the Power Platform*

12
Dynamics 365 Business Central APIs

In the previous chapter, we saw how we can use DevOps techniques with Dynamics 365 Business Central projects, and we focused on aspects such as source control management and CI/CD pipelines.

In this chapter, we'll see how to integrate Dynamics 365 Business Central with external applications by using the RESTful APIs exposed by the platform, and the focus will be on the following topics:

- Comparing OData and RESTful APIs
- Using the Dynamics 365 Business Central standard
- Creating custom APIs with Dynamics 365 Business Central for new and existing entities
- Creating applications that use Dynamics 365 Business Central APIs
- Using bound actions
- Using Dynamics 365 Business Central webhooks
- Working with Dynamics 365 Business Central APIs in Microsoft Graph automation APIs

By the end of this chapter, you will be able to create RESTful APIs for Dynamics 365 Business Central and use them to integrate with external applications.

Comparing OData and APIs in Dynamics 365 Business Central

Every client that can make HTTP calls can consume RESTful APIs. Using the GET, POST, PATCH, and DELETE verbs of the HTTP protocol, entities can be **Created, Read, Updated, and Deleted** (**CRUD**). To make integrations with Dynamics 365 Business Central, OData and RESTful APIs are the recommended tools to work with.

Open Data Protocol (**OData**) is a web protocol that permits you to perform CRUD operations on tabular data with HTTP calls by using URIs for resource identification. Exposing an object as OData in Dynamics 365 Business Central is quite simple: open the **WEB SERVICES** page, insert a new record with the **Page** type, select the page you want to expose, and click on **Publish**.

Dynamics 365 Business Central automatically assigns to the published entity an OData and OData V4 URL, and then you can use this published entity (our page) as a web service by performing HTTP REST calls (GET, POST, PUT, DELETE, and PATCH) to the provided endpoints (as you can see in the following screenshot):

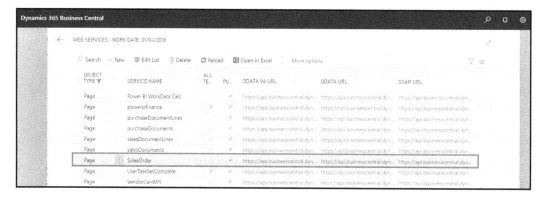

When calling an OData endpoint, you can apply filters, use grouping, use Flow Filters, and call business logic by using bound actions (we'll discuss them later in this chapter, in the *Using bound actions* section).

APIs in Dynamics 365 Business Central use the same OData stack under the hood, but they have three main advantages when we talk about integration:

- They have **versioning** (one of the most important things when doing service integration, because you will need a stable contract).
- They are **webhook supported** (you can publish your API page and then call `/api/microsoft/runtime/beta/webhookSupportedResources` to verify that the entity is supported by webhooks).
- They have **namespaces** so you can isolate and group your APIs according to their scope or functional area: `{{shortUrl}}/api/APIPublisher/APIGroup/v1.0/mycustomers('0 1121212')`.

The fixed contract is the main reason that Microsoft prevents the opportunity to extend standard API pages. If you try to extend a standard API page (for example, the `Customer Entity` page), Visual Studio Code throws an error:

```
                                      Page "Customer Entity"

                                      The Page "Customer Entity" of type API cannot be extended AL(AL0454)

0 references                          Quick Fix...  Peek Problem
pageextension 50103 MyExtension extends "Customer Entity"
{
    layout
    {
        // Add changes to page layout here
    }
}
```

 For more information on how to use RESTful APIs in general, I recommend the following link: `https://www.odata.org/getting-started/basic-tutorial/`.

Now that we have explained the main differences between OData web services and RESTful APIs, in the next sections, we'll see how to use the Dynamics 365 Business Central APIs in your applications.

Using Dynamics 365 Business Central standard APIs

The Dynamics 365 Business Central platform exposes some standard entities as RESTful APIs. The exposed entities are summarized in the following table:

Company	Finance	Sales	Purchasing	Reports
company	accounts	customers	irs1099Codes (US only)	agedAccountsPayable
companyInformation	dimensions	customerPayments	purchaseInvoices	agedAccountsReceivable
countriesRegions	dimensionLines	customerPaymentJournals	purchaseInvoiceLines	balanceSheet
currencies	dimensionValues	salesInvoices	vendors	cashFlowStatement
employees	generalLedgerEntries	salesInvoiceLines		incomeStatement
items	journals	salesOrders		retainedEarningsStatement
itemCategories	journalLines	salesOrderLines		customerSales
paymentMethods		salesQuotes		vendorPurchases
paymentTerms		salesQuoteLines		trialBalance
shipmentMethods		salesCreditMemos		
taxAreas		salesCreditMemoLines		
taxGroups				
unitsOfMeasure				
picture, defaultDimension, attachments, pdfDocument				

Dynamics 365 Business Central API endpoints have the following format:

Endpoint URL section	Description
`https://api.businesscentral.dynamics.com`	Dynamics 365 Business Central base URL (the same for standard and custom APIs)
`/v2.0`	API version
`/your tenant domain`	Domain name or ID of the Dynamics 365 Business Central tenant
`/environment name`	Name of the environment (production, sandbox, and so on). This can be retrieved from the Dynamics 365 Business Central Admin portal
`/api`	Fixed value
`/beta`	Indicates the version of the API in use

At the time of writing, Dynamics 365 Business Central APIs are on endpoint version 2.0, and API `version_number = 1.0`.

The tenant ID is needed when using basic authentication. This is how you do it:

```
GET https://api.businesscentral.dynamics.com/v2.0/{tenant
Id}/{environment name}/api/v1.0/$metadata
```

If you're using OAuth authentication, the tenant ID is not needed:

```
GET https://api.businesscentral.dynamics.com/v2.0/{environment
name}/api/v1.0/$metadata
```

Version 1.0 of the Dynamics 365 Business Central APIs only supports production and primary sandbox environments. If you need to use the APIs in a sandbox environment that's different than the default one (which is called `Sandbox`) or in a different production environment, you need to use version 2.0 of the APIs, as shown in the following endpoint:

```
https://api.businesscentral.dynamics.com/v2.0/{tenant
Id}/OtherSandboxName/api/
```

When using APIs, the first thing you have to do is use a specific company ID. To retrieve the list of available companies on your Dynamics 365 Business Central tenant, you need to send an HTTP GET request to the `/companies` API endpoint. An example of this API call is as follows:

```
GET
https://api.businesscentral.dynamics.com/v2.0/<tenantID>/production/api/beta/companies
Content-Type: application/x-www-form-urlencoded
Authorization: Basic sdemiliani <YourWebServiceAccessKey>
```

This is the response we receive:

```
1   HTTP/1.1 200 OK
2   Content-Length: 283
3   Content-Type: application/json; odata.metadata=minimal; odata.streaming=true
4   Content-Encoding: gzip
5   Server: Microsoft-HTTPAPI/2.0
6   Access-Control-Allow-Headers: Origin, X-Requested-With, Authorization
7   Access-Control-Allow-Origin: *
8   Access-Control-Allow-Credentials: true
9   ms-correlation-x: 44a36631-cfff-4441-bf48-2269d9b8dd48
10  OData-Version: 4.0
11  request-id: e9a3612f-7ca8-4669-a0e0-87f69a338662
12  Strict-Transport-Security: max-age=31536000; includeSubDomains
13  x-content-type-options: nosniff
14  Access-Control-Expose-Headers: Date, Content-Length, Server, OData-Version, ms-correlation-x
15  Date: Mon, 15 Jul 2019 08:27:18 GMT
16  Connection: close
17
18  {
19    "@odata.context": "https://api.businesscentral.dynamics.com/v2.0/194a87bd-73c6-43c6-95d7-1ca48985db5e/production/api/beta/$metadata#companies",
20    "value": [
21      {
22        "id": "80d28ea6-02a3-4ec3-98f7-936c2000c7b3",
23        "systemVersion": "34093",
24        "name": "CRONUS IT",
25        "displayName": "CRONUS IT",
26        "businessProfileId": ""
27      },
28      {
29        "id": "2f8ea8a1-549d-414e-9ced-aeb0dc7bf3d7",
30        "systemVersion": "34093",
31        "name": "My Company",
32        "displayName": "",
33        "businessProfileId": ""
34      }
35    ]
36  }
```

If we want to retrieve the list of `Customer` records for a specific company (for example, `Cronus IT`), we need to send an HTTP GET request to the following API endpoint:

```
GET
https://api.businesscentral.dynamics.com/v2.0/<tenantID>/production/api/beta/companies(80d28ea6-02a3-4ec3-98f7-936c2000c7b3)/customers
Content-Type: application/x-www-form-urlencoded
Authorization: Basic sdemiliani <YourWebServiceAccessKey>
```

This is the response we receive from it:

```
Response(1021ms) ✕
297                              :
298          }
299      },
300  ⊟   {
301                    : "W/\"JzQ0O1haOXpkNk14dXpYTE1OSy9TbGVPcmgxUmdVVmd4TGVYTXJpMUx1R2hZTnc9MTswMDsn\"",
302           : "410de1ce-9971-45f7-a196-d1b56e777fc4",
303           : "10000",
304                    : "Adatum Corporation",
305           : "Company",
306                    : "+390322845333",
307           : "andrea.ricci@contoso.com",
308           : "www.demiliani.com",
309           : false,
310           : "a5775c77-c940-41aa-a3fe-9602881892cd",
311                    : "Clienti e fornitori nazionali",
312                    : "789456278",
313           : "00000000-0000-0000-0000-000000000000",
314           : "EUR",
315                    : "b22af43b-a12a-482d-a498-ba0e0e33c821",
316                    : "00000000-0000-0000-0000-000000000000",
317           : "00000000-0000-0000-0000-000000000000",
318           : " ",
319           : 0,
320           : 0,
321                    : 215507.8,
322                    : "2019-05-21T12:57:05.93Z",
323  ⊟             : {
324           : "Station Road, 23",
325           : "Genova",
326           : "",
327           : "IT",
328           : "16100"
329      }
330      },
331  ⊟   {
332                    : "W/\"JzQ0O1JGUHYzdFVMWHBWYnRhTzEzdXI2eXd3ZGZ5Z3purlVoY3JvYT17LMHg5UUU9MTswMDsn\"",
333           : "c5de0fdf-3b5b-4b6e-a69e-ee0ef6a4a99e",
334           : "C00038",
335                    : "Vendi SR 2",
336           : "Company",
337                    : "",
```

You can also apply filters when calling the APIs. For example, here, we retrieve all `Item` records where `unitPrice` is greater than 100:

```
GET
https://api.businesscentral.dynamics.com/v2.0/<tenantID>/production/ap
i/beta/companies(80d28ea6-02a3-4ec3-98f7-936c2000c7b3)/items?$filter=u
nitPrice%20gt%20100
Content-Type: application/x-www-form-urlencoded
Authorization: Basic sdemiliani <YourWebServiceAccessKey>
```

This is the response:

Dynamics 365 Business Central standard APIs also support features such as **expand**, in which, in a single call, you can expand the relationships between entities, and retrieve the main entity along with the related entities. For example, to retrieve a sales invoice and all of its sales invoice line records in a single HTTP call, you can perform an HTTP GET call to the following API endpoint:

```
GET
https://api.businesscentral.dynamics.com/v2.0/<tenantID>/production/ap
i/beta/companies(80d28ea6-02a3-4ec3-98f7-936c2000c7b3)/salesInvoices(0
34a122b-962b-4007-b3d1-00718c2f21ff)?$expand=salesInvoiceLines
Content-Type: application/x-www-form-urlencoded
Authorization: Basic sdemiliani <YourWebServiceAccessKey>
```

As a result, you have a single JSON response object with the sales invoice header and its related sales invoice line detail. Here is the header object:

Also, here is the related line's details:

```
Response(1255ms)  ✕

51       "state": "",
52       "countryLetterCode": "",
53       "postalCode": ""
54       }
55       "salesInvoiceLines": [
56       {
57           "@odata.etag": "W/\"JzQ00tJVlozL1NUb1ZnMjY5UG1ySX8oZG0vekJvTG1KVW9xMmJPcnI0UjZFVHc9MTswMDsn\"",
58           "documentId": "034a122b-962b-4007-b3d1-00718c2f21ff",
59           "sequence": 10000,
60           "itemId": "70546a5e-d776-4268-a3e3-feac1702f1ca",
61           "accountId": "00000000-0000-0000-0000-000000000000",
62           "lineType": "Item",
63           "description": "Cassettiera ATENE",
64           "unitOfMeasureId": "3696d816-643b-4144-909b-edf17d235c2a",
65           "unitPrice": 435.8,
66           "quantity": 8,
67           "discountAmount": 0,
68           "discountPercent": 0,
69           "discountAppliedBeforeTax": false,
70           "amountExcludingTax": 3486.4,
71           "taxCode": "STANDARD",
72           "taxPercent": 20,
73           "totalTaxAmount": 697.28,
74           "amountIncludingTax": 4183.68,
75           "invoiceDiscountAllocation": 0,
76           "netAmount": 3486.4,
77           "netTaxAmount": 697.28,
78           "netAmountIncludingTax": 4183.68,
79           "shipmentDate": "2018-03-21",
80           "itemDetails": {
81               "number": "1906-S",
82               "displayName": "Cassettiera ATENE"
83           },
84           "unitOfMeasure": {
85               "code": "PZ",
86               "displayName": "Pezzo",
87               "symbol": null,
88               "unitConversion": null
89           }
90       },
```

You can now parse this JSON object and use its data as per your needs.

In the next section, we will see how to create a custom API page for a new entity added to Dynamics 365 Business Central and how to create a new API page for an existing entity.

Creating a custom API in Dynamics 365 Business Central

With Dynamics 365 Business Central extensions, you can create custom entities and you can expose a custom entity as a RESTful API.

To create a new API in Dynamics 365 Business Central, you need to define a new `Page` object with `PageType = API`. To do this, you can use the `tpage` snippet and then select **Page of type API**, as follows:

```
tpage
    □ tpage, Page                            Snippet: Page of type API (AL Languag  ×
    □ tpage, Page of type API                e)
    □ tpage, Page of type list
    □ tpage, Variable Template: Page         page Id ApiPageName
    □ tpagecust                              {
    □ tpageext                                   PageType = API;
    □ tpagefield                                 Caption = 'apiPageName';
    □ TestPage                                   APIPublisher = 'publisherName';
    □ ttestpage                                  APIGroup = 'groupName';
                                                 APIVersion = 'VersionList';
                                                 EntityName = 'entityName';
                                                 EntitySetName = 'entitySetName';
```

When creating API pages, remember the following:

- Fields must have a name in the REST-API-compliant format (only alphanumeric values, and no spaces or special characters (`camelCase`)).
- You should use the ID of the entity (`SystemId`).
- When you insert modify, or delete an entity through APIs, triggers on the underlying table are not executed. You need to call the table's trigger by handling the corresponding triggers at the page level.
- In the `OnModify` trigger of the API page, you need to handle the possibility of renaming a record (an API call via a record ID can issue a primary key rename).

Here, we'll see two main scenarios:

- How to implement an API for a custom entity (assuming that there's an extension that adds the `Car` entity to Dynamics 365 Business Central for managing car details inside the ERP)
- How to implement a new API for an existing entity

We will look into each of these scenarios in the following sections.

Implementing a new API for a custom entity

In this example, we will be creating a new entity in Dynamics 365 Business Central to handle the details of `Cars`, and this entity will also be exposed as an API for external applications:

1. To do this, we first create a new `Car` table, as follows:

```
table 50111 Car
{
    DataClassification = CustomerContent;
    Caption = 'Car';
    LookupPageId = "Car List";
    DrillDownPageId = "Car List";
    fields
    {
        field(1; ModelNo; Code[20])
        {
            Caption = 'Model No.';
            DataClassification = CustomerContent;
        }
        field(2; Description; Text[100])
        {
            Caption = 'Description';
            DataClassification = CustomerContent;
        }
        field(3; Brand; Code[20])
        {
            Caption = 'Brand';
            DataClassification = CustomerContent;
        }
        field(4; Power; Integer)
        {
            Caption = 'Power (CV)';
            DataClassification = CustomerContent;
        }
```

```
            field(5; "Engine Type"; Enum EngineType)
            {
                Caption = 'Engine Type';
                DataClassification = CustomerContent;
            }
            field(10; ID; Guid)
            {
                Caption = 'ID';
                DataClassification = CustomerContent;
            }
        }

        keys
        {
            key(PK; ModelNo)
            {
                Clustered = true;
            }
        }

        trigger OnInsert()
        begin
            ID := CreateGuid();
        end;
    }
```

The `Car` table has the required fields, and it has an `ID` field defined as `Guid` that is automatically assigned in the `OnInsert` trigger.

2. The `Engine Type` field is of the `Enum EngineType` type, and the `enum` is defined as follows:

```
enum 50111 EngineType
{
    Extensible = true;
    value(0; Petrol)
    {
        Caption = 'Petrol';
    }
    value(1; Diesel)
    {
        Caption = 'Diesel';
    }
    value(2; Electric)
    {
        Caption = 'Electric';
    }
    value(3; Hybrid)
```

```
    {
        Caption = 'Hybrid';
    }
}
```

3. We also create a `Car List` page (a standard list page) for managing `Car` data in Dynamics 365 Business Central. The `Car List` page is defined as follows:

```
page 50112 "Car List"
{
    PageType = List;
    SourceTable = Car;
    Caption = 'Car List';
    ApplicationArea = All;
    UsageCategory = Lists;
    layout
    {
        area(content)
        {
            repeater(General)
            {
                field(ModelNo;ModelNo)
                {
                    ApplicationArea = All;
                }
                field(Description;Description)
                {
                    ApplicationArea = All;
                }
                field(Brand;Brand)
                {
                    ApplicationArea = All;
                }
                field("Engine Type";"Engine Type")
                {
                    ApplicationArea = All;
                }
                field(Power;Power)
                {
                    ApplicationArea = All;
                }
            }
        }
    }
}
```

4. Now, we need to create the API page (by using the `tpage` snippet and then selecting the **Page of type API**). The `CarAPI` page is defined as follows:

```
page 50111 CarAPI
{
    PageType = API;
    Caption = 'CarAPI';
    APIPublisher = 'sd';
    APIGroup = 'custom';
    APIVersion = 'v1.0';
    EntityName = 'car';
    EntitySetName = 'cars';
    SourceTable = Car;
    DelayedInsert = true;
    ODataKeyFields = ID;

    layout
    {
        area(Content)
        {
            repeater(GroupName)
            {
                field(id; ID)
                {
                    Caption = 'id', Locked = true;
                }
                field(modelno; ModelNo)
                {
                    Caption = 'modelNo', Locked = true;
                }
                field(description; Description)
                {
                    Caption = 'description', Locked = true;
                }
                field(brand; Brand)
                {
                    Caption = 'brand', Locked = true;
                }
                field(engineType; "Engine Type")
                {
                    Caption = 'engineType', Locked = true;
                }
                field(power; Power)
                {
                    Caption = 'power', Locked = true;
                }
            }
        }
```

```
       }

       trigger OnInsertRecord(BelowxRec: Boolean): Boolean
       begin
            Insert(true);
            Modify(true);
            exit(false);
       end;

       trigger OnModifyRecord(): Boolean
       var
            Car: Record Car;
       begin
            Car.SetRange(ID, ID);
            Car.FindFirst();
            if ModelNo <> Car.ModelNo then begin
                Car.TransferFields(Rec, false);
                Car.Rename(ModelNo);
                TransferFields(Car);
            end;
       end;

       trigger OnDeleteRecord(): Boolean
       begin
            Delete(true);
       end;
   }
```

This page exposes the fields that we want to have in our API by applying the naming rules according to the OData specifications.

We then handle the `OnInsertRecord`, `OnModifyRecord`, and `OnDeleteRecord` page triggers to call the table's triggers and to handle renaming a record.

5. Now, press *F5* in Visual Studio Code and publish your extension. When it's published, search for `Car List` and then insert some example `Car` records, such as the following:

6. Now, we can test our custom API. When published in a SaaS tenant, a custom API endpoint has the following format:

```
{BaseURL}/v2.0/<your tenant id>/<environment name>/api/<api
publisher>/<api group>/<api version>
```

If you're testing it on a Docker-based sandbox (for example, on an Azure VM as I'm doing here), the API endpoint is like this:

```
{BaseServerUrl:ODATA_Port}/{ServerInstance}/api//<api
publisher>/<api group>/<api version>
```

You can check the metadata for the published API with the following URL (here, d365bcita0918vm is the name of my Azure VM that's hosting the container):

```
https://d365bcita0918vm.westeurope.cloudapp.azure.com:7048/BC/
api/sd/custom/v1.0/$metadata
```

The APIs are invoked per company. To have the list of companies on your database, you have to send a GET request to the following URL:

```
{baseUrl}/{D365BCInstance}/api/sd/custom/v1.0/companies
```

To have the list of cars for the selected company, you need to send a GET request to the following URL (by passing the company ID that was retrieved with the preceding call):

```
{baseUrl}/{D365BCInstance}/api/sd/custom/v1.0/companies({id})/
cars
```

In our environment, the URL is as follows:

```
GET
https://d365bcita0918vm.westeurope.cloudapp.azure.com:7048/BC/
api/sd/custom/v1.0/companies(ecdc7cd0-
ab75-4d40-8d0e-80d2471c4378)/cars
```

This is the response that we get:

```
Response(50ms)  ×

  5    Server: Microsoft-HTTPAPI/2.0
  6    OData-Version: 4.0
  7    Access-Control-Allow-Origin: *
  8    Access-Control-Allow-Credentials: true
  9    Access-Control-Expose-Headers: Date, Content-Length, Server, OData-Version
 10    request-id: a8b5b1a9-0ff8-40de-b89b-eb0ec5e31335
 11    Date: Thu, 27 Jun 2019 13:07:10 GMT
 12    Connection: close
 13
 14  ⊟ {
 15        "@odata.context": "https://d365bcita0918vm.westeurope.cloudapp.azure.com:7048/NAV/api/sd/custom/v1.0/$metadata#companies(ecdc7cd0-ab75-4d
          40-8d0e-80d2471c4378)/cars",
 16  ⊟     "value": [
 17  ⊟         {
 18                "@odata.etag": "W/\"JzQ0O1TyOTU2QS9wVS96SVFpT2w3Tko4WWRMT29MWlVuRkpadHZaVzFDdmxiSHc9MTswMDsn\"",
 19                "modelno": "M001",
 20                "id": "0237f4af-3422-41b3-94aa-81196346460e",
 21                "description": "Mercedes GLC",
 22                "brand": "MERCEDES",
 23                "engineType": "Diesel",
 24                "power": 180
 25            },
 26  ⊟         {
 27                "@odata.etag": "W/\"JzQ0O3ZTdUg2VzBiNGtlbGtaOTl1MXVQl2NUbVFyUHlWZjhxUVowVIFQSlpLbzQ9MTswMDsn\"",
 28                "modelno": "M002",
 29                "id": "e02d9a68-900a-4af1-aee7-723692389479",
 30                "description": "BMW 3 Series",
 31                "brand": "BMW",
 32                "engineType": "Diesel",
 33                "power": 145
 34            }
 35        ]
 36    }
```

As you can see, we have the JSON representation of the inserted records, and every field (JSON token) has the name that we assigned in our API definition.

To insert a new `Car` record via our previously published custom `cars` API, you need to send a POST request to the following URL by passing the JSON record to create in the body:

```
{baseUrl}/{D365BCInstance}/api/sd/custom/v1.0/companies({id})/cars
```

This is the HTTP request we send:

```
#Insert a new Car
POST https://d365bcita0918vm.westeurope.cloudapp.azure.com:7048/NAV/api/sd/custom/v1.0/companies(ecdc7cd0-ab75-4d40-8d0e-80d2471c4378)/cars
Content-Type: application/json
Authorization: Basic admin Z1JkubB/3epQOtfnBph04rcNgyFpaEuB9OVTnrd0VPs=

{
    "modelno": "M003",
    "description": "Fiat 500",
    "brand": "FIAT",
    "engineType": "Petrol",
    "power": 75
}
```

The response received is as follows:

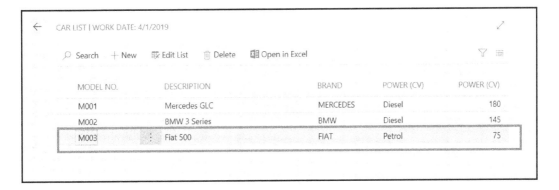

We receive `HTTP/1.1 201 Created` and the JSON details of the `Car` record are added to Dynamics 365 Business Central.

If you look at `Car List` in Dynamics 365 Business Central, you can see that the new record has been created:

When sending a POST request, remember to correctly set the content type of the request to `application/json`. Otherwise, you can receive a quite confusing error in the response message, such as `{"error":{"code":"BadRequest","message":"Cannot create an instance of an interface."}}`.

To retrieve the details of a specific car record, just send a GET request to the following URL:

```
{baseUrl}/{D365BCInstance}/api/sd/custom/v1.0/companies({id})/cars({id})
```

This is done by passing the GUID of the car record to retrieve.

In our example, if we want to retrieve the details of the Mercedes record, we have to send an HTTP GET request to the following URL:

```
https://d365bcita0918vm.westeurope.cloudapp.azure.com:7048/BC/api/sd/custom/v1.0/companies(ecdc7cd0-ab75-4d40-8d0e-80d2471c4378)/cars(0237f4af-3422-41b3-94aa-81196346460e)
```

This is the response we receive:

```
1   HTTP/1.1 200 OK
2   Transfer-Encoding: chunked
3   Content-Type: application/json; odata.metadata=minimal; odata.streaming=true
4   Content-Encoding: gzip
5   Server: Microsoft-HTTPAPI/2.0
6   OData-Version: 4.0
7   Access-Control-Allow-Origin: *
8   Access-Control-Allow-Credentials: true
9   Access-Control-Expose-Headers: Date, Content-Length, Server, OData-Version
10  request-id: f33693a8-e950-48cc-84e8-ab0d848b4f78
11  Date: Thu, 27 Jun 2019 13:37:24 GMT
12  Connection: close
13
14  {
15      "@odata.context": "https://d365bcita0918vm.westeurope.cloudapp.azure.com:7048/NAV/api/sd/custom/v1.0/$metadata#companies(ecdc7cd0-ab75-4
        d40-8d0e-80d2471c4378)/cars/$entity",
16      "@odata.etag": "W/\"JzQ0QzQ4TzZDejJRcktucG1TSnJGVnpRT0tLSF10ejgxYXFiYzRzQWd4RV10ZGs9MTswMDsn\"",
17      "id": "0237f4af-3422-41b3-94aa-81196346460e",
18      "modelno": "M001",
19      "description": "Mercedes GLC",
20      "brand": "MERCEDES",
21      "engineType": "Diesel",
22      "power": 180
23  }
```

As you can see, we have retrieved the JSON representation of the `Car` record.

Implementing a new API for an existing entity

As we discussed in the *Comparing OData and APIs in Dynamics 365 Business Central* section, you cannot extend an existing standard Dynamics 365 Business Central API page. If you need to retrieve new fields for a standard Dynamics 365 Business Central entity, you need to create a new API page in your namespace.

For example, here, I am creating a simple new API that retrieves a customer's details, which are not natively exposed in the standard `Customer` API. The API page is defined as follows:

```
page 50115 MyCustomerAPI
{
    PageType = API;
    Caption = 'customer';
    APIPublisher = 'SD';
    APIVersion = 'v1.0';
    APIGroup = 'customapi';
    EntityName = 'customer';
    EntitySetName = 'customers';
    SourceTable = Customer;
    DelayedInsert = true;
    ODataKeyFields = SystemId;
//URL:
//https://api.businesscentral.dynamics.com/v2.0/TENANTID/sandbox/api/S
D/customapi/v1.0/customers

    layout
    {
        area(Content)
        {
            repeater(GroupName)
            {
                field(no; "No.")
                {
                    Caption = 'no', Locked = true;
                }
                field(name; Name)
                {
                    Caption = 'name', Locked = true;
                }
                field(Id; SystemId)
                {
                    Caption = 'Id', Locked = true;
                }
                field(balanceDue; "Balance Due")
                {
```

```
            Caption = 'balanceDue', Locked = true;
        }
        field(creditLimit; "Credit Limit (LCY)")
        {
            Caption = 'creditLimit', Locked = true;
        }
        field(currencyCode; "Currency Code")
        {
            Caption = 'currencyCode', Locked = true;
        }
        field(email; "E-Mail")
        {
            Caption = 'email', Locked = true;
        }
        field(fiscalCode; "Fiscal Code")
        {
            Caption = 'fiscalCode', Locked = true;
        }
        field(balance; "Balance (LCY)")
        {
            Caption = 'balance', Locked = true;
        }
        field(countryRegionCode; "Country/Region Code")
        {
            Caption = 'countryRegionCode', Locked = true;
        }
        field(netChange; "Net Change")
        {
            Caption = 'netChange', Locked = true;
        }
        field(noOfOrders; "No. of Orders")
        {
            Caption = 'noOfOrders', Locked = true;
        }
        field(noOfReturnOrders; "No. of Return Orders")
        {
            Caption = 'noOfReturnOrders', Locked = true;
        }
        field(phoneNo; "Phone No.")
        {
            Caption = 'phoneNo', Locked = true;
        }
        field(salesLCY; "Sales (LCY)")
        {
            Caption = 'salesLCY', Locked = true;
        }
        field(shippedNotInvoiced; "Shipped Not Invoiced")
        {
```

```
                                Caption = 'shippedNotInvoiced', Locked = true;
                              }
                        }
                  }
            }
      }
```

When this is published on our Dynamics 365 Business Central tenant, we can reach this API at the following endpoint:

```
{baseUrl}/{D365BCInstance}/api/sd/customapi/v1.0/companies({id})/custo
mers
```

If we send an HTTP GET request to this endpoint to retrieve the Customer records, we get the following API response:

As you can see, the custom API shows all of the Customer fields we have added to our API page (the Normal and Flowfields fields).

In the next section, we'll see how to use Dynamics 365 Business Central APIs from an external application.

Creating an application that uses Dynamics 365 Business Central APIs

As we've mentioned in this chapter, APIs are extremely useful for integrating external applications with Dynamics 365 Business Central (they permit us to use simple HTTP calls to manage ERP entities and business logic). As an example, here, we will create a C# .NET application that creates Customer records in a Dynamics 365 Business Central SaaS tenant.

This scenario is very useful for implementing custom data loading procedures. By using APIs, you can create very powerful data transfer routines that permit you to load tons of data by avoiding standard tools such as configuration packages.

This application is a .NET Console application that does the following:

- Connects to a Dynamics 365 Business Central tenant by using basic authentication (a username and a web service access key)
- Reads the company in this tenant and retrieves the company IDs
- Creates a JSON object that represents a Customer record
- Sends a POST request to the Customer API endpoint by passing the JSON of the Customer record to create

The complete source code is on the GitHub repository of this book.

The main function of this application is defined as follows:

```
static HttpClient client = new HttpClient();
static string baseURL, user, key;
static string workingCompanyID;

static void Main(string[] args)
{
    GetSettingsParameters();
    RunAsync().GetAwaiter().GetResult();
}

static async Task RunAsync()
{
    client.BaseAddress = new Uri(baseURL);
    client.DefaultRequestHeaders.Accept.Clear();
    client.DefaultRequestHeaders.Accept.Add(
        new MediaTypeWithQualityHeaderValue("application/json"));
```

```
    string userAndPasswordToken =
        Convert.ToBase64String(Encoding.UTF8.GetBytes(user + ":" +
key));
client.DefaultRequestHeaders.TryAddWithoutValidation("Authorization",
        $"Basic {userAndPasswordToken}");
    try
    {
        //Reads D365BC tenant companies
        await GetCompanies(baseURL);
        //Creates a D365BC customer
        await CreateCustomer(baseURL, workingCompanyID);
    }
    catch (Exception e)
    {
        Console.WriteLine(e.Message);
    }
    Console.ReadLine();
}
```

In the `Main` method, we read the application settings parameters by calling the `GetSettingsParameters` function, and then we asynchronously start the tasks that read the companies (`GetCompanies`) and create the `Customer` record (`CreateCustomer`) via the API.

The `GetSettingsParameters` function defines the mandatory parameters for using the Dynamics 365 Business Central APIs (such as tenant ID, API URL, user, and access key), and it's defined as follows:

```
static void GetSettingsParameters()
{
    string tenantID = "<YourTenantIDHere>";
    baseURL = "https://api.businesscentral.dynamics.com/v2.0/" +
tenantID +
        "/production/api/beta";
    user = "<YourUsernameHere>";
    key = "<YourUserWebServiceAccessKeyHere>";
}
```

We invoke the Dynamics 365 Business Central APIs in the `GetCompanies` and `CreateCustomer` methods.

In the `GetCompanies` method, we send an HTTP GET request to the following endpoint:

```
https://api.businesscentral.dynamics.com/v2.0/{tenantID}/production/api/{APIversion}/companies
```

Then, we retrieve the list of companies in the specified tenant. The response is in JSON format, so we need to parse it (we are retrieving the id and name tokens). The code for this is as follows:

```
static async Task GetCompanies(string baseURL)
{
    HttpResponseMessage response = await client.GetAsync(baseURL +
"/companies");
    JObject companies = JsonConvert.DeserializeObject<JObject>
        (response.Content.ReadAsStringAsync().Result);
    JObject o = JObject.Parse(companies.ToString());
    foreach (JToken jt in o.Children())
    {
        JProperty jProperty = jt.ToObject<JProperty>();
        string propertyName = jProperty.Name;
        if (propertyName == "value")
        {
            foreach (JToken jt1 in jProperty.Children())
            {
                JArray array = new JArray(jt1.Children());
                for (int i = 0; i < array.Count; i++)
                {
                    string companyID = array[i].Value<string>("id");
                    string companyName = array[i].Value<string>("name");
                    Console.WriteLine("Company ID: {0}, Name: {1}",
companyID, companyName);
                    if (companyName == "CRONUS IT")
                    {
                        workingCompanyID = companyID;
                    }
                }
            }
        }
    }
}
```

Here, we want to work with a specific company, so we save the desired company ID in a global variable called workingCompanyID to use that company ID on the entire application.

In the CreateCustomer method, we send a POST request to the following API endpoint:

```
https://api.businesscentral.dynamics.com/v2.0/{tenantID}/production/ap
i/{APIversion}/customers
```

This is done by passing a JSON object in the request body. This object is a JSON representation of a `Customer` record (the request's content type must be `application/json`). Then, the API response is read.

The `CreateCustomer` method's code is as follows:

```
static async Task CreateCustomer(string baseURL, string companyID)
{
    JObject customer = new JObject(
        new JProperty("displayName", "Stefano Demiliani API"),
        new JProperty("type", "Company"),
        new JProperty("email", "demiliani@outlook.com"),
        new JProperty("website", "www.demiliani.com"),
        new JProperty("taxLiable", false),
        new JProperty("currencyId",
"00000000-0000-0000-0000-000000000000"),
        new JProperty("currencyCode", "EUR"),
        new JProperty("blocked", " "),
        new JProperty("balance", 0),
        new JProperty("overdueAmount", 0),
        new JProperty("totalSalesExcludingTax", 0),
        new JProperty("address",
            new JObject(
                new JProperty("street", "Viale Kennedy 87"),
                new JProperty("city", "Borgomanero"),
                new JProperty("state", "Italy"),
                new JProperty("countryLetterCode", "IT"),
                new JProperty("postalCode", "IT-28021")
                )
            )
    );
    HttpContent httpContent = new StringContent(customer.ToString(),
Encoding.UTF8,
        "application/json");
    HttpResponseMessage response = await client.PostAsync(baseURL +
        "/companies("+companyID+")/customers", httpContent);
    if (response.Content != null)
    {
        var responseContent = await
response.Content.ReadAsStringAsync();
        Console.WriteLine("Response: " + responseContent);
    }
}
```

Here, we create a JSON object that represents a `Customer` entity, we send (asynchronously) this JSON object as the body of an HTTP POST request to the Dynamics 365 Business Central `/customers` API, and we read the API response. When this is invoked, the `Customer` record is created in Dynamics 365 Business Central.

Remember that Dynamics 365 Business Central limits the number of simultaneous API calls that you can perform in a certain sliding window. If you have an external service that performs too many requests on a tenant, you could receive an HTTP 429 error (`Too Many Requests`):

```
{
    "error":
    {
      "code": "Application_TooManyRequests",
      "message": "Too many requests reached. Actual (101). Maximum
(100)."
    }
}
```

The purpose of this is mainly to avoid things such as **Denial-of-Service (DoS)** attacks and insufficient resources in the tenant.

The actual permitted maximum number of requests per minute is as follows:

- Sandbox environment: 300 requests/minute for OData (5 requests per second), and 300 requests/minute for SOAP
- Production environment: 600 requests/minute for OData (10 requests per second), and 600 requests/minute for SOAP

To avoid this situation, you should handle how you perform requests to a Dynamics 365 Business Central API endpoint and, if you receive this error, you should adopt something such as a retry policy on the API calls in your external application.

This is an example of how you can use Dynamics 365 Business Central APIs on your custom applications. The example provided uses .NET and C#, but you can use the APIs on every platform and with every language that supports HTTP calls.

Using bound actions

We can use **bound actions** to use RESTful APIs not only to perform CRUD operations but also to invoke standard business logic defined in the application (both custom and standard code).

Bound actions can be used in the OData V4 endpoint (as described at `https://demiliani.com/2019/06/12/dynamics-365-business-central-using-odata-v4-bound-actions/`) and standard Dynamics 365 Business Central APIs.

Imagine you have a codeunit (in the example described here, it's called `CustomerWSManagement`) that defines a business logic (a set of functions) to work on the `Customer` entity and you want to call some of these methods from APIs. Our codeunit has two business functions:

- `CloneCustomer`: This creates a new customer based on an existing customer record.
- `GetSalesAmount`: This gives the total sales amount for a given customer.

The `CustomerWSManagement` codeunit code is defined as follows:

```
codeunit 50102 CustomerWSManagement
{
    procedure CloneCustomer(CustomerNo: Code[20])
    var
        Customer: Record Customer;
        NewCustomer: Record Customer;
    begin
        Customer.Get(CustomerNo);
        NewCustomer.Init();
        NewCustomer.TransferFields(Customer, false);
        NewCustomer.Name := 'CUSTOMER BOUND ACTION';
        NewCustomer.Insert(true);
    end;

    procedure GetSalesAmount(CustomerNo: Code[20]): Decimal
    var
        SalesLine: Record "Sales Line";
        total: Decimal;
    begin
        SalesLine.SetRange("Document Type", SalesLine."Document
Type"::Order);
        SalesLine.SetRange("Sell-to Customer No.", CustomerNo);
        SalesLine.SetFilter(Type, '<>%1', SalesLine.Type::" ");
        if SalesLine.FindSet() then
        repeat
```

```
                total += SalesLine."Line Amount";
            until SalesLine.Next() = 0;
            exit(total);
        end;
}
```

To use OData V4 bound actions, you need to declare a function in a page, and this function must have the [ServiceEnabled] attribute.

 If you declare a [ServiceEnabled] function in a pageextension object and you try to access the metadata of the OData endpoint (baseurl/ODataV4/$metadata), you will not see the action published.

To publish your action attached to the Customer entity, you need to create a new page like the following and then publish it as a web service:

```
page 50102 "My Customer Card"
{
    PageType = Card;
    ApplicationArea = All;
    UsageCategory = Administration;
    SourceTable = Customer;
    ODataKeyFields = "No.";
    layout
    {
        area(Content)
        {
            group(GroupName)
            {
                field(Id; Id)
                {
                    ApplicationArea = All;
                }
                field("No."; "No.")
                {
                    ApplicationArea = All;
                }
                field(Name; Name)
                {
                    ApplicationArea = All;
                }
            }
        }
    }
}
```

Here, the `ODataKeyFields` property specifies the field to use as the key when calling the OData endpoint (I want the `No.` field of the `Customer` record).

Inside this page, I am declaring two procedures to call the two methods defined in our AL codeunit:

```
[ServiceEnabled]
procedure CloneCustomer(var actionContext: WebServiceActionContext)
var
    CustomerWSMgt: Codeunit CustomerWSManagement;
begin
    CustomerWSMgt.CloneCustomer(Rec."No.");
    actionContext.SetObjectType(ObjectType::Page);
    actionContext.SetObjectId(Page::"My Customer Card");
    actionContext.AddEntityKey(Rec.FIELDNO("No."), Rec."No.");
    //Set the result code to inform the caller that the record is
created
    actionContext.SetResultCode(WebServiceActionResultCode::Created);
end;

[ServiceEnabled]
procedure GetSalesAmount(CustomerNo: Code[20]): Decimal
var
    actionContext: WebServiceActionContext;
    CustomerWSMgt: Codeunit CustomerWSManagement;
    total: Decimal;
begin
    actionContext.SetObjectType(ObjectType::Page);
    actionContext.SetObjectId(Page::"My Customer Card");
    actionContext.AddEntityKey(Rec.FIELDNO("No."), rec."No.");
    total := CustomerWSMgt.GetSalesAmount(CustomerNo);
    //Set the result code to inform the caller that the result is
retrieved
    actionContext.SetResultCode(WebServiceActionResultCode::Get);
    exit(total);
end;
```

From the preceding code, we can see the following:

- `CloneCustomer` is a procedure called without parameters. It takes the context of the call and calls the `CloneCustomer` method defined in our codeunit.
- `GetSalesAmount` is a procedure that takes a code parameter, calls the `GetSalesAmount` procedure defined in our codeunit, and returns the result as a response.

What happens with these procedure definitions when we publish the `MyCustomerCard` page as a web service (called `MyCustomerCardWS` here)?

If we go to the OData V4 metadata endpoint, we can now see that the actions are published:

Now, we can try to call our bound actions via OData. As the first step, we want to call the `CloneCustomer` function. To do this, we need to send an HTTP POST request to the following endpoint:

```
https://yourbaseurl/ODataV4/Company('CRONUS%20IT')/MyCustomerCardWS('1
0000')/NAV.CloneCustomer
```

The following is the output we get after the call:

```
Response(82ms) ✕

1   HTTP/1.1 201 Created
2   Transfer-Encoding: chunked
3   Content-Encoding: gzip
4   Location: https://d365bcita0918vm.westeurope.cloudapp.azure.com:7048/NAV/ODataV
    4/Company('CRONUS%20IT')/MyCustomerCardWS('10000')
5   Server: Microsoft-HTTPAPI/2.0
6   Access-Control-Allow-Origin: *
7   Access-Control-Allow-Credentials: true
8   Access-Control-Expose-Headers: Date, Content-Length, Server, OData-Version
9   request-id: a722b82b-3b72-4ba1-919a-c47aab8e46a3
10  Date: Wed, 12 Jun 2019 14:51:39 GMT
11  Connection: close
12
13
```

The code in our codeunit is called and a `Customer` record has been created (that is, cloned by the customer with `"No."` = `10000` as the input):

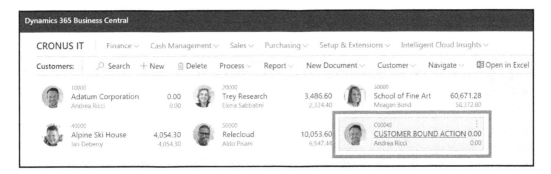

Our second function to call (`GetSalesAmount`) wants a `Code[20]` parameter as input (it's not strictly necessary; it's only to show how to pass parameters to a bound action). We need to send a POST request to the following endpoint:

```
https://yourbaseurl/ODataV4/Company('CRONUS%20IT')/MyCustomerCardWS('1
0000')/NAV.GetSalesAmount
```

As we can see, it is done by passing a JSON body with the required parameter.

This is the POST request that was sent:

```
POST
https://d365bcita0918vm.westeurope.cloudapp.azure.com:7048/NAV/ODataV4
/Company('CRONUS%20IT')/MyCustomerCardWS('10000')/NAV.GetSalesAmount
Content-Type: application/json
Authorization: Basic admin
Z1JkubB/3epQOtfnBph04rcNgyFpaEuB9OVTnrd0VPs=

{
  "customerno": "10000"
}
```

The following is the response received from the POST request:

```
Response(48ms) ✕                                          🖫 📄 🗍 ▥ ⋯

 1   HTTP/1.1 200 OK
 2   Transfer-Encoding: chunked
 3   Content-Type: application/json; odata.metadata=minimal
 4   Content-Encoding: gzip
 5   Server: Microsoft-HTTPAPI/2.0
 6   OData-Version: 4.0
 7   Access-Control-Allow-Origin: *
 8   Access-Control-Allow-Credentials: true
 9   Access-Control-Expose-Headers: Date, Content-Length, Server, OData-Version
10   request-id: 46a68ab7-4cb7-4017-aa94-2a7fbfc0ab14
11   Date: Wed, 12 Jun 2019 14:57:36 GMT
12   Connection: close
13
14 ⊟ {
15       "@odata.context": "https://d365bcita0918vm.westeurope.cloudapp.azure.com:704
         8/NAV/ODataV4/$metadata#Edm.Decimal",
16       "value": 19148.0
17   }
```

As you can see, the response is a JSON object with the value of the total sales amount for the given customer (retrieved by calling our codeunit method).

 The name of the parameter to pass in the JSON object must match the OData metadata, not your function's parameters.

In the next section, we'll examine the concept of webhooks inside Dynamics 365 Business Central and we'll explore how to subscribe to notifications sent from a Dynamics 365 Business Central entity.

Using Dynamics 365 Business Central webhooks

Webhooks are a way to create event-driven service integrations: instead of polling another system to check whether there are any changes in entities with webhooks, a client subscribes to events that will be pushed to it from the source system. Dynamics 365 Business Central supports webhooks, so a client can subscribe to a webhook notification (event) and will then automatically receive notifications if an entity in Dynamics 365 Business Central changes.

To use webhooks with Dynamics 365 Business Central, we need to perform the following steps:

1. A subscriber must register the webhook subscription with Dynamics 365 Business Central by making a POST request to the **subscription** API and by passing a notification URL in the request body. The endpoint URL is as follows:

   ```
   https://api.businesscentral.dynamics.com/v2.0/TENANTID/product
   ion/api/v1.0/subscriptions
   ```

The request body to establish a subscription is the following (here, we're using the `customers` entity as an example):

```
{
    "notificationUrl": "YourAplicationUrl",
    "resource":
"https://api.businesscentral.dynamics.com/v2.0/TENANTID/produc
tion/api/v1.0/companies(COMPANYID)/customers",
    "clientState": "SomeSharedSecretForTheNotificationUrl"
}
```

2. Dynamics 365 Business Central returns a validation token to the subscriber.
3. The subscriber needs to return the validation token in the response body and provide status code `200` (this is the mandatory handshake phase).
4. If Dynamics 365 Business Central receives the validation token in the response body, the subscription is registered and notifications will be sent to the notification URL.

When a subscription is established, the subscriber receives a notification for every update on the subscribed entity. Webhook subscriptions expire after 3 days if they are not renewed before that.

To renew a webhook subscription, a subscriber must send a PATCH request to the subscription endpoint (this request requires the handshake phase too). The request endpoint to renew a webhook subscription is as follows:

```
https://api.businesscentral.dynamics.com/v2.0/TENANTID/production/api/
v1.0/subscriptions('SUBSCRIPTIONID')
```

To renew a webhook subscription, you need to pass the `@odata.etag` tag of your previously established subscription as an `If-Match` block in the PATCH request header.

This is the HTTP response that you receive when the subscription is established:

```
Response(1635ms)  ✕                                        🖫  🗋  🗗  ⊞
  6    Server: Microsoft-HTTPAPI/2.0
  7    Access-Control-Allow-Headers: Origin, X-Requested-With, Authorization
  8    Access-Control-Allow-Origin: *
  9    Access-Control-Allow-Credentials: true
 10    ms-correlation-x: 1a6e52dd-fccc-4692-800f-f7e705b9ed9c
 11    OData-Version: 4.0
 12    request-id: 28fc1b91-d868-49f4-bc31-c733984438ec
 13    Strict-Transport-Security: max-age=31536000; includeSubDomains
 14    x-content-type-options: nosniff
 15    Access-Control-Expose-Headers: Date, Content-Length, Server, OData-Version, ms-correl
       ation-x
 16    Date: Wed, 10 Jul 2019 15:45:42 GMT
 17    Connection: close
 18
 19 ⊟ {
 20      "@odata.context": "https://api.businesscentral.dynamics.com/v1.0/194e87bd-73c6-43c6
         -95d7-1ca48985db5e/api/beta/$metadata#subscriptions/$entity",
 21      "@odata.etag": "W/\"JzQ00lyemdod1UxaWduR3NZaUp2aW9oVTFERU5qV1JDQXpLQi8rU3NyVzBsNmM
         9MTswMDsn\"",
 22      "subscriptionId": "84765ab3c48c4bb0beeb789f936a8c71",
 23      "notificationUrl": "https://d365bcwebhooks.azurewebsites.net/api/D365BCListener?cod
         e=MJ4Y2PltvuOOp/4qz8GbDIQ56LtJqBPiV6Y1fP16cQvXIZL4oA2NRQ==&testerId=subscriber1",
 24      "resource": "api/beta/companies(80d28ea6-02a3-4ec3-98f7-936c2000c7b3)/customers",
 25      "userId": "10cb2537-0adf-4a69-97e5-894c60788667",
 26      "lastModifiedDateTime": "2019-07-10T15:45:41Z",
 27      "clientState": "",
 28      "expirationDateTime": "2019-07-13T15:45:41Z"
 29    }
```

If you try to issue a subscription request again to the same endpoint where an active subscription has been established, you receive the following error:

```
   Response(975ms) ×

1   HTTP/1.1 400 Bad Request
2   Content-Length: 132
3   Content-Type: application/json; odata.metadata=minimal
4   Content-Encoding: gzip
5   Server: Microsoft-HTTPAPI/2.0
6   Access-Control-Allow-Headers: Origin, X-Requested-With, Authorization
7   Access-Control-Allow-Origin: *
8   Access-Control-Allow-Credentials: true
9   ms-correlation-x: 9fdc1cb1-8a27-4c93-ad40-df76bed3f98c
10  OData-Version: 4.0
11  request-id: 14327997-7d34-4efc-85b4-564bb79594de
12  Strict-Transport-Security: max-age=31536000; includeSubDomains
13  x-content-type-options: nosniff
14  Access-Control-Expose-Headers: Date, Content-Length, Server, OData-Version, ms-correlation-x
15  Date: Wed, 17 Jul 2019 15:39:32 GMT
16  Connection: close
17
18  {
19      "error": {
20          "code": "BadRequest",
21          "message": "A subscription already exist for the values provided in the 'notificationUrl' and 'resource'."
22      }
23  }
```

When a subscription is established, a subscriber can receive notifications when the subscribed entities in Dynamics 365 Business Central are modified. This is an example of a notification sent to a subscriber (the notification is a JSON object that contains all of the modified entities):

```
{
  "value": [
    {
      "subscriptionId": "customers",
      "clientState": "someClientState",
      "expirationDateTime": "2019-07-20T07:52:31Z",
      "resource": "api/beta/companies(80d28ea6-02a3-4ec3-98f7-
936c2000c7b3)/customers(26814998-936a-401c-81c1-0e848a64971d)",
      "changeType": "updated",
      "lastModifiedDateTime": "2019-07-19T12:54:20.467Z"
    },
    {
      "subscriptionId": "webhookCustomersId",
      "clientState": "someClientState",
      "expirationDateTime": "2019-07-20T07:52:31Z",
      "resource": "api/beta/companies(80d28ea6-02a3-4ec3-98f7-
```

```
                        936c2000c7b3)/customers(130bbd17-
    dbb9-4790-9b12-2b0e9c9d22c3)",
            "changeType": "created",
            "lastModifiedDateTime": "2019-07-19T12:54:26.057Z"
        }
    ]
}
```

Webhooks are also exposed for custom objects in our extensions. A page with `PageType = API` will expose webhooks with the following limitations (these also apply to standard API pages):

- The page cannot have composite keys.
- The page cannot use temporary tables or system tables as `SourceTable`.

A subscription to a webhook can be deleted by sending a DELETE request to the `/subscriptions({id})` endpoint. Also, to delete a subscription, you need to send a request with the `If-Match` header containing `@odata.etag` of the subscription to delete.

For more information about Dynamics 365 Business Central webhooks, I recommend checking this post:

`http://demiliani.com/2019/12/10/webhooks-with-dynamics-365-business-central/`

In this section, you saw how webhooks work in Dynamics 365 Business Central. In the next section, we'll see how to use Microsoft Graph APIs with Dynamics 365 Business Central.

Working with Dynamics 365 Business Central APIs in Microsoft Graph

Microsoft Graph (`https://graph.microsoft.io/`) is an interesting platform that provides a unique gateway for RESTful APIs that spans multiple Microsoft services. Dynamics 365 Business Central is now one of the endpoints available in Microsoft Graph.

To work with Dynamics 365 Business Central in Graph, you first need to change your Dynamics 365 Business Central user's permission in Graph and then enable the **Financials.ReadWrite.All** permission scope. You can do that by using the **Graph Explorer** tool:

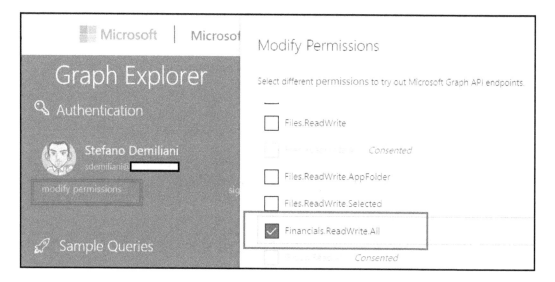

After setting the permissions, you can start using the Dynamics 365 Business Central APIs available in Graph (actually, you need to use the **BETA** API endpoint).

As an example, to retrieve the available companies in your Dynamics 365 Business Central tenant, you need to send an HTTP GET request to `https://graph.microsoft.com/beta/financials/companies`, as follows:

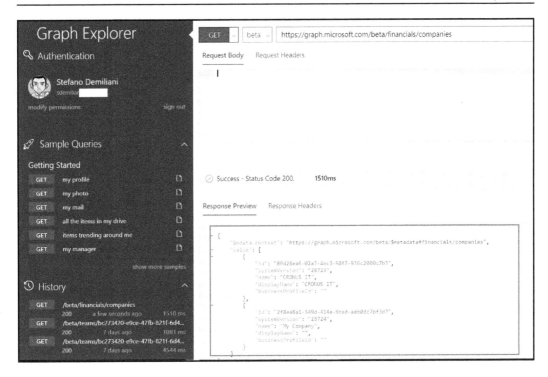

You can parse this JSON response and retrieve the company's ID, which you will use in all of the next API calls.

To retrieve the list of `Customer` records for a given company, you need to send an HTTP GET request to the following URL (by passing the company's ID):

```
https://graph.microsoft.com/beta/financials/companies('80d28ea6-02a3-4
ec3-98f7-936c2000c7b3')/customers
```

As a response, you will get some JSON data with the list of all of your customers:

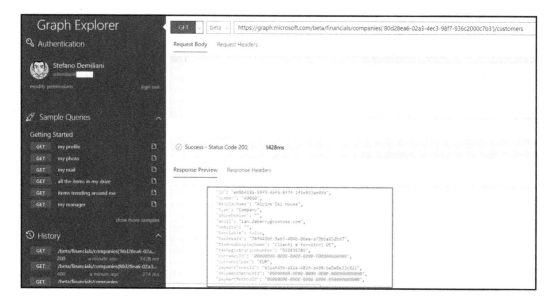

To retrieve general ledger entries for a given company ordered by descending posting date, you can perform an HTTP GET request to the following URL:

```
https://graph.microsoft.com/beta/financials/companies('80d28ea6-02a3-4
ec3-98f7-936c2000c7b3')/generalLedgerEntries?$orderby=postingDate desc
```

This is the response received from the API:

To retrieve, for example, the details for a certain `Currency` (for example, USD), you need to send an HTTP GET request to the following URL:

```
https://graph.microsoft.com/beta/financials/companies('80d28ea6-02a3-4
ec3-98f7-936c2000c7b3')/currencies?$filter=code eq 'USD'
```

The response retrieved will be like the following:

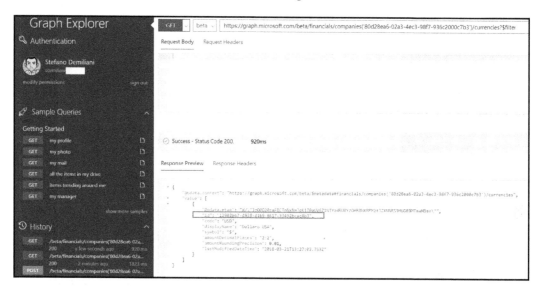

From this response, we can retrieve the ID of the currency because we can use it later to create a new `Customer` record in Dynamics 365 Business Central by using Graph APIs.

To create a `Customer` record in a company with `Currency Code` set to USD, you need to send an HTTP POST request to the following endpoint and set `Content-type` to `application/json`:

```
https://graph.microsoft.com/beta/financials/companies('80d28ea6-02a3-4
ec3-98f7-936c2000c7b3')/customers
```

The request body of this POST request must be JSON content with the customer's details that we want to create, as in the following:

```
{
  "displayName": "Graph Customer",
  "type": "Company",
  "address": {
  "street": "V.le Kennedy 8",
  "city": "Novara",
  "state": "IT",
  "countryLetterCode": "IT",
  "postalCode": "28021"
  },
```

```
      "phoneNumber": "",
      "email": "graph@packtpub.com",
      "website": "",
      "currencyId": "12902bb7-4938-41b9-8617-33492bcac8b3",
      "currencyCode": "USD",
      "blocked": " ",
      "overdueAmount": 0
}
```

As a response, we get some JSON data with the created `Customer` record:

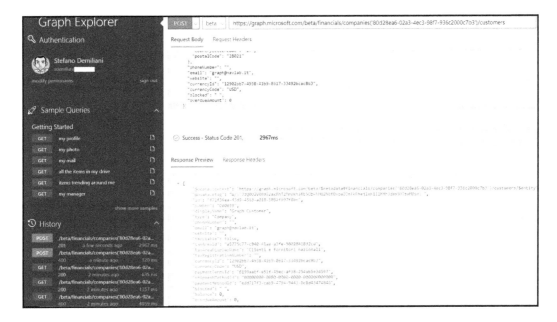

If you now open Dynamics 365 Business Central, you will see that the new `Customer` record has been created:

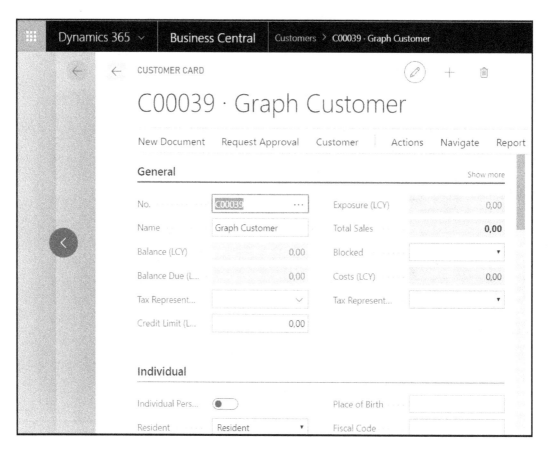

The Dynamics 365 Business Central APIs available in Graph are listed at `https://docs.microsoft.com/en-us/graph/api/resources/dynamics-graph-reference?view=graph-rest-beta`.

Consider them as beta versions for now, as they will be improved in the future.

We've covered how to use Graph APIs to interact with Dynamics 365 Business Central. In the next section, we'll get an overview of the automation APIs.

Automation APIs in Dynamics 365 Business Central

Dynamics 365 Business Central also exposes APIs for automating tenant-related tasks, such as the following:

- Creating companies
- Managing users, groups, and permissions
- Handling extensions (the installation/uninstallation of per-tenant extensions)
- Importing and applying configuration packages

Automation APIs are under the `/microsoft/automation` namespace. For example, to create a company in a Dynamics 365 Business Central tenant, you can send an HTTP POST request to the following endpoint:

```
POST
https://api.businesscentral.dynamics.com/v2.0/api/microsoft/automation
/{apiVersion}/companies({companyId})/automationCompanies
Authorization: Bearer {token}
Content-type: application/json
{
    "name": "PACKT PUB",
    "displayName": "PACKT Publishing",
    "evaluationCompany": false,
    "businessProfileId": ""
}
```

To retrieve users on your tenant, you need to send a GET request to the following endpoint:

```
GET
https://api.businesscentral.dynamics.com/v1.0/api/microsoft/automation
/beta/companies({id})/users
```

When you have retrieved your user's details, to assign a permission set to a user via an automation API, you need to send a POST request to the following endpoint:

```
POST
https://api.businesscentral.dynamics.com/v1.0/api/microsoft/automation
/{apiVersion}/companies({companyId})//users({userSecurityId})/userGrou
pMembers
Authorization: Bearer {token}
```

```
{
  "code": "D365 EXT. ACCOUNTANT",
  "companyName" :"CRONUS IT"
}
```

To modify the details of a Dynamics 365 Business Central user, you need to send an HTTP PATCH request to the following endpoint:

```
PATCH
https://api.businesscentral.dynamics.com/v1.0/api/microsoft/automation
/beta/companies({id})/users({userSecurityId})
Content-type: application/json
If-Match:*
{
 "state": "Enabled",
 "expiryDate": "2021-01-01T21:00:53.444Z"
}
```

To get a list of the extensions installed on a tenant, you can send a GET request to the following endpoint:

```
GET
https://api.businesscentral.dynamics.com/v1.0/api/microsoft/automation
/{apiVersion}/companies({{companyid}})/extensions
```

To handle the installation and uninstallation of extensions, you can send a POST request to the following bound actions:

- `Microsoft.NAV.install`
- `Microsoft.NAV.uninstall`

For example, to uninstall a previously installed extension, you can send a POST request to the following endpoint:

```
POST
https://api.businesscentral.dynamics.com/v1.0/api/microsoft/automation
/{apiVersion}/companies({companyId})//extensions({extensionId})/Micros
oft.NAV.uninstall
Authorization: Bearer {token}
```

AppSource extensions must be previously installed on the tenant; then, you can install/uninstall them via the automation API.

If you have a per-tenant extension, you can upload and install it on the SaaS tenant by sending a PATCH request to the following endpoint:

```
PATCH
https://api.businesscentral.dynamics.com/v1.0/api/microsoft/automation
/beta/companies({companyId})/extensionUpload(0)/content
Authorization : Bearer {token}
Content-type : application/octet-stream
If-Match:-*
```

Here, the request body content must have the `.app` package file (binary) to upload on the tenant. With automation APIs, authentication must be OAuth 2.0 Authorization (Bearer Token).

More information about Dynamics 365 Business Central APIs can be found at `https:/ /docs.microsoft.com/en-us/dynamics365/business-central/dev-itpro/ administration/itpro-introduction-to-automation-apis`.

Automation APIs are extremely important and powerful if you need to activate a CI/CD pipeline and if you need to hydrate tenants.

Summary

In this chapter, we gave an overview of how to use the OData stack (and RESTful APIs, in particular) for integration with Dynamics 365 Business Central. We saw how to use standard APIs, create custom APIs, create applications that use Dynamics 365 Business Central APIs, and use advanced concepts such as webhooks and Graph APIs. Then, we gave an overview of automation APIs.

At the end of this chapter, you were given a complete overview of how to expose Dynamics 365 Business Central business logic and entities and how to handle integrations with external applications by using REST HTTP calls. APIs are the future of Dynamics 365 Business Central integrations, and here, you have learned how to use them on your applications and extensions.

In the next chapter, we'll see how to use Azure Functions and other serverless services with Dynamics 365 Business Central extensions.

13
Serverless Business Processes with Business Central and Azure

In Chapter 12, *Dynamics 365 Business Central APIs*, we looked at an overview of the various APIs that are exposed by Dynamics 365 Business Central. We learned how to use them in our applications, as well as how to create our custom APIs.

In this chapter, we'll cover an important concept that arises when we architect business applications in a cloud environment: *serverless processing*. As you already know, with SaaS, you cannot use all the functionalities that are available in an on-premise environment (such as files and .NET DLLs), and, in a cloud environment, you need to rethink about these functionalities by using services that are provided by the cloud infrastructure.

In this chapter, we will learn about the following topics:

- An overview of the serverless functionalities offered by the Azure platform
- Using Azure Functions with Dynamics 365 Business Central
- Serverless processing scenarios with Dynamics 365 Business Central in real-world applications

By the end of this chapter, you will have a clear understanding of how you can implement serverless processes with Dynamics 365 Business Central by using Azure Functions.

Technical requirements

In order to follow this chapter, you'll need the following:

- A valid Azure subscription (a paid subscription, or a trial subscription that you can activate for free at `https://azure.microsoft.com/free/`)
- Visual Studio or Visual Studio Code
- The Azure Functions extensions for Visual Studio or Visual Studio Code

Overview of Microsoft Azure serverless services

Serverless technologies are key in the cloud world. They allow you to focus on your business application and your code instead of taking care of provisioning and managing resources, scaling, and, more generally speaking, handling the underlying infrastructure that's needed to run your apps.

Azure offers a full suite of managed serverless services that you can use as building blocks of your applications, and these services include compute resources, database, storage, orchestration, monitoring, intelligence, and analytics.

The Azure serverless offering can be grouped into the following categories:

- Compute:
    - Serverless functions (Azure Functions)
    - Serverless application environments (Azure App Service)
    - Serverless Kubernetes (Azure Kubernetes Service)
- Storage:
    - Azure serverless storage (Blob Storage)
- Database
- Workflow and integration:
    - Azure Logic Apps
    - Azure API Management
    - Azure Event Grid
- Monitoring:
    - Azure Monitor

- Analytics:
  - Azure Stream Analytics
- AI and machine learning:
  - Azure Cognitive Services
  - Azure Machine Learning Service
  - Azure Bot Service
- DevOps:
  - Azure DevOps

The infrastructure that's needed to handle your service is fully managed by Microsoft in its data centers around the globe. You have these main three advantages when you use serverless processing in your applications with Azure:

- **You can scale your service as needed**: You can scale a service in/out (add more instances or reduce the number of instances) or you can scale up/down a service (increase/decrease resources).
- **Pay per use**: You only pay for the time your code is running or for the resources you use when executing your code.
- **Integrated security and monitoring** features managed by the Azure platform.

 More information about the serverless offering provided by Azure can be found at `https://azure.microsoft.com/en-us/solutions/serverless/`.

Now that we've had an overview of Microsoft Azure Serverless services, let's look at an overview of Azure Functions.

Getting an overview of Azure Functions

Azure Functions is a service offered by Azure that provides functions as a service. You write code (in different languages) without worrying about the infrastructure, and your code executes in the cloud. With Azure Functions, you can run your code on demand (after a request to the function), on schedule, or automatically in response to different events.

You can write an Azure function directly via the Azure portal or you can develop it locally on your development machine. You can also debug and test an Azure function locally before deploying it to the cloud.

Azure Functions has the following key features:

- Develop in the language you are most familiar with or reuse your existing code in the cloud
- Integrated security; you can specify what security you want to have and the platform will handle it
- Scalability management; you can have service tiers according to your loads and usage
- Pay-per-use pricing model

At the time of writing, the following Azure function types are available:

- **HTTPTrigger**: This is the classical function, where your code execution is triggered using an HTTP request.
- **TimerTrigger**: Your code is executed on a predefined schedule.
- **BlobTrigger**: Your code is executed when a blob is added to an Azure Blob Storage container.
- **QueueTrigger**: Your code is executed when a message arrives in an Azure Storage queue.
- **EventGridTrigger**: Your code is executed when events are delivered to a subscription in Azure Event Grid (event-based architectures).
- **EventHubTrigger**: Your code is executed when events are delivered to an Azure Event Hub (frequently used in IoT scenarios).
- **ServiceBusQueueTrigger**: Your code is executed when a message arrives in an Azure Service Bus queue.
- **ServiceBusTopicTrigger**: Your code is executed when a message for a subscribed topic arrives at the Azure Service Bus.
- **CosmosDBTrigger**: Your code is executed when documents are added or updated in a document collection stored in Azure Cosmos DB.

Azure Functions has the following pricing plans:

- **Consumption plan**: You pay for how long your code is being executed for in the cloud.
- **App Service plan**: You pay for the hosting plan, just like a normal web app. You can run different functions on the same app service plan.

As we mentioned previously, direct usage of .NET DLLs (.NET variables in AL) is not available on the SaaS environment. Azure Functions is the recommended way to use .NET code with Dynamics 365 Business Central in a SaaS environment.

In the following sections, we'll look at the implementation of an Azure function that validates email addresses. We'll use this function to validate the email address associated with a customer record in Dynamics 365 Business Central. This function will be developed using Visual Studio and then Visual Studio Code.

Developing an Azure function with Visual Studio

To create an Azure function with Visual Studio, you need to have the Azure SDK tools installed. These tools can be installed directly when installing Visual Studio or later, by going to `https://azure.microsoft.com/en-us/downloads/`.

Now, follow these steps to learn how to develop an Azure function:

1. With Visual Studio (I'm using the 2019 version), create a new project and select the **Azure Functions** template:

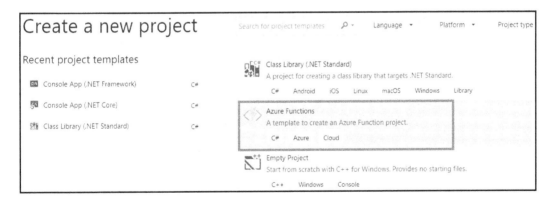

2. Choose a name for your project (here, I'm using **EmailValidator**), choose a location to save the project files in, and click **Create**:

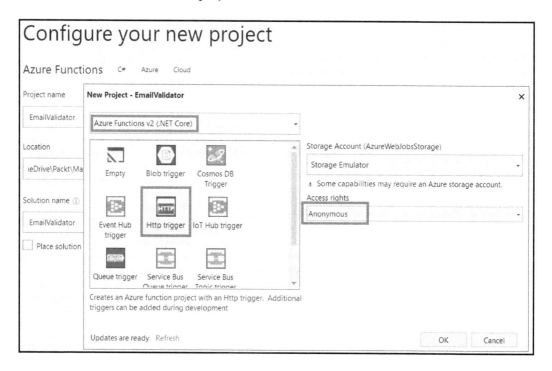

3. Next, you have to select the runtime version of your Azure function:
   - **Azure Functions v2 (.NET Standard)**: Based on .NET Core (cross-platform), this is the new available runtime.
   - **Azure Functions v1 (.NET Framework)**: Based on .NET Framework, this only supports development and hosting in the Azure portal or on Windows computers.

Here, I've selected Azure Functions v2 (.NET Core).

4. Then, you have to select the Azure function type (I selected **Http trigger** because I want a function that can be called via HTTP) and for simplicity, I have selected *Anonymous* as the Access rights for our function (no authentication and everyone can use it; we'll talk about this in the *Managing Azure function keys* section of this chapter).

5. Now, click **OK** to create the solution. This is the project tree that you will see in Visual Studio:

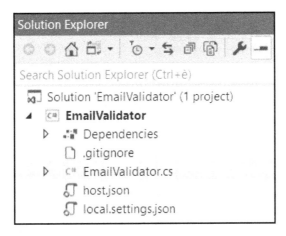

Here, you have the following files:

- `host.json`: This file contains global configuration options that affect all the functions in your project. In our project, we have the runtime version (2.0).
- `local.settings.json`: This file contains the settings of your project.
- `EmailValidator.cs`: This is your function's source code (C#).

Our function's implementation is quite simple. It receives an `email` parameter as input (via a GET or POST request), it validates the email address, and it returns a JSON response stating whether the address is valid or not (this is a custom object called `EmailValidationResult`).

The function code is defined as follows:

```
[FunctionName("EmailValidator")]
public static async Task<IActionResult> Run(
    [HttpTrigger(AuthorizationLevel.Anonymous, "get", "post", Route =
null)] HttpRequest req,
    ILogger log)
{
    log.LogInformation("C# HTTP trigger function processed a
request.");
    string email = req.Query["email"];
    string requestBody = await new
StreamReader(req.Body).ReadToEndAsync();
    dynamic data = JsonConvert.DeserializeObject(requestBody);
    email = email ?? data?.email;

    //Validating the email address
    EmailValidationResult jsonResponse = new EmailValidationResult();
    jsonResponse.Email = email;
    jsonResponse.Valid = IsEmailValid(email);
    string json = JsonConvert.SerializeObject(jsonResponse);

    return email != null
        ? (ActionResult)new OkObjectResult($"{json}")
        : new BadRequestObjectResult("Please pass a email parameter
on the query string or in the request body");
}
```

This function retrieves the `email` parameter from the input and calls the
`IsEmailValid` function.

This function validates an email address by using the
`System.Net.Mail.MailAddress` class, as follows:

```
static bool IsEmailValid(string emailaddress)
{
    try
    {
        System.Net.Mail.MailAddress m = new
System.Net.Mail.MailAddress(emailaddress);
        return true;
    }
    catch (FormatException)
    {
        return false;
    }
}
```

After email validation, the function creates an `EmailValidationResult` object with the response values, serializes it, and returns the JSON response. This `EmailValidationResult` object is defined as follows:

```
public class EmailValidationResult
{
    public string Email { get; set; }
    public bool Valid { get; set; }
}
```

Now that we've tested the function, it's time to publish it locally.

Testing the Azure function locally

Visual Studio provides an emulator that we can use to test and debug our Azure function before deploying it to Azure. If you run the project, the emulator starts and you have a local URL to use for testing your function:

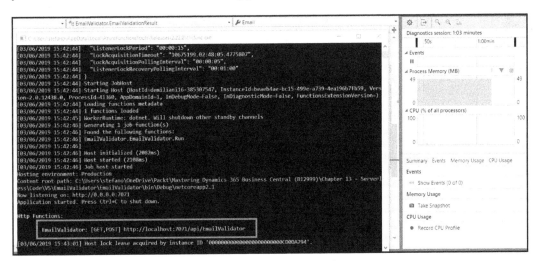

We can test our function by opening a browser and calling a URL, such as `http://localhost:7071/api/EmailValidator?email=masteringd365bc@packt.com`.

When invoked, the emulator shows the request details:

```
Application started. Press Ctrl+C to shut down.

Http Functions:

        EmailValidator: [GET,POST] http://localhost:7071/api/EmailValidator

[03/06/2019 15:43:01] Host lock lease acquired by instance ID '000000000000000000000000CD0DA794'.
[03/06/2019 15:45:18] Executing HTTP request: {
[03/06/2019 15:45:18]    "requestId": "653b9bfb-5730-4947-9022-eccfebdac2ce",
[03/06/2019 15:45:18]    "method": "GET",
[03/06/2019 15:45:18]    "uri": "/api/EmailValidator"
[03/06/2019 15:45:18] }
[03/06/2019 15:45:20] Executing 'EmailValidator' (Reason='This function was programmatically called via the host APIs.',
 Id=560277ae-131f-4740-81da-f51d8a10a6d1)
[03/06/2019 15:45:20] C# HTTP trigger function processed a request.
[03/06/2019 15:45:21] Executed 'EmailValidator' (Succeeded, Id=560277ae-131f-4740-81da-f51d8a10a6d1)
[03/06/2019 15:45:21] Executed HTTP request: {
[03/06/2019 15:45:21]    "requestId": "653b9bfb-5730-4947-9022-eccfebdac2ce",
[03/06/2019 15:45:21]    "method": "GET",
[03/06/2019 15:45:21]    "uri": "/api/EmailValidator",
[03/06/2019 15:45:21]    "identities": [
[03/06/2019 15:45:21]      {
[03/06/2019 15:45:21]        "type": "WebJobsAuthLevel",
[03/06/2019 15:45:21]        "level": "Admin"
[03/06/2019 15:45:21]      }
[03/06/2019 15:45:21]    ],
[03/06/2019 15:45:21]    "status": 200,
[03/06/2019 15:45:21]    "duration": 2976
[03/06/2019 15:45:21] }
```

We can see the JSON response in the browser. The previous call gives us the following response object:

```
{"Email":"masteringd365bc@packt.com","Valid":true}
```

If we call the function with a bad email address, such as `http://localhost:7071/api/EmailValidator?email=masteringd365bc`, we get the following response object:

```
{"Email":"masteringd365bc","Valid":false}
```

Our function is working correctly.

Now that we've tested the Azure function, we are ready to deploy it.

Deploying the function to Azure

Now, we need to deploy our function to Azure. We can do this directly from Visual Studio, as follows:

1. Begin by right-clicking on the project and selecting **Publish...**:

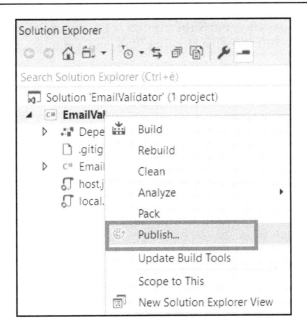

2. We need to choose an **Azure App Service** to deploy the function to. To do this, we can select an existing one or create a new one. Here, I have created a new **Azure App Service** instance for this function:

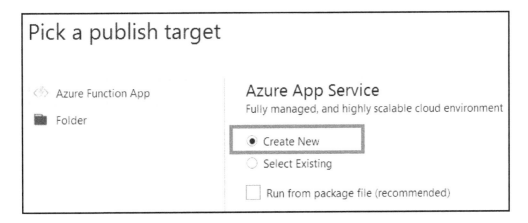

Click on **Publish**.

3. After this, we select the **Subscription**, a **Resource Group** (create a new one or use an existing one), a **Hosting Plan**, and a storage account to use for the deployment:

Now, click **Create** – our function (and all the associated resources) will be deployed to Azure.

4. Now, our function has been published on the Azure data centers and we have a public URL so that we can use it, as shown in the following screenshot:

In my example, the public URL is `https://emailvalidator20190603055323.azurewebsites.net` (you can customize it).

To test your function, use the following URL: `https://emailvalidator20190603055323.azurewebsites.net/`**`api/EmailValidator?email=masteringd365bc@packt.com`**.

The function now runs in the Azure cloud and you're ready to use it.

There is an alternative way of developing an Azure function that's extremely important for any Dynamics 365 Business Central developer. We'll take a look at this in the next section.

Developing an Azure function with Visual Studio Code

To start developing Azure functions with Visual Studio Code, you need to install the following extensions:

- **Azure Account**, which you can download from `https://marketplace.visualstudio.com/items?itemName=ms-vscode.azure-account`.
- **Azure Functions**, which you can download from `https://marketplace.visualstudio.com/items?itemName=ms-azuretools.vscode-azurefunctions`.

You also need to install **Azure Functions Core Tools**, a set of tools that allow you to develop and test your functions on your local machine.

 You need to install the version that supports the Azure Functions runtime you're using. You can install this at `https://github.com/Azure/azure-functions-core-tools`.

To develop Azure functions with Visual Studio Code, follow these steps:

1. The first thing you need to do is log into your Azure subscription by using the **Azure: Sign In** command from the Visual Studio Code Command Palette:

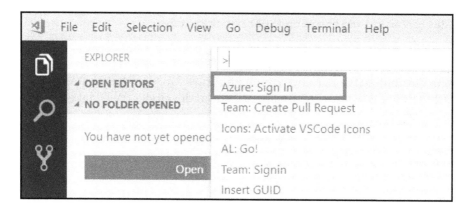

After entering your credentials, you will see the account connected to your subscription at the bottom bar of Visual Studio Code.

2. Now, on the Visual Studio Code sidebar, select the Azure Functions extension and click on the **Create New Project** button:

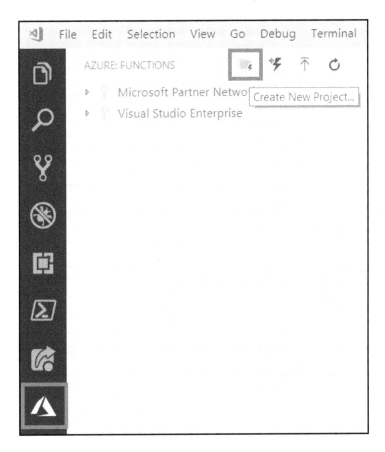

Select a folder that you want to place your Azure Functions project in.

3. Then, you will be prompted to choose a language to develop your function in. From the list of supported languages, I've selected C#, as shown here:

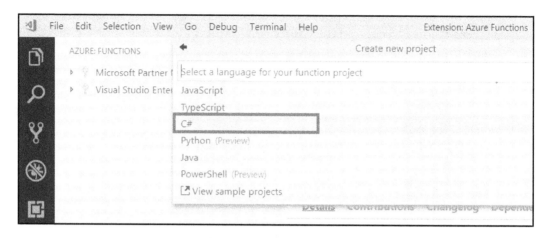

4. Next, you have to select either of the following runtime versions for your Azure function:

- **Azure Functions v2 (.NET Standard)**: Based on .NET Core (cross-platform), this is the new available runtime.
- **Azure Functions v1 (.NET Framework)**: Based on .NET Framework, this only supports development and hosting in the Azure portal or on Windows computers.

Here, I've selected **Azure Functions v2 (.NET Standard)**:

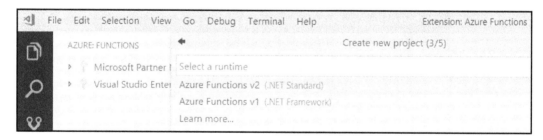

5. Now, set a name for your Azure Functions project (here, I've named it `EmailValidatorCore`):

6. After naming the project, provide a namespace:

7. Now, you need to select the authentication type for your function. For simplicity, I've selected **Anonymous** (everyone can call our function):

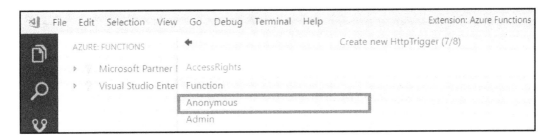

8. Now, choose where to open the project that will be created (**Current window**, **New window**, and **Add to workspace** are the available options).

Visual Studio Code will start downloading the required packages for your Azure Functions project, and, when it's finished, a set of files will be created. The following is the template of your Azure function:

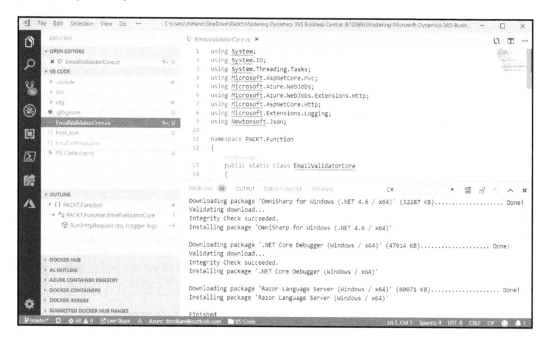

Here, you have the following files:

- `host.json`: This file contains the global configuration options that affect all the functions in your project. In our project, we have the runtime version (2.0).
- `local.settings.json`: This file contains the settings of your project.
- `EmailValidatorCore.cs`: This is your function's source code (C#).

Please note that you may have some temporary errors in your code (missing references). This occurs when Visual Studio Code needs to download all the .NET Core packages. To get the correct references, you need to execute the **.NET: Restore Project** command from the Command Palette, as follows:

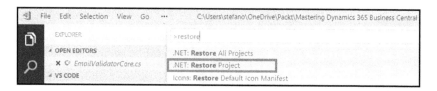

Select the proposed option and click **OK**, as follows:

Your project's references are now fixed and you can start coding your function.

As in the previous example, we want to create a function for validating email addresses, and we can reuse the same C# code to do so. Here, you've seen how to start creating an Azure Functions project by using Visual Studio Code directly.

Testing your Azure function locally

To test your function locally, you need to install the **Azure Functions Core Tools**. This can be installed using the following command on the Command Prompt (or from the Visual Studio Code Terminal):

```
npm i -g azure-functions-core-tools --unsafe-perm true
```

To use npm with Visual Studio Code, you need to have Node.js installed on your machine. You can install it from `https://nodejs.org/en/`.

When you run the npm command, some packages will be downloaded and installed on your local machine:

```
C:\Users\stefano>npm i -g azure-functions-core-tools --unsafe-perm true
C:\Users\stefano\AppData\Roaming\npm\func -> C:\Users\stefano\AppData\Roaming\npm\node_modules\azure-functions-core-tool
s\lib\main.js
C:\Users\stefano\AppData\Roaming\npm\azurefunctions -> C:\Users\stefano\AppData\Roaming\npm\node_modules\azure-functions
-core-tools\lib\main.js
C:\Users\stefano\AppData\Roaming\npm\azfun -> C:\Users\stefano\AppData\Roaming\npm\node_modules\azure-functions-core-too
ls\lib\main.js

> azure-functions-core-tools@2.7.1158 postinstall C:\Users\stefano\AppData\Roaming\npm\node_modules\azure-functions-core
-tools
> node lib/install.js

attempting to GET "https://functionscdn.azureedge.net/public/2.7.1158/Azure.Functions.Cli.win-x64.2.7.1158.zip"
[=================] Downloading Azure Functions Core Tools
+ azure-functions-core-tools@2.7.1158
added 52 packages from 32 contributors in 26.176s

C:\Users\stefano>_
```

After installing the tools, you need to restart Visual Studio Code in order for this to take effect.

To start testing your function locally, you can press *F5* directly in Visual Studio Code. The local Azure Function Host environment will start and Visual Studio Code will give you a local URL so that you can call your function:

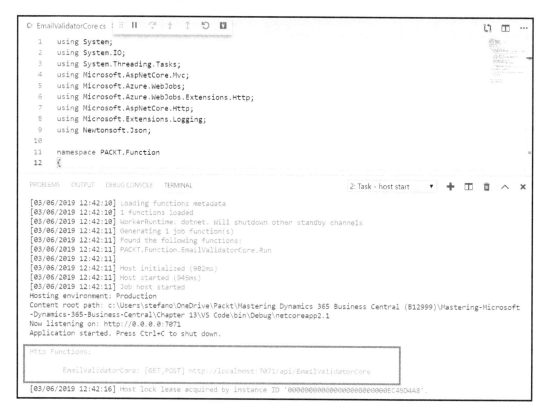

Now, we can test the function by passing the email parameter via a URL in a browser (like we did in the *Deploying the function to Azure* section).

Along with this, we can debug the code directly from Visual Studio Code by placing breakpoints, moving step by step, checking variables and outputs, and so on, as shown in the following screenshot:

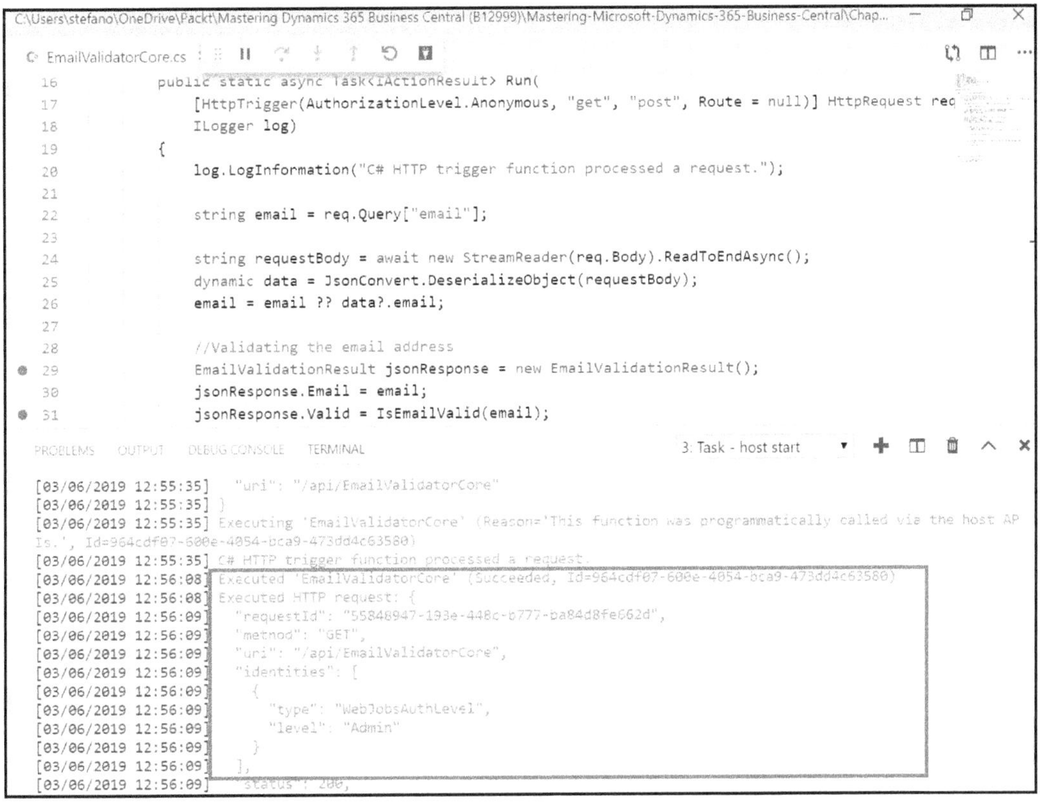

Now, you've debugged and tested your Azure function in your local environment. In the next section, we'll learn how to publish the function to the Azure cloud.

Publishing your function to Azure

To deploy your Azure function to Azure, follow these simple steps:

1. Click on the Azure Functions icon in the Visual Studio Code sidebar and click on the blue arrow icon called **Deploy to Function App**, as shown here:

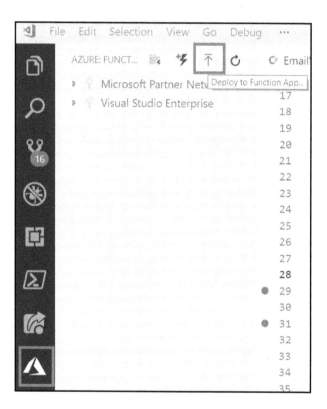

2. Visual Studio Code will ask you to choose an Azure subscription as the location to deploy your function to from the list of the available subscriptions for your account, as shown here:

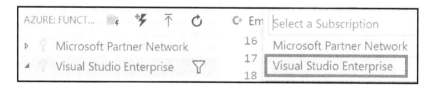

3. Now, select **Create New Function App in Azure** and give it a globally unique name:

I've called it `SDEmailValidatorCore`.

4. From here, you can create a new resource group and a new storage account. Choose the region where you want to deploy your function. Then, resource deployment will start.

5. When the deployment process is finished, Visual Studio Code will show you a confirmation message in the bottom-right corner. You can see the deployed function in the subscription tree view on the left:

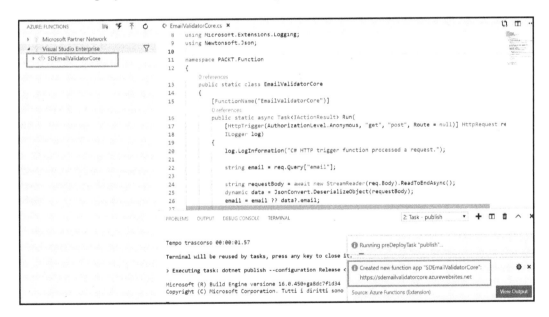

Now, your Azure function is running on an Azure data center and you can start using it with AL code. We will look at this in more detail in the next section.

Calling an Azure function from AL

Now that we have deployed our function to Azure, we can use it from the AL code in our extensions.

As we explained in Chapter 6, *Advanced AL Development*, in the *Consuming web services and APIs from AL* section, we can call an Azure function with AL by using the HttpClient data type, which provides a data type for sending HTTP requests and receiving HTTP responses from a resource that's been identified by a URI.

To test our Azure function, we will create a simple extension (a new project with **AL:Go!**) that allows us to validate an email address associated with a customer record. Our CustomerEmailValidation extension is made up of a single codeunit object where we define an event subscriber to the OnAfterValidate event of the **E-Mail** field in the Customer table. In this EventSubscriber procedure (called ValidateCustomerEmail), we do the following:

- Call the Azure function using the HttpClient object.
- Read the response from the Azure function using the HttpResponse object.
- Parse the JSON response in order to extract the Valid token.
- Throw an error if Valid = false.

The code for this is as follows:

```
codeunit 50100 EmailValidation_PKT
{
    [EventSubscriber(ObjectType::table, Database::Customer,
'OnAfterValidateEvent', 'E-Mail', false, false)]
    local procedure ValidateCustomerEmail(var Rec: Record Customer)
    var
        httpClient: HttpClient;
        httpResponse: HttpResponseMessage;
        jsonText: Text;
        jsonObj: JsonObject;
        funcUrl: Label
'https://sdemailvalidatorcore.azurewebsites.net/api/emailvalidatorcore
?email=';
        InvalidEmailError: Label 'Invalid email address.';
        InvalidJonError: Label 'Invalid JSON response.';
        validationResult: Boolean;
    begin
        if rec."E-Mail" <> '' then begin
            httpClient.Get(funcUrl + rec."E-Mail", httpResponse);
```

```
                httpResponse.Content().ReadAs(jsonText);
                //Response JSON format:
{"Email":"test@packt.com","Valid":true}
                if not jsonObj.ReadFrom(jsonText) then
                    Error(InvalidJonError);
                //Read the Valid token from the response
                validationResult := GetJsonToken(jsonObj,
'Valid').AsValue().AsBoolean();
            if not validationResult then
                    Error(InvalidEmailError);
        end;
    end;

    local procedure GetJsonToken(jsonObject: JsonObject; token: Text)
jsonToken: JsonToken
    var
        TokenNotFoundErr: Label 'Token %1 not found.';
    begin
        if not jsonObject.Get(token, jsonToken) then
            Error(TokenNotFoundErr, token);
    end;
}
```

Press *F5* and deploy your extension.

If you open a customer card, go to the **Address & Contact** tab and insert a value into the **Email** field. You will receive the following message:

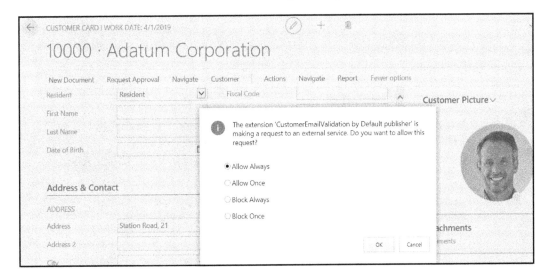

This happens the first time you do this because outbound HTTP calls are blocked by default in a sandbox environment. Select **Allow Once** and click **OK**.

Then, our Azure function is called, the JSON response is retrieved and parsed, and the validation occurs. If you insert a valid email address, the value is correctly inserted into the **Email** field; otherwise, you will receive an error, as shown in the following screenshot:

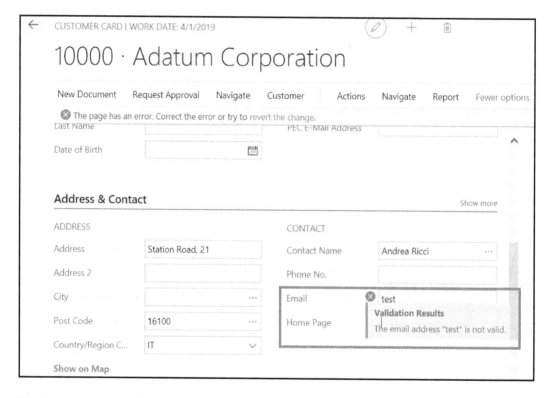

To allow external calls in a sandbox environment automatically, in the `NAV App Settings` table, there is a Boolean field called `Allow HttpClient Requests`, and, when the user selects one of the **Always** options (**Allow Always** or **Block Always**), then a record is inserted into this table with the field set to `true` or `false`.

You can also control this setting programmatically in your AL code. In our extension, we have added the following procedure:

```
local procedure EnableExternalCallsInSandbox()
    var
        NAVAppSetting: Record "NAV App Setting";
        EnvironmentInformation: Codeunit "Environment Information";
        ModInfo: ModuleInfo;
    begin
        NavApp.GetCurrentModuleInfo(ModInfo);
        if EnvironmentInformation.IsSandbox() then begin
            NAVAppSetting."App ID" := ModInfo.Id();
            NAVAppSetting."Allow HttpClient Requests" := true;
            if not NAVAppSetting.Insert() then
                NAVAppSetting.Modify();
        end;
    end;
```

The preceding code retrieves the information about the current extension (`ModuleInfo`) and then checks whether the extension is running in a sandbox environment. If so, it sets the `Allow HttpClient Requests` field to `true`.

In our previous event subscriber (`ValidateCustomerEmail` procedure), we enable the external calls when needed by calling the `EnableExternalCallsInSandbox` procedure, as follows:

```
begin
    if rec."E-Mail" <> '' then begin
        EnableExternalCallsInSandbox();
        httpClient.Get(funcUrl + rec."E-Mail", httpResponse);
```

This allows you to avoid seeing the confirmation request on every external HTTP call.

In the next section, we'll learn how to use Azure Functions and Azure Blob Storage to handle files in the cloud.

Interacting with Azure Blob Storage to handle files in the cloud

One of the main problems we have in the cloud environment with Dynamics 365 Business Central is related to saving files. As we mentioned previously, in the cloud environment, you don't have a filesystem and you cannot access local resources such as network shares or local disks.

If you want to save files with Dynamics 365 Business Central SaaS, the solution is to call an Azure function and store the file in cloud-based storage. You can create a function that saves a file in Azure Blob Storage, and from here you can share Azure Storage as a network drive. This is the scenario that we will cover in this section.

Creating an Azure Blob Storage account

As the first step in implementing our solution, we need to have a storage account on Azure and we need to create a Blob container inside that storage account.

To manually create an Azure Storage account (called `d365bcfilestorage`, in this case), follow these steps:

1. Select **Storage Accounts** from the Azure portal, click **Create**, and follow the instructions on the screen. To create a Blob container inside this storage account, select **Blobs** from the **Services** section:

2. Then, click on **Container**, give it a name (here, I've chosen **d365bcfiles**), select the public access level (by default, container data is private to the account owner), and click **OK**:

Now, the Blob container has been created in your Azure Storage account.

The connection string for accessing your Azure Storage account (which must be used in your Azure functions) can be retrieved by selecting the storage account and clicking on **Access keys**:

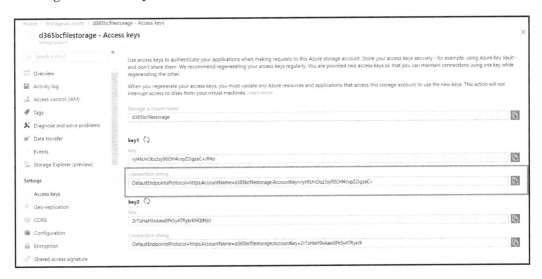

Here, we'll embed this connection string inside the function project, but, in a production environment, you can store it in an Azure Key Vault and retrieve it from there for better security.

In our Blob container, I've manually uploaded a file (PNG image) in order to store a file:

Now, we have created a Blob container on Azure Storage so that we can host our files. In the next section, we'll create an Azure function for saving and retrieving files from this Blob storage.

Creating Azure functions with Visual Studio

Open Visual Studio and create a new Azure Functions project by selecting the **HttpTrigger** template. Name your function `SaaSFileMgt`.

In our project, we want to create the following functions:

- `UploadFile`: This function will receive an object with binary data (file content) and some metadata (file details) via an HTTP POST request. It will store the file in a container in an Azure Blob Storage account.
- `DownloadFile`: This function will receive an object with the URI of the file to download and its details (via an HTTP POST request) and returns the binary of the file stored in the Azure Blob Storage container.
- `ListFiles`: This function will retrieve (via an HTTP GET request) a list of all the URIs of the files stored in the Azure Blob Storage container. These files will be explained in the upcoming sections.

The functions to upload/download a file must only support the HTTP POST method, so, in the `HttpTrigger` definition template, we have removed the `get` parameter. The signatures of these functions are as follows:

```
[FunctionName("UploadFile")]
public static async Task<IActionResult> Upload(
    [HttpTrigger(AuthorizationLevel.Function, "post", Route = null)]
HttpRequest req, ILogger
    log)
```

```
[FunctionName("DownloadFile")]
public static async Task<IActionResult> Download(
    [HttpTrigger(AuthorizationLevel.Function, "post", Route = null)]
HttpRequest req, ILogger
    log)
```

The function to list files in Blob storage must only support the GET method, and the signature is as follows:

```
[FunctionName("ListFiles")]
public static async Task<IActionResult> Dir(
    [HttpTrigger(AuthorizationLevel.Function, "get", Route = null)]
HttpRequest req,
  ILogger log)
```

Let's explore each of these functions.

The UploadFile function

The `UploadFile` function receives a JSON object in the body via an HTTP POST request, as follows:

```
{
    "base64":
"data:image/png;base64,iVBORw0KGgoAAAANSUhEUgAAAJAAAACVCAYAAAC3i3MLAA"
,
    "fileName": "MyFile.png",
    "fileType": "image/png",
    "fileExt": "png"
}
```

The `UploadFile` function parses the JSON in the request body and then calls the `UploadBlobAsync` function. In this function, we upload the file to the Azure Blob Storage container and we return the URI of the uploaded file.

The `UploadFile` function's code is as follows:

```
[FunctionName("UploadFile")]
public static async Task<IActionResult> Upload(
    [HttpTrigger(AuthorizationLevel.Function, "post", Route = null)]
HttpRequest req,
    ILogger log)
    {
        log.LogInformation("C# HTTP trigger function processed a
request.");
        string requestBody = await new
```

```
StreamReader(req.Body).ReadToEndAsync();
        dynamic data = JsonConvert.DeserializeObject(requestBody);
        string base64String = data.base64;
        string fileName = data.fileName;
        string fileType = data.fileType;
        string fileExt = data.fileExt;
        Uri uri = await UploadBlobAsync(base64String, fileName,
fileType,
                    fileExt);
        return fileName != null
            ? (ActionResult)new OkObjectResult($"File {fileName}
stored. URI = {uri}")
            : new BadRequestObjectResult("Error on input parameter
(object)");
    }
```

UploadBlobAsync is a function that performs the Blob upload to the d365bcfiles container in the Azure Storage account. Its code is as follows:

```
public static async Task<Uri> UploadBlobAsync(string base64String,
string fileName, string fileType, string fileExtension)
{
    string contentType = fileType;
    byte[] fileBytes = Convert.FromBase64String(base64String);
    CloudStorageAccount storageAccount =
        CloudStorageAccount.Parse(BLOBStorageConnectionString);
    CloudBlobClient client = storageAccount.CreateCloudBlobClient();
    CloudBlobContainer container =
client.GetContainerReference("d365bcfiles");
    await container.CreateIfNotExistsAsync(
        BlobContainerPublicAccessType.Blob,
        new BlobRequestOptions(),
        new OperationContext());
    CloudBlockBlob blob = container.GetBlockBlobReference(fileName);
    blob.Properties.ContentType = contentType;
    using (Stream stream = new MemoryStream(fileBytes, 0,
fileBytes.Length))
    {
        await
blob.UploadFromStreamAsync(stream).ConfigureAwait(false);
    }
    return blob.Uri;
}
```

The DownloadFile function

The DownloadFile function receives a JSON object in the body via an HTTP POST request, as follows:

```
{
    "url":
"https://d365bcfilestorage.blob.core.windows.net/d365bcfiles/Mastering
D365BC.png",
    "fileType": "image/png",
    "fileName": "MasteringD365BC.png"
}
```

This function retrieves the details of the file to download from the request body and calls the DownloadBlobAsync function. Then, it returns the content of the downloaded file (Base64-encoded string):

```
[FunctionName("DownloadFile")]
public static async Task<IActionResult> Download(
    [HttpTrigger(AuthorizationLevel.Function, "post", Route = null)]
HttpRequest req,
    ILogger log)
{
    log.LogInformation("C# HTTP trigger function processed a
request.");
    try
    {
        string requestBody = await new
StreamReader(req.Body).ReadToEndAsync();
        dynamic data = JsonConvert.DeserializeObject(requestBody);
        string url = data.url;
        string contentType = data.fileType;
        string fileName = data.fileName;
        byte[] x = await DownloadBlobAsync(url, fileName);
        //Returns the Base64 string of the retrieved file
        return (ActionResult)new
OkObjectResult($"{Convert.ToBase64String(x)}");
    }
    catch(Exception ex)
    {
        log.LogInformation("Bad input request: " + ex.Message);
        return new BadRequestObjectResult("Error on input parameter
(object): " +
            ex.Message);
    }
}
```

`DownloadBlobAsync` is the function that connects to the Azure Storage Blob container, checks for the file, and (if it is found) returns the byte array (stream) of this file:

```
public static async Task<byte[]> DownloadBlobAsync(string url, string
fileName)
{
    CloudStorageAccount storageAccount =
        CloudStorageAccount.Parse(BLOBStorageConnectionString);
    CloudBlobClient client = storageAccount.CreateCloudBlobClient();
    CloudBlobContainer container =
client.GetContainerReference("d365bcfiles");
    CloudBlockBlob blob = container.GetBlockBlobReference(fileName);
    await blob.FetchAttributesAsync();
    long fileByteLength = blob.Properties.Length;
    byte[] fileContent = new byte[fileByteLength];
    for (int i = 0; i < fileByteLength; i++)
    {
        fileContent[i] = 0x20;
    }
    await blob.DownloadToByteArrayAsync(fileContent, 0);
    return fileContent;
}
```

The ListFiles function

The `ListFiles` function is called via an HTTP GET request (no parameters). It calls the `ListBlobAsync` function and then returns the list of the URI of the files in the blob container (JSON format).

Its code is defined as follows:

```
[FunctionName("ListFiles")]
        public static async Task<IActionResult> Dir(
            [HttpTrigger(AuthorizationLevel.Function, "get", Route =
null)] HttpRequest req,
            ILogger log)
        {
            log.LogInformation("C# HTTP trigger function processed a
request.");
            string requestBody = await new
StreamReader(req.Body).ReadToEndAsync();
            dynamic data = JsonConvert.DeserializeObject(requestBody);
            var URIfileList = await ListBlobAsync();
            string json = JsonConvert.SerializeObject(URIfileList);
            return URIfileList != null
```

```
                ? (ActionResult)new OkObjectResult($"{json}")
                : new BadRequestObjectResult("Bad request.");
    }
```

The `ListBlobAsync` function connects to the Azure Storage container and retrieves the list of blob files stored on it by using the `ListBlobsSegmentedAsync` method.

This method returns the list of files in segments by using a `BlobContinuationToken`. When this token is `null`, all the files are retrieved:

```
public static async Task<List<Uri>> ListBlobAsync()
{
    CloudStorageAccount storageAccount =
        CloudStorageAccount.Parse(BLOBStorageConnectionString);
    CloudBlobClient client = storageAccount.CreateCloudBlobClient();
    CloudBlobContainer container =
client.GetContainerReference("d365bcfiles");
    List<Uri> URIFileList = new List<Uri>();
    BlobContinuationToken blobContinuationToken = null;
    do
    {
        var resultSegment = await
container.ListBlobsSegmentedAsync(prefix: null,
                                        useFlatBlobListing: true,
                                        blobListingDetails:
BlobListingDetails.None,
                                        maxResults: null,
                                        currentToken:
blobContinuationToken,
                                        options: null,
                                        operationContext: null);
        // Get the value of the continuation token returned by the
listing call.
        blobContinuationToken = resultSegment.ContinuationToken;
        foreach (IListBlobItem item in resultSegment.Results)
        {
            URIFileList.Add(item.Uri);
        }
    } while (blobContinuationToken != null); //Loop while the
continuation token is not null.

    return URIFileList;
}
```

Now, that we've created our Azure functions, it's time to deploy them. We'll learn how to do this in the next section.

Deploying the Azure functions

Our Azure functions can be deployed to our Azure subscription directly from Visual Studio. To deploy these functions to Azure, you need to create a new **Azure App Service** instance, as follows:

After that, publish your functions to this Azure App Service:

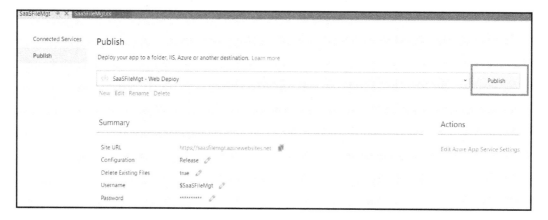

If you go to the Azure portal, you will see that the functions have been published and that you now have a public URL to test them:

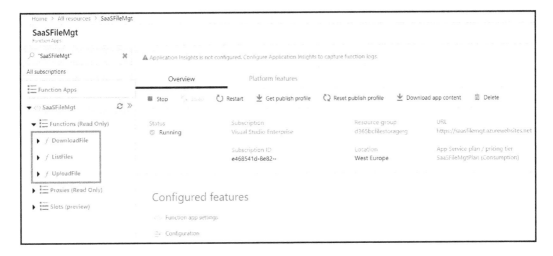

Now, the functions run on an Azure data center. In the next section, we'll learn how we can manage the access keys of our deployed functions (authorization).

Managing Azure Functions keys

Azure Functions uses authorization keys to protect access to your HTTP-triggered functions. When you deploy a function, you can choose between the following authorization levels:

- **Anonymous**: No access key is required.
- **Function**: A specific access key is required in order to access the function.
- **Admin**: A master host key is required.

You can manage these access keys directly from the Azure portal by selecting your function and clicking on **Manage**:

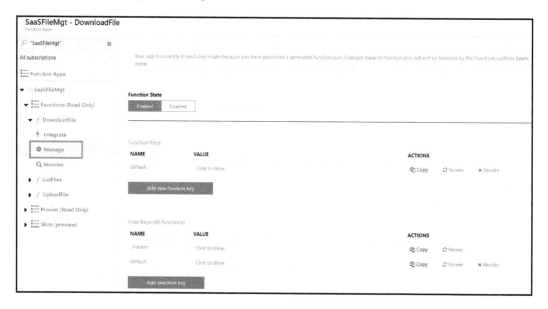

You can also use the **Key Management API** (https://github.com/Azure/azure-functions-host/wiki/Key-management-API) if you want to manage keys programmatically.

 More information on how you can manage the authorization keys for your Azure Functions can be found here: https://docs.microsoft.com/en-us/azure/azure-functions/functions-bindings-http-webhook#authorization-keys.

In this section, you've learned how to handle access keys for our Azure function. In the next section, we'll learn how to test our previously deployed Azure function (uploading and downloading files from Blob storage).

Testing the Azure functions

In our scenario, the Azure functions have been deployed with the **Function** authorization level, so we need to call the desired function by passing a `code` parameter with the function key (which we can obtain from the portal). For example, to test the `ListFiles` function, we need to call the following URL: `https://saasfilemgt.azurewebsites.net/api/ListFiles?code=FUNCTIONKEY`.

This is the response we get (a list of our Blob files' URIs):

To test the `DownloadFile` function, we need to send a POST request to the function's URL by passing a JSON object with the following parameters (which identify the file to retrieve):

```
{
    "url":
"https://d365bcfilestorage.blob.core.windows.net/d365bcfiles/Mastering
D365BC.png",
    "fileType": "image/png",
    "fileName": "MasteringD365BC.png"
}
```

Launching the HTTP request from Visual Studio Code gives us the following response:

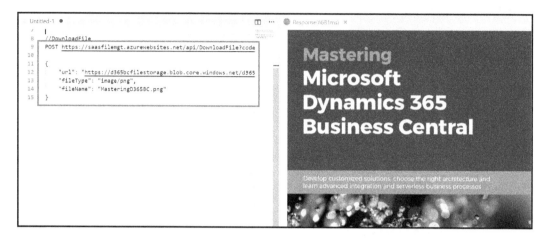

As you can see, the function downloads the requested file from Azure Blob Storage (the function returns the Base64 string).

In the next section, we'll learn how to call our Azure function from an AL extension in Dynamics 365 Business Central.

Writing the Dynamics 365 Business Central extension

The extension we want to create here is a simple application that adds two actions to the *Item List* page for uploading and downloading files to/from Azure Blob Storage.

This AL extension will define two objects:

- A `codeunit` object with the logic to call our Azure functions that handle the files with Azure Blob Storage
- A `pageextension` object that adds the actions on the **Item List** page and calls the relative procedures defined in our codeunit

Let's look at these in more detail.

Codeunit definition

The codeunit is called `SaaSFileMgt` and contains two procedures:

- `UploadFile`: This function will handle the file upload to Azure Blob Storage.
- `DownloadFile`: This function will handle the file download from Azure Blob Storage.

In the codeunit, we have two global variables, both of which contain the URLs of the Azure functions to call:

```
var
        BaseUrlUploadFunction: Label
'https://saasfilemgt.azurewebsites.net/api/UploadFile?code=YOURFUNCTIO
NKEY';
        BaseUrlDownloadFunction: Label
'https://saasfilemgt.azurewebsites.net/api/DownloadFile?code=YOURFUNCT
IONKEY';
```

Here, `YOURFUNCTIONKEY` is the key we use to access the Azure function (retrieved from the Azure portal by selecting the function and clicking on **Manage**).

The `UploadFile` procedure is defined as follows:

```
procedure UploadFile()
var
  fileMgt: Codeunit "File Management";
  selectedFile: Text;
  httpClient: HttpClient;
  httpContent: HttpContent;
  jsonBody: text;
  httpResponse: HttpResponseMessage;
  httpHeader: HttpHeaders;
  fileName: Text;
  fileExt: Text;
```

```
        base64Convert: Codeunit "Base64 Convert";
        instr: InStream;
    begin
        UploadIntoStream('Select a file to
upload','','',selectedFile,instr);
        fileName := delchr(fileMgt.GetFileName(selectedFile), '=', '.'
+
                fileMgt.GetExtension(selectedFile));
        fileExt := fileMgt.GetExtension(selectedFile);
        jsonBody := ' {"base64":"' + tempblob.ToBase64String() +
                '","fileName":"' + fileName + '.' + fileExt +
                '","fileType":"' + GetMimeType(selectedFile) + '",
"fileExt":"' +
                fileMgt.GetExtension(selectedFile) + '"}';
        httpContent.WriteFrom(jsonBody);
        httpContent.GetHeaders(httpHeader);
        httpHeader.Remove('Content-Type');
        httpHeader.Add('Content-Type', 'application/json');
        httpClient.Post(BaseUrlUploadFunction, httpContent,
httpResponse);
        //Here we should read the response to retrieve the URI
        message('File uploaded.');
    end;
```

From the preceding code, we can see the following:

1. We ask for a file to upload.
2. We read the file into a `Stream` object.
3. We retrieve some parameters related to the file (name and extension).
4. We create a JSON message, as requested by the function (as we described previously).
5. Then, we send an HTTP POST request to our Azure function (by using the `HttpClient` object), passing the JSON in the body.

The `DownloadFile` procedure is defined as follows:

```
    procedure DownloadFile(fileName: Text; blobUrl: Text)
    var
        tempblob: Codeunit "Temp Blob";
        httpClient: HttpClient;
        httpContent: HttpContent;
        jsonBody: text;
        httpResponse: HttpResponseMessage;
        httpHeader: HttpHeaders;
        base64: Text;
        fileType: Text;
```

```
        fileStream: InStream;
        base64Convert: Codeunit "Base64 Convert";
        outstr: OutStream;
    begin
        fileType := GetMimeType(fileName);
        jsonBody := ' {"url":"' + blobUrl + '","fileName":"' +
fileName + '", "fileType":"' +
                    fileType + '"}';
        httpContent.WriteFrom(jsonBody);
        httpContent.GetHeaders(httpHeader);
        httpHeader.Remove('Content-Type');
        httpHeader.Add('Content-Type', 'application/json');
        httpClient.Post(BaseUrlDownloadFunction, httpContent,
httpResponse);
        httpResponse.Content.ReadAs(base64);
        base64 := DelChr(base64, '=', '"');
        base64Convert.FromBase64(base64);
        tempblob.CreateOutStream(outstr);
        outstr.WriteText(base64);
        tempblob.CreateInStream(fileStream);
        DownloadFromStream(fileStream, 'Download file from Azure
Storage', '', '', fileName);
    end;
```

This procedure receives the name of the file to retrieve as input. This is how it works:

1. It calls a custom function (GetMimeType) that returns the content type of this file, and then we compose the JSON message for the request.
2. Then, we send an HTTP POST request to our Azure function (by using the HttpClient object), passing the JSON in the body.
3. We read the HttpResponse object (Base64 of the retrieved file) and download it to the client-side by using an InStream object and calling the DownloadFromStream method.

The GetMimeType utility is defined as follows:

```
local procedure GetMimeType(selectedFile: Text): Text
var
    fileMgt: Codeunit "File Management";
    mimeType: Text;
begin
    case lowercase(fileMgt.GetExtension(selectedFile)) of
        'pdf':
            mimeType := 'application/pdf';
        'txt':
            mimeType := 'text/plain';
```

```
            'csv':
                mimeType := 'text/csv';
            'png':
                mimeType := 'image/png';
            'jpg':
                mimeType := 'image/jpg';
            'bmp':
                mimeType := 'image/bmp';
            'gif':
                mimeType := 'image/gif';
            else
                Error('File Format not supported!');
        end;
        EXIT(mimeType);
    end;
```

This simply receives a filename as input, retrieves the file extension, and then returns the MIME type associated with the file.

The pageextension definition

The pageextension object extends the **Item List** page by adding the two actions we described previously. The object definition is as follows:

```
pageextension 50103 ItemListExt extends "Item List"
{
    actions
    {
        addlast(Creation)
        {
            Action(Upload)
            {
                ApplicationArea = All;
                Caption = 'Upload file to Azure Blob Storage';
                Image = Add;
                Promoted = true;
                trigger OnAction();
                var
                    SaaSFileMgt: Codeunit SaaSFileMgt;
                begin
                    SaaSFileMgt.UploadFile();
                end;
            }

            Action(Download)
            {
                ApplicationArea = All;
```

```
                    Caption = 'Download file from Azure Blob Storage';
                    Image = MoveDown;
                    Promoted = true;
                    trigger OnAction();
                    var
                        SaaSFileMgt: Codeunit SaaSFileMgt;
                    begin
                        SaaSFileMgt.DownloadFile('TEST.txt',
'https://d365bcfilestorage.blob.core.windows.net/d365bcfiles/TEST.txt'
);
                    end;
                }
            }
        }
    }
```

These two actions simply call the methods defined in our codeunit by passing the required parameters.

In the next section, we'll test the integrated solution (an Azure function being called by Dynamics 365 Business Central).

Testing our application

Now, it's time to test our application and see how it works. When published, our extension adds two functions to the **Item List** page for uploading/downloading files:

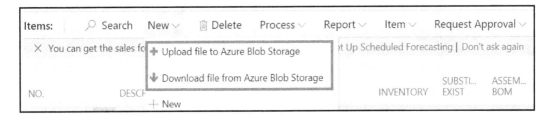

If you click the **Upload file to Azure Blob Storage** action, you can select a file from your local machine:

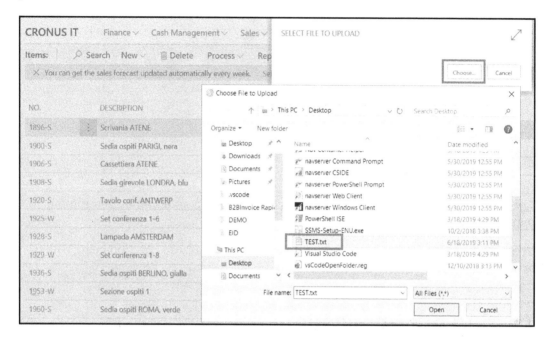

This file will be uploaded to the Azure Blob Storage container via an HTTP POST request to our Azure function. We can debug the `httpResponse` object and see that it returns `HttpStatusCode = 200 (success)`:

```
jsonBody := ' {"base64":"' + tempblob.ToBase64String() +
'","fileName":"' + fileName + '.' + fileExt +
'","fileType":"' + GetMimeType(selectedFile) + '", "fileEx
                                                              200 OK
                                                                 HttpStatusCode: 200
httpContent.WriteFrom(jsonBody);                                 ReasonPhrase: OK
httpContent.GetHeaders(httpHeader);                              IsSuccessStatusCode: True
httpHeader.Remove('Content-Type');                               IsBlockedByEnvironment: False
httpHeader.Add('Content-Type', 'application/json');            ▸ Headers
httpClient.Post(BaseUrlUploadFunction, httpContent, httpResponse);
//Here we should read the response to retrieve the URI
message('File uploaded.');
```

We will receive a message that tells us that the file has been uploaded to Azure Blob
Storage, as shown here:

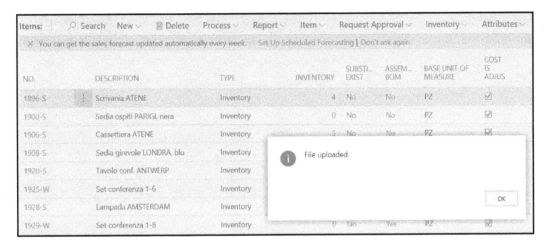

If we check the blob container in our Azure Storage account, we will see that the file
has been uploaded into the blob storage correctly:

When you click on the **Download file from Azure Blob Storage** action,
an HTTP POST request to the `DownloadFile` Azure function is performed (by
passing a JSON body, as we described previously) and the `httpResponse` object
returns `HttpStatusCode = 200 (success)`.

The `httpResponse` object is a Base64 encoding of the retrieved file. Here, the Base64 string is decoded and the file is downloaded to the client-side by using an `InStream`:

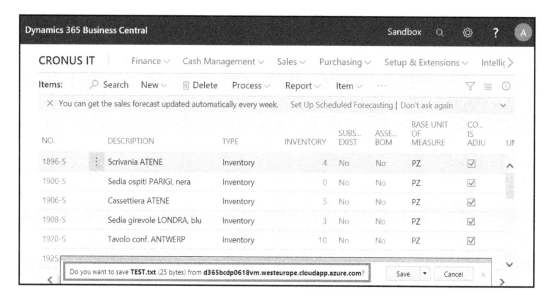

As you can see, the file is retrieved from the stream and the browser prompts the user to download it locally.

Now, you can handle files in a cloud environment (upload and download). Azure also allows us to map the Blob storage to our on-premise network so that we can have a serverless filesystem that's totally transparent for the end user.

Summary

In this chapter, we looked at what Azure functions are and how we can use them in our Dynamics 365 Business Central extensions to execute .NET code on a cloud environment and to implement serverless processes.

We learned how to create a simple Azure function using Visual Studio and Visual Studio Code and how to use Azure Functions with other Azure services (in particular, how to use Azure Functions and Azure Blob Storage to implement a filesystem in the cloud with Dynamics 365 Business Central).

After reading this chapter, you should understand how to develop, deploy, and use Azure functions to implement business tasks in the cloud in a totally serverless way. In a modern cloud-based ERP, this is a really important feature to master in order to extend the platform's functionalities and to embrace other cloud services.

In the next chapter, we'll learn how to monitor and scale our functions in the cloud and how to apply DevOps techniques (continuous integration and continuous deployment) to our Azure Functions projects by using Azure DevOps.

14
Monitoring, Scaling, and CI/CD with Azure Functions

In the previous chapter, we learned how to create Azure Functions with Visual Studio and Visual Studio Code, how to publish a function on Azure, and how to call an Azure function from a Dynamics 365 Business Central extension.

We also learned how to use Azure Functions to implement serverless processes on Azure and execute .NET code in the cloud by looking at a real-life example of how to handle files in a SaaS environment. These topics are extremely important to understand so that you can execute custom code in a cloud environment and interact with external services in a serverless way.

In this chapter, we'll explore other important aspects related to Azure Functions, including the following:

- Monitoring a function published in the Azure cloud
- Scaling an Azure function
- Applying DevOps and CI/CD to Azure Functions

By the end of this chapter, you will have had a complete and in-depth overview of the Azure Functions service and you will be confident with using this service on your Microsoft Dynamics 365 Business Central projects to execute complex code and serverless tasks from a cloud tenant.

Technical requirements

To follow the content in this chapter, you need to have the following:

- A valid Azure subscription (a paid or a trial subscription that you can activate for free at `https://azure.microsoft.com/free/`)
- A valid account in Azure DevOps (`https://azure.microsoft.com/en-in/services/devops/`)

Monitoring Azure Functions

Monitoring Azure Functions is an important task when you're managing your serverless services on Azure. If you want to have a reliable service that always works, you need to have a policy for checking incoming calls on a function, errors, the need for scalability of particular functions, and so on.

From the Azure portal, select your Azure function. By clicking on *Monitor*, you will be able to see the logged requests (success and errors). The following screenshot shows this:

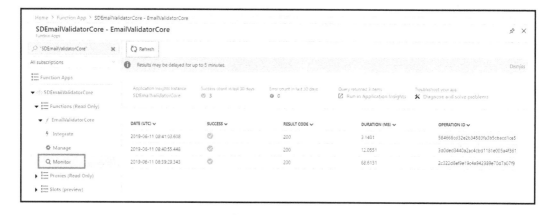

If you select a single request, you can see its **Invocation Details**:

For more advanced logging, you can click on **Run** in **Application Insights** (this must be activated from the portal):

Here, you can also perform custom queries inside the function's telemetry. For example, this is a query on the telemetry log that displays the number of requests per worker role (function) over the last 20 minutes:

```
requests
| where timestamp > ago(20m)
| summarize count() by cloud_RoleInstance, bin(timestamp, 1m)
| render timechart
```

The following is the output of this:

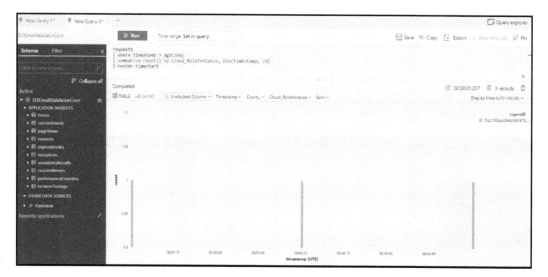

The following is a useful query that you can perform on **Application Insights** to retrieve errors in your function:

```
traces
| where customDimensions.LogLevel == "Error"
```

When **Application Insights** is configured, you'll have a nice panel where you can immediately see everything that occurs in your function (failed requests, server response time, number of server requests, availability, and so on):

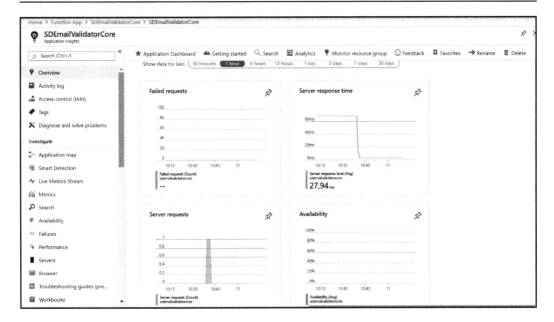

Application Insights is an important section to check if you wish to discover failures and discover whether the function is performing well or needs to be scaled. The following screenshot shows this:

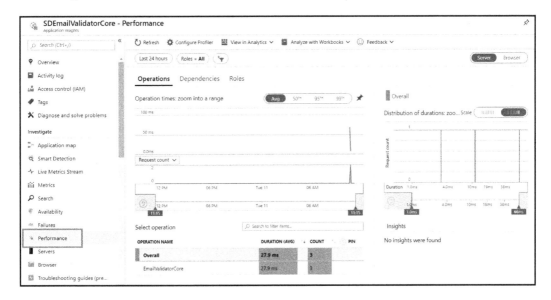

More information about working efficiently with **Application Insights** can be found at `https://docs.microsoft.com/en-us/azure/azure-functions/functions-monitoring`.

As you can see, **Application Insights** is an extremely powerful tool for monitoring your live services and managing your function's logs. I recommend that you always activate it in order to keep your serverless platform on Azure under control. Next, let's learn how Azure Functions work.

Scaling Azure Functions

When using Azure Functions in a production environment, scalability is an important aspect to check because it allows you to tune up your service and avoid bottlenecks or resource deficits.

Azure Functions are executed on two different plans:

- **Consumption plan**: You pay for what you consume. Your app is scaled up or down according to your power requirements. Your billing depends on the number of executions, the execution time, and the memory that the app is using.
- **Premium plan**: This is quite similar to the consumption plan (scaling up and down is handled automatically according to the requested power). Your billing depends on the amount of core per second and the GB of memory per second that's used across all of your instances. The Premium plan adds the following features:
  - Always warm instances to avoid cold starts
  - VNet connectivity
  - Unlimited execution duration
  - Premium instance sizes (one core, two core, and four core instances)
  - Predictable pricing options
  - High-density app allocation for plans with multiple function apps

You can check the hosting plan that's used by your function via the **Overview** tab in the Azure portal:

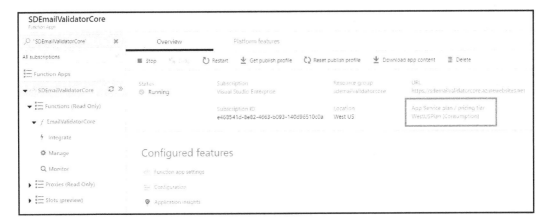

Your Azure function can also run on the same dedicated environment as other cloud applications (App Service apps). This is called an **App Service plan**, and you pay the same quota for all the functions in the same **App Service plan**. When you use an **App Service plan**, you can handle scaling manually (by adding, for example, more VM instances) or automatically (by enabling autoscale).

 For more information about this plan, see `https://docs.` `microsoft.com/en-us/azure/app-service/overview-hosting-` `plans`.

Now, you have a clear overview of the scaling and related billing options that you have when you deploy your functions on Azure. You should select the plan you wish to use according to your business needs.

Azure Functions and DevOps

In this section, we will discuss DevOps techniques and, in particular, how you can create a CI/CD process for your Azure Functions with Azure DevOps.

First, to have source code management, your function's code must be hosted on a Git repository. Here, we're using Azure DevOps as a repository for our CI/CD process:

1. To start, create a new project in Azure DevOps. This project will contain a Git repository for your source code. By clicking on the **Repos** menu on the left, you will see the URL of this repository. Clone it into your local folder with the following command:

   ```
   Git clone
   https://demiliani@dev.azure.com/demiliani/AzureFunctionDevOps/
   _git/AzureFunctionDevOps
   ```

2. In this local repository, I've placed all the project files for our `EmailValidator` Azure function that we previously developed with Visual Studio and committed. Then, we pushed all the files to our online Azure DevOps repository, as shown in the following screenshot:

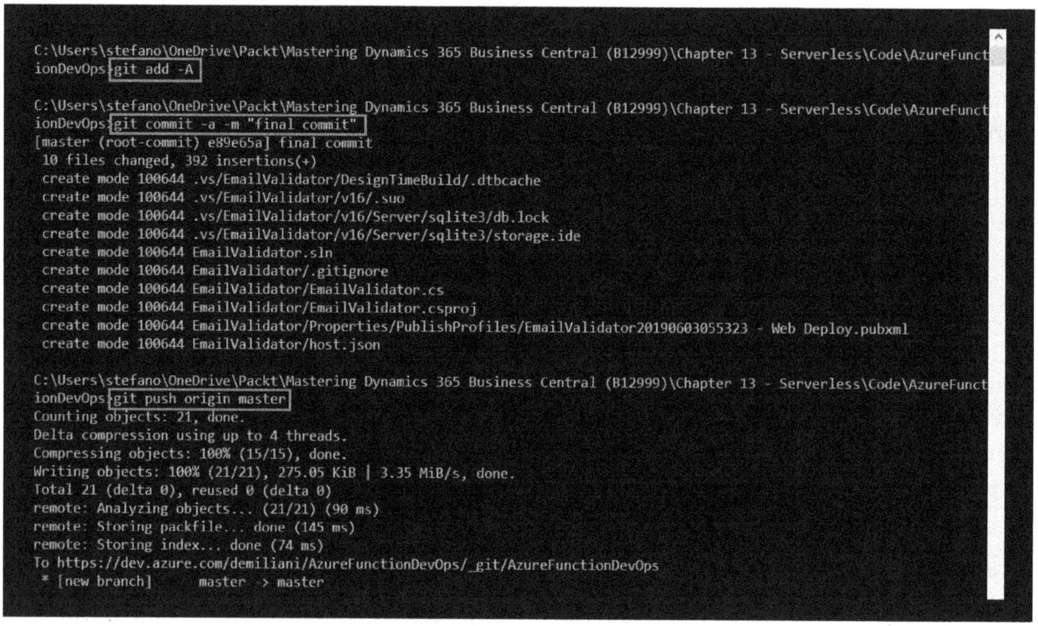

Our code is now on Azure DevOps.

3. Now, we want to create a build pipeline for our Azure Functions project. From the **Azure DevOps** project page, select **Pipelines | Builds** and click on **New Pipeline**. On the **Where is your code?** page, click on **Use the classic editor** to create a pipeline without YAML:

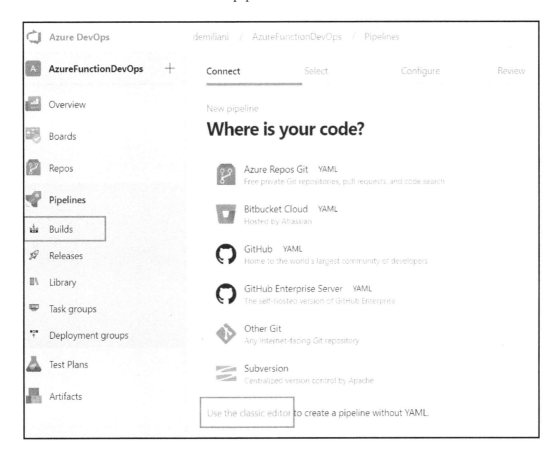

4. Now, you have to choose where your code is going to be hosted. Select **Azure Repos Git** and select a repository from the list (you should have only one repository for the selected project) and a branch to use:

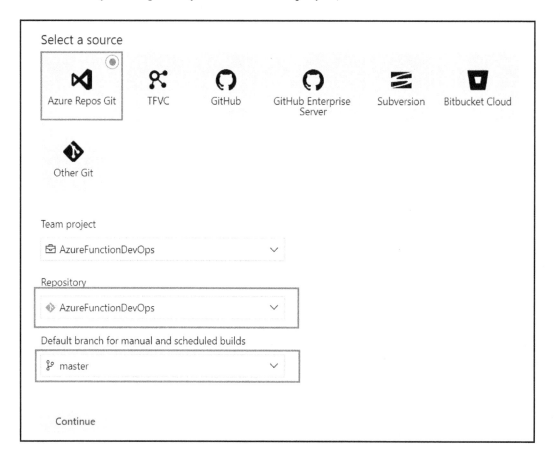

5. Click on **Continue**. On the **Choose a template** page, you need to select a template for your build pipeline. Scroll down the list, select **Azure Functions for .NET**, and click **Apply**:

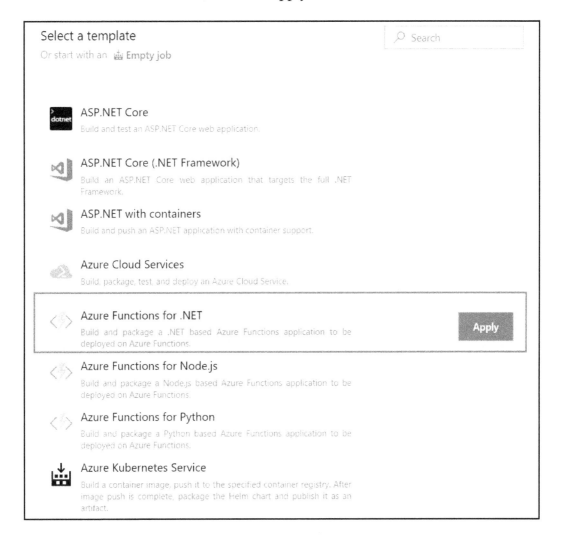

Your build pipeline will be created according to the template you've selected.

6. Click on **Save & queue**:

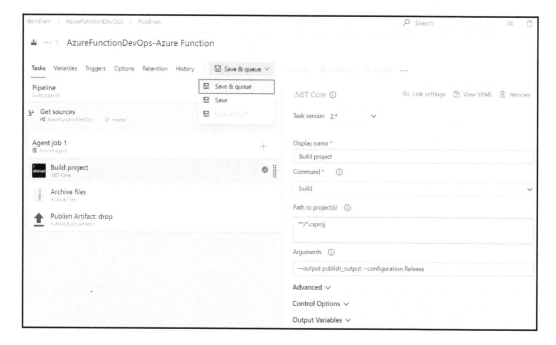

7. Now, a new **Save build pipeline and queue** window will appear. Here, click on **Save & queue** again:

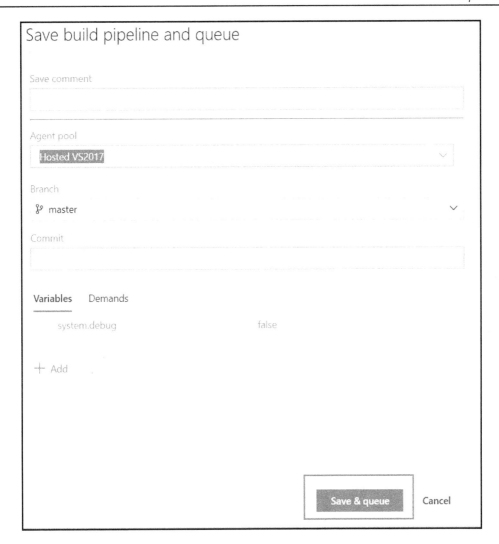

8. Now, your build pipeline has been queued. At the top of your screen, you should see something similar to the following message:

9. If you click on the build number, you will see the build steps that have been performed:

The build process is working, and the nice thing is that you also receive an email, notifying you about the build result.

We have triggered the build manually, but a good developer is often a lazy developer, and so we want to trigger the build automatically on every commit on the repository in the master branch. Let's take a look at how to do this:

1. To define a build trigger, select the build pipeline and click **Edit**:

2. Here, select **Triggers** and click on **Enable continuous integration**:

3. Click on **Save & queue** and select the **Save** option.

Now, when you push a new code modification to your code repository, the build is automatically triggered.

If we want to have an automatic deployment to Azure for our function project upon every commit, we have to create a release pipeline. Let's learn how to do this:

1. To create a release pipeline on Azure DevOps, select **Pipelines | Releases** and click on **New Pipeline**. Then, select **Azure App Service deployment** and click **Apply**:

2. On the next screen, click on **Add** in the **Artifacts** section on the left:

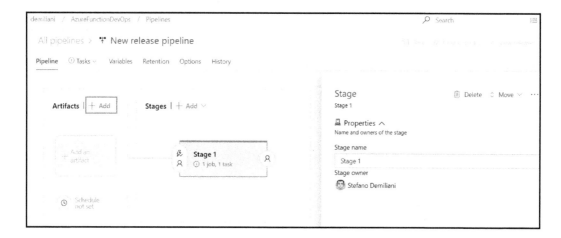

3. On the **Add an Artifact** page, select **Build** as the **Source Type**. Then, select your build pipeline and click on **Add**:

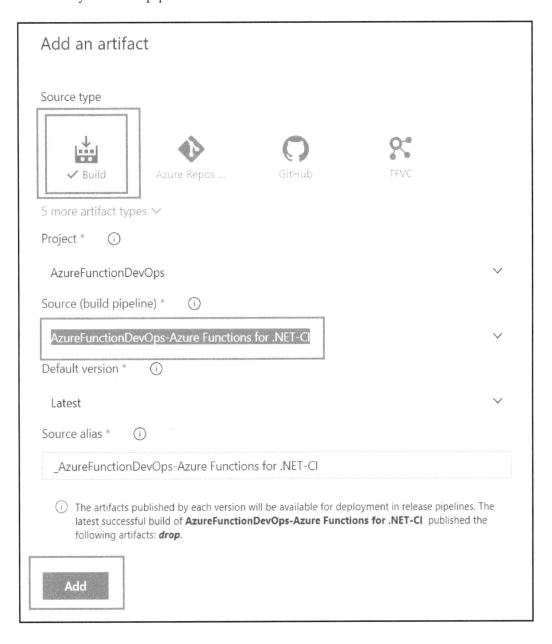

4. Now, click the red exclamation mark on **Stage 1** to view the build tasks:

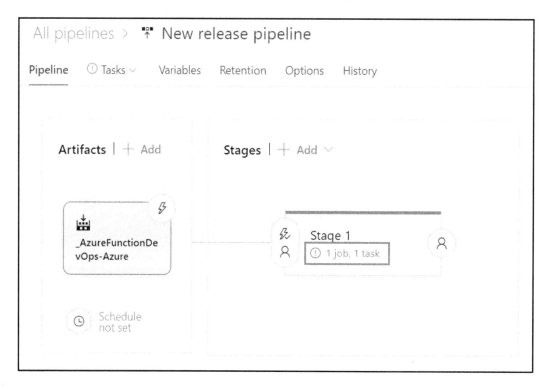

Here, you have to select an Azure subscription and set **App Type** to **Function App on Windows**.

5. To use the Azure subscription, you need to click the **Authorize** button after you've made your selection (you need to disable your popup blocker if it's active):

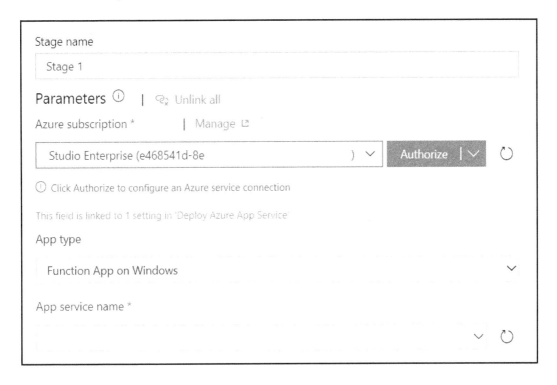

6. When your subscription has been authorized, select the **App Service name**:

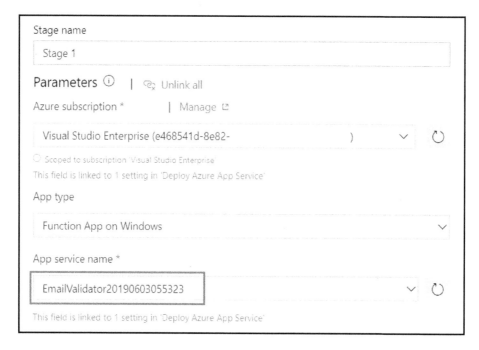

7. Then, click on **Save**. By doing this, your release pipeline will be saved and ready:

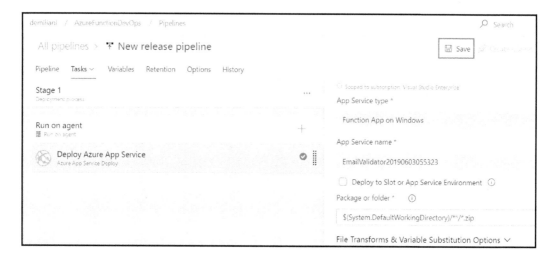

8. To create a new release manually on Azure DevOps, select **Pipelines |
Releases** and click on **Create a release**. On the **Create a new release** page,
don't change anything and just click on **Create**:

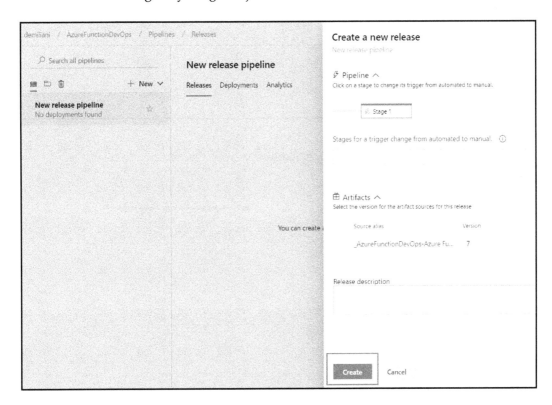

9. A new release will be queued:

10. If you click the release name, you will be redirected to the release progress page:

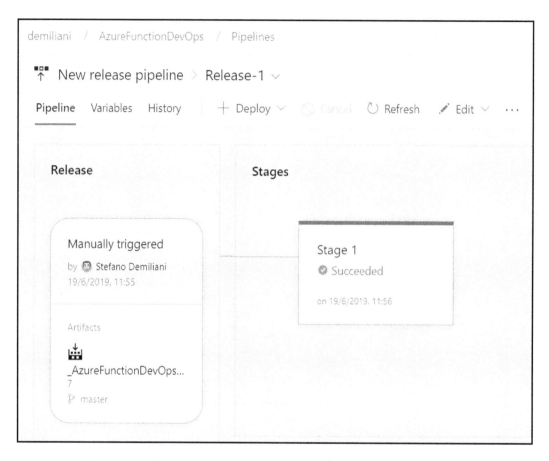

11. If your release pipeline succeeds, your function will be automatically deployed to the Azure App Service:

12. Finally, to fully enable a continuous deployment process, we need to edit the release pipeline again and click on the continuous deployment icon:

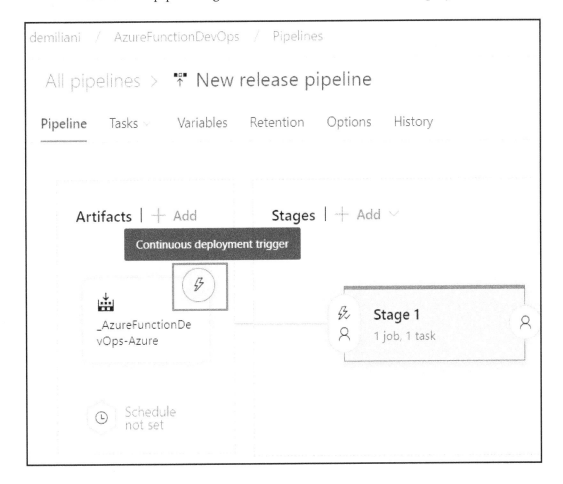

13. Here, we need to enable the **Continuous deployment trigger** option:

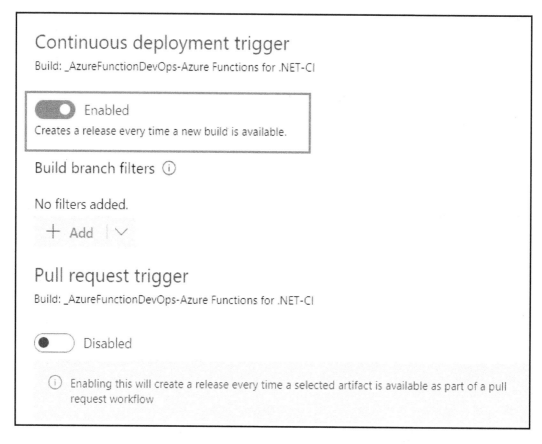

That's it! We have a CI/CD process in place for our Azure function.

With this process, and by using Azure DevOps, you can automatically build and release (deploy) an Azure function onto your cloud environment, all from a managed platform.

Summary

In this chapter, we learned how to monitor an Azure function, how to monitor incoming calls and logs, and how to use Application Insights for advanced analysis.

In all, we learned how to select the best service plan for the functions that we'll be deploying in the cloud, and then we learned how to implement CI/CD techniques to create a smart deployment process of our functions in the cloud.

Now, you have a clear overview of the options that are available for deploying and monitoring services on Azure and for selecting the best deployment model for your business case. You've also learned how you can activate a CI/CD process on your development pipeline so that you can build and deploy functions on Azure.

In the next chapter, we'll talk about how to integrate Dynamics 365 Business Central with the *Microsoft Power Platform* and, in particular, how to use *Flow* and *PowerApps* with Dynamics 365 Business Central to implement "zero-coding" business processes.

15
Business Central and Integration with the Power Platform

In the previous chapter, we saw how to use Azure Services combined with Dynamics 365 Business Central to implement modern serverless business processes and we had an extensive overview of how to use Azure Functions from AL.

In this chapter, we will introduce an important part of the Dynamics 365 family: *Microsoft Power Platform*. We'll cover the following topics:

- An introduction to Microsoft Power Platform
- Microsoft Flow and PowerApps overview
- Implementations of real-world scenarios by using Flow and PowerApps integrated with the Dynamics 365 Business Central ecosystem

By the end of this chapter, you will have a complete overview of Power Platform and be able to use Flow and PowerApps to implement custom solutions and workflows with Dynamics 365 Business Central in a low-coding way.

Technical requirements

To follow the examples described in this chapter, you'll need the following:

- An Office 365 subscription with access to Flow and PowerApps
- An active Dynamics 365 Business Central online tenant

Introducing the Power Platform

Power Platform combines the features of applications such as **Flow**, **PowerApps**, and **PowerBI** into a unified business application platform. The importance of this platform in the Microsoft ecosystem has been explained many times directly by Satya Nadella in his talks. In a modern business application's implementation, we need to seriously consider the Power Platform.

The platform embraces the *Analyze, Act, and Automate* paradigm. Each component of the Power Platform is built on top of the *Common Data Service for Apps* (a platform that allows users to quickly integrate programs, build new custom applications, and create automated workflows), and the platform brings data together into what is called the *Common Data Model*.

A schema of this platform is displayed in the following diagram:

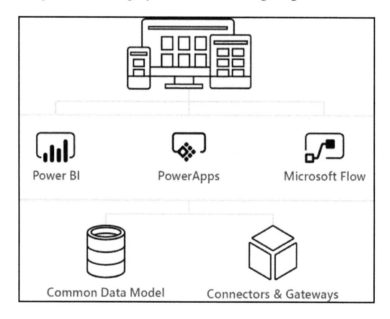

Flow and **PowerApps** are low-code development-based platforms made by Microsoft to provide powerful tools for what we call **power users** – users that usually don't have a technical background, but work and are totally involved with a business, so they know all the business rules, processes exceptions, and other business aspects that allow them to know what a system can do from an end user's point of view.

So, we have explained what Power Platform is and what its building blocks are. Since these tools are already available, why not use it in combination with Dynamics 365 Business Central to provide even more power for those power users to create apps, integrations, and business logic workflows, and build a fully integrated and managed platform for our businesses?

In the upcoming sections, we'll look at an overview of Flow and PowerApps, and we'll see some real-world solutions that involve Dynamics 365 Business Central in tandem with Power Platform.

Understanding Flow

Flow is a platform that was built with the purpose of providing a way to create automated workflows and integrating Microsoft and non-Microsoft technologies through connectors and triggers. These tools are available for the end user so that they can build business processes in a visual way. More information can be found at `https://us.flow.microsoft.com/en-us/`.

Flow has more than 180 different connectors that you can use through actions and triggers to build automated workflows. One of these connectors is the **Dynamics 365 Business Central connector**, and it's the standard connector for interacting with Dynamics 365 Business Central from Flow. The connector is available at `https://us.flow.microsoft.com/en-us/connectors/?filter=business+centralcategory=all`.

One of the biggest advantages of using Flow is that it gives us a visual way to build automated workflows that can make our data from our Dynamics environment interact with external platforms, create approval process, send notification actions, and other applications in an easy way.

As shown in the following screenshot, Microsoft also gives us a bunch of existing templates that will help us create our first Flow workflow quickly:

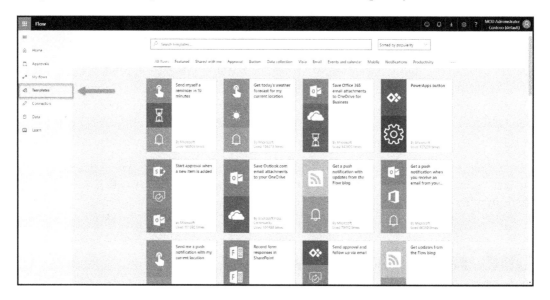

More information can be found at https://us.flow.microsoft.com/en-us/templates/.

Filtering the templates by business central, you can see all the available templates (you can also submit templates that you create for the technical community), as follows:

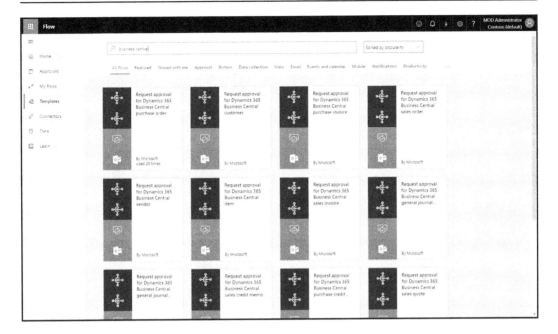

With these templates, you are able to play around with workflows that will integrate Dynamics 365 Business Central with other platforms, and you can start using a template that can be changed so that it suits your needs in an easy way.

These templates are always improved and developed by the community and by the Flow team.

> Start creating a workflow using a template to see how it works and then change it to fit your needs by adding other actions and integrations.

As you can see, with Flow, you have lots of pre-built tasks (workflows) that you can immediately use in your existing Dynamics 365 Business Central solutions without writing a single line of code. Just use the connector and start your workflow with a few mouse clicks.

In the next section, we'll look at an overview of PowerApps and see what it can offer with regard to implementing your solutions.

Understanding PowerApps

PowerApps is a platform that was built with the purpose of creating business applications that can be used on mobile phones, tablets, and web browsers, all using a very easy user interface. It also uses connectors to integrate those apps with Microsoft and non-Microsoft platforms.

The distribution, permission, licensing, and authentication for the use of those apps is based on Microsoft 365 licenses, so it is already totally integrated with your Microsoft 365 environment.

 More information about PowerApps and its licensing can be found at `https://powerapps.microsoft.com/`.

In the **PowerApps Studio** (`https://web.powerapps.com`), you can create apps easily:

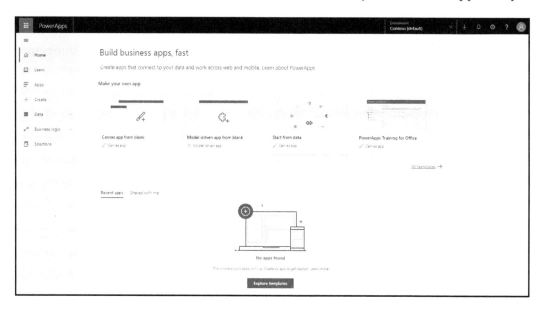

Since PowerApps also work with the same connector concept that's in Flow, we can also create apps that connect and interact with our data on Dynamics 365 Business Central environments, giving us a way to create business apps that can work on a browser and on a mobile device and that can also execute business logic inside Dynamics 365 Business Central.

In the next section, we'll learn how to use Flow and PowerApps with Dynamics 365 Business Central in real-world scenarios and implement a modern business solution.

Integration scenarios with Power Platform

Now that we have had an overview of **Flow** and **PowerApps** and we know that they allow us to build powerful integrated solutions with Dynamics 365 Business Central to provide more control, integration, and extension, let's discuss and learn how to combine these technologies to do more with our environment.

The following scenarios are just ideas to help you brainstorm and to show you some of the features that are available to you. However, the platforms are so flexible and adaptable to different use cases to the extent that we would need an entire book to cover all the bases, so remember to use these scenarios to extract some ideas for your daily needs.

Scenario 1 – creating a human resources recruiting/onboarding process

In this scenario, we will create a recruiting/onboarding process that will make it easy for a human resources department to send a form to a new employee so that they can fill it in. This data, after an approval process, will be automatically registered to Dynamics 365 Business Central.

Technologies Used: Microsoft Forms, Flow, Teams, and Dynamics 365 Business Central.

First of all, let's create our form on Microsoft Forms. The goal here is to give a human resources manager a way to generate an external form with a link that can be sent to a new employee, who can then add their data, avoiding the bureaucracy of having this form filled in manually in person.

To create this form, follow these steps:

1. Open **Forms** with your Office 365 Account at `http://forms.microsoft.com` and then click on **New Form**.
2. Add the name and description of your form.
3. Now, let's add some fields to our form, thinking about all the fields that we need/want on Dynamics 365 Business Central. To create a new field, you just need to click on the **+ Add New** button:

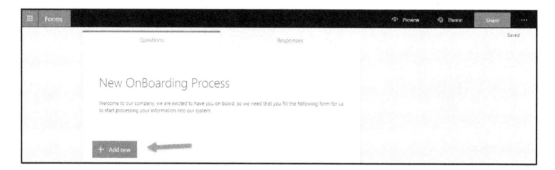

4. Then, select the type of field to create (here, I've selected **Choice**):

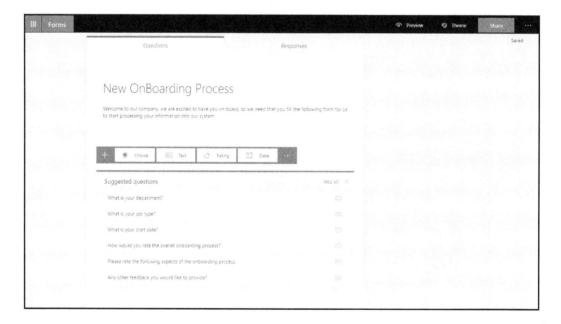

5. Then, select the label:

Let's create the following fields:

- **First Name** (text)
- **Last Name** (text)
- **E-mail** (text)
- **Address** (text)
- **Address City** (text)
- **Address State** (text)
- **Address Postal Code** (text)
- **Phone Number** (text)
- **Birth Date** (date)

6. The final form will be as follows:

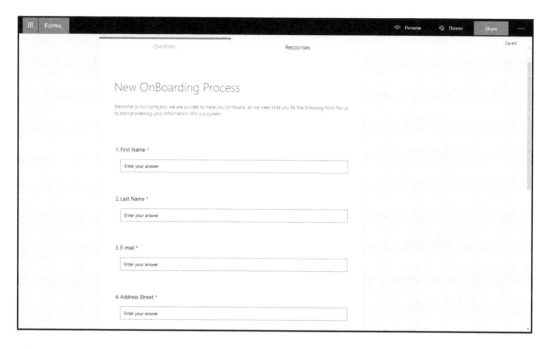

After creating our form on Forms, we can create our Flow workflow:

1. Open the Microsoft Flow site (`https://flow.microsoft.com`), log in with your Office 365 account, and go to **My Flows**.

2. Click on **+ New** | **Create from blank**:

3. Let's look for more triggers. Click on **Search hundreds of connectors and triggers**.

4. Search for `Microsoft Forms` and then select the **When a new response is submitted** trigger:

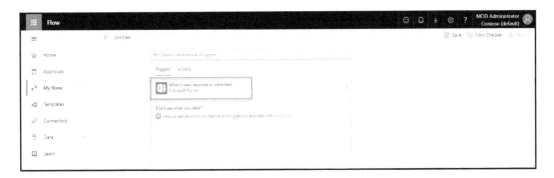

5. On the trigger action, pick your form from the **Form Id** field (**New Onboarding Process**):

6. Now, let's add a new step. Click on **+ New Step**:

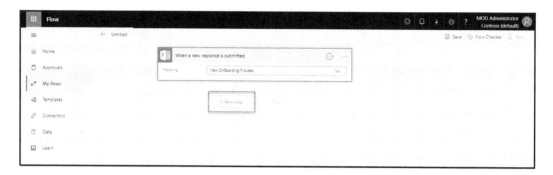

7. Select **Built-in** and then **Apply to each**:

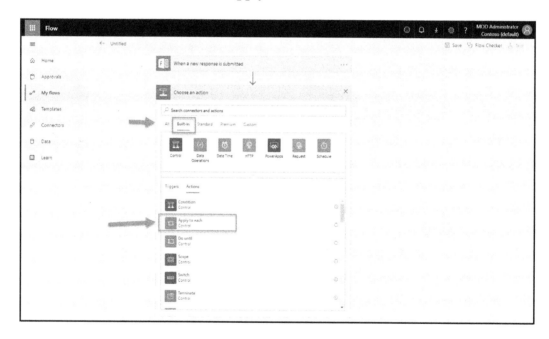

We will select the Form responses from the **When a new response is submitted** trigger as the output for this **Apply to each** action. Basically, for each response that's submitted (in this case, it will be always one; that's just the way that Flow handles the execution), we will do something on the workflow's execution:

8. Now, we can create an approval process to validate any response that's submitted before it goes to Dynamics 365 Business Central. Click on **Add an Action**:

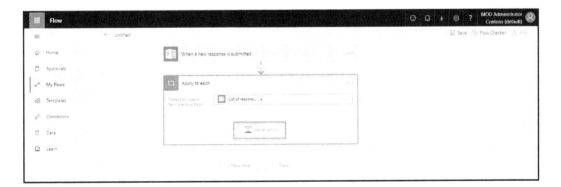

9. Search for `Microsoft Forms` and select **Get response details**:

10. Select the form that we've created in the **Form Id** field and add **List of response notifications Response Id** as the **Response Id**. This action will fill in all the fields on the form:

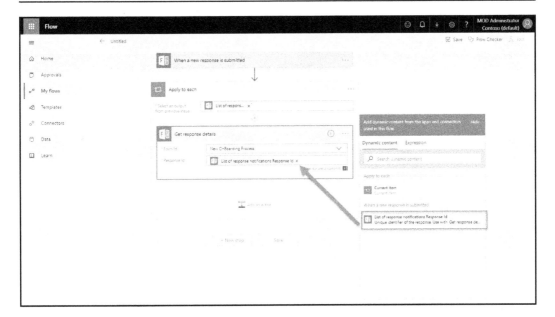

11. Now, add a new step by clicking on **Add an action**:

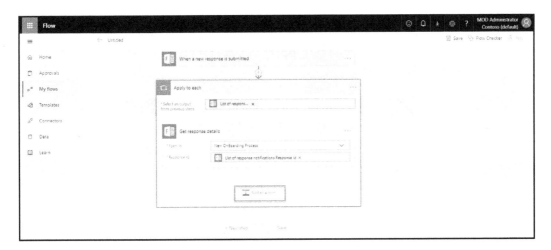

12. Search for `Approvals` and then **Start and Wait for approval**:

13. The **Approval Type** will be **Approve/Reject – First to respond** (you can change it to the other one if you want):

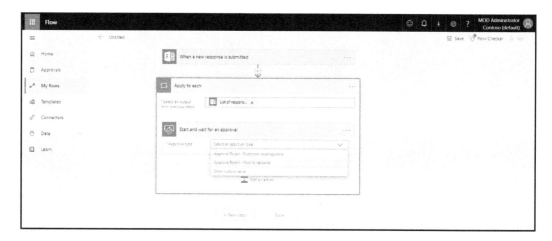

14. You can personalize the approval information that will be sent for the human resources person who's responsible for making a decision about approval:

In the **Assigned To** field, I've used a fixed person, but, if you want, you can create an integration with another application that will set the approver automatically.

15. With the approval configured, we need to handle when the approver completes the approval process. In this example, if it gets approved, we will create this entry on Dynamics 365 Business Central. If it gets rejected, we will send an email to the employee to fill the form in again. For this, add an action:

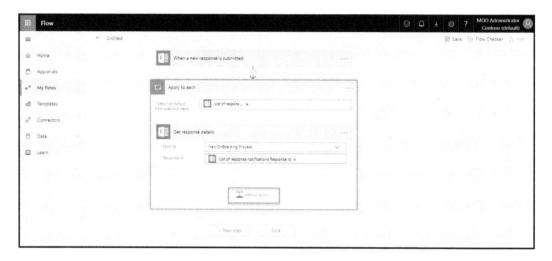

16. Then, select **Condition**:

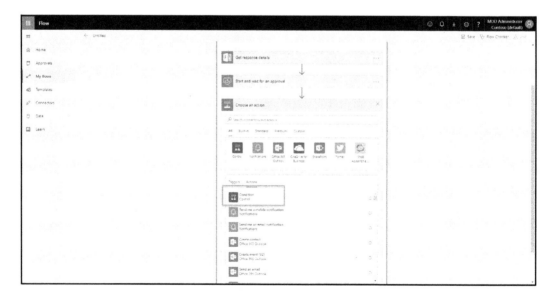

17. The condition must use the value from **Response** (this is a collection of the responses if the approval process handles multiple approvals):

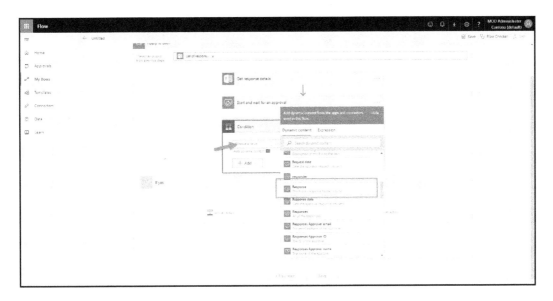

18. We need to check whether the value of this response is equal to **Approve**:

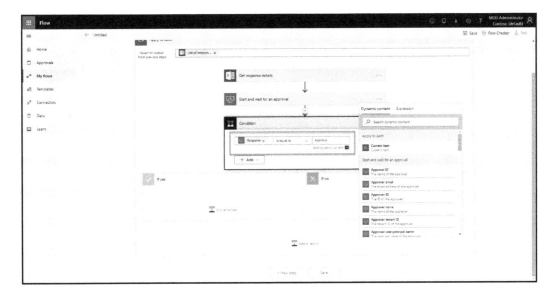

19. If the statement is true, we will create the entry on Dynamics 365 Business Central and post a message to our Teams channel for onboarding. In the **If yes** box, let's add an action:

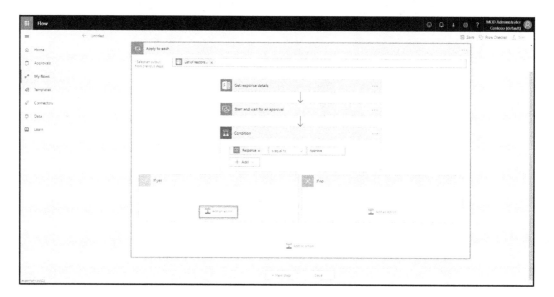

20. Search for `Dynamics 365 Business Central` and then select **Create item**:

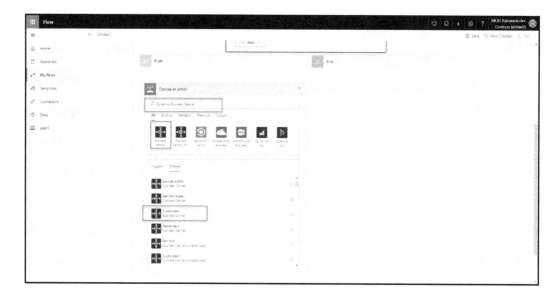

21. Select your company name. Under **Table name**, you can see all the tables that we can interact with using Flow. For this scenario, we will use the employees table:

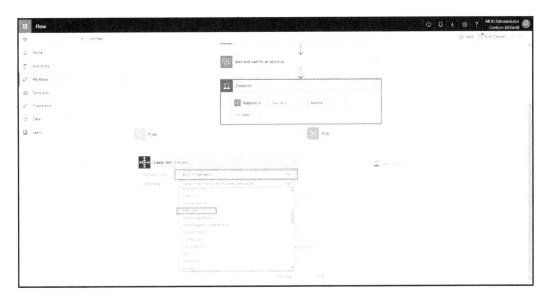

22. After selecting the employees table, we will be able to see all the available fields (all the fields that we can use to send information through **Flow**):

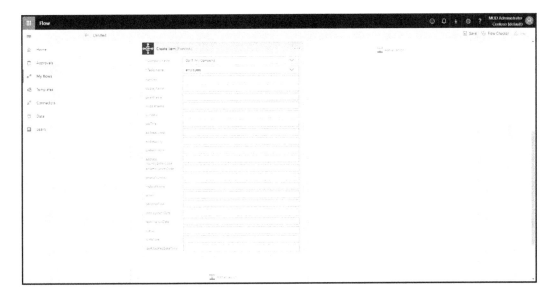

23. Let's start picking the data from the Forms response and add it to the right places on the Dynamics 365 Business Central action:

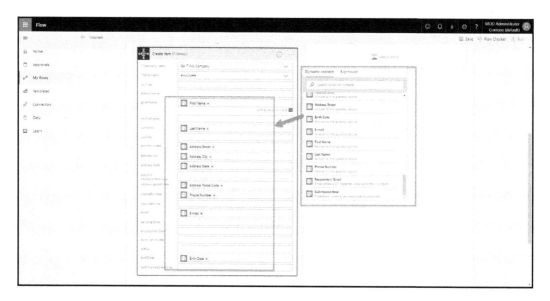

24. Now, we will create a post on a Teams channel to inform our human resources team that a new onboarding process has been filed and approved and that the entry has been created on Dynamics 365 Business Central. Go to **Add an Action**:

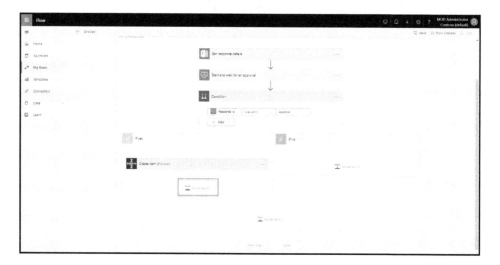

25. Search for `Microsoft Teams` and then click on **Post a message as the Flow bot to a channel**. This will automatically post into a Teams channel as a Flow bot user:

26. Select the team and the channel that you want to post to:

27. Under **Message**, you can add the text that you want to post to Teams:

28. Done! Now, let's add an action when the approval process is rejected. Under **If no**, click on **Add an Action**:

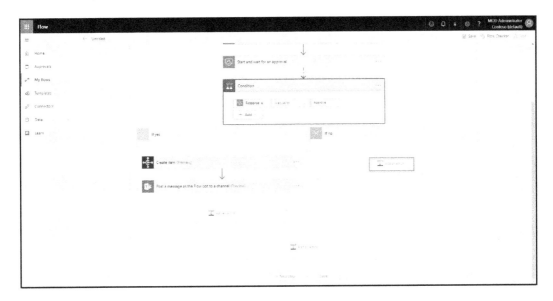

29. After this, search for `Office 365 Outlook` and then select **Send an email**:

In the **To** field, add the email that was on the form (remember that we are sending an email to the employee, asking them to fill in the form again):

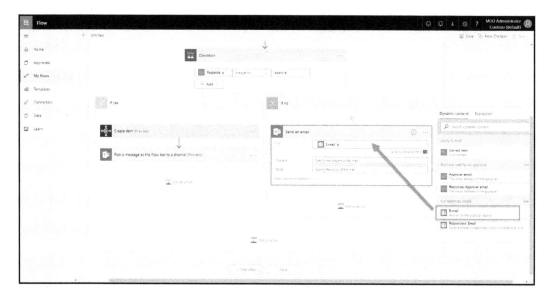

You can change the **Subject** and **Body** so that it contains the content that you want:

You can also change the configuration so that this email can handle HTML by setting the **Is HTML** option to **Yes**.

Now, we have the final flow, as shown in the following screenshot. To save it, give this flow a **Name** in the top bar and click on **Save**. This is shown as follows:

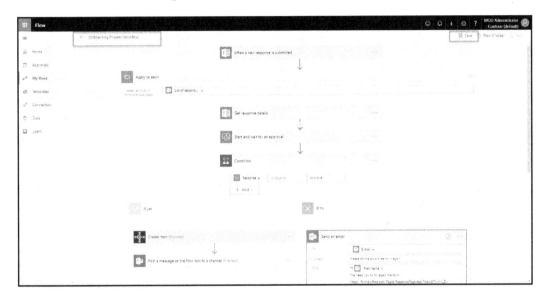

Now, let's try it out:

1. Open the Form that we've created in preview mode, fill it in, and click **Submit**:

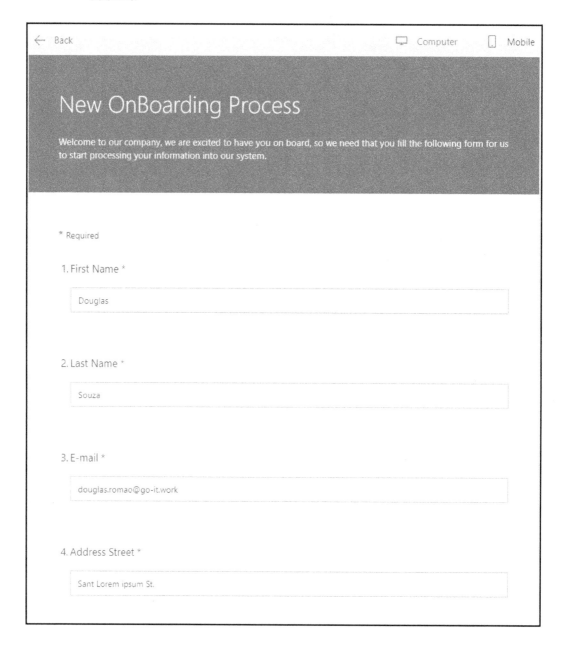

After submitting, this is the response you will obtain:

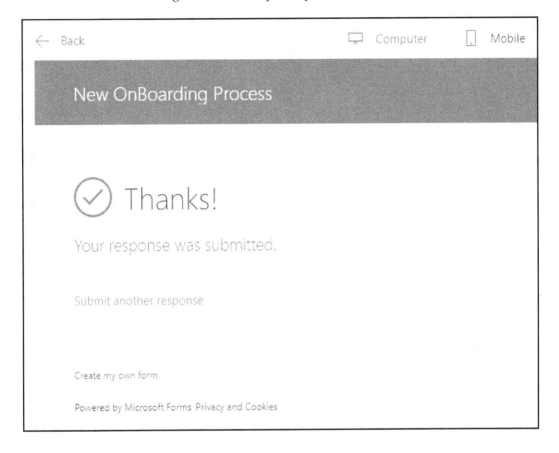

2. Access the human resources account (the one that you selected to be responsible for approving the form) to check that you've received an approval email:

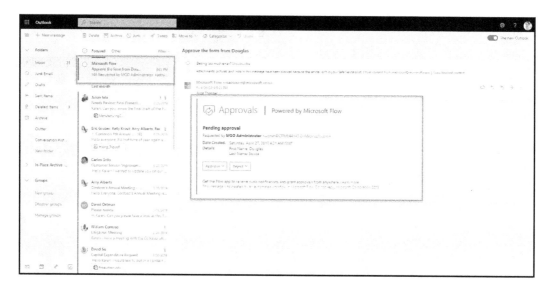

If you click on **Approve**, the workflow will continue creating the employee on Dynamics 365 Business Central with all the data from the form, and it will be posted on Teams:

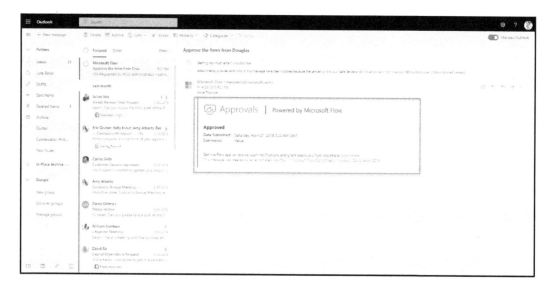

3. If you have access to your Dynamics 365 Business Central tenant, you will be able to see the **Employee** record that's been created:

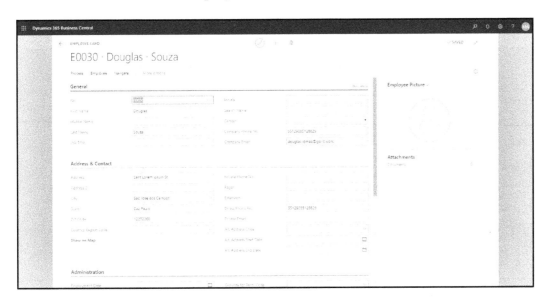

4. Then, if you access your Teams channel, you will be able to see that the approval notification has been posted, as follows:

5. If you click on **Reject**, an email will be sent to the employee, asking them to fill in the form again:

This is the email that was sent to the employee:

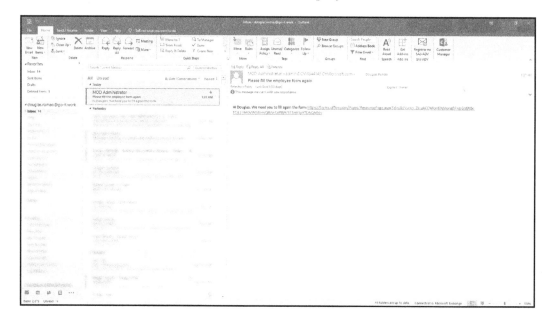

With that, we have a completely automated workflow for the onboarding process that can be connected with the recruiting process. It can register the new employee on the ERP, notify the IT manager, and so on.

The same approach for creating an item in a table on Dynamics 365 Business Central can also be used for sales order information, purchases, tax, and other data types that you have on Dynamics 365 Business Central.

In this section, you've seen how easy it is to create custom workflows by using Flow with Dynamics 365 Business Central. We've successfully completed this scenario without writing a single line of code.

In the next section, we'll learn how to implement an approval workflow for sales orders in the Dynamics 365 Business Central ERP using Flow.

Scenario 2 – creating a simple sales order approval workflow

In this scenario, we will create a simple sales order approval workflow in Dynamics 365 Business Central using the templates provided by Microsoft to handle an approval for our sales orders.

Technologies Used: Flow and Dynamics 365 Business Central.

To start creating a custom approval workflow, you can start directly from the ERP side, as follows:

1. On Dynamics 365 Business Central, go to the **Sales** menu and click on **Sales Orders**. Now, click on **New** and, on the **New Order** page, click on **Request Approval** and then click on **Create a Flow**:

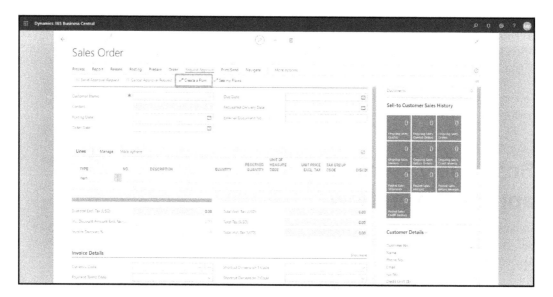

2. Flow templates will be presented to you, and you can select the templates that are the best fit for your process. Let's select the workflow called **Request Approval for Dynamics 365 Business Central sales order**:

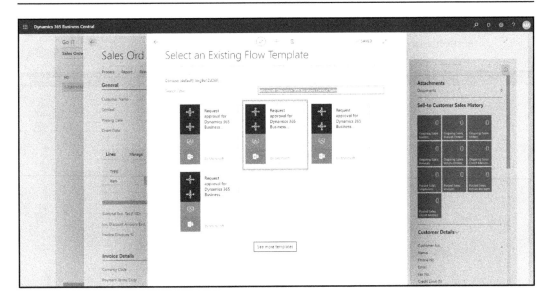

3. You can change the workflow so that it does exactly what your process needs, including the information related to the sales order, the approvers for the approval process, and the path that the workflow will take (depending on the replies):

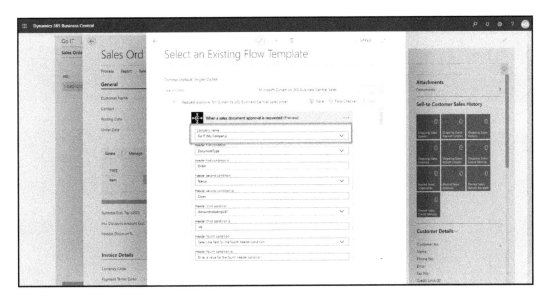

4. Here, we can select the details of the request (see the fields in the following screenshot):

5. Then, we can select the action (if approved) and save the workflow:

6. Now, go back to the Sales Order screen. Let's select an existing sales order, select **Request Approval**, and then click on **Send Approval Request** (Dynamics 365 Business Central will check if a workflow has already been configured and will use it when the user clicks on **Send Approval Request**):

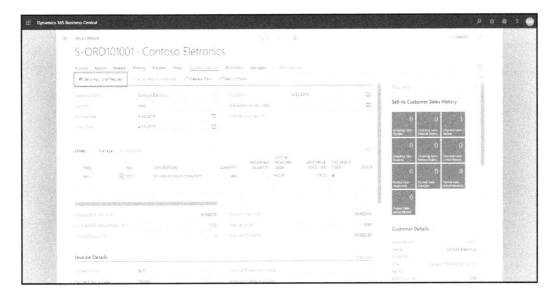

7. The workflow has started, and the approver should receive a notification to approve/reject that sales order:

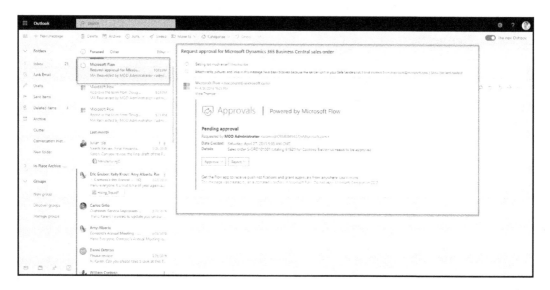

As a final result, we have created with few simple steps a workflow that permits to approve Dynamics 365 Business Central documents (like Sales Orders) directly via email. As mentioned previously, we can change the entire behavior of this approval process with a few clicks and make this workflow work in whatever way best suits our business needs.

This is a simple way of creating a workflow for a sales order that can be easily used for other types of data on Dynamics 365 Business Central.

Scenario 3 – creating a simple app to list all customers and sales quotes

In this scenario, we are going to create an app on PowerApps that will connect to our Dynamics 365 Business Central environment, list all customers, and, for the selected customer, list their sales quotes. This app can be used in a browser or a mobile device.

 Technologies Used: PowerApps and Dynamics 365 Business Central.

To start creating our application, perform the following steps:

1. Open **PowerApps Studio** with your Office 365 account at `http://web.powerapps.com`. There are different ways to build apps in PowerApps; we are going to use the **Canvas** app from a blank template so that we can build an app for a mobile phone layout from scratch. Click on **Canvas app from blank**:

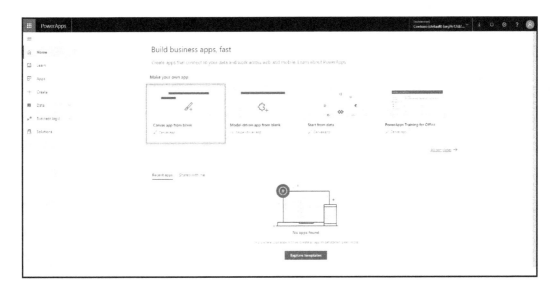

2. Come up with a name for your app, select the format that you want (in this example, we will use the **Phone** format), and click on **Create**:

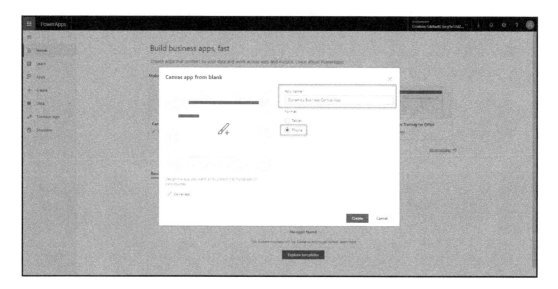

As soon as the application is created, you will be redirected to **PowerApps Studio**, where we will start to build the components for our app.

We need to connect our app to Dynamics 365 Business Central by adding a data source on PowerApps using an existing connector. The *connector* concept here is the same as it is in Flow. Microsoft uses the same concept in all of the Power Platform applications.

3. From the top navigation menu, select **View** and then click on **Data Sources**:

4. Now, add a data source. If you have already created a connection with Dynamic 365 Business Central (or other platforms) in any other Power Platform application, you can select the connection directly from the list that appears.

5. If you haven't created a connection with Dynamics 365 Business Central (or other platforms) in any other Power Platform application previously, click on **+ New connection**, search for `Business Central`, and select the **Business Central Connector**, as follows:

6. Now, click on **Create**. By creating the connection (or selecting an existing one) with Dynamics 365 Business Central, you need to select the dataset that you want to use:

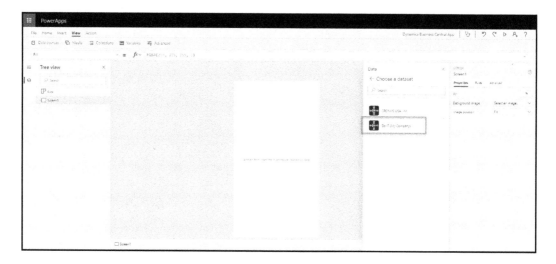

7. Now, we can select which table from Dynamics 365 Business Central we want to use in the app. In our example, we will select the **customers** table and the **salesQuotes** table, and then click on **Connect**:

The connection has been made. Now, we can start adding the controls to our app to consume those connections.

8. In the top navigation menu, go to the **Insert** tab and, in **Controls**, select the **Drop down** control:

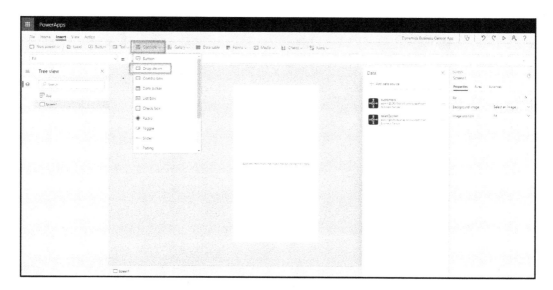

9. By default, the data source for this dropdown will be an example, but we can change this by going to the right panel, going to the **Items** property, and selecting the customers table from Dynamics 365 Business Central:

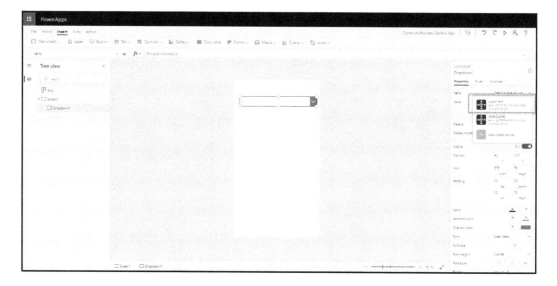

10. In the **Value** property, we can select which value from the customers table we want to display to the end user on the dropdown; let's select **displayName**:

11. At this point, we are going to add a new control to show all the sales orders to that selected customer so that, every time we change the customer on the dropdown, it loads all the sales orders for the selected customer. In the **Insert** tab, click on the **Gallery** and select **Vertical Gallery**:

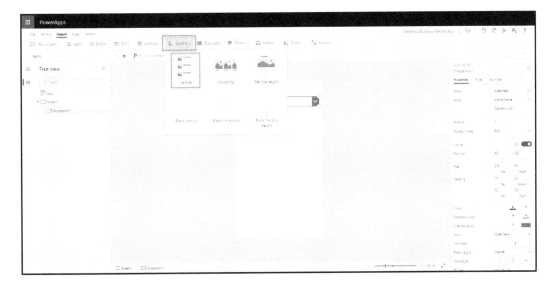

Once you have selected the gallery, you need to select the data source for this gallery. This is pretty much the same concept that we covered for the dropdown menu a few steps ago.

12. In the **Items** property, select the **salesOrder** data source:

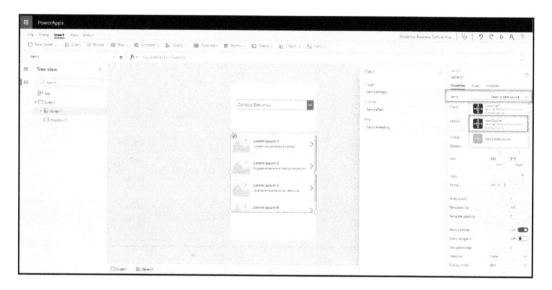

13. Now, we can select which layout our gallery will use and which fields will be displayed there. In the **Layout** property, select the template called **Title, subtitle, and body**:

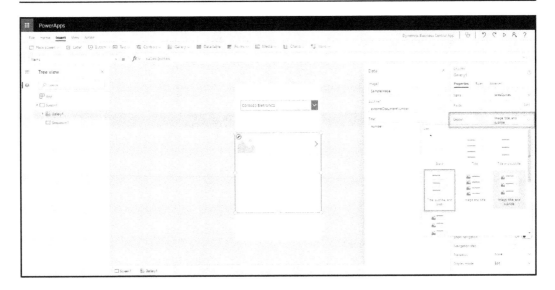

14. In the **Data** section, select **number** for the **Title2** property. In the **Subtitle2** property, select **status**:

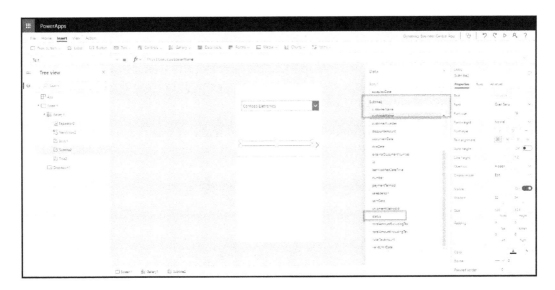

In the same way, in the **Body1** property, select **totalAmountExcludingTax**.

Now, we need to make sure that a filter will be applied to show only the sales orders for the customer that's selected from the dropdown. By default, when we select a data source, the data will be retrieved without any filters.

To do that, refer to the following screenshot:

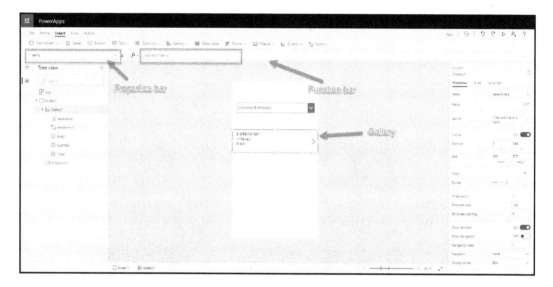

Click on the **gallery**. In the control properties pane, select the **Items** property. In the functions bar, we need to change the function to filter the data from the data source by using a command called `Filter()`.

You can find more detailed information about this at `https://docs.microsoft.com/en-us/powerapps/maker/canvas-apps/functions/function-filter-lookup`.

Let's use the following `Filter` formula:

```
Filter(salesOrders, Text(customerId) = Text(Dropdown1.Selected.id))
```

The filter formula is shown here:

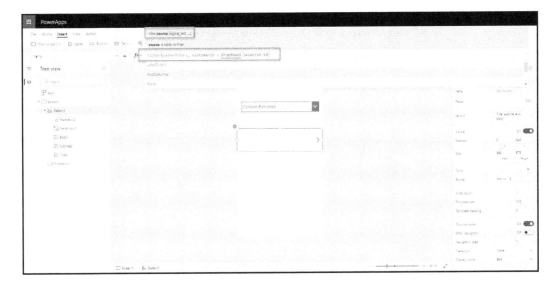

Let's take a look at what this formula is all about.

The `Filter` function requires the data source as its first parameter, which, in this case, will be the **salesOrder** table from Dynamics 365 Business Central.

The second parameter for the `Filter` function is the logical test. In this case, we will check whether the `customerId` from the `salesOrder` table is equal to the `id` from the item we selected in `Dropdown1`, which is the item we selected from the customers table on Dynamics 365 Business Central.

In this case, we are using the `Text()` function to convert both parameters into text so that they can be compared.

Now, every time the dropdown is changed for the user, the filter will be applied and the sales orders will be filtered by the value that's selected in the dropdown.

Now, we just need to save the app. To do this, follow these steps:

1. In the top navigation menu, go to **File**, type in the name of your app, change the icon (if you want), and click on **Save**:

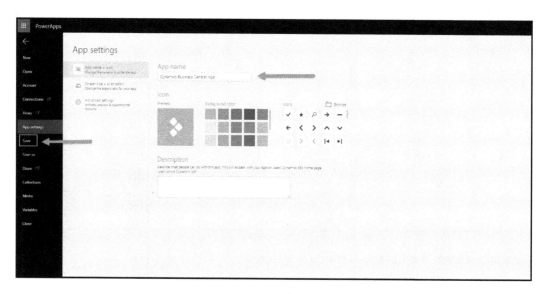

2. Now, go back to the app and run our application. To start the app, click on the play icon in the top-right corner:

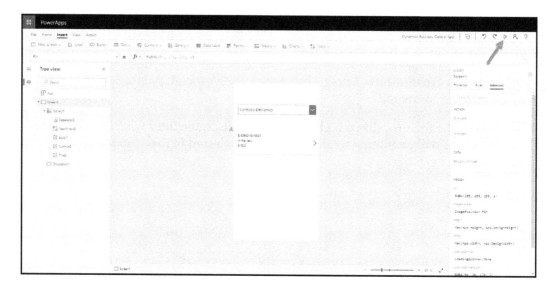

3. Select some other customers from the dropdown to check that the filter has been applied:

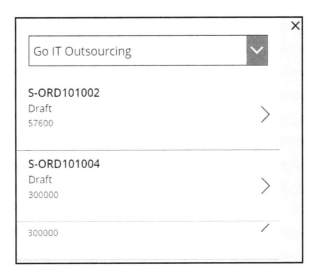

With that, we have an app that's integrated with Dynamics 365 Business Central that can be changed to fit the other processes and needs of our business.

With PowerApps, we have quickly implemented an application that is able to work on a browser and on a mobile device that can be shared with our entire organization and that can be secured by our IT administrator.

Summary

In this chapter, we had an overview of the Microsoft Power Platform, with a special focus on two important applications: Microsoft Flow and Microsoft PowerApps.

We saw the implementation of three real-world business scenarios by integrating Microsoft Dynamics 365 Business Central with *Flow* and *PowerApps*, and all of this was done with zero coding. This is the power of this business platform!

We also learned how to embrace the entire Dynamics 365 platform in order to extend our ERP solutions and create modern business applications.

In the next chapter, we'll look at another interesting integration scenario: how to use Dynamics 365 Business Central with machine learning.

Section 5: Moving Solutions to the New Extension Model

In this section, we will cover the integration of machine learning functionalities into a Dynamics 365 Business Central solution, the aspect of taking an existing ISV solution (written with old C/AL code) and moving it to the new extension model, the architectural aspects of this, and tips on how to start this process in the right way. We will also look at the famous set of third-party tools for AL developers that can be useful for developing Dynamics 365 Business Central applications.

This section comprises the following chapters:

- Chapter 16, *Integrating Machine Learning into Dynamics 365 Business Central*
- Chapter 17, *Moving Existing ISV Solutions to the New Extension Model*
- Chapter 18, *Useful and Proficient Tools for AL Developers*

16
Integrating Machine Learning into Dynamics 365 Business Central

In the previous chapter, we gave an overview of the Microsoft Power Platform, and we saw how to use Dynamics 365 Business Central with Flow and PowerApps to solve business tasks with zero coding.

In this chapter, we'll talk about a topic that has been emerging over the last few years: **Machine Learning** (**ML**) with Dynamics 365 Business Central. The year 2019 is the year of **Artificial Intelligence** (**AI**). You hear about AI everywhere. The world is telling us: *If you want to be on top, apply AI*. But what is AI? How does it differ from classical programming? What is going on behind the scenes?

The aim of this chapter is not for you to become a true data scientist or ML master, but to get a clear understanding of the basics of AI and some experience of how to embed AI into your Dynamics 365 Business Central projects.

In this chapter, we cover the following topics:

- What ML is and an overview of its main processes
- Dynamics 365 Business Central ML Framework overview
- Using ML in your Dynamics 365 Business Central applications
- Understanding the Prediction API

What are AI and ML?

AI consists of tasks that are characteristic of human intelligence, such as language and speech understanding, recognizing objects and sounds, and planning. The word *tasks* is used because, technically, you can complete these tasks with two different approaches: classical programming and ML.

At the beginning of 1990, some companies introduced **Optical Character Recognition (OCR)** software. They invested millions of dollars and hired hundreds of developers who wrote code to recognize handwritten text. This was classical programming with simple tools, such as `if-else`. The approach worked, but the result was quite poor. The accuracy was low and the number of mistakes was high.

Why did this approach fail? Because what is natural for a human brain is very difficult to be programmed.

So, how we can solve this task in another way? The answer is ML!

> *"Machine learning is the process by which a machine (computer) is capable of showing behavior that has not been explicitly programmed into it"*
>
> *– Arthur Samuel, 1959*

Or, in other words: computers learn from data to perform predictive analytics.

As you can see, instead of writing code, to create ML functions, we need something else: data.

So, let's cover this process in detail in the following sections.

An overview of the ML process

According to its definition, ML is an application of AI that provides systems with the ability to learn and improve on their own, from experience, and not by being explicitly programmed.

Here is the classic ML process. It's when you try to predict an answer based on answers from previous experience:

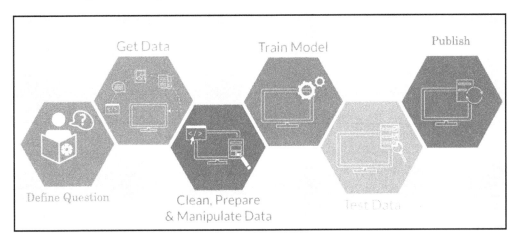

Let's go through the preceding diagram in detail:

1. **Define a question**: ML is not a magic box. To get an answer, you should know the question, and you should build a model that will answer that exact question.

   Remember: the exact question is the key to the right answer!

2. **Find data**: You should find data that will answer your question. The data, which, in (ML) terminology, is usually called a *dataset*, should be relevant, complete, exact, and sufficient. In this chapter, we will use Dynamics 365 Business Central as business-related data storage.

3. **Prepare your data**: To make the ML training process possible, you should join all of your tables in one table (dataset). You should define which field you want to predict (the label) and which fields influence the predictions (the features).

4. **Train the ML model**: During this step, you create ML models by applying a training dataset to the ML algorithm.

5. **Test your trained ML model**: To understand the quality of predictions and to calculate ML model accuracy, you need also a *test dataset*. The test dataset should be different from the training dataset but have the same structure.

For example, here is our training dataset:

Date	Sales Amount
01.11.17	100
18.11.17	150
08.12.17	250
17.12.17	260

This is what we used to create the `F(day)` = `"sales amount"` ML model, and here is our test dataset:

Date	Sales Amount
05.11.17	140
15.12.17	240

We take features from the test dataset and apply them to our trained ML model to predict labels:

Date	Sales Amount	Predicted Sales Amount
05.11.17	140	137
15.12.17	240	245

Then, we compare **Sales Amount** with **Predicted Sales Amount** and get the model's accuracy:

Date	Sales Amount	Predicted Sales Amount	Difference, %
05.11.17	140	137	2.1%
15.12.17	240	245	2.1%

So, the accuracy of our model is 97.9%.

6. **Publish the ML model as a web service**: When you are satisfied with the model's accuracy, you can publish your model as a web service and consume it from everywhere to predict the future from new features. If I call the published model for future dates, the results show predictions for future dates, as shown in the following table:

Date	Predicted Sales Amount
06.11.18	115
16.12.18	255

With a well-trained ML model, you can easily get predictions using your data.

Next, let's see how the Business Central ML Framework works.

Understanding the Business Central ML Framework

Building your own (custom) ML model from scratch could be complicated. It usually requires experience in Python, R, or services such as Azure ML Studio. If you don't want to invest in that but still want to use the power of AI with your data, you can use **Dynamics 365 Business Central ML Framework**.

Technically, it can be divided into four different frameworks:

- The Time Series API
- The ML Prediction API
- The custom Azure ML API
- The custom Vision API

Each framework is intended for its own task and uses different algorithms:

- For example, with the **Time Series API**, you can predict numbers (such as sales and quantities) with the power of regression algorithms just by knowing dates and numbers from the past.
- With the **ML Prediction API**, you can predict classes, such as yes/no or colors.
- The **Custom Azure ML API** allows you to connect to your custom model, built in **Azure ML Studio**.
- The **Custom Vision API** allows you to connect to your custom model, built in **Custom Vision**.

In the next sections, we will focus on the **Time Series** and **ML Prediction APIs**, as they are the simplest and don't require ML experience, but they're still powerful.

The Time Series API

In this example, let's assume that you are the owner of a restaurant and you want to predict how many items from the menu your customers will order in the next 7 days.

You have the following sales history:

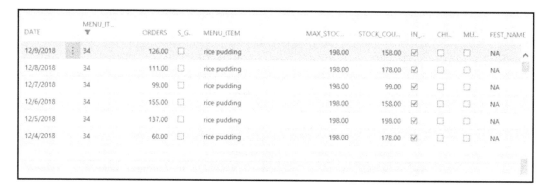

DATE	MENU_IT..	ORDERS	S_G.	MENU_ITEM	MAX_STOC..	STOCK_COU..	IN_..	CHI.	MLE.	FEST_NAME
12/9/2018	34	126.00	☐	rice pudding	198.00	158.00	☑	☐	☐	NA
12/8/2018	34	111.00	☐	rice pudding	198.00	178.00	☑	☐	☐	NA
12/7/2018	34	99.00	☐	rice pudding	198.00	99.00	☑	☐	☐	NA
12/6/2018	34	155.00	☐	rice pudding	198.00	158.00	☑	☐	☐	NA
12/5/2018	34	137.00	☐	rice pudding	198.00	198.00	☑	☐	☐	NA
12/4/2018	34	60.00	☐	rice pudding	198.00	178.00	☑	☐	☐	NA

In this dataset, you have 38,325 rows and 11 columns. The sales history entries exist from January 10, 2015 to December 9, 2018. The dataset can be found at `https://dkatsonpublicdatasource.blob.core.windows.net/machinelearning/AML-restaurant-sales-by-menu-item.csv`.

You can call the **Time Series API** using AL Language code to get predictions about **orders**. Then, we can check the quality of the predictions programmatically before displaying them to the end user. Let's see how to do this.

Step 1 – Downloading the dataset to Dynamics 365 Business Central

Perform the following steps to download the dataset into Business Central:

1. Create a new AL project in Visual Studio Code and clone this GitHub repository: `https://github.com/dkatson/BC-ML-Framework`. You will get a new `RestSalesEntry` table (and a page) where you can save this dataset, and a new codeunit, `RefreshRestSales`, that will upload this dataset from an external source:

```
codeunit 50100 "AIR RefreshRestSales"
{
    procedure Refresh();
    var
        restsales: Record "AIR RestSalesEntry";
        HttpClient: HttpClient;
        ResponseMessage: HttpResponseMessage;
        JsonToken: JsonToken;
        JsonValue: JsonValue;
        JsonObject: JsonObject;
        JsonArray: JsonArray;
        JsonText: text;
        i: Integer;
    begin
        restsales.DeleteAll;

        // Simple web service call
        HttpClient.DefaultRequestHeaders.Add('User-Agent', 'Dynamics 365');
        if not HttpClient.Get('https://dkatsonpublicdatasource.blob.core.windows.net/machinelearning/AML-restaurant
                              ResponseMessage)
        then
            Error('The call to the web service failed.');
```

2. When you publish this app, you'll see this page:

3. Click on the **Refresh restsales** button, and you will see this dataset inside Dynamics 365 Business Central:

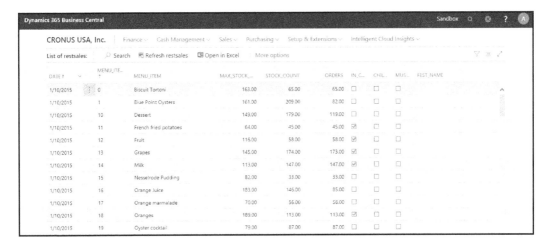

Now, you have data in place, but to make predictions, you need to have an ML model published as a web service, where you will send data to get predictions back. So, for this, we move to the second step.

Step 2 – Publishing a model as a web service from a public template

With a few clicks, you can create a model from a public template and publish an endpoint that serves only your needs. Enter the following URL in your favorite browser:

```
https://gallery.cortanaintelligence.com/Experiment/Forecasting-Model-for-
Microsoft-Dynamics-365-for-Financials-1
```

This is a publicly available model prepared by the Microsoft ERP team and aimed at time series predictions:

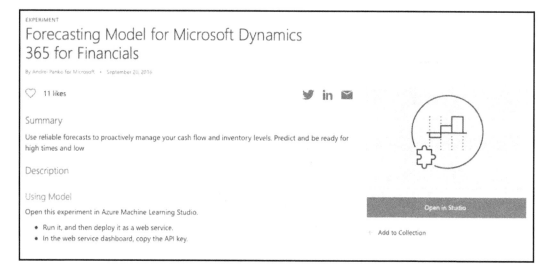

Now, follow these steps:

1. Click on the **Open in Studio** button.
2. Choose **Free Workspace** or **Standard Workspace**.
3. Sign in to your Microsoft account.
4. Click the **OK** button to copy the experiment from the gallery.
5. Keep the default values in the **Region** and **Workspace** fields, unless you are an experienced user of Azure ML.
6. Click on the **Run** button at the bottom of the experiment canvas.
7. Click on the **Deploy Web Service | Deploy Web Service (Classic)** button at the bottom of the experiment canvas.

The system deploys the Azure ML experiment as web services and provides a RESTful API that can be consumed by a wide range of devices and platforms, including Dynamics 365 Business Central:

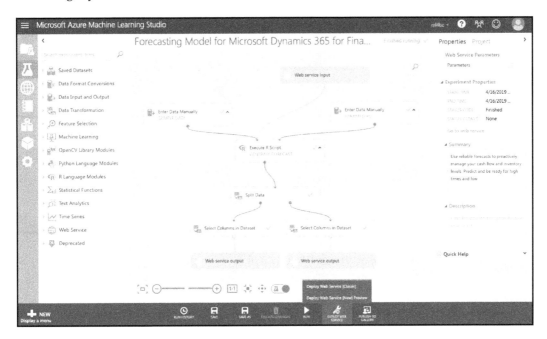

When the deployment is finished, the web services dashboard opens.

Here, you can see the API key and two available APIs: **Request/Response** and **Batch Execution**. The current version of the Time Series API that is shipped with Dynamics 365 Business Central supports the Request/Response API. At the bottom of the API help page, you can find input and output definitions and code samples. However, the request URI is the only thing you need for this example.

Now, follow these steps:

1. Copy and paste the API key in a text file to save it although you can also access it later.
2. Click on the **Request/Response** link to open the API help page:

3. After that, copy and paste the request URI in a text file to save it although you can also access it later:

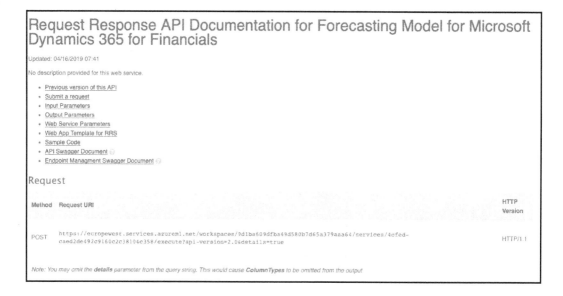

That's it. This ML model, which can predict any figure, including *orders* (from our example) is now published, and you can call it from the Dynamics 365 Business Central Time Series API.

Step 3 – Sending your data from Business Central to the ML endpoint to get predictions

The next step is to send the data to the endpoint to receive predictions. Let's see how that happens:

1. Open your AL project in Visual Studio Code, cloned from `https://github.com/dkatson/BC-ML-Framework`, and switch to the `Time-Series-API` branch. Here, press *Ctrl + Shift + P* and type `checkout`:

2. Now, select a branch:

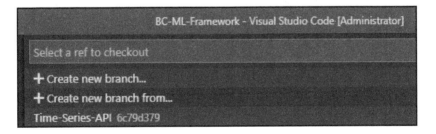

This is the upgraded version of the restaurant example extension.

The differences between this and the previous one are as follows:

- Demonstration data (demo items and sales history) is loaded automatically when you install the app.
- A new action appears in the Item Card – `Update Rest. Forecast`.

Let's look at how it works.

There is a new codeunit called `Calculate Rest. Forecast` with the main function, `CalculateRestForecast`, and two additional functions, `getMLUri` and `getMLKey`. Insert your URI and a key (copied from *step 2*) into these functions:

```
Cod50101.AIRCalculateRestForecast.al ×

     1 reference | You, 3 days ago | 1 author (You)
  1  codeunit 50101 "AIR Calculate Rest. Forecast"
  2  {
  3
         1 reference
  4      procedure CalculateRestForecast(ItemNo: Code[20])
  5      var ···
 12      begin···
 42      end;
 43
 44      local procedure getMLUri(): Text       You, 3 days ago • Time Series Forecast
 45      begin
 46          exit('https://europewest.services.azureml.net/workspaces/9d1ba609dfba49d580b7d65a379aaa64/services/4cfedcaed
 47      end;
 48
                        local procedure getMLKey(): Text
 49      local procedure getMLKey(): Text
 50      begin
 51          exit('eFp5IY7xyMfA99ta1Q3Eqyb/UgigT8U+lZTJfqJcmO2zAvEZLtvG2IylY+Atp1/Fr67pnIwXhFOlafafo6hmzA==')
 52      end;
 53
 54  }
```

Let's investigate the `CalculateRestForecast` function's variables:

```
≡ Cod50101.AIRCalculateRestForecast.al ✕

      1 reference | You, 3 days ago | 1 author (You)
  1   codeunit 50101 "AIR Calculate Rest. Forecast"
  2   {
  3
        1 reference
  4       procedure CalculateRestForecast(ItemNo: Code[20])
  5       var
  6           TimeSeriesMgt: Codeunit "Time Series Management";
  7           RestSalesEntry: Record "AIR RestSalesEntry";
  8           Date: Record Date;
  9           TempTimeSeriesForecast: Record "Time Series Forecast" temporary;
 10           TempTimeSeriesBuffer: Record "Time Series Buffer" temporary;
 11           TimeSeriesModel: Option ARIMA,ETS,STL,"ETS+ARIMA","ETS+STL",ALL;
 12 ⊞     begin ⋯
 42       end;
 43
```

From the preceding screenshot, we understand the following:

- `TimeSeriesMgt` is a time series library, which prepares the data, submits it to the Azure ML, and gets the prediction.
- `RestSalesEntry` is our history dataset, which we will use to prepare the data, and which we will send to the Azure ML web service to get the predictions.
- `TempTimeSeriesForecast` is prepared data that we will send to the Azure ML web service to get the predictions.
- `TimeSeriesModel` is the name (or combination) of regression algorithm(s) that will be applied to the prepared data inside of Azure ML web service to get predictions.
- `TempTimeSeriesBuffer` is our prediction that was received from the Azure ML web service.

Let's investigate the `CalculateRestForecast` function's business logic. The whole task can be done with four functions from the `Time Series Management` variable. Here, `Initialize` is used to set up the connection:

```
Cod50101.AIRCalculateRestForecast.al ×

      1 reference | You, 3 days ago | 1 author (You)
1     codeunit 50101 "AIR Calculate Rest. Forecast"
2     {
3
         1 reference
4         procedure CalculateRestForecast(ItemNo: Code[20])
5  ⊞      var ⋯
12        begin
13
14            //Setup Connection
15            TimeSeriesMgt.Initialize(getMLUri(), getMLKey(), 30, false);
16
```

Now, prepare the historical data that you will use for predictions. In our case, we will predict `orders` by items, which means that one call to the ML web service will return `orders` predictions for one item. So, it makes sense to filter the sales history dataset by one item per call:

```
Cod50101.AIRCalculateRestForecast.al ×

      1 reference | You, 3 days ago | 1 author (You)
1     codeunit 50101 "AIR Calculate Rest. Forecast"
2     {
3
         1 reference
4         procedure CalculateRestForecast(ItemNo: Code[20])
5  ⊞      var ⋯
12        begin
13
14            //Setup Connection
15            TimeSeriesMgt.Initialize(getMLUri(), getMLKey(), 30, false);
16
17            //Get Historical Data
18            RestSalesEntry.SetRange(menu_item_id, ItemNo);
19
```

`PrepareData` transforms any table data into a dataset that is ready for submission. Specify the source table and the field to be used for grouping. Remember that the Time Series API requires the date as the second grouping of fields. Choose a label —the field that you want to predict. It should contain numerical values—decimals or integers.

In our case, we will specify the `date` field from `RestSalesEntry` as a date, `menu_item_id` as a group field, and `orders` as a predictive field.

Also, we specify that `Period type` is equal to `day` (because we have historical transactions for each day), `start day` for the predictions will be the current `work date`, and the number of historical entries that will be used to calculate an `orders` prediction will be all of the entries we have:

```
≡ Cod50101.AIRCalculateRestForecast.al  ×

    1 reference
      procedure CalculateRestForecast(ItemNo: Code[20])
 5 ⊞   var...
12        begin
13
14            //Setup Connection
15            TimeSeriesMgt.Initialize(getMLUri(), getMLKey(), 30, false);
16
17            //Get Historical Data
18  RestSalesEntry procedure PrepareData(RecordVariant: Variant, GroupIDFieldNo: Integer, DateFieldNo: Integer
19                         , ValueFieldNo: Integer, PeriodType: Option, ForecastingStartDate: Date, ObservationPeriod
20            //Prepare data s: Integer)
21            TimeSeriesMgt.PrepareData(RestSalesEntry,
22                             RestSalesEntry.FieldNo(menu_item_id),
23                             RestSalesEntry.FieldNo(date),
24                             RestSalesEntry.FieldNo(orders),
25                             Date."Period Type"::Date,
26                             WorkDate(),  //from which date we want to forecast
27                             RestSalesEntry.Count);  //number of history periods
28
```

The number of historical periods tells the system how many periods it should take from the past, starting from the forecast date. This means that if you have holes in your historic dataset, then it will also include them in the calculation.

In our case, our historical data finishes at 2018-12-09. And we want to forecast starting from 2019-01-05. We have a hole of about 6 months. That means that the `PrepareData` function will fill that hole with zero entries and, as a result, will exclude 6 months of historical data, starting from the beginning (2015-01-10):

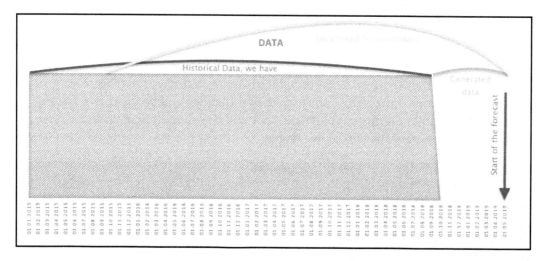

You can avoid that by playing with the `ObservationPeriod` parameter.

Once the data is prepared, you can read it and modify it before sending it to Azure Machine Learning Service. For example, here, we had a missing period in our `RestSalesEntry` dataset. During the `PrepareData` stage, there are system-generated zero (0) entries. If we send this dataset as is, Machine Learning Service will think that we had no sales for that period, and that will dramatically influence sales predictions for the future. To avoid that, we need to exclude zero entries from the prepared dataset:

```al
≡ Cod50101.AIRCalculateRestForecast.al ✕

              1 reference
      4       procedure CalculateRestForecast(ItemNo: Code[20])
      5  ⊞    var ···
     12       begin
     13
     14           //Setup Connection
     15           TimeSeriesMgt.Initialize(getMLUri(), getMLKey(), 30, false);
     16
     17           //Get Historical Data
     18           RestSalesEntry.SetRange(menu_item_id, ItemNo);
     19
     20           //Prepare data for the forecast
     21           TimeSeriesMgt.PrepareData(RestSalesEntry,
     22                               RestSalesEntry.FieldNo(menu_item_id),
     23                               RestSalesEntry.FieldNo(date),
     24                               RestSalesEntry.FieldNo(orders),
     25                               Date."Period Type"::Date,
     26                               WorkDate(),  //from which date we want to forecast
     27                               RestSalesEntry.Count);  //number of history periods
     28
     29           //Get Prepared data and delete empty lines
     30           TimeSeriesMgt.GetPreparedData(TempTimeSeriesBuffer);
     31           TempTimeSeriesBuffer.SetRange(Value, 0);
     32           TempTimeSeriesBuffer.DeleteAll();
```

The Forecast function sends the final prepared dataset to the Azure ML web service, which calculates the forecast according to specified parameters and returns the forecast result. Let's investigate the input parameters:

- ForecastingPeriods: This is the number of days/months/years for the future forecast that you want to get—a specific period type equal to what you specified in the PrepareData function.
- ConfidenceLevel: This is the minimum probability of the forecast result. If you specify 0, it will use 80%, or you can specify the exact percentage. You can try different values and see how it will change. We don't recommend using a value higher than 95.
- TimeSeriesModel: This is a statistical algorithm that is used by the Azure ML web service to create forecasts based on the prepared historical dataset you send. It could be ARIMA, ETS, or STL. It also could be a combination of ETS + ARIMA, ETS + STL, or all three.

In our case, we will calculate an `orders` forecast for the next 7 days with a minimum probability of 80%, and we will apply all of the statistical algorithms and calculate the average result:

```
≡ Cod50101.AIRCalculateRestForecast.al  ✕
   4        procedure CalculateRestForecast(ItemNo: Code[20])
   5 ⊞      var …
  12        begin
  13
  14            //Setup Connection
  15            TimeSeriesMgt.Initialize(getMLUri(), getMLKey(), 30, false);
  16
  17            //Get Historical Data
  18            RestSalesEntry.SetRange(menu_item_id, ItemNo);
  19
  20            //Prepare data for the forecast
  21            TimeSeriesMgt.PrepareData(RestSalesEntry,
  22                                      RestSalesEntry.FieldNo(menu_item_id),
  23                                      RestSalesEntry.FieldNo(date),
  24                                      RestSalesEntry.FieldNo(orders),
  25                                      Date."Period Type"::Date,
  26                                      WorkDate(),   //from which date we want to forecast
  27                                      RestSalesEntry.Count);  //number of history periods
  28
  29            //Get Prepared data and delete empty lines
  30            TimeSeriesMgt.GetPreparedData(TempTimeSeriesBuffer);
  31            TempTimeSeriesBuffer.SetRange(Value, 0);
  32            TempTimeSeriesBuffer.DeleteAll();
  33
  34            //Calculate Forecast
  35            TimeSeriesMgt.Forecast(7, 0, TimeSeriesModel::ALL);        You, 5 days ago • time
  36
```

`GetForecast` populates the `TempTimeSeriesForecast` table with the forecast results, which you can then use anywhere:

```
≡ Cod50101.AIRCalculateRestForecast.al  ✕
 4          procedure CalculateRestForecast(ItemNo: Code[20])
 5  ⊞       var ···
12          begin
13
14              //Setup Connection
15              TimeSeriesMgt.Initialize(getMLUri(), getMLKey(), 30, false);
16
17              //Get Historical Data
18              RestSalesEntry.SetRange(menu_item_id, ItemNo);
19
20              //Prepare data for the forecast
21              TimeSeriesMgt.PrepareData(RestSalesEntry,
22                                        RestSalesEntry.FieldNo(menu_item_id),
23                                        RestSalesEntry.FieldNo(date),
24                                        RestSalesEntry.FieldNo(orders),
25                                        Date."Period Type"::Date,
26                                        WorkDate(),   //from which date we want to forecast
27                                        RestSalesEntry.Count);  //number of history periods
28
29              //Get Prepared data and delete empty lines
30              TimeSeriesMgt.GetPreparedData(TempTimeSeriesBuffer);
31              TempTimeSeriesBuffer.SetRange(Value, 0);
32              TempTimeSeriesBuffer.DeleteAll();
33
34              //Calculate Forecast
35              TimeSeriesMgt.Forecast(7, 0, TimeSeriesModel::ALL);
36
37              //Get Forecast
38              TimeSeriesMgt.GetForecast(TempTimeSeriesForecast);
```

The simplest way to investigate the results is to create a list page with the
`TempTimeSeriesForecast` table:

```
    //Get Forecast
    TimeSeriesMgt.GetForecast(TempTimeSeriesForecast);

    //Show forecast
    Page.Run(Page::"AIR RestForecast", TempTimeSeriesForecast);          You, 5
```

Let's publish this app and investigate the results. Go to the rice pudding item with the **No. 2** field as **34** and click on **Actions | Item | Restaurant | Update Rest. Forecast**:

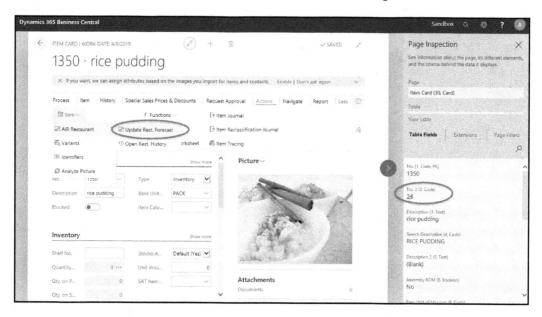

The result will be stored in a temporary table and shown on the screen:

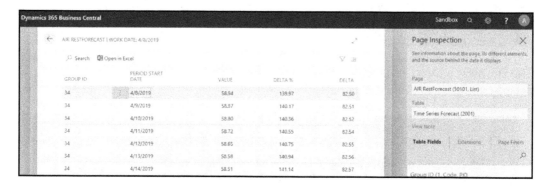

The delta is around 140%, which is quite big. The reason is that we calculated the forecast from April 2019, but our last entry in the past is from September 2018, as shown here:

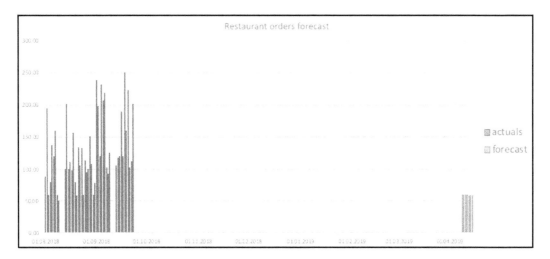

If we change **Work date** to September 24, 2018 (the day just after the last actual prediction we have) and run the forecast, we will see that the delta decreases to 65%:

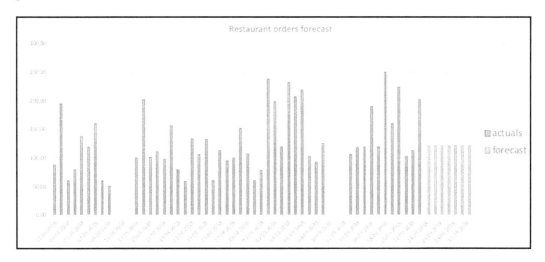

But still, the delta percentage is quite big. Why? That's because of the lack of features used in the forecast.

Time series forecasts use only two features, `item no.` and `date`. But usually, it's required to use more features that influence a forecast.

After understanding how the Time Series API framework works, let's explore its Prediction API.

Understanding the ML Prediction API

In the previous section, we trained an ML model based on the Time Series API. As there is a limit of only two features, the resulting model had poor accuracy. With the **ML Prediction API**, you can set as many features as you want. This approach gives you more flexibility and opportunities to experiment, allowing you to improve model quality by changing features and generating new features.

Also, the ML Prediction API allows you to train a custom ML model directly from AL.

If you are building an industry solution, you can add the `train-ml-model` function directly to your Dynamics 365 Business Central app.

The API is available in codeunit 2003, ML Prediction Management. Let's look at how it works.

In Visual Studio Code, open the project you cloned from `https://github.com/dkatson/BC-ML-Framework` and switch to the `Train-ML-Model-From-AL-API` branch. This is the upgraded version of the previously seen restaurant example extension.

The differences between this and the previous one are as follows:

- We don't use the Time Series API.
- We train an ML model (with eight features) to get the **orders** forecasted directly from AL.

Step 1 – Publishing a general prediction model as a web service from a public template

As a prerequisite for the training from the Business Central process, you still need to publish your general prediction ML web service into your Azure subscription.

Visit `https://gallery.azure.ai/Experiment/Prediction-Experiment-for-Dynamics-365-Business-Central` in your favorite browser.

This is a publicly available model prepared by the Microsoft ERP team and was designed especially for ML prediction management use:

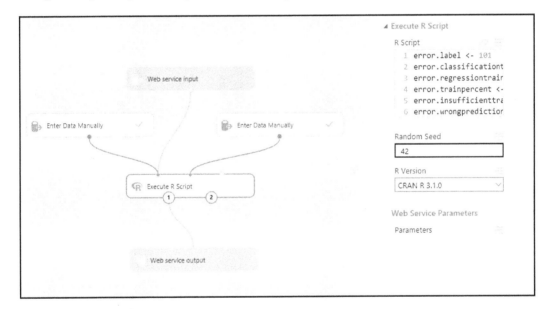

To publish it, follow these steps:

1. Open this experiment in Azure ML Studio.
2. Run it, and then deploy it as a web service.
3. In the web service dashboard, copy the API key.

Step 2 – Training the ML model from AL

In the Visual Studio Code project you cloned earlier, there is a table called **Rest. ML Forecast Setup** with two additional functions, `getMLUri` and `getMLKey`.

Insert your URI and a key (copied from the previous step) into these functions:

```
Tab50101.AIRRestMLForecastSetup.al ×

2 references | You, 3 hours ago | 1 author (You)
table 50101 "AIR Rest. ML Forecast Setup"        You, 3 hours ago • train-my-model
{

    You, 3 hours ago | 1 author (You)
    fields
    {···
    }

    You, 3 hours ago | 1 author (You)
    keys
    {···
    }

    1 reference
    procedure InsertIfNotExists()
    var
    begin···
    end;

    2 references
    procedure getMLUri(): Text
    begin
        exit('https://europewest.services.azureml.net/workspaces/9d1ba609dfba49d580b7d65a379aaa64/services/419fa286d38472cacf7f1
    end;

    2 references
    procedure getMLKey(): Text
    begin
        exit('ZQ8cpUHEpPoej9q/iNqfX2zmfWxbEwmufJddaXRcKvA6aDnO2x107bqO01avgMT0MoJt7stKpaShwa9+eAw45g==')
    end;
```

Open the **Train Rest. Forecast ML** codeunit and find the `Train()` function. Let's investigate how it works. The defined variables are as follows:

```
procedure Train();
var
    MLPrediction: Codeunit "ML Prediction Management";
    MyModel: Text;
    MyModelQuality: Decimal;

    Setup: Record "AIR Rest. ML Forecast Setup";
    RestSalesHistory: Record "AIR RestSalesEntry";
begin···
end;
```

From the preceding screenshot, we observe the following:

- `ML Prediction Management`: This is the main codeunit, which has functions to train, save, and use the ML model.
- `MyModel`: This is the trained model in coded text format.
- `MyModelQuality`: This is the quality of the trained model.
- `Setup`: This is the table where trained models are stored.
- `RestSalesEntry`: This is the historical data used to train an ML model.

Specify connections to your published predictive ML web service, as follows:

```
procedure Train();
var         You, 3 hours ago • train-my-model
begin

    //Setup connection
    MLPrediction.Initialize(Setup.getMLUri(), Setup.getMLKey(), 0);
```

Now, prepare historical data for the training process. You can filter data or add new columns.

The important things to note here are as follows:

- There should not be empty fields in the training dataset. If you have them, fill them with any value, such as `0` or `NA`.
- If you have a `Date` field, split it into two fields (at least): day and month. Usually, the forecast depends on these fields, not on the date itself. The date format is not supported in this API.

Consider the following screenshot:

```
procedure Train();
var ...
begin

    //Setup connection
    MLPrediction.Initialize(Setup.getMLUri(), Setup.getMLKey(), 0);

    //Prepare data for the training
    MLPrediction.SetRecord(RestSalesHistory);
```

Specify the features for the model. Here, you specify the fields that influence the predictions:

```
procedure Train();
var ...
begin

    //Setup connection
    MLPrediction.Initialize(Setup.getMLUri(), Setup.getMLKey(), 0);

    //Prepare data for the training
    MLPrediction.SetRecord(RestSalesHistory);

    //Set features
    MLPrediction.AddFeature(RestSalesHistory.FieldNo(month));
    MLPrediction.AddFeature(RestSalesHistory.FieldNo(day));
    MLPrediction.AddFeature(RestSalesHistory.FieldNo(stock_count));
    MLPrediction.AddFeature(RestSalesHistory.FieldNo(menu_item_id));
    MLPrediction.AddFeature(RestSalesHistory.FieldNo(in_children_menu));
    MLPrediction.AddFeature(RestSalesHistory.FieldNo(fest_name));
    MLPrediction.AddFeature(RestSalesHistory.FieldNo(Children_Event));
    MLPrediction.AddFeature(RestSalesHistory.FieldNo(Music_Event));
    MLPrediction.AddFeature(RestSalesHistory.FieldNo(max_stock_quantity));
```

Then, we specify the label. Here, you specify the fields that you are going to predict:

```
MLPrediction.AddFeature(RestSalesHistory.FieldNo(fest_name));
MLPrediction.AddFeature(RestSalesHistory.FieldNo(Children_Event));
MLPrediction.AddFeature(RestSalesHistory.FieldNo(Music_Event));
MLPrediction.AddFeature(RestSalesHistory.FieldNo(max_stock_quantity));

//Set label
MLPrediction.SetLabel(RestSalesHistory.FieldNo(orders));
```

Next, we train the model. Here, you send a request to the web service with the historical data that's used for training. As a result, you will get a trained model in Base64 text format and the model quality:

```
//Set label
MLPrediction.SetLabel(RestSalesHistory.FieldNo(orders));

//Train model
MLPrediction.Train(MyModel, MyModelQuality);
```

Save your trained model. It will be used later, in the prediction process:

```
//Train model
MLPrediction.Train(MyModel, MyModelQuality);

//Save model
Setup.InsertIfNotExists();
Setup.SetRestaurantModel(MyModel);
Setup.Validate("My Model Quality", MyModelQuality);
Setup.Modify(true);
```

Step 3 – Predicting using the trained model

Open the **Calculate Rest. Forecast ML** codeunit and find the `Predict()` function. Let's see how it works:

1. Check that you have the trained model in place:

```
Setup.Get();
Setup.TestField("My Model");
```

2. Specify the connection to your published predictive ML web service:

```
//Setup connection
MLPrediction.Initialize(Setup.getMLUri(), Setup.getMLKey(), 0);
```

3. Generate a temporary table with data (features), which will be used to get **orders** (predictions). The structure of this table should be the same as the table you used in the training process. Otherwise, the `Prediction` web service will not work properly.

4. Then, pass this table to the ML web service input. It's important to understand that predictions will be calculated for each record (row) of the passed table:

```
//Prepare data for the forecast
PrepareData(Item, RestSalesHistory);
MLPrediction.SetRecord(RestSalesHistory);
```

5. Specify which fields from the table will be the features. List them in the same order as when you trained the model. Otherwise, the `Prediction` web service will not work properly:

```
//Set features
MLPrediction.AddFeature(RestSalesHistory.FieldNo(in_children_menu));
MLPrediction.AddFeature(RestSalesHistory.FieldNo(fest_name));
MLPrediction.AddFeature(RestSalesHistory.FieldNo(children_event));
MLPrediction.AddFeature(RestSalesHistory.FieldNo(music_Event));
MLPrediction.AddFeature(RestSalesHistory.FieldNo(s_month));
MLPrediction.AddFeature(RestSalesHistory.FieldNo(s_day));
MLPrediction.AddFeature(RestSalesHistory.FieldNo(s_go_list));
```

6. Specify which field from the passed table will be a label. Use the same field that you used when you trained the model. You can only mention one field here:

```
//Set label
MLPrediction.SetLabel(RestSalesHistory.FieldNo(orders));
```

The ML Prediction API can make predictions using classification or regression algorithms. You don't control that. If the label field has a type of integer or decimal, then the regression tree algorithm, `annova`, will be applied. Otherwise, it will use a classification algorithm.

If you predict values using classification algorithms, then you can also specify a field to save the confidence percentage of the prediction. This isn't supported for the regression algorithm.

Predict values using the `Predict` function and pass the trained ML model:

```
//Set confidence field (only for classification models)
//MLPrediction.SetConfidence(RestSalesHistory.FieldNo(confidence));

//Predict
MLPrediction.Predict(Setup.GetRestaurantModel());
```

Save the forecast result:

```
//Save forecast
SaveForecastResult(RestSalesHistory, TempTimeSeriesForecast);
```

You now have forecast data to check.

Step 4 – Getting insights into how ML works

When you get predictions from an ML web service, it's always interesting to understand why the model gives some results or makes those decisions. As the ML Prediction API uses tree-based ML algorithms, we can see the decision tree:

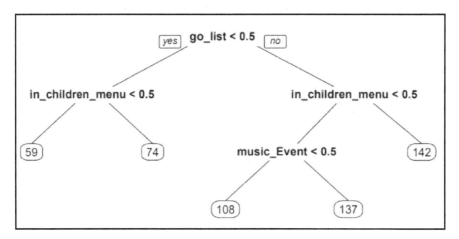

It's important to understand that the decision tree is an artifact of the trained model, not of the predictions made by the trained model.

Open the **Train Rest. Forecast ML** codeunit and find the `DownloatPlotOfTheModel` function. Let's see how it works:

1. Connect to your published ML web service.
2. Get the `.pdf` file with the decision tree calling the `PlotModel` function. You will get it in Base64 text format.

3. Then, use the `DownloadPlot` function to save the `.pdf` file locally. If you don't need to save it, just skip this line of code:

```
procedure DownloadPlotOfTheModel()
var
    MLPrediction: Codeunit "ML Prediction Management";
    PlotBase64: Text;
    Setup: Record "AIR Rest. ML Forecast Setup";
begin
    Setup.Get();
    MLPrediction.Initialize(Setup.getMLUri(), Setup.getMLKey(), 0);

    PlotBase64 := MLPrediction.PlotModel(Setup.GetRestaurantModel(), Setup."My Features", Setup."My Label");

    MLPrediction.DownloadPlot(PlotBase64, 'rest_sales_prediction');
end;
```

You will have a plot of your ML model.

Step 5 – Publishing and running the forecast

When you publish and run the forecast from the **Item** card, you will get this screenshot:

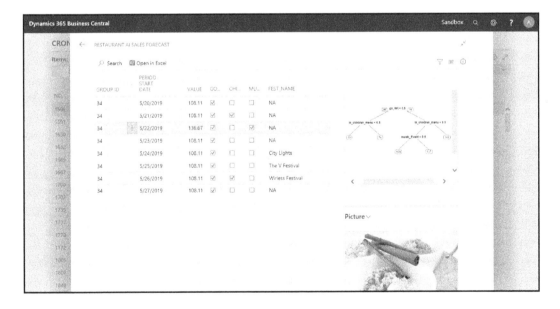

If you to compare the forecast results with the previous models, you will notice that this model gives worse results than the custom-built ML model, but better results than the Time Series API:

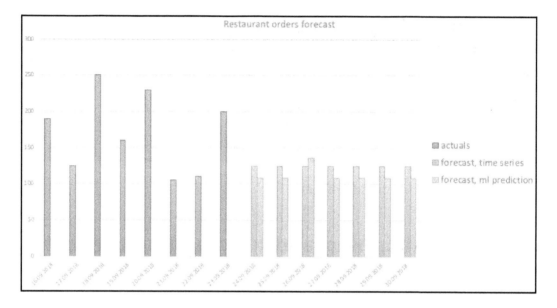

This section explained how ML prediction works and the steps involved in performing it.

Summary

In this chapter, we looked through the ML APIs available with Dynamics 365 Business Central. I've made a comparative analysis of the three ML APIs in the following table:

	The Time Series API	The ML Prediction API	The Custom Azure ML API
ML Experience required	Low	Medium	High
ML Model	Microsoft	Microsoft	Custom
Data preparation level	Low	Medium	High
Max Features	2	Unlimited	Unlimited
Training service	-	Business Central	Azure ML Studio
Trained model storage	-	Business Central	Azure ML Studio

ML Model quality	Low	Medium	High
ML Model usage level	General	Industry	Company

The comparison is based on the example provided in this chapter. Use this table as a guide to help you to choose the best way of applying AI in your app.

As we learned here, building custom ML models is an art that requires creativity, time, and some math skills.

In the next chapter, we'll explore an architectural overview and look at the best practices of moving your existing ISV solutions to extensions.

17
Moving Existing ISV Solutions to the New Extension Model

In this chapter, we'll focus on existing ISV solutions for Dynamics NAV (mainly based on the C/AL language). We'll also look at tips, tricks, and best practices to adopt when moving these solutions to Dynamics 365 Business Central and to the new extension programming paradigm.

The topics we will cover in this chapter are as follows:

- Architectural best practices for moving a C/AL solution to an extension-based one
- Converting existing C/AL code into AL
- Things to check and remember during a solution redesign for SaaS environments

By the end of this chapter, you will have a better understanding of what steps are required to move an existing C/AL solution to AL, the architectural choices when converting a monolithic C/AL solution into extensions (this will affect your final application and how you will sell it), and the tools that can help you in this migration process (code conversion tools).

Preparing the transition from C/AL to AL and extensions

Without a doubt, Dynamics NAV was one of the ERPs in the international market that had the most active community of partners and users. If you are a customer that would like to implement Dynamics NAV, it is really quite easy to find a custom solution that fits and is tailored to your business needs. To do this, just search through one of several add-ons that have been developed by partners or **Independent Software Vendors** (**ISVs**) over the years.

All these solutions are written using the C/AL language. Normally, they contain the following:

- New objects (objects that are created to satisfy a customer's business case)
- Modified standard objects (objects from the standard application base code that have been modified to satisfy a customer's need)

These solutions are always a monolithic solution (everything is packaged into a single codebase inside the database, where an object can reference all the other objects in the solution).

With Dynamics 365 Business Central, CSIDE Development Environment and the C/AL language are available only until version 14.x and only for the on-premise world. From version 15 (wave 2), Microsoft has removed those developer tools, and so existing solutions must now be moved to AL and converted into the new extension model.

Moving an existing C/AL-based solution to AL extensions is not always just an easy *code conversion* process; normally, it requires a redesign and a rethink of the entire application (this is always the approach that's suggested by Microsoft).

When planning to move an existing C/AL solution to AL extensions, on the technical side, there are three main aspects to consider:

- How many extensions should I write to best split the C/AL solution?
- How can I reuse my existing C/AL code?
- What is allowed and not allowed when it comes to targeting a SaaS-based solution?

In the upcoming sections, we will learn how these aspects affect the transition from an existing solution to the new programming model and to the new platform.

Planning the number of extensions to code

As we mentioned in `Chapter 5`, *Developing a Customized Solution for Dynamics 365 Business Central*, extension A cannot reference objects and methods exposed by extension B. This is only possible if extension A explicitly declares a dependency on extension B.

When moving an existing solution to extensions, you have two main choices:

- Create a single monolithic extension
- Create N dependent extensions

Let's explore these concepts in more detail.

A single monolithic extension is an easier choice since developers don't have to think about independent modules. Instead, they just create all the objects and business logic in a single giant AL extension project. In the end, there will be a single `.app` file that does the following:

- Adds new objects
- Extends standard objects
- Adds new business logic
- Raises events
- Subscribes to events raised by the standard business logic

The following diagram shows this solution:

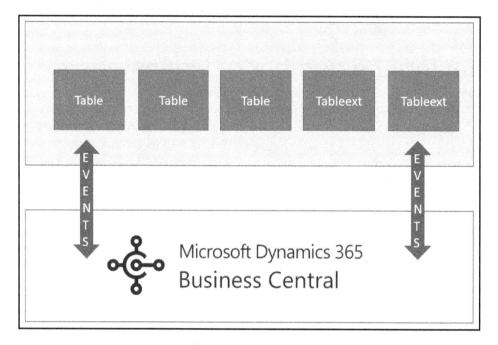

Developers don't have to think about dependencies in this context (all the code is in a single object). However, the disadvantage of this solution is that even a small update of the extension (such as adding a little code change) requires unpublishing and publishing the entire application. This simply means that we update an extension in Dynamics 365 Business Central: unpublish the old version and publish the new version.

Secondly, this is not a solution that can be split into and sold as modules. However, splitting your solution into N separate extensions is a good choice if you want to have a modular solution. When moving an existing C/AL solution to N separate extensions, you typically have the following:

- Independent or standalone extensions (modules that do not require dependencies from other modules)
- Dependent extensions (modules that require dependencies from other modules)

A diagram of this solution is as follows:

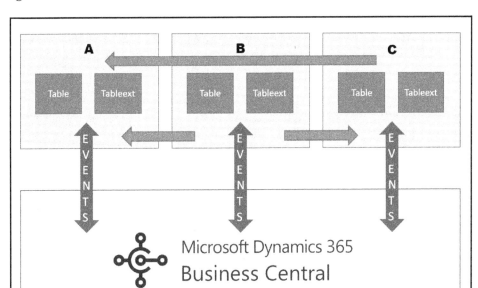

Here, extension A is an independent extension (it can only reference objects from the base module). Extension C depends on extension A, while extension B depends on A and C.

Dependencies have some advantages, such as the following:

- They help us structure more complex deployment scenarios
- They improve code and business logic reusability (avoiding redundancy)
- They increase maintenance
- They enhance deployment flexibility

The drawbacks of dependencies are as follows:

- When you publish the extensions, you must publish the extension that doesn't have any dependencies (the so-called master or parent extension) first. For example, if you try and publish an extension with dependencies first (a child), it will throw an error stating that object references do not exist in the database.
- When you remove extensions, you must remove the dependent extensions first (such as a child) and subsequently the parent extension.

So, we may be wondering which is the better option here.

This is the question that every Microsoft partner is currently asking themselves. There are no rules written in stone about this topic, and what you want to achieve in terms of object modularity, as well as your marketing strategy, depends a lot on your own existing solution.

A best practice and suggestion is to not skip or avoid dependencies. Moving an existing C/AL solution to N different dependent extensions is a good choice as it guarantees modularity and flexibility, but it is also recommended to not create too many micro-extensions. Developers should think about macro functionalities and try to isolate them into featured modules that can be installed when needed by customers.

An important thing to remember within this context is to always add events in order to let others hook your existing codebase.

Only by raising events (*integration* or *business* events) can you have a solution that can interact with other extensions that have been installed in the system and that can also be extended by third parties (other Microsoft partners).

In the next section, we'll learn how to speed up the conversion process (where possible!) of your existing C/AL-based solutions to AL.

Converting existing solutions into AL

Many Microsoft partners that actually work with Dynamics NAV have developed a lot of custom solutions over the years (add-ons, customer solutions, and so on). In order to be ready for the new Dynamics 365 Business Central platform, these must be migrated to AL code.

If you have an existing codebase or an existing solution in place, the first thing you can do when it comes to moving this solution to the extensions world is to try to convert your C/AL objects into AL.

Please keep in mind that conversion is not always the best thing to do, but just a starting point (you can convert all new objects as-is, but you should pay attention and refactor the modified standard objects that your existing solution will certainly have).

So, how can you convert your C/AL solution into AL?

As we mentioned in Chapter 7, *Report Development with AL*, Dynamics 365 Business Central on-premise and Docker images come shipped with a tool that can easily help with converting C/AL objects into AL objects: Txt2AL.exe.

With this tool, you can specify a series of C/AL objects of any kind, export them in TXT format, and automatically convert them into AL format.

To proficiently use this tool, you should perform the following steps:

1. Make an export of all the baseline object of your fresh database into a TXT file (called MyBaseline.txt here) using the following command:

    ```
    finsql.exe Command=ExportToNewSyntax, File=MyBaseline.txt,
    Database="<databasename>", ServerName=<servername>
    ,Filter=Type=table;ID=<tableID>
    ```

 Details of the ExportToNewSyntax command can be found here: https://docs.microsoft.com/en-us/dynamics-nav/ exporttonewsyntax.

2. Import your C/AL solution into a newly created database, compile the objects, and export all new and/or modified objects into a TXT file (called, for example, MyCustomObjects.txt) using the preceding syntax.

3. Execute the Set-ObjectPropertiesFromMenuSuite cmdlet in order to have a conversion from the MenuSuite information to your pages and reports in the generated AL files (remember: MenuSuite objects are not available in Dynamics 365 Business Central).

4. Execute the Compare-NAVApplicationObject cmdlet to compare the base objects with the modified objects and to create the .DELTA files with the differences between them:

    ```
    Compare-NAVApplicationObject -OriginalPath "C:\MyBaseline.txt
    " -ModifiedPath "C:\ MyCustomObjects.txt " -ExportToNewSyntax
    ```

5. Execute the Txt2AL.exe tool using the following syntax:

    ```
    txt2al -source=<DELTAFilePath> --target=<ALOutputFilesPath> --
    rename --type --extensionStartId --injectDotNetAddIns --
    dotNetAddInsPackage --dotNetTypePrefix --translationFormat
    -addLegacyTranslationInfo
    ```

The following table contains a description of all the `Txt2AL.exe` command parameters (some of them are optional). Let's look at how each one functions:

Parameter name	Description
`--source=Path`	The path of the folder containing the `.delta` files. This is a mandatory parameter.
`--target=Path`	The path of the folder that will contain the generated `.AL` files. This is a mandatory parameter.
`--rename`	If used, output files will be automatically renamed as the `.txt` objects.
`--type=ObjectType`	The type of object to convert. Allowed values include Codeunit, Table, Page, Report, Query, and XmlPort.
`--extensionStartId`	This permits you to define the starting ID of the generated extension objects (the default is 70,000,000). It will be incremented by 1 for each generated object.
`--injectDotNetAddIns`	This adds the definition of standard .NET add-ins (a set of add-ins embedded into the platform) in the resulting .NET package.
`--dotNetAddInsPackage=Path`	This specifies the path to an AL file containing a definition for a .NET package containing .NET type declarations that should be included in the .NET package definition produced by the conversion.
`--dotNetTypePrefix`	This allows you to define a prefix to be used for all .NET type aliases that are created during the conversion.
`--translationFormat=ObjectType`	This allows you to specify the translation file format. Allowed values include Xliff and Lcg.

Parameter name	Description
--addLegacyTranslationInfo	This allows you to add information to the translation file. During conversion, XLIFF files from all the CaptionML properties in the app are extracted. If this switch is set, a comment is added in the generated XLIFF files that specify what the ID of the translation item would be in C/SIDE. This acts as a mapping that allows you to convert existing translation resources for your app.

Now that we've explained the tool for converting code from C/AL to AL (Txt2AL), how can we move our existing C/AL solution to the extension-based architecture (AL language) in a semi-automated way?

The first step, and good practice, is to move the existing C/AL solution that you have in place to the last **Cumulative Update** (**CU**) of the last Dynamics 365 Business Central version that supports the CSIDE Development Environment and C/AL language: Dynamics 365 Business Central Spring 2019 update (platform 14.x).

To showcase the semi-automated process, we will use Docker containers with the *NavContainerHelper* PowerShell library, which is available at `https://github.com/microsoft/navcontainerhelper`.

Create a new Docker container with the Dynamics NAV version your C/AL solution is based on (in this example, we will use Dynamics NAV 2018 CU 16) and import the custom or modified TXT objects into this container. The script may look as follows:

```
# Environment Settings
$auth = "NavUserPassword"
$credential = New-Object pscredential 'admin', (ConvertTo-SecureString
-String 'P@ssword1' -AsPlainText -Force)
$licenseFile = "C:\temp\license.flf"
$demoSolutionPath =
"C:\ProgramData\NavContainerHelper\MyNAVSolution.txt"

New-NavContainer -accept_eula `
                 -imageName "mcr.microsoft.com/dynamicsnav:2018-cu16"

                 -containerName "nav2018" `
                 -licenseFile $licenseFile `
                 -auth $auth `
                 -Credential $Credential `
                 -updateHosts `
```

```
                          -includeCSide

# Import and compile objects
Import-ObjectsToNavContainer -containerName "nav2018" -objectsFile
$demoSolutionPath
Compile-ObjectsInNavContainer -containerName "nav2018" -filter
"Modified=Yes"
```

Now, run the following command:

Export—ModifiedObjectsAsDeltas —containerName "nav2018" —openFolder

This will open a local folder (typically
`C:\ProgramData\NavContainerHelper\Extensions\nav2018\delta`) that
contains all the modifications to the base code (called *deltas*). In particular, after
running the preceding command, you will find two types of file in this folder:

- **.TXT** files are your new objects (that you could use as-is).
- **.DELTA** files are the modified objects.

You should always check the `.DELTA` files because they could contain some custom
code modifications that aren't supported in AL anymore. An example of a non-
supported customization could be the code that was previously inserted directly on a
standard table trigger or written inside standard posting routines. This code must be
moved and encapsulated inside event subscribers that have been natively raised by
the Dynamics 365 Business Central platform (as we explained in `Chapter`
`5`, *Developing a Customized Solution for Dynamics 365 Business Central*).

After this (mandatory) code refactoring, we need to create a Dynamics 365 Business
Central container (here, this is called `d365bc`) and we need to import the object's
deltas.

The script is as follows:

```
# Environment Settings
$imageName = "mcr.microsoft.com/businesscentral/onprem:ltsc2019"$auth
= "NavUserPassword"
$credential = New-Object pscredential 'admin', (ConvertTo-SecureString
-String 'P@ssword1' -AsPlainText -Force)
$licenseFile = "C:\temp\license.flf"

# Create Dynamics 365 Business Central container
New-NavContainer -accept_eula `
                -imageName $imageName `
                -containerName "d365bc" `
                -licenseFile "C:\temp\license.flf" `
```

```
        -auth $auth `
        -Credential $Credential `
        -updateHosts `
        -includeCSide

# Import and compile Delta files
Import-DeltasToNavContainer -containerName "d365bc" -deltaFolder
"C:\ProgramData\NavContainerHelper\Extensions\nav2018\delta"
Compile-ObjectsInNavContainer -containerName "d365bc" -filter
"Modified=Yes"
```

Now, you have a container with your C/AL solution in it where you can test your code and (eventually) refactor it over and over again. The previously created NAV container can now be removed from your system by executing the following command:

```
Remove-NavContainer -containerName nav2018
```

Now, we're ready to work on our new AL-based solution.

We now have two possible scenarios when developing (or migrating an existing solution) an application for Dynamics 365 Business Central:

- C/AL to AL conversion (no modifications on standard base objects are required for supporting the SaaS version of the product)
- C/AL to AL code customizations (base AL objects will be changed; this is only available for the on-premise world)

In the upcoming sections, we will learn how to perform in these two C/AL to AL situations.

C/AL to AL conversion

Here, we need to create a Dynamics 365 Business Central development container with our AL solution. This container has no support for C/AL anymore. The script to create this container is as follows:

```
# Environment Settings
$imageName = "mcr.microsoft.com/businesscentral/onprem-ltsc2019"
$auth = "NavUserPassword"
$credential = New-Object pscredential 'admin', (ConvertTo-SecureString
-String 'P@ssword1' -AsPlainText -Force)
$licenseFile = "C:\temp\license.flf"

# Create Business Central container
```

```
New-NavContainer -accept_eula `
                 -imageName $imageName `
                 -containerName "d365bcdev" `
                 -licenseFile $licenseFile `
                 -auth $auth `
                 -Credential $Credential `
                 -updateHosts
```

You now have a working Dynamics 365 Business Central container without the C/AL tools that we'll use in the upcoming steps.

Now, open Visual Studio Code, create a new AL project (*CTRL* + *Shift* + *P* and select **AL:GO!**), give it a name (here, it is called MyALSolution), and modify the launch.json file in your solution in order to connect to this container (here, this is called d365bcdev).

In PowerShell, execute the following command:

```
Convert-ModifiedObjectsToAl -containerName "d365bc" -sqlCredential
$credential -alProjectFolder "C:\Packt\MyALSolution"
```

The NavContainerHelper module has a function called Convert-ModifiedObjectsToAl that allows you to export all the modified objects from the selected container (you can also apply filters to objects if needed) and then run the Convert-Txt2Al command on the resulting files. As a result of this command, you will have a folder (specified by the -alProjectFolder parameter) with many .al files that have been generated in the conversion from the base C/AL solution.

The output will not always be 100% perfect; you need a bit of refactoring and you need to add ApplicationArea and UsageCategory properties to your objects, but the major work has been done. Now, you can compile your AL solution and deploy it on your d365bcdev container. Due to this, your solution is a 100% AL extension on Dynamics 365 Business Central.

C/AL to AL code customizations

When converting C/AL solutions into AL, you may also have cases where you are strictly forced to modify the standard AL code (we suggest avoiding this as much as possible because, if you modify Microsoft's base code, your solution cannot be moved to the Dynamics 365 Business Central SaaS environment). Let's get started:

1. If this is what's happening to you, you can create a Dynamics 365 Business Central development container (d365bcdev) with the -includeAL option:

```
# Environment Settings
$imageName = "mcr.microsoft.com/businesscentral/onprem-
ltsc2019"
$auth = "NavUserPassword"
$credential = New-Object pscredential 'admin', (ConvertTo-
SecureString -String 'P@ssword1' -AsPlainText -Force)
$licenseFile = "C:\temp\license.flf"

# Create Business Central container
New-NavContainer -accept_eula `
                -imageName $imageName `
                -containerName "d365bcdev" `
                -licenseFile $licenseFile `
                -auth $auth `
                -Credential $Credential `
                -updateHosts `
                -includeAL
```

When executing this command, you will find a folder with the baseline of the AL objects in a new folder called Original-<version>-<country>-al (for example, C:\ProgramData\NavContainerHelper\Extensions\Original-14.0.29537.0-W1-al).

2. Now, you can create a new AL project with all the base AL objects you obtained from the previous step. This can be done automatically by executing the following script:

```
Create-AlProjectFolderFromNavContainer -containerName
"d365bcdev" -alProjectFolder
"C:\ProgramData\NavContainerHelper\AL\MyALSolution" -
useBaseLine -addGit
```

In the previous code, we're using the following two parameters:

- The `-useBaseline` option is used to copy the `.AL` base files into our AL solution project.
- The `-addGit` option creates an offline Git repository of the folder and commits all the objects (you need to have Git installed).

3. Now, you can open this folder with Visual Studio Code and compile the solution without publishing (or using the *Ctrl + Shift + B* shortcut). This compilation process can take a few minutes. You can also compile the solution without opening Visual Studio Code by executing the following command:

```
Compile-AppInNavContainer -containerName "d365bcdev" -
credential $credential -appProjectFolder
"C:\ProgramData\NavContainerHelper\AL\MyALSolution"
```

You may see some deprecation warnings during compilation. After compilation, you need to commit these modifications to your local Git repository.

You now have a full AL app (with all the standard AL objects).

In the next step, you have to replace the C/AL objects in the container database with this newly compiled AL app. To do that, execute the following command:

```
Publish-NewApplicationToNavContainer -containerName "d365bcdev" -
appDotNetPackagesFolder
"C:\ProgramData\NavContainerHelper\AL\MyALSolution\.netpackages" -
appFile
"C:\ProgramData\NavContainerHelper\AL\MyALSolution\output\SD_myalapp_1
.0.0.0.app" -credential $credential -useCleanDatabase
```

`Publish-NewApplicationToNavContainer` is a cmdlet that uninstalls all the apps from the database, removes all C/AL objects, and uses the development endpoint of the container to publish the new `.app` file. We use the `-useCleanDatabase` flag to remove C/AL objects and uninstall the existing apps.

Now that you have a Docker container that runs a full AL base app, you need to import your AL custom solution (extension). To do this, execute the following command:

```
Convert-ModifiedObjectsToAl -containerName "d365bc" -sqlCredential
$credential -doNotUseDeltas -alProjectFolder "C:\Packt\MyALSolution" -
alFilePattern "*.al,*.xlf"
```

This will work on the container where you've previously imported your custom C/AL solution (here, this is called d365bc). Now, the conversion runs on all the objects (the full database, except for the report layout files).

After this step, you have a full base app that contains your custom objects and your modifications inside the standard .AL objects. You can now compile the objects and deploy them on your Dynamics 365 Business Central container for testing. You now have a code-customized AL solution (again, it is highly advisable to avoid this if possible).

These are the steps that are required if you wish to start a code conversion. As a general rule, remember to always take the SaaS environment as your reference and target point.

Upgrading from Dynamics 365 Business Central version 14 to version 15

Microsoft's recommended path for migrating your solution to the new refactored Dynamics 365 Business Central version 15 is to start from your solution that was previously moved to version 14 (moving to version 14 and AL is the first step).

Microsoft's official migration path is represented in the following diagram:

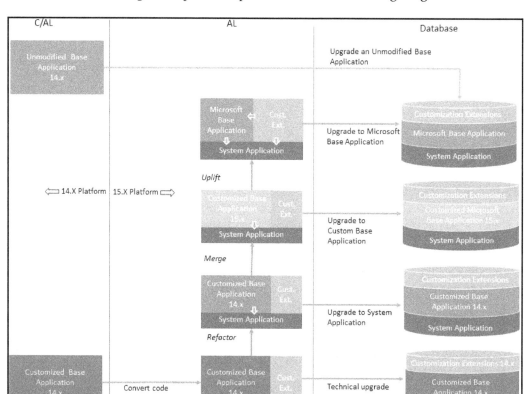

 More information on this can be found at `https://docs.microsoft.` `com/en-us/dynamics365/business-central/dev-itpro/upgrade/` `upgrade-overview-v15`.

To start a technical upgrade from a version 14 database to version 15, you can execute the following PowerShell command:

```
Invoke-NAVApplicationDatabaseConversion -DatabaseServer <database
server name>\<database server instance> -DatabaseName "<database
name>"
```

The conversion updates the system tables of the database to the new schema (data structure) and provides the latest platform features and performance enhancements.

For migrating to version 15, detailed steps are described in the following official Microsoft pages:

- Upgrading an unmodified application to Dynamics 365 Business Central 2019 Release Wave 2: `https://docs.microsoft.com/en-us/dynamics365/business-central/dev-itpro/upgrade/upgrade-unmodified-application`.
- Technical Upgrade to Dynamics 365 Business Central 2019 Wave 2: `https://docs.microsoft.com/en-us/dynamics365/business-central/dev-itpro/upgrade/upgrade-technical-upgrade-v14-v15`.

In the next section, we'll look at another important aspect to take into consideration when architecting solutions for the new Dynamics 365 Business Central platform: how to handle customer requests for customizations.

Handling customer-specific personalization's

You've worked hard so far, and now your solution has finished moving from the old C/AL to the new extension's architecture. Now, a common business scenario occurs when you sell your solution to a customer: they want some specific customizations of your solution to satisfy their particular business needs. Here, we immediately have a problem: how can you handle customizations for your customers?

The extension model has some rules, and you need to absolutely avoid the situation represented in the following diagram:

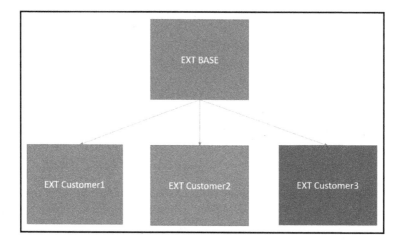

In the preceding diagram, we can see that EXT BASE is the standard solution and its base code is modified for every customer that acquires the solution.

You don't need to directly customize your extension code for every customer you have. Forking your solution's base code is absolutely a bad practice (it hurts the extension's principles; that is, the base code must never be changed).

What you need to do is represented in the following diagram:

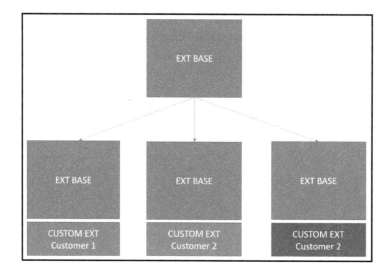

Here, your extension's base code (called EXT BASE, in the preceding diagram) is the same for every customer. To handle customizations for each customer, you create a new extension for each customer (CUSTOM EXT, in the preceding diagram) that will be *dependent* on your base extension (it will be a new layer above the standard layer). This is a best practice and what the extension model wants: you don't modify base code, you *extend* base code. So, aside from these, what are the other solutions for extensions that we need to remember? Let's check them out.

Other things to remember

When moving a solution to extensions, there are other things to remember and aspects that you need to handle or rethink. In the upcoming sections, you will find a summary of some of the most common ones.

Handling the MenuSuite

With Dynamics NAV, pages and reports can be searched in the web client by adding them to a *MenuSuite* object (a standard object that defines the functional menu of the application). With Dynamics 365 Business Central, the `MenuSuite` object is not supported, and pages and reports can be searchable and visible by setting the `UsageCategory` and `ApplicationArea` properties.

If you convert objects from C/AL, you need to set these properties on the converted objects. You can automate the process of setting these properties on your objects by using a PowerShell module called `TransitionMenuSuiteObjectsForSearch.psm1`, which you can find on the Dynamics 365 Business Central DVD image.

You can import this module on PowerShell as follows:

```
Import-Module -Name
c:\dvd\WindowsPowerShellScripts\WebSearch\TransitionMenuSuiteObjectsFo
rSearch.psm1
```

Then, execute the following command:

```
Set-ObjectPropertiesFromMenuSuite -RoleTailoredClientFolder
"C:\Program Files (x86)\Microsoft Dynamics NAV\140\RoleTailored
Client" -DataBaseName "YourDatabase" -OutPutFolder "C:\temp"
```

Now, `UsageCategory` and `ApplicationArea` are set on all your converted objects.

.NET variables and add-ins

If your existing code uses .NET variables, these objects are not supported in a SaaS environment. If you want to use .NET on SaaS, you need to wrap your DLLs (or your .NET code) into an Azure function and call that function from your AL code. `Chapter 6`, *Advanced AL Development*, and `Chapter 13`, *Serverless Business Processes with Business Central and Azure*, show you how to handle these situations.

If your extension targets the on-premise world (`Target = Internal` in the `app.json` file), then you can use .NET assemblies in your AL code (but this code can never be moved into a SaaS environment). More information on how to use .NET variables in AL for the on-premise world can be found at `https://docs.microsoft.com/en-us/dynamics365/business-central/dev-itpro/developer/devenv-get-started-call-dotnet-from-al` and `https://demiliani.com/2019/06/04/dynamics-365-business-central-using-dotnet-assemblies-on-a-docker-container-sandbox/`.

Another possible problem occurs if you have a solution that uses .NET visual add-ins, such as the following **Sales Order** page:

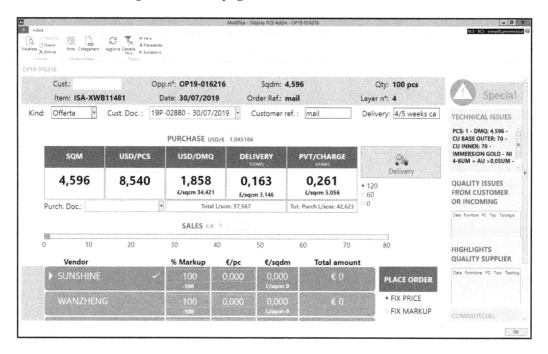

The following is a custom **Sales Order** page we have implemented that uses a .NET **Windows Presentation Foundation** (**WPF**) add-in that's been declared in C/AL as follows:

RowSpan	<Undefined>
ColumnSpan	<Undefined>
DateFormula	<No>
ControlAddIn	**EID.PCBAddinDemoControl;PublicKeyToken=ac092374586fd254**
Style	<None>
StyleExpr	<FALSE>
ExtendedDatatype	<None>
Image	<Stack>

To move this solution to Dynamics 365 Business Central, you need to remake the visual add-in as a JavaScript add-in, as described in `Chapter 6`, *Advanced AL Development*.

File management

With Dynamics 365 Business Central, files are only supported on-premises. If you're targeting the SaaS environment, you should handle files in a different way by using *Streams* (as described in `Chapter 6`, *Advanced AL Development*, in the *Handling files* section) or by using *Azure Functions* for file storage (a complete solution is described in `Chapter 13`, *Serverless Business Processes with Business Central and Azure*).

Printing

Direct printing (sending a document to a printer on the local network directly) is not available in the SaaS environment. A possible solution to this problem is described here: `https://demiliani.com/2019/01/29/dynamics-365-business-central-and-direct-printing/`.

Microsoft is also working on supporting direct printing in the near future in the SaaS environment. The wave 2 release will have a new reporting event called `OnDocumentReady`, which exposes a data stream and the context of a document. A document can then be picked up by an extension that can handle printing.

In the next section, we'll learn how the Dynamics 365 Business Central wave 2 release architecture could affect your extension's development in the near future.

Dynamics 365 Business Central wave 2 release changes

Dynamics 365 Business Central Wave 2 release (platform 15) is AL- and web-client-only. You will not find support for C/AL and CSIDE anymore. Instead, if you go to the *Extensions Management* page in Dynamics 365 Business Central platform 15, you will find the following two Microsoft extensions:

- **Base Application** (version 15.0.<build>.0): This extension contains all the business logic that was moved to AL.
- **System Application** (version 15.0.<build>.0): This extension handles the system layer.

In addition to simplifying the entire codebase, the main benefits of this new structure are that you can move away from code customizations and start making vertical or horizontal solutions based on the Dynamics 365 Business Central platform. You can set up a staging environment and practice with the breaking changes that will be introduced officially in the new version by following these two official articles:

- https://freddysblog.com/2019/07/31/preview-of-dynamics-365-business-central-2019-release-wave-2/
- https://freddysblog.com/2019/08/02/organizing-your-al-files/

All the new extensions that you will create for Dynamics 365 Business Central must be dependent on these Microsoft apps. In Visual Studio Code, when you start a new extension project, you need to add the following dependencies to your extension's `app.json` file:

```json
{} app.json    ✕

{} app.json ▸ ...
  1   {
  2       "id": "06c02671-ee53-46e8-9e5a-92ee6db7e06f",
  3       "name": "TEST3",
  4       "publisher": "SD",
  5       "version": "1.0.0.0",
  6       "brief": "",
  7       "description": "",
  8       "privacyStatement": "",
  9       "EULA": "",
 10       "help": "",
 11       "url": "",
 12       "logo": "",
 13       "dependencies": [
 14           {
 15               "appId": "63ca2fa4-4f03-4f2b-a480-172fef340d3f",
 16               "name": "System Application",
 17               "publisher": "Microsoft",
 18               "version": "1.0.0.0"
 19           },
 20           {
 21               "appId": "437dbf0e-84ff-417a-965d-ed2bb9650972",
 22               "name": "BaseApp",
 23               "publisher": "Microsoft",
 24               "version": "15.0.0.0"
 25           }
 26       ],
 27       "screenshots": [],
 28
 29       "idRanges": [
```

Those dependencies will be automatically added if you select **4.0** as the target platform in Visual Studio Code.

After that, you can download symbols from your environment and start coding:

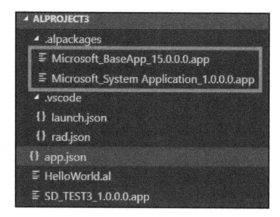

This is the recommended way to develop extensions for the SaaS and the on-premise world.

In the Dynamics 365 Business Central wave 2 release, Microsoft permits you to also modify the base code (now, it's full AL converted) and the links at the beginning of this section explain how to extract the .al files to a local folder and start working on those files to create your new custom *BaseApp*.

As an example, here, I'm directly modifying the standard *Sales-Post* codeunit by adding a custom function:

More information on how to modify the *Base Application* can be found here: `https://demiliani.com/2019/09/24/dynamics-365-business-central-wave-2-customizing-the-base-application/`.

As we mentioned previously, in many sources by community experts, *just because you can, it doesn't mean you should*. Modifying base code is actually permitted to help partners move solutions to AL and the new platform as soon as possible, but, in the long term, on-premise will follow cloud rules, so Microsoft's base code modifications may become more restricted in the future.

With the new platform, you can also build extensions on top of the *System Application* itself. Just remove the dependency from the *BaseApp*, download some symbols, and you're ready to go. As shown in the following screenshot, now, you have only downloaded two app packages (no BaseApp):

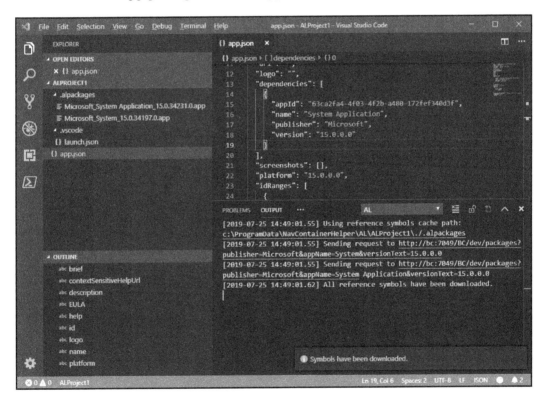

Now, you can start coding an extension that depends only on the *System Application*.

The *System Application* is actually a work in progress and could change in the future (new modules will be added). The latest version is always available on GitHub at `https://github.com/Microsoft/alappextensions`.

As you've seen in this section, from the Dynamics 365 Business Central 15.x platform, all the base code has been moved to AL and you need to create extensions with AL and Visual Studio Code, starting with the Microsoft Base and System apps.

Summary

In this chapter, we looked at the best practices of moving an existing monolithic C/AL solution to the new extension architecture and to the AL language. We also saw the best practices of architecting your solution, such as how to convert existing C/AL code into AL in a semi-automatic way, and how to handle common problems during the migration phase of your existing solution.

Toward the end of this chapter, you learned how to migrate to the new Dynamics 365 Business Central platform and the best practices to adopt when starting a project for a new solution. Now, you have a clear vision of the tools to use to migrate existing code to AL and the steps that are required to start this migration activity.

In the next chapter, we'll learn how third-party tools can help us work with AL and extensions, and also help us move our existing solutions to the new Dynamics 365 Business Central architecture.

18
Useful and Proficient Tools for AL Developers

In the previous chapter, we provided some guidance and best practices on moving existing ISV solutions to the new Dynamics 365 Business Central development model based on extensions.

Having the correct tools when working with extensions and Visual Studio Code can save you lots of time and energy. In this chapter, we want to give you an overview of some third-party development tools that you can use in your everyday developer life with AL to be more proficient in many tasks. We will focus here on tools developed by a famous name in the Microsoft Dynamics ERP world: Waldo.

We'll cover the following topics in this chapter:

- Who is Waldo?
- What tools to use

Who is Waldo?

Waldo's real name is Eric Wauters and he is one of the founding partners of *iFacto Business Solutions* and *Cloud Ready Software*. With his 18 years of technical expertise, he is an everyday inspiration to its development teams. As a development manager, he continually acts upon the technical readiness of iFacto and CRS.

Apart from that, Eric is also very active in the Microsoft Dynamics 365 Business Central community, where he tries to solve technical issues and shares his knowledge with other Dynamics enthusiasts. Surely, a lot of you will have read some of Eric's posts, which he invariably signs with `waldo`.

Lots of people have been using and even contributing to tools he shares for free on MiBuSo, GitHub, the PowerShell Gallery, and the Visual Studio Marketplace.

His proven track record led to him being given a **Microsoft Most Valuable Professional** (**MVP**) award each year since 2007.

After learning about Waldo, in the next section, we'll see an overview of most of his tools for AL developers.

What tools to use

Over the years, Waldo has created quite a lot of tools. The first tool Waldo ever put online was back in 2004, `WaldoNavPad`, a tool that helps to work with bigger texts in Microsoft Dynamics NAV. It helped to break up code into smaller pieces, which was necessary because, back then, we could only have a maximum of 250 characters in one field.

The tool was downloaded over 11,000 times from MiBuSo. Because of its popularity, Waldo updated the tool to a version that worked in the RTC and as an AL extension, where he extended the functionality a bit to have an HTML editor inside Business Central.

Following this tool, quite a few minor tools made it to the download list of MiBuSo, which you can find at `https://mibuso.com/downloads/results?keywords=waldo`.

Since 2013, when Microsoft released more and more PowerShell building blocks, Waldo decided to dive into that to help the uptake in the community. This resulted in some very extended libraries of helper functions, which are categorized and published on the PowerShell Gallery. Just search for `waldo` (`https://www.powershellgallery.com/packages?q=waldo`) and you will find six PowerShell modules:

- `Ready.Software.SQL`: These include some functions that help you to work with SQL Server (and Business Central), such as taking backups and restoring them.
- `Ready.Software.PowerShell`: This is a very small set of functions for some PowerShell-related challenges.
- `Ready.Software.Windows`: These include Windows-related functions such as zipping and unzipping items.
- `Ready.Software.NAV`: This module contains most functions, all related to NAV (Business Central):
    - Working with objects (upgrade, version list, languages, and so on)
    - Working with servers (such as permissions and companies)

- `RemoteNAVDockerHostHelper`: This is a module to help you to work with a `DockerHost` when that `DockerHost` is not on your local PC (hence the word `Remote` in `RemoteNAVDockerHost`).
- `NavContainerHelperExtension`: This is just a set of functions that Waldo needed to work with Docker. Similar to `NavContainerHelper`, these functions were not part of that module at the time they were created.

All of these functions have had a purpose in Waldo's life as a developer. Every single script in which he uses these modules is online on his GitHub: `https://github.com/waldo1001/Cloud.Ready.Software.PowerShell`. You will find all modules there and the scripts in which he puts these modules to use.

A large number of these PowerShell scripts were created to be able to help the development of V1 Extensions. But when these were discontinued (for the better), there was a new kid on the block: Visual Studio Code, in which we can develop for what we call Extensions V2. In Waldo's opinion, this tool needed some help with the following:

- Automatically naming files
- Running objects
- Snippets

So, Waldo started to build an extension for Visual Studio Code to help AL developers to do their jobs more efficiently. The **CRS AL Language Extension** was born: `https:/ /marketplace.visualstudio.com/items?itemName=waldo.crs-al-language- extension`.

This is just a peek at Waldo's tools and how he came to build them. Here are a few resources where you can find his tools:

- MiBuSo: `https://mibuso.com/downloads/results?keywords=waldo`
- The PowerShell Gallery: `https://www.powershellgallery.com/packages? q=waldo`
- GitHub: `https://github.com/waldo1001`
- DevOps: `https://dev.azure.com/waldo1001/WaldoDemos`

In this chapter, we will talk about a few of his tools, focused on making your life as an AL developer a little bit easier.

The AL Extension Pack

The smallest tool that Waldo ever built is the **Visual Studio Code | Extension Packs**. In fact, it's a collection of all of the **Visual Studio Code** extensions that Waldo values and uses in everyday development tasks.

You can find the **Extension Packs** on the Marketplace under the name **AL Extension Pack**. Here is a direct link:

```
https://marketplace.visualstudio.com/items?itemName=waldo.al-extension-
pack
```

This is what the home page looks like:

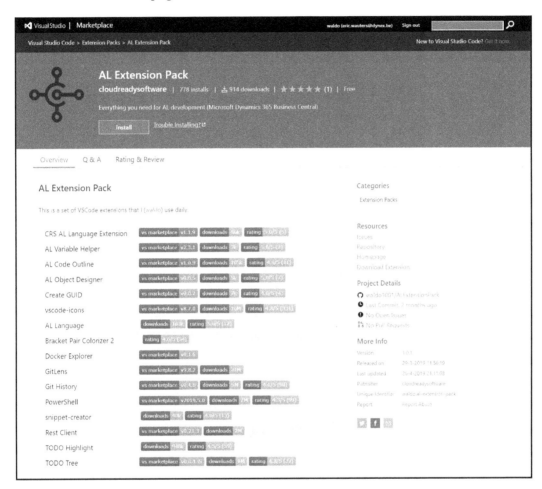

By simply installing this extension, it will automatically install all extensions that are in the pack, and when Waldo adds an extension, it will automatically be installed on your system as well.

There's also a similar package that we highly recommend installing if you want to have a full-featured Visual Studio Code environment:

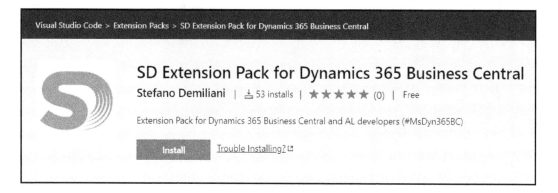

You can find this tool at the following link:

```
https://marketplace.visualstudio.com/items?itemName=StefanoDemiliani.sd-extpack-d365bc
```

The CRS AL Language Extension

A somewhat bigger extension that Waldo has written for the community is the **CRS AL Language Extension**:

The extension can be found at the following link:

```
https://marketplace.visualstudio.com/items?itemName=waldo.crs-al-language-
extension
```

The main reason why so many people are using it is that it manages filename conventions: developers don't have to worry anymore about how to name their files—this extension can take care of that automatically. But it does a lot more.

Let's have an overview of its functionality.

Run objects

We all know that we can run a table or page whenever we publish an app by changing some settings in the `launch.json` file. But that's not convenient.

In a way, we need to be able to do the following:

- Run any object in the windows, web, tablet, or phone client.
- Run some tools directly, such as the following:
  - Test Tool
  - Event Subscribers
  - Database Locks Page
- Run the current object that is open in the client.

The `launch.json` way of running objects isn't going to help us here.

The CRS AL Language Extension comes with these new commands, which can be found in the command palette:

- CRS: Run Object (Web Client).
- CRS: Run Object (Tablet Client).
- CRS: Run Object (Phone Client).
- CRS: Run Object (Windows Client).
- CRS: Run Current Object (Web Client) (*Ctrl* + *Shift* + *R*)—this runs the object from the open file (the extension needs to be published first). You can also run this command from the status bar (**Run In Web Client**) and the context menu from the explorer.
- CRS: Run CAL Test Tool in Web Client.
- CRS: Run Event Subscribers Page in Web Client.
- CRS: Run Database Locks Page in Web Client.

The nice thing is it will find the settings in `launch.json` and use these to run the actual objects.

Renaming/reorganizing files

As mentioned earlier, this is the most widely used functionality of the tool:

- `Renaming` is renaming the file.
- `Reorganizing` is renaming the file AND placing it in a subfolder that matches its object type.

The essence is captured in four commands that are again available from the Visual Studio Code command palette:

- CRS: Rename – Current File.
- CRS: Rename – All Files.
- CRS: Reorganize – Current File.
- CRS: CRS: Reorganize – All Files—note that `Reorganize` will move a test codeunit to the test folder.

There's also a setting to start the file renaming/reorganizing automatically when saving a `.al` file:

```
"CRS.OnSaveAlFileAction": "Rename"
```

Another interesting functionality of rename/reorganize is the ability to change the patterns of filenames:

```
"CRS.FileNamePattern":
"<ObjectNameShort>.<ObjectTypeShort><ObjectId>.al",
 "CRS.FileNamePatternExtensions":
"<ObjectNameShort>.<ObjectTypeShort><BaseId>-Ext<ObjectId>.al",
 "CRS.FileNamePatternPageCustomizations":
"<ObjectNameShort>.<ObjectTypeShort><BaseId>-PageCust.al"
```

Here is an overview of all of the available tool settings:

- `CRS.nstfolder`: This is the folder of the NST.
- `CRS.WebServerInstancePort`: This is the port number for the web client.
- `CRS.WinServer`: This is the server that the Windows client is connecting to.

- CRS.WinServerInstance: This is the server instance that the windows client is connecting to.
- CRS.WinServerInstancePort: This is the port number of the server instance that the Windows client is connecting to.
- CRS.PublicWebBaseUrl: Override Launch.json settings with this setting if necessary to run objects from VS Code.
- CRS.ExtensionObjectNamePattern: This is the pattern for the object name; if set (it's not set by default), it will perform an automatic object name for extension objects:
    - <Prefix>
    - <Suffix>
    - <ObjectType>
    - <ObjectTypeShort>: A short notation of the object type
    - <ObjectTypeShortUpper>: The same as ObjectTypeShort but uppercase
    - <ObjectId>
    - <BaseName>: Weird characters are removed—does NOT include prefix or suffix
    - <BaseNameShort>: Does NOT include prefix or suffix
    - <BaseId>: If you want this to work, you need to put Id in a comment after the base name

- CRS.FileNamePattern: This is the pattern of the filename for non-extension objects. These variables can be used:
    - <Prefix>: Just the prefix separately
    - <Suffix>: Just the suffix separately
    - <ObjectType>
    - <ObjectTypeShort>: A short notation of the object type
    - <ObjectTypeShortUpper>: The same as ObjectTypeShort but uppercase
    - <ObjectId>
    - <ObjectName>: Weird characters are removed, including prefix and suffix
    - <ObjectNameShort>

- `CRS.FileNamePatternExtensions`: This is the pattern of the filename for extension objects. These variables can be used:
  - `<Prefix>`: Just the prefix separately
  - `<Suffix>`: Just the suffix separately
  - `<ObjectType>`
  - `<ObjectTypeShort>`: A short notation of the object type
  - `<ObjectTypeShortUpper>`: The same as `ObjectTypeShort` but uppercase
  - `<ObjectId>`
  - `<ObjectName>`: Weird characters are removed, including prefix and suffix
  - `<ObjectNameShort>`
  - `<BaseName>`: Weird characters are removed, but this does not include prefix nor suffix
  - `<BaseNameShort>`: Does not include prefix nor suffix
  - `<BaseId>`: If you want this to work, you need to put `Id` in a comment after the base name, like in this example:

```
tableextension 50100 "Just Some Table Extension"
extends Customer //18
{
    fields
    {
        // Add changes to table fields here
        field(50100;"Just Some field";Code[10]){
            TableRelation="Just Some Table"."No.";
        }
    }
}
```

- `CRS.FileNamePatternPageCustomizations`: This is the pattern of the filename for page customizations. These variables can be used:
  - `<Prefix>`: Just the prefix separately
  - `<Suffix>`: Just the suffix separately
  - `<ObjectType>`
  - `<ObjectTypeShort>`: A short notation of the object type
  - `<ObjectTypeShortUpper>`: The same as `ObjectTypeShort` but uppercase

- `<ObjectName>`: Weird characters are removed—includes prefix and suffix
- `<ObjectNameShort>`: Includes prefix and suffix
- `<BaseName>`: Weird characters are removed and does NOT include prefix nor suffix
- `<BaseNameShort>`: Does NOT include prefix nor suffix
- `<BaseId>`: Same remarks as before

- `CRS.ObjectNamePrefix`: When using the reorganize/rename commands, this setting will make sure the object name (and filename) will have a prefix:
    - Tip 1: Use as a workspace setting
    - Tip 2: Use an ending space if you want the prefix to be separated by a space
- `CRS.ObjectNameSuffix`: When using the reorganize/rename commands, this setting will make sure the object name (and filename) has a suffix:
    - Tip 1: Use as a workspace setting
    - Tip 2: Use a start space if you want the suffix to be separated by a space
- `CRS.RemovePrefixFromFilename`: When using the reorganize/rename commands, this setting will remove any prefix from the filename (but keep it in the object name). Tip: Use as a workspace setting.
- `CRS.RemoveSuffixFromFilename`: When using the reorganize/rename commands, this setting will remove any suffix from the filename (but keep it in the object name). Tip: Use as a workspace setting.
- `CRS.AlSubFolderName`: This is the variable subfolder name. "None" means you want to disable the command to move files to a subfolder.
- `CRS.OnSaveAlFileAction`: This will automatically rename/reorganize the file you are editing. This takes into account the prefix/suffix as well.
- `DisableDefaultAlSnippets`: This disables the default snippets that come with the `Microsoft.al-language` extension. When you change the setting, you need to restart Visual Studio Code twice—once to disable the snippets on activation (at that time, the snippets are still loaded), and once to not load the snippets anymore.

- `DisableCRSSnippets`: This disables the CRS snippets that come with this extension. When you change the setting, you need to restart Visual Studio Code twice—once to disable the snippets on activation (at that time, the snippets are still loaded), and once to not load the snippets anymore.
- `RenameWithGit`: Use `git mv` to rename a file. This keeps the history of the file but stages the rename, which you should commit separately. **The feature is still in preview-mode, therefore the default value is** `false`.

Search on Google/Microsoft Docs

A small addition, but very handy when coding, is being able to easily find documentation using two new commands in the command palette:

- CRS: Search Microsoft Docs
- CRS: Search Google

It will take the selected word, and search that word on Google or Microsoft Docs, with Business Central as the main topic.

Snippets

Last, but definitely not least, several snippets are included in the CRS AL Language extension.

First of all, there are improved versions of the Microsoft snippets:

- Removed unused triggers
- Improved tab stops
- Improved uncompilable code
- Removed default global variables

There are also new snippets that implement some default design patterns:

- `tmynotifications` (CRS): The implementation of my notifications for your own notifications
- `tassistedsetup` (CRS): The implementation of the assisted setup for your own wizards
- `tcodeunit` (CRS Method): Snippets for implementing a default encapsulated method design pattern that implements an `OnBefore` and `OnAfter` event by default

It's a good thing to explore all snippets and familiarize yourself with them.

Feedback

If you have feedback, or you want to contribute to this project, then don't hesitate to fork or create issues on the repository for the CRS AL Language extension, which you can find on GitHub at `https://github.com/waldo1001/crs-al-language-extension`.

WaldoNavPad

The goal of `WaldoNavPad` has always been to be able to easily work with an unlimited amount of text by easily splitting the text into pieces to save in a Business Central (or NAV) database (not just by saving it as a BLOB, but as text) so that you can still filter and search for parts of the texts.

On top of this, the text should be split intelligently by preserving paragraphs, carriage returns, and full words. This still preserves the format of the text as much as possible, which makes it as readable as possible in the small field lengths that NAV had at its disposal.

How to get it to work

The latest version of `WaldoNavPad` can be found on Waldo's GitHub:

`https://github.com/waldo1001/Waldo.NAV.Pad`

It can easily be downloaded, forked, or cloned from there.

If you do so, you'll have the AL code of an app that implements `WaldoNavPad`:

This set of files is intended to allow you to copy, renumber, rename, and do more to your own project. It's not intended to be created as an app, nor has it been uploaded to AppSource, so you can use it as a dependency from your own app.

Running the app for the first time

Once in Visual Studio Code, the app builds and publishes as is. You can simply create your `launch.json`, download the symbols, and build the app right away. This will get you to the **Customer List** page, where there are the following two new actions:

- **Open WaldoNAVPad Text**: A normal page with a multiline textbox to handle large texts
- **Open WaldoNAVPad HTML**: A JavaScript-based HTML editor (based on TinyMCE)

The actions appear as follows:

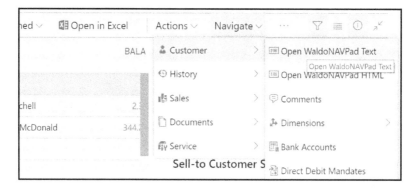

Here is the text editor on the normal page:

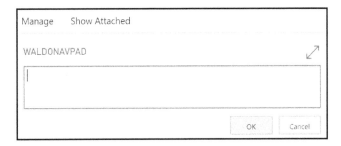

The HTML text editor is as follows:

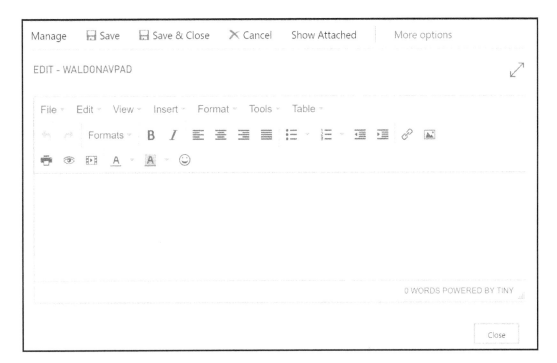

Next, let's see how the background for the text appears.

The background

When you dive into the code, you'll see that the app consists of two parts:

- **NAVpad Handling**: This subfolder contains the code to handle the NAVpad. The idea is you only use the `WaldoNAVPad` Class codeunit, where you can show/save/get the texts from the NAVpad. To save the texts, it will use the text handling functionality.
- **Text Handling**: This subfolder contains the code to intelligently handle the texts that have to be saved to the database or have to be loaded from the database. If you want to use the NAVPad text-tables, there is no need to use these methods. However, if you want to save texts to your own table, you can simply use the functions in the `WaldoNAVPad` Text Class codeunit, which lets you get text and loop through it to save it to your own tables.

By looping through your text, the system is going to cut sentences at spaces or carriage returns to preserve the formatting of your text as much as possible.

In the following example, you see the NAVPad Handling routine looping through the text to save the text:

```
local procedure InsertWPNTextForRecord(var WaldoNAVPadTextClass: Codeunit "WaldoNAVPad Text Class"; var RecRef: RecordRef);
begin
    with WaldoNAVPadTextClass do
        if FINDFIRST() then
            repeat
                InsertWPNText(GetCurrentTextLine(), RecRef);
            until NEXT() < 1;
end;
```

By default, the system saves the text in two tables:

- `WaldoNAVPad` Blobstore: This is a table with formatted HTML tags to preserve all of the formatting the user has been doing to the text.
- `WaldoNAVPad` Textstore: This is a table where all of the HTML tags are stripped to be able to show it decently in Business Central.

To show the content of these tables, the app has two pages in the `_JustForTexting` folder:

- page 82,150 WaldoNAVPad Blobs
- page 82,149 WaldoNAVPad Texts

Here is an example of how the records are saved by running the page called **WaldoNAVPad Texts**:

Next, we will see how to implement these actions.

Implementing the logic

To show you how to implement this in your own business logic, the app has a
_JustForTesting subfolder, which contains a page extension for page 22 (**Customer List**) that shows how you can simply create an action on a page and implement WaldoNAVPad by calling the class functions:

```
action(OpenWaldoNAVPadTextHTML)
{
    Caption = 'Open WaldoNAVPad HTML';
    Image = Text;
    Promoted = true;
    ApplicationArea = All;

    trigger OnAction()
    var
        WaldoNAVPadClass: Codeunit "WaldoNAVPad Class";
    begin
        //Example code to implement the WaldoNAVPad on a Record, using the generic Text tables
        WaldoNAVPadClass.Initialize(Rec);
        WaldoNAVPadClass.ShowAndSaveTexts(true, true);
    end;
}
```

The Initialize function will load the text that is linked to the current record. The ShowAndSaveTexts method will show the texts (in this case, in the HTML editor) if the user chooses to see it.

MostUselessAppEver

A not-so-important, but rather interesting, repository of Waldo is something he calls *the most useless app ever*. It is an AL app intended for demos, prototyping, tryouts, or tests—you name it. It contains a lot of different tryouts and demos of different parts and topics of AL development.

A few examples of this are as follows:

- Translations
- The different .NET wrappers
- Some editing hacks to work with Visual Studio Code
- Included SQL files to check the tables of an app
- Publish web services
- Included HTTP files to check web services

- Function overloading
- The Tenant Management codeunit

You can find `MostUselessAppEver` on Waldo's GitHub at `https://github.com/waldo1001/MostUselessAppEver`.

You can simply clone the repository and start working with it. There is not a single piece of business logic that is useful, but it will show you some tricks to work with AL development.

PowerShell tools

As mentioned before, Waldo has been diving into PowerShell quite heavily. There has been a strong focus on C/AL and merging, upgrading, and all that, but for AL, there hasn't been much need in terms of PowerShell (yet).

Still, let's point out a few areas in his scripts that can be of any use in terms of AL development.

GitHub

All of Waldo's PowerShell modules and scripts can be found on GitHub at `https://github.com/waldo1001/Cloud.Ready.Software.PowerShell`.

You will see two folders:

- `PSModules`: This contains all of the code for the modules. These modules can be found on the PowerShell Gallery as well: `https://www.powershellgallery.com/packages?q=waldo`.
- `PSScripts`: This contains scripts that mostly put the functions of these modules to work.

Docker scripts

Waldo has been using Docker in quite a number of ways. First, he ran a Windows 2016 Server VM on his laptop, where he had installed Docker—so, in a way, it was a remote Docker host. Then, he moved to Docker on his own PC, which simplified the development experience a bit. All of his scripts to manage Docker are in the `PSScripts/NAVDocker` folder.

Here, you find scripts to create containers, but also to work with apps in these Docker containers, such as the following:

- `CleanApp`: This will remove all apps from a Docker container.
- `InstallApp`: This will install an app with PowerShell.
- `ExportObjectsAsAL`: This will export objects as an AL file. It's very convenient to use for reports, which you can export, rename, and replace easily.

Publishers

In another repository (`blog.CALAnalysis`), Waldo has been documenting all of the publishers from a certain version of NAV or Business Central, which results in a file that lists all of the event publishers and where they are called.

Following is an example of the publishers:

```
3337 published events found.
Number of times a publisher was raised:
1 : Codeunit<Calc. G/L Acc. Where-Used>.PROCEDURE<OnAfterCheckPostingGroups>
1 : Codeunit<Calc. G/L Acc. Where-Used>.PROCEDURE<OnBeforeShowGLAccWhereUsed>
1 : Codeunit<Calc. G/L Acc. Where-Used>.PROCEDURE<OnShowExtensionPage>
1 : Codeunit<Job Calculate WIP>.PROCEDURE<OnInsertWIPGLOnBeforeGenJnPostLine>
1 : Codeunit<Job Post-Line>.PROCEDURE<OnAfterJobPlanningLineModify>
1 : Codeunit<Job Post-Line>.PROCEDURE<OnAfterPostInvoiceContractLine>
1 : Codeunit<Job Post-Line>.PROCEDURE<OnBeforePostInvoiceContractLine>
1 : Codeunit<Job Post-Line>.PROCEDURE<OnBeforePostJobOnPurchaseLine>
1 : Codeunit<Job Post-Line>.PROCEDURE<OnPostInvoiceContractLineBeforeCheckJobLine>
1 : Codeunit<Job Post-Line>.PROCEDURE<OnPostPurchaseGLAccountsOnBeforeJobJnlPostLine>
1 : Codeunit<Job Post-Line>.PROCEDURE<OnPostSalesGLAccountsOnBeforeJobJnlPostLine>
1 : Codeunit<Job Create-Invoice>.PROCEDURE<OnAfterTestSalesHeader>
1 : Codeunit<Job Create-Invoice>.PROCEDURE<OnBeforeGetCrMemoNo>
1 : Codeunit<Job Create-Invoice>.PROCEDURE<OnBeforeGetInvoiceNo>
1 : Codeunit<Job Create-Invoice>.PROCEDURE<OnBeforeInsertSalesHeader>
1 : Codeunit<Job Create-Invoice>.PROCEDURE<OnBeforeInsertSalesLine>
1 : Codeunit<Job Create-Invoice>.PROCEDURE<OnBeforeModifySalesHeader>
1 : Codeunit<Job Create-Invoice>.PROCEDURE<OnBeforeModifySalesLine>
1 : Codeunit<Job Create-Invoice>.PROCEDURE<OnBeforeUpdateSalesHeader>
1 : Codeunit<Job Create-Invoice>.PROCEDURE<OnCreateSalesHeaderOnBeforeUpdateSalesHeader>
1 : Codeunit<Job Create-Invoice>.PROCEDURE<OnCreateSalesInvoiceJobTaskOnBeforeCreateSalesLine>
1 : Codeunit<Job Create-Invoice>.PROCEDURE<OnCreateSalesInvoiceLinesOnBeforeCreateSalesLine>
1 : Codeunit<Job Create-Invoice>.PROCEDURE<OnCreateSalesInvoiceLinesOnBeforeGetCustomer>
1 : Codeunit<Job Transfer Line>.PROCEDURE<OnAfterFromGenJnlLineToJnlLine>
1 : Codeunit<Job Transfer Line>.PROCEDURE<OnAfterFromJnlLineToLedgEntry>
1 : Codeunit<Job Transfer Line>.PROCEDURE<OnAfterFromJnlToPlanningLine>
1 : Codeunit<Job Transfer Line>.PROCEDURE<OnAfterFromJobLedgEntryToPlanningLine>
1 : Codeunit<Job Transfer Line>.PROCEDURE<OnAfterFromPlanningLineToJnlLine>
1 : Codeunit<Job Transfer Line>.PROCEDURE<OnAfterFromPlanningSalesLineToJnlLine>
1 : Codeunit<Job Transfer Line>.PROCEDURE<OnAfterFromPurchaseLineToJnlLine>
```

This is where they are called:

```
DETAILS:
Codeunit<Calc. G/L Acc. Where-Used>.PROCEDURE<OnAfterCheckPostingGroups>
  Raised in: Codeunit<Calc. G/L Acc. Where-Used>.PROCEDURE<CheckPostingGroups>
    Code lines:
    ...
    CheckICPartner(GLAccNo);
    CheckPaymentMethod(GLAccNo);
    CheckSalesReceivablesSetup(GLAccNo);
    CheckEmployeePostingGroup(GLAccNo);

    OnAfterCheckPostingGroups(GLAccWhereUsed,GLAccNo); <=====================
Codeunit<Calc. G/L Acc. Where-Used>.PROCEDURE<OnBeforeShowGLAccWhereUsed>
  Raised in: Codeunit<Calc. G/L Acc. Where-Used>.PROCEDURE<ShowGLAccWhereUsed>
    Code lines:
    OnBeforeShowGLAccWhereUsed(GLAccWhereUsed); <=====================

    GLAccWhereUsed.SETCURRENTKEY("Table Name");
    PAGE.RUNMODAL(0,GLAccWhereUsed);
Codeunit<Calc. G/L Acc. Where-Used>.PROCEDURE<OnShowExtensionPage>
  Raised in: Codeunit<Calc. G/L Acc. Where-Used>.PROCEDURE<ShowSetupForm>
    Code lines:
    ...
          BEGIN
            PaymentMethod.Code := COPYSTR("Key 1",1,MAXSTRLEN(PaymentMethod.Code));
            PAGE.RUN(0,PaymentMethod);
          END;
        ELSE
          OnShowExtensionPage(GLAccWhereUsed); <=====================
      END;
Codeunit<Job Calculate WIP>.PROCEDURE<OnInsertWIPGLOnBeforeGenJnPostLine>
  Raised in: Codeunit<Job Calculate WIP>.PROCEDURE<InsertWIPGL>
    Code lines:
    ...
    END;
    CLEAR(DimMgt);
    DimMgt.UpdateGlobalDimFromDimSetID(GenJnlLine."Dimension Set ID",GenJnlLine."Shortcut Dimension 1 Code",
      GenJnlLine."Shortcut Dimension 2 Code");

    OnInsertWIPGLOnBeforeGenJnPostLine(GenJnlLine); <=====================
    GenJnPostLine.RunWithCheck(GenJnlLine);
Codeunit<Job Post-Line>.PROCEDURE<OnAfterJobPlanningLineModify>
  Raised in: Codeunit<Job Post-Line>.PROCEDURE<PostInvoiceContractLine>
    Code lines:
    ...
    END;

    JobPlanningLine.UpdateQtyToInvoice;
    JobPlanningLine.MODIFY;

    OnAfterJobPlanningLineModify(JobPlanningLine); <=====================

    IF JobPlanningLine.Type <> JobPlanningLine.Type::Text THEN
      PostJobOnSalesLine(JobPlanningLine,SalesHeader,SalesLine,EntryType::Sale);
```

Quite a lot of people refer to this for trying to find out that the event that they are about to use is actually being called on the place they expect.

ALOps

ALOps is the current tool Waldo is working on. The goal of this tool is to provide the easiest way possible for Dynamics 365 Business Central partners to set up build and release pipelines in Azure DevOps.

In essence, build and release pipelines are a crucial part of **continuous integration/continuous deployment** (**CI/CD**), but very far from the daily knowledge of an AL developer. `ALOps` is there to close that bridge: with very limited knowledge, you can set up your own build pipeline in a matter of minutes.

DevOps extension

ALOps is a DevOps extension that is available on the Marketplace for Azure DevOps:

And it is free for any open source repository.

The extension is actually a structured collection of PowerShell scripts. And the nice thing is, the user does not have to have any PowerShell knowledge to set up the most complex build pipeline, including the signing of apps, compilations, tests, and so on.

Steps

As `ALOps` is there to set up pipelines, it includes what we call steps. The steps it includes today are as follows:

1. Compile app
2. Sign app
3. Verify signed app
4. Publish app
5. Test app
6. Clean apps from the environment
7. Copy app between environments
8. Import a RapidStart package
9. Import a license
10. Build a Docker container
11. Wait for a Docker container to finish building
12. Remove a Docker container
13. Import **for side-by-side development** (**fob**)
14. Export objects (`txt` or `fob`)
15. Compile (C/AL)

All of these steps work on Docker or non-Docker environments if you wish.

Documentation on GitHub

Waldo documents ALOps on GitHub, in a repository that is also used to gather issues or other feedback. You can find it at `https://github.com/HodorNV/ALOps`.

That repository is actually just a set of documents that describe the DevOps extension.

App templates

To make it even easier for app developers to set up build and release pipelines, there is an ever-developing repository with template apps including build pipelines that app developers can simply use to import so they start with a ready-made set of files, including a working build pipeline.

All of the repositories are being hosted in this public project on DevOps:

```
https://dev.azure.com/HodorNV/ALOps%20Templates
```

Example of using ALOps

The `WaldoNavPad` app we talked about earlier is actually set up with a working build pipeline in Azure DevOps, even while the repository of `WaldoNavPad` is on GitHub. Waldo has set it up in this public repository:

```
https://dev.azure.com/msdyn365bc/WaldoGitHubBuilds/
```

Just navigate to the builds and click one of the builds to see the details:

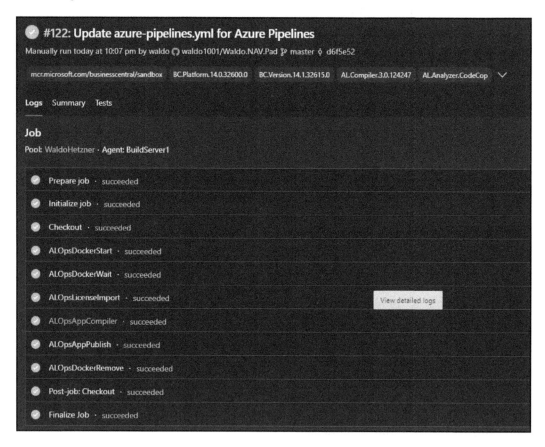

For the settings of this build, you have to open the `azure-pipelines.yml` file in the repository here:

`https://github.com/waldo1001/Waldo.NAV.Pad`

It gives you a readable, ready-to-go build pipeline that is part of the repository. All of the settings and steps required to build the app are there:

```
name: $(Build.BuildId)
variables:
- group: 'ALOps Build Pipeline Variables'
- name: 'AppVersion'
 value: '1.0.[yyyyWW].*'
- name: 'dockerimage'
 value: 'mcr.microsoft.com/businesscentral/sandbox'

pool:
 name: WaldoHetzner

steps:
- checkout: self
 clean: true

- task: ALOpsDockerStart@1
  inputs:
    docker_image: $(dockerimage)
    docker_pull: true
    docker_login: 'Insider Docker Registry'

- task: ALOpsDockerWait@1
  inputs:
     search_string: 'Ready for connections!'

- task: ALOpsLicenseImport@1
  inputs:
    usedocker: true
    license_path: $(bc.license)

- task: ALOpsAppCompiler@1
  inputs:
    usedocker: true
    nav_app_version: $(AppVersion)
    failed_on_warnings: true

- task: ALOpsAppPublish@1
  inputs:
     usedocker: true
     nav_artifact_app_filter: '*.app'
```

```
      skip_verification: true

- task: ALOpsDockerRemove@1
  enabled: true
  condition: always()
  inputs:
      docker_login: 'Insider Docker Registry'

- task: PublishBuildArtifacts@1
  enabled: false
  inputs:
    PathtoPublish: '$(Build.ArtifactStagingDirectory)'
    ArtifactName: 'Base'
    publishLocation: 'Container'
```

For any more information on how to set it up, the place to be is the app on the Marketplace or the GitHub repository mentioned before, which can get you to all of the information you need to set it up.

Summary

In this chapter, we saw an interesting set of third-party tools that can help you to increase your productivity when developing extensions for Dynamics 365 Business Central.

This is the last chapter of this book. In all of these chapters, we've covered all of the topics needed to master every Dynamics 365 Business Central implementation, from the basic to the most complex. Now it's your turn: start developing extensions, embracing the SaaS, and putting all of these topics into practice.

Other Books You May Enjoy

If you enjoyed this book, you may be interested in these other books by Packt:

Microsoft Dynamics 365 Business Central Cookbook
Michael Glue

ISBN: 978-1-78995-854-6

- Build and deploy Business Central applications
- Use the cloud or local sandbox for application development
- Customize and extend your base Business Central application
- Create external applications that connect to Business Central
- Create automated tests and debug your applications
- Connect to external web services from Business Central

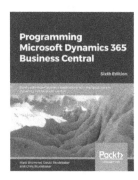

Programming Microsoft Dynamics 365 Business Central - Sixth Edition
Mark Brummel, David Studebaker, Et al

ISBN: 978-1-78913-779-8

- Programming using the AL language in the Visual Studio Code development environment
- Explore functional design and development using AL
- How to build interactive pages and learn how to extract data for users
- How to use best practices to design and develop modifications for new functionality integrated with the standard Business Central software
- Become familiar with deploying the broad range of components available in a Business Central system
- Create robust, viable systems to address specific business requirements

Leave a review - let other readers know what you think

Please share your thoughts on this book with others by leaving a review on the site that you bought it from. If you purchased the book from Amazon, please leave us an honest review on this book's Amazon page. This is vital so that other potential readers can see and use your unbiased opinion to make purchasing decisions, we can understand what our customers think about our products, and our authors can see your feedback on the title that they have worked with Packt to create. It will only take a few minutes of your time, but is valuable to other potential customers, our authors, and Packt. Thank you!

Index

CPSIA information can be obtained
at www.ICGtesting.com
Printed in the USA
BVHW08203615050520
579773BV00003B/67